MEDICAL SCHOOL PROFILES

Medical School
Admissions Data and Analysis

Rachel A. Winston, Ph.D.

Lizard Publishing is not sponsored by any college. While data was derived by school, state, or nationally published sources, some statistics may be out of date as published sources vary widely based upon the date of submission and currency of numbers. Attempts were made to obtain the best information during the writing of this book from American Medical Association, Liaison Committee for Medical Education (LCME), Association of American Medical Colleges, American Medical College Application Service, American Medical Student Association, The Student Doctor Network, NCES, U.S. Census Bureau, U.S. Department of Education, Common Data Set, College Board, U.S. News & World Report, college, and organizational sites. Descriptions of colleges are a compilation of college website information as well as student, faculty, and staff interviews with individuals and often from unique experiences and impressions. Attempts were made to triangulate multiple points of light. If you would like to share program information, data, or an impression of a specific college, please write to Lizard Publishing at the address below or at the e-mail address: *info@mylizard.org.*

ISBN 978-1946432414 (hardback); 978-1946432377 (paperback); 978-1946432407 (e-book)
LCCN: 2021923429

Lizard Publishing® 7700 Irvine Center Drive, Suite 800, Irvine, CA 92618 *www.lizard-publishing.com*

Lizard Publishing creates, designs, produces, and distributes books and resources to provide academic, admissions, and career information. Our mental process is fueled by three tenets:

- Ignite the hunger to learn and the passion to make a difference

- Illuminate the expanse of knowledge by sharing cutting edge thinking

- Innovate to create a world that makes the transition from dreams to reality

We work with academic leaders who transform the educational landscape to publish relevant content and advise students of their educational and professional options, with the aim of developing 21st-century learners and leaders. We also work with students to publish their books and present widely diverse ideas to the college/graduate school-bound community. With headquarters in Irvine, California, Lizard Publishing works virtually with authors to edit, publish, and distribute both hard copy and paperback books.

This book was published in the U.S.A. Lizard Publishing is a premium quality provider of educational reference, career guidance, and motivational publications/merchandise for global learners, educators, and stakeholders in education.

Book design by Michelle Tahan *www.michelletahan.com*

Book formatting by Obinna Chinemerem Ozuo

Book website: *www.medschoolexpert.com*

LIZARD PUBLISHING

This book is dedicated to students who seek to become patient-centered physicians and are passionately devoted to their pursuit of compassionate, ethical, and service-oriented medicine. This book was inspired by Zenobia Miro, Harrison White, Ida Ramezani, Nadia Aluzri, and Sean Wong.

Working at hospitals and conducting research in neurobiochemistry at Upstate Medical School and genetics at Syracuse University, I was surrounded by pre-med hopeful students eagerly pursuing their medical career. Subsequently, I spent most of my life helping students gain admission to medical school and working with authors who wrote books on medical school admission and MCAT prep.

Surrounded by students and teaching college for thirty-five years provided a keen insight into the student pursuit. I have also completed more than a dozen degrees and certificates and know the challenge and rigor of meshing rigorous coursework with a full complement of activities. Supporting students in their quest to attend medical school further inspired me to continuously adapt to changes in medical school admissions as well as investigate the broader picture of cutting-edge medical research.

ACKNOWLEDGMENTS

There is never enough room to acknowledge every person. Many people contributed to my perspective about medicine, assisted in the development of my knowledge base, or taught me indelible lessons. In a lifetime of experiences working with students, I am wiser and more worldly.

I gratefully acknowledge Michelle Tahan, Jasmine Jhunjhnuwala, and E. Liz Kim, as well as my family, friends, colleagues, and professors. It is with profound gratitude that I mention and acknowledge the many physicians with whom I studied, collaborated, and mentored.

As a faculty member in the UCLA College Counseling Certificate Program, I met numerous dedicated counselors who spend their life serving and supporting students. Meaningful contributions to the book have been made indirectly by admissions representatives, college counselors, faculty members who took a special interest in this book's success.

I would also like to thank the thousands of students I have taught, counseled, or supported in my nearly four decades of service.

Isaac Newton once said, "If I see so far, it is because I stand on the shoulders of giants."

A few of those giants whose broad shoulders lifted me higher and helped teach invaluable lessons include: David, Malka, and Steven Waugh, Zenobia Miro, Harrison White, Dania Baseel, Hyojung Lee, Maya Abdulridha, Miriam Bargout, Casey Duan, Alizeh Ahmedani, Taya Salman, Gabrielle McGahey, Kelvin Wong, Pria Chawla, Ria Chawla, Sydney Inouye, Joseph Inouye, Patrick Bayeh, Ritika Singh, Kelly Gee, Nathan Mermilliod, John Abdelmakek, Viren Abhyankar, Mehr Bawa, Natalie Moshayedi, Desiree Moshayedi, Nayer Toma, Tarika Gujral, Ryan Johnson, Andersen Cheong, Anabella Cheong, and Sabrina Wang.

> *"If I see so far, it is because I stand on the shoulders of giants."*
> *Isaac Newton*

Finally, there would be no book on medical school and no career college admissions counseling, without the support of Robert Helmer whose tireless efforts support me every single day.

ABOUT THE AUTHOR

D r. Rachel A. Winston is a tireless student advocate. She has served the educational community as a university professor, college advisor, statistician, researcher, author, cryptanalyst, motivational speaker, publishing executive, and lifelong student. As one of the leading experts in college counseling and an award-winning faculty member, Dr. Winston has spent her lifetime learning, teaching, mentoring, and coaching students. Much of her counseling practice is focused on admissions to medical, dental, vet, and engineering schools.

She started college at thirteen and graduated from college programs in such widely ranging disciplines as chemistry, mathematics, computers, liberal arts, international relations, negotiation, conflict resolution, peace building, business administration, higher education leadership, interpreting, college counseling, and publishing. Throughout her education, she attended and graduated from Harvard, University of Chicago, GWU, UCLA, Syracuse, CSUF, CSUDH, Pepperdine, Claremont Graduate University, and Gallaudet University.

Her position working in Washington, D.C. on Capitol Hill and with the White House in the 1980s took her to approximately a hundred universities training campaign managers at colleges from Colorado to California, thoroughly dotting the western states. Later, she led college tours with students and their families on road trips throughout the United States. She has taught or counseled thousands of students over her career and speaks at conferences and academic programs throughout the world.

As a professor and avid writer for numerous publications, she won the 2012 McFarland Literary Achievement Award, Bletchley Park Cryptanalyst Award, and numerous other awards, including Faculty Member of the Year, Leadership Tomorrow Leader of the Year, and college service and leadership awards. While studying Human Capital at Claremont Graduate University, she was a scholarship recipient at the Drucker School of Management. She was also elected to the statewide Board of Governors for the Faculty Association for California Community Colleges, where she served on their executive committee.

She served as a faculty member for the UCLA College Counselor Certificate Program, the Director of Mathematics at Brandman University, and Embry Riddle Aeronautical University, Chapman University, Cal State Fullerton, and a handful of California Community Colleges, including Cerro Coso College where she also served as the Academic Senate President and retired in 2016. Over her career, she taught mathematics online, on television, live interactive satellite, telecourses, and in large and small lecture halls.

AUTHORS' NOTE

You are reading this book because you are considering admission to medical school. Whatever route you took to get to this point, you are in the right place. Right now, you need to gather information to make informed decisions.

While many people offer advice, suggestions differ. Friends will tell you the 'right' way or the way their neighbor was accepted. Graciously accept this anecdotal information while you commit to learning more. This opportunity to pursue medicine is your future.

Dig deeper to consider both expert and current information from counselors who have worked with hundreds of students. Changes in programs, curricula, requirements, and links happen each year.

Double check each program's specifics yourself. This guide is current as of September 2021, with each school's profile information. However, since researching this book, changes may have taken place. There are other medical school books written by talented and experienced counselors. We admire and cheer on their efforts.

> *"We are what we think. All that we are arises with our thoughts. With our thoughts, we make the world."*
> *Buddha*

This set of profiles and lists is different in that it also provides unique tidbits. We hope you find this information valuable. Your job is to begin early by assembling information for the schools you are considering. Create a road map and set yourself on a clear path.

If you see an error in this book or even a suggestion for a future edition, please write to Rachel Winston at collegeguide@yahoo.com. We will fix the entry with the next printed version. All of that said, this book was written with you in mind.

There is a wealth of information on the Internet with free downloads, FAQs, testimonials, and offers to help you with your applications. Some of these advisors are knowledgeable and could help you. Students and parents hunt around the web, searching for a tremendous number of hours to seek the information they need.

This book of profiles was designed to make your search easier. For now, though, we will assume that you are reasonably confident that you want to attend medical school and are exploring this avenue as a possible way to take advantage of a program that will get you on your way toward your goal.

We assume that you are a highly academic candidate who is willing to work very hard. You may be fascinated with the human body, human physiology, or holistic health. Selflessly serving others is virtually a prerequisite for medical programs. This book will help you get to your goal. Applying to and writing essays for each medical school will require research.

While you might believe that medical school programs are relatively similar, each program's nuances make them very different. These small differences may seem confusing. My goal with this book is to demystify the information and process.

CONTENTS

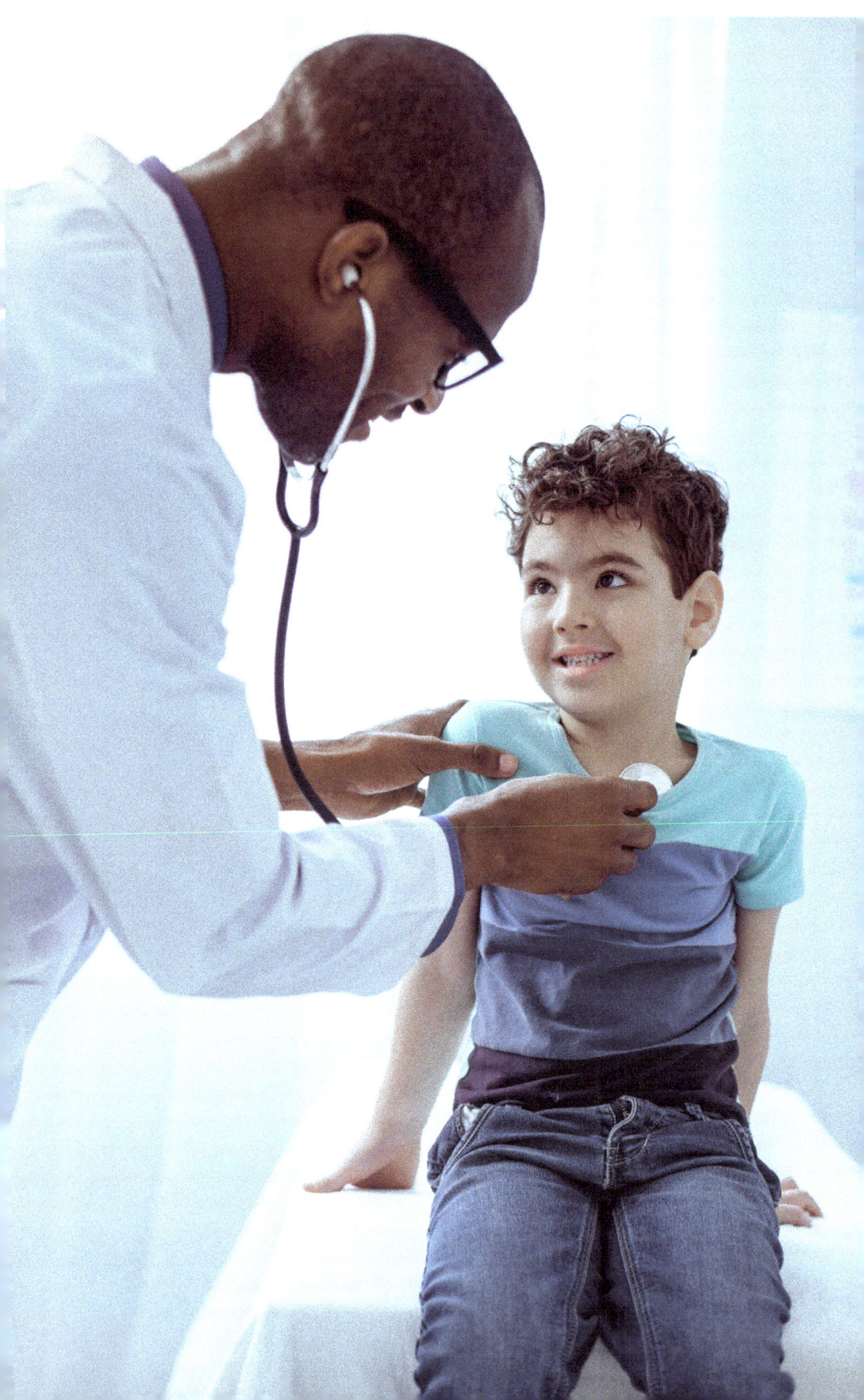

CHAPTER 1

INTRODUCTION TO MEDICAL SCHOOL EDUCATION

I n one precipitating moment, students know they want to attend medical school. That could be the tragic illness, pain, or death of a friend or family member. On the other hand, the decision to pursue medicine could be due to the onset of a disease, disorder, or pain. Occasionally, this event happens in childhood, though often the journey begins in high school or college. While it is never too late to begin this journey, the number of prerequisites required and the foundation needed favors those who know when they begin college.

Nevertheless, while medical school is challenging and the time requirement is daunting, the profession is rewarding. You will directly impact a person's present and future, making a significant impact on a family and community. From bringing a newborn into the world as he or she takes its first breaths to surgery that will save life, you will contribute to the world and become a colleague to those with similar goals and aspirations.

NUMEROUS AREAS TO EXPLORE

Whether you want to pursue primary care, cardiology, dermatology, oncology, neurology, or psychiatry, you are on the right path. Often medical school applicants have an idea of the direction they want to pursue. However, medical school offers numerous opportunities to explore new areas. Furthermore, after medical school, you can choose from many paths. For example, students may head into private practice, community clinic, or pursue other areas such as public health, research, teaching, or community-based service.

APPLYING TO MEDICAL SCHOOL

Applying to medical school is a process that requires more work than you may expect. Students spend more than a year in the application process. Students start with developing an organized method to approach the application process and a timeline to follow. This effort is typically followed by research on medical school programs and prerequisite requirements yet to be completed. Every school is different. There are no two schools with precisely the exact same course requirements, admissions dates, GPA/MCAT profiles, interview schedules, and essays. Next, students need to determine who will serve as their recommenders, make formal requests to professors/practitioners, and secure the recommendations. Some schools have formal committee letters.

AAMC MEDICAL COLLEGE FAIRS
(AMERICAN ASSOCIATION OF MEDICAL COLLEGES)

You may find it valuable to attend the AAMC Medical College Fairs. I do. I learn something new each time. Some of the changes are alarming, like the 2021 announcement of artificial intelligence determining some aspects of admissions at NYU. The reasons given were to avoid bias and improve NYU's process. Announcements, changes, and general information are also helpful. Students have the chance to talk with admissions officers and ask specific questions. More than 130 medical schools were in attendance in the fall of 2021. These fairs are offered virtually quite a few times a year. Find one or two that are convenient for you. You may find that the time you spent was worth the effort.

MSAR (MEDICAL SCHOOL ADMISSIONS REQUIREMENTS)
ADMISSIONS DATA WEBSITE

MSAR is comprehensive with information from every medical school in the U.S. and Canada that offers an MD degree. After each MCAT, MSAR is updated with new data from the MCAT, AMCAS (American Medical College Admission Service), and medical school admissions offices. At some point, you will inevitably use this site, which allows you considerable freedom in researching and comparing medical schools. This site is almost always up-to-date.

ORGANIZE YOUR EFFORT

I typically make charts of medical schools for those students I counsel, though you can do this on your own. Here is one of the charts I create. You do not need to hire an advisor to create solid materials that make your work organized and efficient. You can create your own charts. Choose the schools you are interested in attending and fill in the data from various online sources.

Condense the data. There are numerous variables for you to consider. You can get lost in the volumes of information available. For example, each school has a range of GPAs and MCAT scores. This effort may seem overwhelming, but I use simple, colorful charts/tables in Microsoft Word that I can color-code. Some people like Excel, though I find it clunky and uninviting. Remember applying to medical school is a long process. It is helpful if you can see and code the information for your own purposes.

Medical Schools	USNWR Primary Care	USNWR Rank Research	GPA	MCAT	Attendance Rate Class Size/ Applications	Percent In-State Matriculants	# Inter-viewed	# Accept	# In Class	Accept Rate	Other Imp Info

The AAMC and AMCAS websites are very helpful. Note that statistical information and cost of attendance change from year to year. Thus, when you begin to make your chart, you may find that the data from last month is not the same. Don't worry. For now you just need to get a general idea of where you stand, what you need to do, how you need to do it, and track what you need to remember.

Another chart I make for my students is also very helpful for your planning purposes. Again, you can construct this from scratch using information from this book and other sources. Planning, organization, and one-stop informational charts will save you a ton of time. Every time you contact a med school (student, faculty, admissions, or alumnus) or learn details about the school, input the information into the chart. Small fonts are okay so you can fit more information.

Medical Schools	Prerequisite Requirements	Recommended Classes	Key Dates, Logins, Interview Type	Contact w/ Med School, Follow Up Rules

While students are quick to start working on their essays, this endeavor may not be prudent. There is much to learn before you know what to tell a medical school about yourself. The best way to start is by constructing a chart using the data from this book. This data is current for the 2021-2022 admissions cycle. However, there are rarely significant changes from one year to the next, though dates, costs, and statistics will change. The pandemic has altered admissions, but requirements are likely to remain. However, the grace colleges allowed at a few schools with pass/fail classes, community college courses, delays, waivers etc., are unlikely to continue a few years from now.

WHAT MAJOR SHOULD I CHOOSE?

One question students always ask is whether or not the choice of a major is more important than GPA and MCAT scores. Actually, students can major in anything and attend medical school provided they complete the required courses for entrance. GPA and MCAT scores are most important. I have had students get accepted to medical school in anthropology, political science, music, Spanish, and philosophy, while others major in chemistry, biology, engineering, and public health. Either way, they are in medical school now.

The point is that if you are genuinely interested in the subject you are studying, you will be motivated to persist in the most demanding classes. When you are passionate about your classes, you dive into the material with true appreciation for the subject. Additionally, you will have numerous experiences that allow you to reflect on the world and solidify your decision to serve communities, help patients, and live your life as a physician. Otherwise, you can get lost in the checklist approach to medical school admissions. If you only go through the motions, you will not enjoy the journey along the way. Instead, know your why; take action on your how; invent your future.

Especially if you are majoring in a non-science subject, make sure that you have medical service, clinical experience, and community health experiences. You can shadow physicians. However, this passive experience, while illuminating, has little involvement. Serving as a scribe is more active while working as a medical assistant or EMT is immersive and invaluable in your preparation. International medical experiences also provide a valuable foundation.

Research aids in gaining awareness for medicine and its advances on the whole. The fine detail and continuous repetition of scientific work provide an appreciation for the field and the outcomes of science. Besides, furthering science by taking innovations one step further is beneficial to all of society. Getting published, presenting at conferences, and expanding the field are all noble goals.

One of the reasons why some students who major in a non-traditional subject have difficulties is that, with fewer science courses, a different mindset is needed to be re-oriented toward science as opposed to the orientation of, let's say, the analysis of literature. Note that your BCPM GPA is a key component in the admissions process. The BCPM (Biology, Chemistry, Physics, and Math) GPA is recomputed based on AMCAS guidelines and acceptable classes they choose to include.

With the ability to go back and forth between science and societal issues, medical schools get a student who can access more of the humanistic side of academia as well. Having a broader background and deeper connections to the world is invaluable for medicine. Besides, more well-rounded students with varied backgrounds add a different type of diversity to the school and contribute an engaging intellectual exchange between students.

Nearly all medical schools require a year of each of the following: Biology, General Chemistry, Organic Chemistry, Physics, Mathematics (Calculus, Statistics), English, Humanities, and Social Science. Most also require Biochemistry and two other semesters of Biology. Review the chart you create and work with your academic advisor to determine what classes you need and how they will fit into your college experience. In the end, your academic performance matters the most.

INTERVIEWS

If you are invited to interview, you will most likely have the Multiple Mini Interview or MMI for short. You can think of it as many shorter interviews with different people who evaluate your quick thinking, attitude, judgments, behaviors, ethical decision-making, and overall answers. The interview is your 'win it or blow it' chance.

- What ethical dilemma was most impactful to you?
- How would you handle a situation where you knew a person was unvaccinated and not wearing a mandated mask?
- What would you do if you knew that insurance would not allow a patient to get the medicine they need and forced you to prescribe one or two others first?
- If you were Anthony Fauci, what would you have done regarding vaccinations at the beginning and during the pandemic?

The challenge in these interviews is that multiple people will assess you on your strengths and weaknesses and give you scores. For most people, interviews of any type are uncomfortable, although there are advantages to the MMI. For example, you can prepare with scenarios and determine how to respond in general and what not to say. Longer explanations and preparation are found in my book, *Medical School: Preparation, Application, Admission.*

Nonetheless, in short, the MMI includes multiple stations that have various formats, from pre-reading and writing to situational activities followed by an interview. These are short, and each has a rubric from which the evaluator gives you a ranking or score. The rubric is standardized and formatted, so that much of the intrinsic bias is removed. Interviewers objectively provide an evaluation that is combined with the rest of the results to earn a composite score. Some of the areas that may be considered include:

Communication	Empathy
Relationship	Compassion
Connection	Awareness
Critical Thinking	Self-description
Problem Solving	Maturity
Reaction to Setbacks	

DEMAND FOR PHYSICIANS

No matter what specialty you pursue, the demand for physicians will continue to outweigh the supply. At this point in time, data show a shortage of physicians. This situation will only worsen. First, there are more people with healthcare needs, which was exacerbated by the pandemic. Second, the population of older people will increase demand. Third, many physicians will retire in the upcoming years and new physicians will be needed. Finally, global demand for healthcare professionals is increasing, particularly in areas like Africa, where the population is expected to double by 2050.

PRIMARY CARE NEEDS

New MD and DO programs have opened in the last five years due to the increasing shortage of primary care physicians. Especially in rural and other underserved areas, comprehensive healthcare is essential. The concern is so great that the federal government provides scholarships to encourage medical school students to serve this need. Investigate possibilities with the National Health Service Corps for programs which have been created in conjunction with the U.S. Department of Health and Human Services. With the high costs of medical school education, these scholarships are extremely helpful.

A FINAL NOTE

This handy resource was designed to be read in conjunction with my companion book, *Medical School: Preparation, Application, Admission*. In that book, you will find hints and information on the entire application process, as well as detailed information on alternative medical programs, what happens after the interview, and how to strengthen your application.

Best wishes in your pursuit of an amazing career and your commitment to serving the healthcare needs of our society.

5
Regions

155
Programs

COLLEGE PROFILES AND REQUIREMENTS

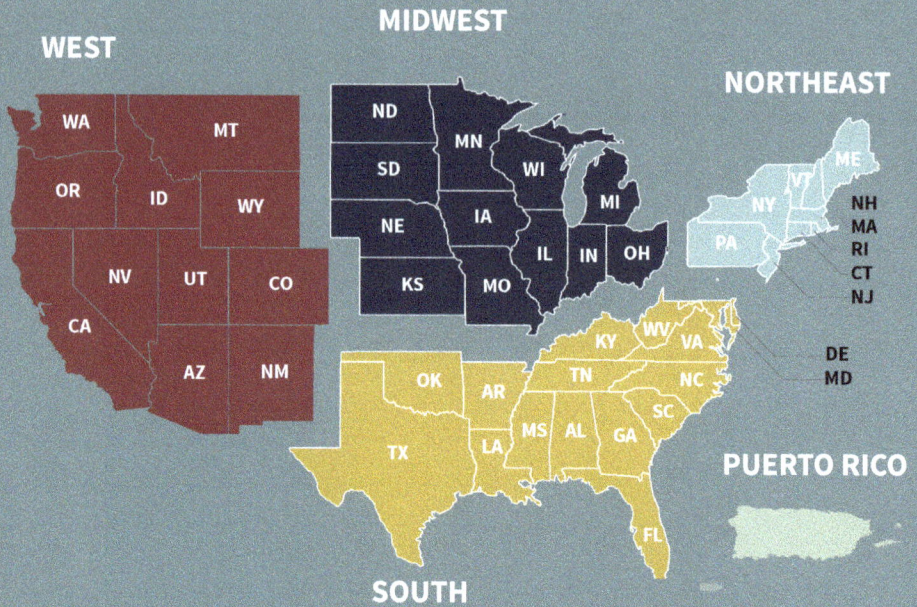

WEST · MIDWEST · NORTHEAST · SOUTH · PUERTO RICO

MD PROGRAMS BY REGION
U.S. CENSUS BUREAU CLASSIFICATIONS

REGION 1 – NORTHEAST

Connecticut, Maine, Massachusetts, New Hampshire, New Jersey, New York, Pennsylvania, Rhode Island, and Vermont

REGION 2 – MIDWEST

Illinois, Indiana, Iowa, Kansas, Michigan, Minnesota, Missouri, Nebraska, North Dakota, Ohio, South Dakota, and Wisconsin

REGION 3 – SOUTH

Alabama, Arkansas, Delaware, District of Columbia, Florida, Georgia, Kentucky, Louisiana, Maryland, Mississippi, North Carolina, Oklahoma, South Carolina, Tennessee, Texas, Virginia, and West Virginia

REGION 4 – WEST

Alaska, Arizona, California, Colorado, Hawaii, Idaho, Montana, Nevada, New Mexico, Oregon, Utah, Washington, and Wyoming

REGION 5 – U.S. TERRRITORIES

Puerto Rico

LIST OF MD PROGRAMS

The programs listed in the following pages include MD programs. This book also provides lists of DMD and DDS, DO, dental, PharmD, and vet schools, since many students interested in medical school are also interested in healthcare. There are many facets of the healthcare world. One of these other areas might be a good option for you.

Medical school is not for everyone.

Thus, this book aims to provide you with a more comprehensive set of lists so that you can explore your options. Keep the book handy. You may find that even after you begin college, if you choose a traditional pre-med path, you may find the additional programs in the back a good option for you.

Creating lists is often tedious and cumbersome. These lists were gathered to help you with this task.

These descriptions of the college programs, tuition, requirements, and deadlines are accurate as of April 2021. Requirements may have changed somewhat due to the pandemic, but all of this information is a great place to start!

Note: To simplify the text and fit information into the charts and descriptions, abbreviations were used as well as shortened sentences and acronyms.

CONNECTICUT

MAINE

MASSACHUSETTS

NEW HAMPSHIRE

NEW JERSEY

NEW YORK

PENNSYLVANIA

RHODE ISLAND

VERMONT

CHAPTER 2

REGION ONE

NORTHEAST

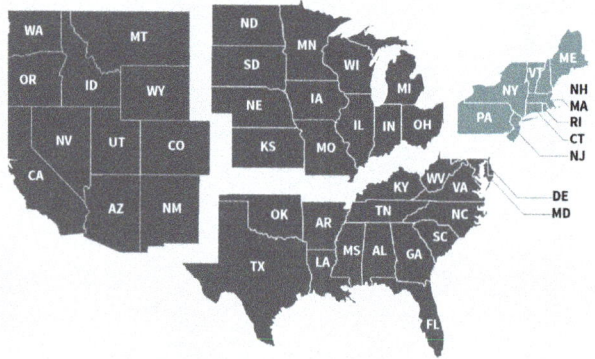

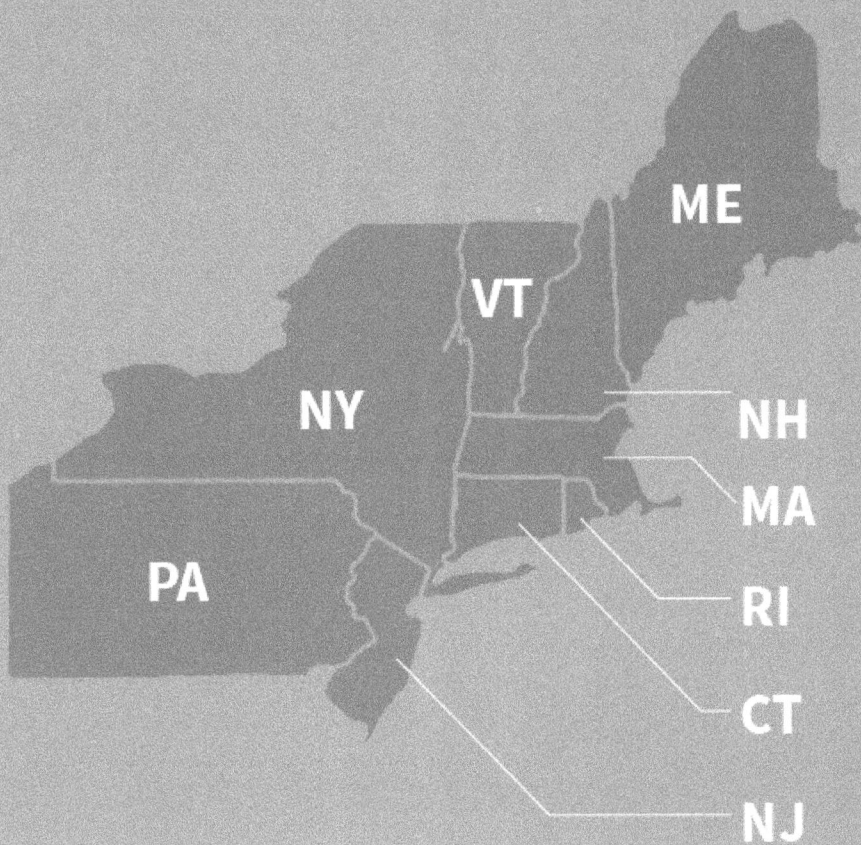

36 Programs | 9 States

MEDICAL PROGRAMS

Medical School	Ave. GPA & MCAT Early Decision (ED): Yes/No Int'l Students: Yes/No Reapps: Yes/No	Admissions Statistics	Science Req. Other than Gen Chem, OChem, Physics, Bio
Quinnipiac University 275 Mount Carmel Avenue, Hamden, CT 06518	3.71 (overall) 3.63 (science) MCAT: 514 ED: No Int'l Student: Yes Reapps: N/A	**(2019)** Apps Received: 7,701 Interview Received: 343 Number Enrolled: 94 Admitted Rate: 1.2% **(2020)** Apps Received: 7214 Interview Received: 405 Number Enrolled: 94 Admitted Rate: 1.3%	Biochem.
University of Connecticut School of Medicine 263 Farmington Avenue, Farmington, CT 06030	3.82 (overall) 3.77 (science) MCAT: 513 ED: Yes Int'l Student: Yes Reapps: Yes	**(2019)** Apps Received: 3,286 Interview Received: 331 Number Enrolled: 110 Admitted Rate: 3.25% **(2020)** Apps Received: 3,727 Interview Received: 318 Number Enrolled: 110 Admitted Rate: 3%	Zoology (sub. Bio) Anatomy w/ Lab Microbio. w/ Lab Biochem. Additional Bio., Chem., Calc., or Physics (12 cred.)
Yale School of Medicine 333 Cedar Street, New Haven, CT 06510	3.93 (overall) 3.92 (science) MCAT: 521 ED: Yes Int'l Student: Yes Reapps: N/A	**(2019)** Apps Received: 5,776 Interview Received: 642 Number Enrolled: 104 Admitted Rate:1.8% **(2020)** Apps Received: 5,332 Interview Received: 648 Number Enrolled: 100 Admitted Rate: 1.9%	Biochem. w/ Lab

Medical School	Ave. GPA & MCAT Early Decision (ED): Yes/No Int'l Students: Yes/No Reapps: Yes/No	Admissions Statistics	Science Req. Other than Gen Chem, OChem, Physics, Bio
Boston University School of Medicine 72 East Concord St., Boston, MA 02118	3.86 (overall) 3.82 (science) MCAT: 518 ED: Yes Int'l Student: Yes Reapps: N/A	**(2019)** Apps Received: 9,151 Interview Received: 1,015 Number Enrolled: 160 Admitted Rate: 1.75% **(2020)** Apps Received: 9,456 Interview Received: 1,005 Number Enrolled: 152 Admitted Rate: 1.6%	Biochem. Molecular Bio.
Harvard Medical School 25 Shattuck St., Boston, MA 02115	3.94 (overall) 3.93 (science) MCAT: 520 ED: No Int'l Student: Yes Reapps: N/A	**(2019)** Apps Received: 7,613 Interview Received: 948 Number Enrolled: 165 Admitted Rate: 2.2% **(2020)** Apps Received: 7,463 Interview Received: 798 Number Enrolled: 168 Admitted Rate: 2.3%	Biochem. w/ Lab
Tufts University School of Medicine 136 Harrison Ave., Boston, MA 02111	3.78 (overall) 3.74 (science) MCAT: 515 ED: Yes Int'l Student: Yes Reapps: N/A	**(2019)** Apps Received: 12,764 Interview Received: 829 Number Enrolled: 200 Admitted Rate: 1.6% **(2020)** Apps Received: 13,279 Interview Received: 821 Number Enrolled: 200 Admitted Rate: 1.5%	N/A See Chart.

NORTHEAST

MEDICAL PROGRAMS

Medical School	Ave. GPA & MCAT Early Decision (ED): Yes/No Int'l Students: Yes/No Reapps: Yes/No	Admissions Statistics	Science Req. Other than Gen Chem, OChem, Physics, Bio
University of Massachusetts Medical School 55 Lake Ave., North Worcester, MA 01655	3.82 (overall) 3.79 (science) MCAT: 516 ED: Yes Int'l Student: No Reapps: N/A	**(2019)** Apps Received: 4,094 Interview Received: 928 Number Enrolled: 162 Admitted Rate: 3.9% **(2020)** Apps Received: ,4484 Interview Received: 834 Number Enrolled: 162 Admitted Rate: 3.6%	Biochem.
Geisel School of Medicine at Dartmouth 3 Rope Ferry Road, Hanover, NH 03755	3.77 (overall) 3.73 (science) MCAT: 516 ED: No Int'l Student: Yes Reapps: N/A	**(2019)** Apps Received: 8,399 Interview Received: 857 Number Enrolled: 92 Admitted Rate: 1.1% **(2020)** Apps Received: 8,308 Interview Received: 709 Number Enrolled: 92 Admitted Rate: 1.1%	Biochem.
Cooper Medical School of Rowan University 401 South Broadway, Camden, NJ 08103	3.79 (overall) 3.75 (science) MCAT: 512 ED: Yes Int'l Student: No Reapps: N/A	**(2019)** Apps Received: 6,826 Interview Received: 381 Number Enrolled: 111 Admitted Rate: 1.6% **(2020)** Apps Received: 5,985 Interview Received: 394 Number Enrolled: 111 Admitted Rate: 1.9%	N/A See Chart.
Seton Hall University 340 Kingsland St., Nutley, NJ 07110	3.71 (overall) 3.63 (science) MCAT: 513 ED: No Int'l Student:No Reapps: N/A	**(2019)** Apps Received: 4,654 Interview Received: 240 Number Enrolled: 91 Admitted Rate: 1.9% **(2020)** Apps Received: 5,490 Interview Received: 320 Number Enrolled: 122 Admitted Rate: 2.2%	N/A See Chart.

Medical School	Ave. GPA & MCAT / Early Decision (ED): Yes/No / Int'l Students: Yes/No / Reapps: Yes/No	Admissions Statistics	Science Req. Other than Gen Chem, OChem, Physics, Bio
Rutgers New Jersey Medical School 185 South Orange Avenue, Newark, NJ 07107	3.82 (overall) 3.79 (science) MCAT: 515 ED: Yes Int'l Student: Yes Reapps: N/A	**(2019)** Apps Received: 5,112 Interview Received: 714 Number Enrolled: 178 Admitted Rate: 3.5% **(2020)** Apps Received: 5,509 Interview Received: 774 Number Enrolled: 178 Admitted Rate: 3.2%	N/A See Chart.
Rutgers, Robert Wood Johnson Medical School One Robert Wood Johnson Place, New Brunswick, NJ 08901	3.75 (overall) 3.70 (science) MCAT: 514 ED: No Int'l Student: Yes (case by case) Reapps: N/A	**(2019)** Apps Received: 5,689 Interview Received: 500 Number Enrolled: 165 Admitted Rate: 2.9% **(2020)** Apps Received: 5,599 Interview Received: 532 Number Enrolled: 174 Admitted Rate: 3.1%	Biochem.
Albany Medical College 47 New Scotland Avenue, Albany, NY 12208	3.74 (overall) 3.69 (science) MCAT: 511 ED: No Int'l Student: No Reapps: N/A	**(2019)** Apps Received: 10,247 Interview Received: 739 Number Enrolled: 139 Admitted Rate: 1.4% **(2020)** Apps Received: 11,344 Interview Received: 726 Number Enrolled: 143 Admitted Rate: 1.3%	N/A See Chart.

NORTHEAST

MEDICAL PROGRAMS

Medical School	Ave. GPA & MCAT Early Decision (ED): Yes/No Int'l Students: Yes/No Reapps: Yes/No	Admissions Statistics	Science Req. Other than Gen Chem, OChem, Physics, Bio
Albert Einstein College of Medicine 1300 Morris Park Avenue, Bronx, NY 10461	3.81 (overall) 3.77 (science) MCAT: 515 ED: Yes Int'l Student: No Reapps: N/A	**(2019)** Apps Received: 8,088 Interview Received: 1,000 Number Enrolled: 183 Admitted Rate: 2.3% **(2020)** Apps Received: 8,072 Interview Received: 938 Number Enrolled: 183 Admitted Rate: 2.3%	N/A See Chart.
Columbia University Vagelos College of Physicians and Surgeons 630 West 168th Street, New York, NY 10032	3.92 (overall) 3.91 (science) MCAT: 522 ED: No Int'l Student: Yes Reapps: N/A	**(2019)** Apps Received: 7,855 Interview Received: 1,073 Number Enrolled: 138 Admitted Rate: 1.8% **(2020)** Apps Received: 7,293 Interview Received: 857 Number Enrolled: 138 Admitted Rate: 1.9%	N/A See Chart.
CUNY School of Medicine 160 Convent Ave., New York, NY 10031	N/A (overall) N/A (science) MCAT: N/A ED: No Int'l Student: No Reapps: N/A	**(2019)** Apps Received: N/A Interview Received: N/A Number Enrolled: 75 Admitted Rate: N/A **(2020)** Apps Received: 76 Interview Received: 304 Number Enrolled: 76 Admitted Rate: 100%	N/A This is a BS/MD program intended for high school applicants.
Zucker School of Medicine at Hofstra/Northwell 500 Hofstra University, Hempstead, NY 11549	3.84 (overall) 3.81 (science) MCAT: 518 ED: Yes Int'l Student: No Reapps: N/A	**(2019)** Apps Received: 5,316 Interview Received: 874 Number Enrolled: 99 Admitted Rate: 1.9% **(2020)** Apps Received: 4,877 Interview Received: 840 Number Enrolled: 99 Admitted Rate: 2%	N/A See Chart.

Medical School	Ave. GPA & MCAT / Early Decision (ED): Yes/No / Int'l Students: Yes/No / Reapps: Yes/No	Admissions Statistics	Science Req. Other than Gen Chem, OChem, Physics, Bio
Icahn School of Medicine at Mount Sinai One Gustave L. Levy Place, New York, NY 10029	3.87 (overall) 3.86 (science) MCAT: 519 ED: No Int'l Student: Yes Reapps: N/A	**(2019)** Apps Received: 6,592 Interview Received: 956 Number Enrolled: 140 Admitted Rate: 2.1% **(2020)** Apps Received: 7,153 Interview Received: 761 Number Enrolled: 140 Admitted Rate: 2%	N/A See Chart.
University at Buffalo 955 Main St, Buffalo, NY 14203	3.75 (overall) 3.68 (science) MCAT: 512 ED: Yes Int'l Student: No Reapps: Yes	**(2019)** Apps Received: 3,823 Interview Received: 581 Number Enrolled: 180 Admitted Rate: 4.7% **(2020)** Apps Received: 4,360 Interview Received: 770 Number Enrolled: 182 Admitted Rate: 4.2%	N/A See Chart.
New York Medical College 40 Sunshine Cottage Road, Valhalla, NY 10595	3.72 (overall) 3.64 (science) MCAT: 513 ED: Yes Int'l Student: Yes (case by case) Reapps: Yes	**(2019)** Apps Received: 12,714 Interview Received: 995 Number Enrolled: 215 Admitted Rate: 1.7% **(2020)** Apps Received: 12,022 Interview Received: 989 Number Enrolled: 212 Admitted Rate: 1.8%	Biochem.

NORTHEAST

MEDICAL PROGRAMS

Medical School	Ave. GPA & MCAT Early Decision (ED): Yes/No Int'l Students: Yes/No Reapps: Yes/No	Admissions Statistics	Science Req. Other than Gen Chem, OChem, Physics, Bio
New York University Grossman 550 First Avenue New York, NY 10016	3.95 (overall) 3.95 (science) MCAT: 522 ED: No Int'l Student: No Reapps: N/A	**(2019)** Apps Received: 8,937 Interview Received: 1,062 Number Enrolled: 103 Admitted Rate: 1.2% **(2020)** Apps Received: 9,238 Interview Received: 1,000 Number Enrolled: 102 Admitted Rate: 1.1%	N/A See Chart.
New York University Long Island 259 1st St, Mineola, NY 11501	3.81 (overall) 3.77 (science) MCAT: 515 ED: No Int'l Student: No Reapps: N/A	**(2019)** Apps Received: 2,390 Interview Received: 387 Number Enrolled: 24 Admitted Rate: 1% **(2020)** Apps Received: 4,342 Interview Received: 512 Number Enrolled: 24 Admitted Rate: 0.6%	N/A See Chart.
Stony Brook University 101 Nicolls Road, Health Sciences Center, Stony Brook, NY 11794	3.86 (overall) 3.85 (science) MCAT: 516 ED: Yes Int'l Student: Yes Reapps: N/A	**(2019)** Apps Received: 5,241 Interview Received: 776 Number Enrolled: 136 Admitted Rate: 2.6% **(2020)** Apps Received: 5,164 Interview Received: 757 Number Enrolled: 136 Admitted Rate: 2.6%	Biochem.

Medical School	Ave. GPA & MCAT / Early Decision (ED): Yes/No / Int'l Students: Yes/No / Reapps: Yes/No	Admissions Statistics	Science Req. Other than Gen Chem, OChem, Physics, Bio
SUNY Downstate 450 Clarkson Ave., Brooklyn, NY 11203	3.74 (overall) 3.68 (science) MCAT: 514 ED: Yes Int'l Student: No Reapps: Yes	**(2019)** Apps Received: 5,761 Interview Received: 1,066 Number Enrolled: 200 Admitted Rate: 3.5% **(2020)** Apps Received: 6,142 Interview Received: 1,296 Number Enrolled: 207 Admitted Rate: 3.4%	N/A See Chart.
SUNY Upstate 766 Irving Avenue, Syracuse, NY 13210	3.77 (overall) 3.72 (science) MCAT: 513 ED: Yes Int'l Student: Yes Reapps: N/A	**(2019)** Apps Received: 4,482 Interview Received: 875 Number Enrolled: 169 Admitted Rate: 3.8% **(2020)** Apps Received: 4,350 Interview Received: 725 Number Enrolled: 160 Admitted Rate: 3.7%	Biochem.
University of Rochester 601 Elmwood Ave, Rochester, NY 14642	3.84 (overall) 3.80 (science) MCAT: 518 ED: No Int'l Student: Yes (case by case) Reapps: N/A	**(2019)** Apps Received: 5,803 Interview Received: 674 Number Enrolled: 102 Admitted Rate: 1.8% **(2020)** Apps Received: 5,651 Interview Received: 607 Number Enrolled: 102 Admitted Rate: 1.8%	Biochem. w/ Lab

NORTHEAST

MEDICAL PROGRAMS

Medical School	Ave. GPA & MCAT Early Decision (ED): Yes/No Int'l Students: Yes/No Reapps: Yes/No	Admissions Statistics	Science Req. Other than Gen Chem, OChem, Physics, Bio
Weill Cornell Medicine 1300 York Avenue, New York, NY 10065	3.91 (overall) 3.90 (science) MCAT: 519 ED: No Int'l Student: Yes Reapps: N/A	**(2019)** Apps Received: 6,385 Interview Received: 798 Number Enrolled: 106 Admitted Rate: 1.7% **(2020)** Apps Received: 6,878 Interview Received: 813 Number Enrolled: 106 Admitted Rate: 1.5%	N/A See Chart.
Drexel University 2900 W. Queen Lane, Philadelphia, PA 19129	3.75 (overall) 3.69 (science) MCAT: 512 ED: Yes Int'l Student: No Reapps: N/A	**(2019)** Apps Received: 14,0671 Interview Received:1,506 Number Enrolled: 254 Admitted Rate: 1.8% **(2020)** Apps Received: 13,482 Interview Received: 1,619 Number Enrolled: 267 Admitted Rate: 2%	N/A See Chart.
Geisinger Commonwealth 525 Pine Street, Scranton, PA 18509	3.76 (overall) 3.68 (science) MCAT: 512 ED: Yes Int'l Student: No Reapps: N/A	**(2019)** Apps Received: 5,781 Interview Received: 811 Number Enrolled: 115 Admitted Rate: 2% **(2020)** Apps Received: 6,142 Interview Received: 808 Number Enrolled: 115 Admitted Rate: 1.9%	N/A See Chart.

Medical School	Ave. GPA & MCAT Early Decision (ED): Yes/No Int'l Students: Yes/No Reapps: Yes/No	Admissions Statistics	Science Req. Other than Gen Chem, OChem, Physics, Bio
Temple University 3500 N. Broad Street, Philadelphia, PA 19140	3.77 (overall) 3.71 (science) MCAT: 513 ED: Yes Int'l Student: No Reapps: N/A	**(2019)** Apps Received: 11,059 Interview Received: 919 Number Enrolled: 195 Admitted Rate: 1.8% **(2020)** Apps Received: 11,198 Interview Received: 989 Number Enrolled: 218 Admitted Rate: 1.9%	N/A See Chart.
Penn State 500 University Drive, Hershey, PA 17033	3.81 (overall) 3.77 (science) MCAT: 512 ED: Yes Int'l Student: No Reapps: N/A	**(2019)** Apps Received: 11,827 Interview Received: 779 Number Enrolled: 152 Admitted Rate: 1.3% **(2020)** Apps Received: 11,742 Interview Received: 721 Number Enrolled: 152 Admitted Rate: 1.3%	N/A See Chart.
Thomas Jefferson University 1015 Walnut Street, Philadelphia, PA 19107	3.80 (overall) 3.76 (science) MCAT: 514 ED: Yes Int'l Student: Yes Reapps: N/A	**(2019)** Apps Received: 9443 Interview Received: 749 Number Enrolled: 270 Admitted Rate: 2.9% **(2020)** Apps Received: 9,916 Interview Received: 674 Number Enrolled: 270 Admitted Rate: 2.7%	N/A See Chart.

NORTHEAST

MEDICAL PROGRAMS

Medical School	Ave. GPA & MCAT Early Decision (ED): Yes/No Int'l Students: Yes/No Reapps: Yes/No	Admissions Statistics	Science Req. Other than Gen Chem, OChem, Physics, Bio
University of Pennsylvania 3400 Civic Center Boulevard, Building 421, Philadelphia, PA 19104	3.94 (overall) 3.95 (science) MCAT: 522 ED: Yes Int'l Student: Yes Reapps: N/A	**(2019)** Apps Received: 6,578 Interview Received: 707 Number Enrolled: 150 Admitted Rate: 2.3% **(2020)** Apps Received: 6,040 Interview Received: 734 Number Enrolled: 155 Admitted Rate: 2.6%	N/A See Chart.
University of Pittsburgh 3550 Terrace Street, Pittsburgh, PA 15261	3.86 (overall) 3.84 (science) MCAT: 518 ED: No Int'l Student: Yes Reapps: N/A	**(2019)** Apps Received: 7,013 Interview Received: 665 Number Enrolled: 147 Admitted Rate: 2% **(2020)** Apps Received: 7,174 Interview Received: 734 Number Enrolled: 149 Admitted Rate: 2.1%	Biochem.
Brown University 222 Richmond Street, Providence, RI 02912	3.83 (overall) 3.77 (science) MCAT: 517 ED: No Int'l Student: Yes Reapps: N/A	**(2019)** Apps Received: 7,770 Interview Received: 366 Number Enrolled: 144 Admitted Rate: 1.9% **(2020)** Apps Received: 6,751 Interview Received: 375 Number Enrolled: 144 Admitted Rate: 2.1%	Biochem.
University of Vermont 89 Beaumont Ave., Burlington, VT 05405	3.70 (overall) 3.63 (science) MCAT: 512 ED: No Int'l Student: No Reapps: Yes	**(2019)** Apps Received: 6,759 Interview Received: 599 Number Enrolled: 122 Admitted Rate: 1.8% **(2020)** Apps Received: 6,902 Interview Received: 630 Number Enrolled: 124 Admitted Rate: 1.8%	N/A See Chart.

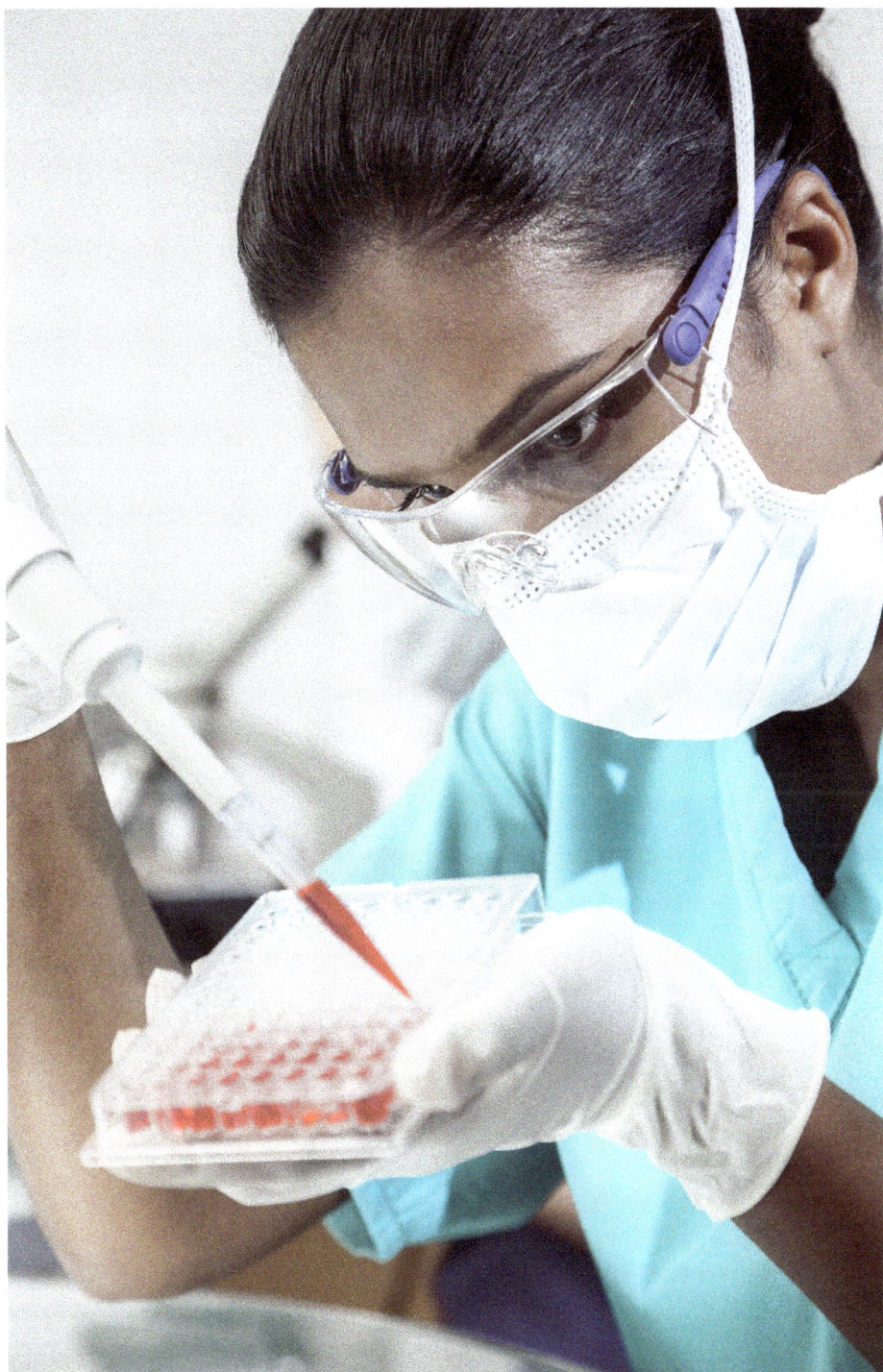

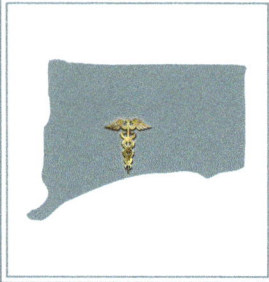

FRANK H. NETTER MD SCHOOL OF MEDICINE AT QUINNIPIAC UNIVERSITY

Address: 275 Mount Carmel Avenue, Hamden, CT 06518
Website: *https://www.qu.edu/schools/medicine.html*
Contact: *https://www.qu.edu/contact-us.html*
Phone: (855) 582-7766

COST OF ATTENDANCE

Tuition: $61,040
Fees & Expenses: $26,838
Total: $87,878

Financial Aid: https://www.qu.edu/schools/medicine/financial-aid.html

Percent Receiving Aid: 83%

ADDITIONAL INFORMATION

Interesting tidbit: A highlight of the curriculum during the first two years is the Medical Student Home (MeSH) program, a longitudinal, mentored clinical experience that acts as a "practical laboratory" for students to work with patients in a community practice.In September of the first year, each medical student is paired with a practicing community physician to provide each medical student with a supervised environment to practice fundamental clinical skills with patients.

What percent of students participate in global health experiences? 22%

What service learning opportunities exist? Bobcat Community Health Alliance, Primary Care Progress (PCP), Science Fridays, etc. For more information, visit:https://www.qu.edu/schools/medicine/life.html

What dual degree options exist? No dual degree options listed.

Important Updates due to COVID-19: All required courses and labs administered online as well as those graded as Pass/Fail or Pass/No Credit as a result of the COVID-19 pandemic are acceptable to meet Netter requirements.

Were tests required? MCAT required.

Are tests expected next year? Yes.

Postgraduate Training Match Rate: 100%

USMLE First-Time Pass Rate

Step 1: 99%

Step 2 CK: 99%

Step 2 CS: 99%

CONNECTICUT

MAINE

MASSACHUSETTS

NEW HAMPSHIRE

NEW JERSEY

NEW YORK

PENNSYLVANIA

RHODE ISLAND

VERMONT

ME
VT
NY
NH
MA
PA
RI
CT
NJ

UNIVERSITY OF CONNECTICUT SCHOOL OF MEDICINE

Address: 263 Farmington Avenue, Farmington, CT 06030
Website: *https://medicine.uconn.edu/*
Contact: *https://medicine.uconn.edu/about-us/contact-us/*
Phone: (860) 679-4713

COST OF ATTENDANCE

In-State Tuition: $40,287
Fees & Expenses: $32,393
Total: $72,681

Out-of-State Tuition: $74,367
Fees & Expenses: $32,393
Total: $106,761

*NE Regional tuition $70,502, making NE Regional COA $102,896.

Financial Aid:http: //health.uconn.edu/student-services/financial-aid/

Percent Receiving Aid: 84%

ADDITIONAL INFORMATION

Interesting tidbit: The medical school's advanced MDelta curriculum, implemented in 2016, employs team-based learning instruction and is focused on shaping and refining students' problem-solving, diagnostic, and treatment skills. Humanism in medicine and the health systems sciences are integral components of MDelta.

What percent of students participate in global health experiences? 19%

What service learning opportunities exist? Migrant Farm Workers Clinic, Hartford Health Education Program, Bridge to the Future Science Mentoring Program and more. For more information, visit:https://medicine.uconn.edu/student-life/community-programs/

What dual degree options exist? BS/MD, MD/PhD, MD/MBA, and MD/MPH. For more information, visit:https://medicine.uconn.edu/prospective-students/

Important Updates due to COVID-19: Pass-Fail grades are only accepted for coursework completed in the college setting for the winter/spring /summer of 2020, not after summer 2020. All on-line courses are accepted if completed between spring 2020 and summer 2021.

Were tests required? MCAT required.

Are tests expected next year? Yes.

Postgraduate Training Match Rate: 98%*

* Reported by school with no known reference year.
USMLE First-Time Pass Rate (2019)

Step 1: 96%
Step 2 CK: 99%
Step 2 CS: 97%

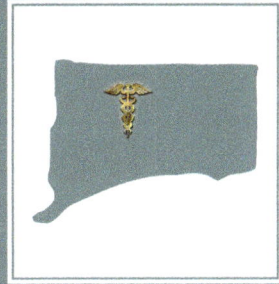

CONNECTICUT

MAINE

MASSACHUSETTS

NEW HAMPSHIRE

NEW JERSEY

NEW YORK

PENNSYLVANIA

RHODE ISLAND

VERMONT

NORTHEAST

CONNECTICUT

MAINE

MASSACHUSETTS

NEW HAMPSHIRE

NEW JERSEY

NEW YORK

PENNSYLVANIA

RHODE ISLAND

VERMONT

YALE SCHOOL OF MEDICINE

Address: 333 Cedar Street, New Haven, CT 06510
Website: *https://medicine.yale.edu/*
Contact: *https://medicine.yale.edu/contact/*
Phone: (203) 785-2696

COST OF ATTENDANCE

Tuition: $66,160
Fees & Expenses: $31,189
Total: $97,349

Financial Aid: https://medicine.yale.edu/education/financialaid/scholarships/

Percent Receiving Aid: 84%

ADDITIONAL INFORMATION

Interesting tidbit: Yale School of Medicine's historical contributions to medicine include the first X-ray performed in the United States, the first successful use of penicillin in America, the first use of cancer chemotherapy, and the introduction of fetal heart monitoring, natural childbirth and newborn rooming-in. Yale doctors designed the first artificial heart pump and the first insulin infusion pump for diabetes.

What percent of students participate in global health experiences? 30%

What service learning opportunities exist? Free medical care in the surrounding communities and students volunteer in various settings. For more information, visit:https://medicine.yale.edu/about/community/

What dual degree options exist? MD/PhD, MD/MPH, MD/MHS, MD/JD, MD/MBA, and MD/MDiv. For more information, visit:https://medicine.yale.edu/edu/md/

Important Updates due to COVID-19: Honor each college/university's response to grading policies, and those of students, with regard to the entirety of 2020 and 2021 (spring, summer, and fall). Permit applicants to take pre-medical requirements online provided the courses include laboratory work and ask applicants to specify any pre-medical courses taken online when filling out the YSM Secondary Application.

Were tests required? MCAT required.

Are tests expected next year? Yes.

Postgraduate Training Match Rate: N/A

USMLE First-Time Pass Rate

Step 1: N/A

Step 2 CK: N/A

Step 2 CS: N/A

BOSTON UNIVERSITY SCHOOL OF MEDICINE

Address: 72 East Concord St., Boston, MA 02118
Website: *https://www.bumc.bu.edu/busm/*
Contact: *https://www.bumc.bu.edu/busm/about/contact-us/*
Phone: (617) 358-9540

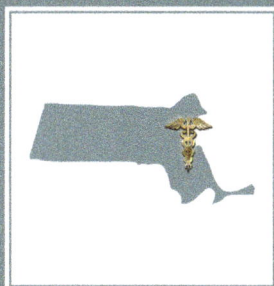

COST OF ATTENDANCE

Tuition: $66,702
Fees & Expenses: $25,168
Total: $91,870

Financial Aid:https: //www.bumc.bu.edu/busm/admissions/
financial-aid/

Percent Receiving Aid: 81%

ADDITIONAL INFORMATION

Interesting tidbit: Created by a merger of Boston University and
the New England Female Medical College in 1873, BUMS was the
first institution in the United States to offer medical education to
women. Its alumni include the first black female physician and the
first Native American physician.

**What percent of students participate in global health
experiences?** 18%

What service learning opportunities exist? Outreach Van Project,
Global Health Program, Flu Shot Program, and more. For more
information, visit:https://www.bumc.bu.edu/busm/education/
medical-education/enrichment/

What dual degree options exist? BS/MD, MD/PhD, MD/MPH, MD/
JD and MD/MBA, MD/MSCR, and MD/OMFS. For more information,
visit:https://www.bumc.bu.edu/busm/admissions/degree-programs/

Important Updates due to COVID-19: Flexible in evaluating the
timing of MCAT tests, the number of P/F grades in Spring 2020 thru
Spring 2021, the abrupt discontinuation of some activities and
other elements impacted by the current pandemic; however a final
admissions decision will not be made without an MCAT score on file.

Were tests required? MCAT and CASPer required.

Are tests expected next year? Yes.

Postgraduate Training Match Rate: 91%*

USMLE First-Time Pass Rate

Step 1: 92-99%*

Step 2 CK: 99-100%*

Step 2 CS: 99-100%*

*Pass rates over the past few years, as reported by Boston
University.

Other: Early Medical School Selection Program (EMSSP) for
students at partnered schools to apply for early admission during
sophomore year of college. For more information, visit:https://
www.bumc.bu.edu/busm/about/diversity/
programs/emssp/

CONNECTICUT

MAINE

MASSACHUSETTS

NEW HAMPSHIRE

NEW JERSEY

NEW YORK

PENNSYLVANIA

RHODE ISLAND

VERMONT

NORTHEAST

CONNECTICUT

MAINE

MASSACHUSETTS

NEW HAMPSHIRE

NEW JERSEY

NEW YORK

PENNSYLVANIA

RHODE ISLAND

VERMONT

HARVARD MEDICAL SCHOOL

Address: 25 Shattuck St., Boston, MA 02115
Website: https://hms.harvard.edu/
Contact:https: //hms.harvard.edu/about-hms/contact-harvard-medical-school
Phone: (617) 432-1550

COST OF ATTENDANCE

Tuition: $66,284
Fees & Expenses: $33,132
Total: $99,146

Financial Aid: https://meded.hms.harvard.edu/md-financial-aid

Percent Receiving Aid: 72%

ADDITIONAL INFORMATION

Interesting tidbit: In 1799, Harvard Medical School Professor Benjamin Waterhouse introduced the smallpox vaccine to the United States. Since then, 15 researchers have shared in nine Nobel prizes for work completed while at the School.

What percent of students participate in global health experiences? 29%

What service learning opportunities exist? Local and other community outreach opportunities available. Students may also participate in Away Rotations or International Rotations. For more information, visit:https://meded.hms.harvard.edu/away-rotations

What dual degree options exist? MD/PhD, MD/MAD, MD/MBA, MD/MMSc, MD/MPH, and MD/MPP. For more information, visit:https://meded.hms.harvard.edu/combined-degrees

Important Updates due to COVID-19: Accept pass/fail grading for spring, summer and fall coursework during 2020. Accept MCAT scores at a later time once the testing sites have reopened.

Were tests required? MCAT required.

Are tests expected next year? Yes.

Postgraduate Training Match Rate: 100%

USMLE First-Time Pass Rate

Step 1: N/A

Step 2 CK: N/A

Step 2 CS: N/A

Note: Applicants choose to apply to one of or both of the following curriculum tracks: Pathways and HST. Pathways allows every student to plan an individual pathway to the MD degree. 135 students are admitted into this track. HST allows students to collaborate with Harvard and MIT faculty on research. 30 students are admitted into the HST track. As such, prerequisites may vary between the two tracks. For more information on these tracks, visit:https://meded.hms.harvard.edu/admissions-choosing-track

TUFTS UNIVERSITY SCHOOL OF MEDICINE

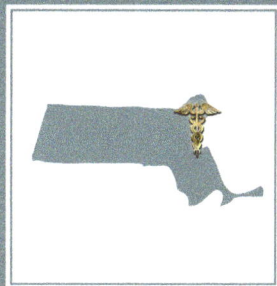

Address: 136 Harrison Ave., Boston, MA 02111
Website: *https://medicine.tufts.edu/*
Contact: *https://medicine.tufts.edu/contact*
Phone: (617) 636-6571

COST OF ATTENDANCE

Tuition: $66,354
Fees & Expenses: $29,183
Total: $95,537

Financial Aid:https: //medicine.tufts.edu/admissions-aid/financial-aid

Percent Receiving Aid: 71%

ADDITIONAL INFORMATION

Interesting tidbit: Tufts College Medical School opened in 1893 and the first-year class is more than 25 percent women.

What percent of students participate in global health experiences? 16%

What service learning opportunities exist? Students work with medically underserved populations, patient support and advocacy initiatives, youth science and health education programs, and more. For more information, visit:https://medicine.tufts.edu/local-global-engagement/CSL

What dual degree options exist? MD/MA in International Relations, MD/MBA, Accelerated MD/MPH, and MD/PhD. https://medicine.tufts.edu/education/dual-degrees

Important Updates due to COVID-19: Considered P/F (pass/no-pass) grades for coursework taken between the winter of 2020 and the summer of 2021. For students who submit P/F grades, a statement from your school documenting your school's grading system during this time frame will be required. Allowed to submit a later MCAT score through the fall of 2020.

Were tests required? MCAT required.

Are tests expected next year? Yes.

Postgraduate Training Match Rate: 100% (2021)

USMLE First-Time Pass Rate

Step 1: N/A

Step 2 CK: N/A

Step 2 CS: N/A

Other: Early Assurance Program available to undergraduate applicants. For more information, visit:https://medicine.tufts.edu/admissions-aid/admissions-program/special-options/early-assurance

Note: Maine Track available. This track is in partnership with Maine Medical Center, where students are dedicated to pursuing a career in rural medicine. For more information, visit:https://medicine.tufts.edu/education/MD-maine-track

CONNECTICUT

MAINE

MASSACHUSETTS

NEW HAMPSHIRE

NEW JERSEY

NEW YORK

PENNSYLVANIA

RHODE ISLAND

VERMONT

NORTHEAST

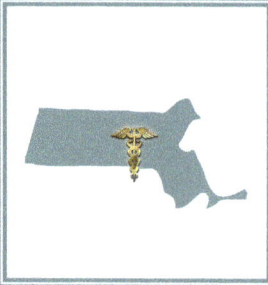

CONNECTICUT

MAINE

MASSACHUSETTS

NEW HAMPSHIRE

NEW JERSEY

NEW YORK

PENNSYLVANIA

RHODE ISLAND

VERMONT

UNIVERSITY OF MASSACHUSETTS MEDICAL SCHOOL

Address: 55 Lake Ave., North Worcester, MA 01655
Website: *https://www.umassmed.edu/*
Contact: *https://www.umassmed.edu/contact-us/*
Phone: (508) 856-2323

COST OF ATTENDANCE

In-State Tuition: $36,570
Fees & Expenses: $33,466
Total: $70,036

Out-of-State Tuition: $62,899
Fees & Expenses: $33,466
Total: $96,365

Financial Aid: https: //www.umassmed.edu/financialaid/currentstudents/

Percent Receiving Aid: 75%

ADDITIONAL INFORMATION

Interesting tidbit: The University of Massachusetts Medical School (UMMS) is the commonwealth's first and only public academic health sciences center.Its founding goal is to provide affordable, high-quality medical education to qualified residents of the commonwealth.

What percent of students participate in global health experiences? 28%

What service learning opportunities exist? For more information, visit:https://www.umassmed.edu/advocacy/service-learning/

What dual degree options exist? MD/PhD:https://www.umassmed.edu/mdphd/

MD/MBA: https://www.umassmed.edu/mba/

Important Updates due to COVID-19: Allow both pass/fail grades and on-line courses for pre-requisites for the Spring, Summer and Fall 2020 semesters. Applications are not considered complete and ready for review by the Admissions Committee until all MCAT scores have been received and are on file.

Were tests required? MCAT required.

Are tests expected next year? Yes.

Postgraduate Training Match Rate: N/A

USMLE First-Time Pass Rate

Step 1: N/A

Step 2 CK: N/A

Step 2 CS: N/A

GEISEL SCHOOL OF MEDICINE AT DARTMOUTH

Address: 3 Rope Ferry Road, Hanover, NH 03755
Website: *https://geiselmed.dartmouth.edu/*
Contact: *https://geiselmed.dartmouth.edu/admissions/contact-us/*
Phone: (603) 650-1505

COST OF ATTENDANCE

Tuition: $67,532
Fees & Expenses: $23,211
Total: $90,743

Financial Aid: https://geiselmed.dartmouth.edu/admissions/costs-and-financial-aid/

Percent Receiving Aid: 80%

ADDITIONAL INFORMATION

Interesting tidbit: The Geisel School of Medicine is the fourth oldest medical school in the nation. The Geisel School poet-physician faculty member, Oliver Wendell Holmes introduced the first use of the stethoscope in medical education.

What percent of students participate in global health experiences? 19%

What service learning opportunities exist? Community Service Committee is a student-run organization that sponsors over 24 community education programs. For more information, visit:https://geiselmed.dartmouth.edu/admissions/medical-education-at-geisel/community-service/

What dual degree options exist? MD/PhD and MD/MBA:https://geiselmed.dartmouth.edu/ed_programs/

Important Updates due to COVID-19: Accept online prerequisite coursework and labs for the 2020-2021 academic year as long as they are from an accredited institution. Accept credit (Pass/Fail) as reported from your school for the 2020-2021 academic year. This includes prerequisite courses.

Were tests required? MCAT required.

Are tests expected next year? Yes.

Postgraduate Training Match Rate: N/A

USMLE First-Time Pass Rate

Step 1: N/A

Step 2 CK: N/A

Step 2 CS: N/A

Other: Early Assurance Program available to Dartmouth College junior undergraduates. For more information, visit:https://www.dartmouth.edu/prehealth/applying/geisel_early.html

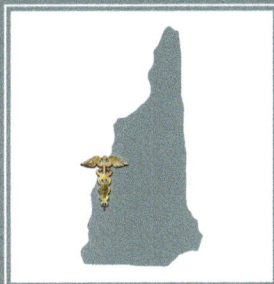

CONNECTICUT

MAINE

MASSACHUSETTS

NEW HAMPSHIRE

NEW JERSEY

NEW YORK

PENNSYLVANIA

RHODE ISLAND

VERMONT

NORTHEAST

CONNECTICUT

MAINE

MASSACHUSETTS

NEW HAMPSHIRE

NEW JERSEY

NEW YORK

PENNSYLVANIA

RHODE ISLAND

VERMONT

COOPER MEDICAL SCHOOL OF ROWAN UNIVERSITY

Address: 401 South Broadway, Camden, NJ 08103
Website: *https://cmsru.rowan.edu/*
Contact: *https://cmsru.rowan.edu/about/contact/*
Phone: (856) 361-2850

COST OF ATTENDANCE

In-State Tuition: $40,479
Fees & Expenses: $25,341
Total: $65,820

Out-of-State Tuition: $62,240
Fees & Expenses: $25,341
Total: $89,581

Financial Aid: https://cmsru.rowan.edu/students/financial_aid/

Percent Receiving Aid: 85%

ADDITIONAL INFORMATION

Interesting tidbit: Officially launched in 2012, CMSRU was the first new medical school in New Jersey in more than 35 years and the only four-year M.D. degree-granting medical school in southern New Jersey.

What percent of students participate in global health experiences? 19%

What service learning opportunities exist? Cathedral Kitchen, Street Medicine Outreach, Playpals, etc. For more information, visit:https://cmsru.rowan.edu/diversity/service_learning/

What dual degree options exist? MD/PhD.

Important Updates due to COVID-19: Allow both pass/fail grades and on-line courses for pre-requisites.

Were tests required? MCAT required.

Are tests expected next year? Yes.

Postgraduate Training Match Rate: N/A

USMLE First-Time Pass Rate

Step 1: N/A

Step 2 CK: N/A

Step 2 CS: N/A

Other: BS/MD available. Cooper Medical School is in partnership with certain undergraduate colleges. For more information, visit:https://csm.rowan.edu/preprofessional/articulation.html

HACKENSACK-MERIDIAN SCHOOL OF MEDICINE AT SETON HALL UNIVERSITY

Address: 340 Kingsland St., Nutley, NJ 07110
Website: *https://www.shu.edu/medicine/*
Contact: *https://www.shu.edu/medicine/admissions/request-information.cfm*
Phone: (973) 761-9000

COST OF ATTENDANCE

Tuition: $65,404
Fees & Expenses: $35,135
Total: $100,539

Financial Aid: https://www.shu.edu/medicine/admissions/financial-aid-and-cost.cfm

Percent Receiving Aid: 100%

ADDITIONAL INFORMATION

Interesting tidbit: Central to the curriculum will be a thread called the Human Dimension. Through immersive and longitudinal experiences, students will come to understand the role of community and context in health and wellbeing, as well as the role of the physician in all elements that contribute to promoting health and preventing disease.

What percent of students participate in global health experiences? N/A

What service learning opportunities exist? Community service projects through student organizations. For more information, visit:https://www.shu.edu/medicine/student-affairs/student-life.cfm

What dual degree options exist? No dual degree options listed.

Important Updates due to COVID-19: N/A

Were tests required? MCAT required.

Are tests expected next year? Yes.

Postgraduate Training Match Rate: N/A

USMLE First-Time Pass Rate

Step 1: N/A

Step 2 CK: N/A

Step 2 CS: N/A

CONNECTICUT

MAINE

MASSACHUSETTS

NEW HAMPSHIRE

NEW JERSEY

NEW YORK

PENNSYLVANIA

RHODE ISLAND

VERMONT

NORTHEAST

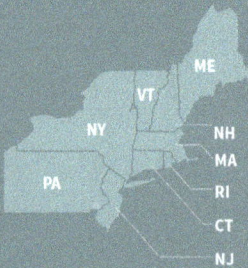

RUTGERS NEW JERSEY MEDICAL SCHOOL

Address: 185 South Orange Avenue, Newark, NJ 07107
Website: *http://njms.rutgers.edu/*
Contact: *http://njms.rutgers.edu/admissions/programs_7_8_year.cfm*
Phone: (973) 972-4631

COST OF ATTENDANCE

In-State Tuition: $43,345
Fees & Expenses: $33,938
Total: $77,283

Out-of-State Tuition: $66,882
Fees & Expenses: $33,938
Total: $100,820

Financial Aid: https://financialaid.rutgers.edu/types-of-aid/

Percent Receiving Aid: 75%

ADDITIONAL INFORMATION

Interesting tidbit: Rutgers New Jersey Medical School developed an Accelerated 3-Year MD Program in an effort to address the national shortage of primary care physicians and particularly the needs of the Newark community. The program allows students who have a strong interest in a primary care career to complete their MD degree in an accelerated 3-year program of study. Application to the Accelerated 3-year Primary Care MD Program is limited to students who have already been accepted to the traditional 4-year MD program.

What percent of students participate in global health experiences? 14%

What service learning opportunities exist? The Young Fathers' Program, RESPIRA, and various pipeline programs. For more information, visit:http://njms.rutgers.edu/community/index.cfm

What dual degree options exist? MD/PhD:http://njms.rutgers.edu/admissions/MD_PhD.cfm

MD/MBA: http://njms.rutgers.edu/admissions/MD_MBA.cfm

MD/MPH: http://njms.rutgers.edu/admissions/MD_MPH.cfm

MD with Thesis: http://njms.rutgers.edu/admissions/MD_Thesis.cfm

Important Updates due to COVID-19: Accept online courses and "Pass" (P/F) grades without prejudice, for courses taken in the Spring and Summer 2020 semesters. Before making interview and admissions decisions, an MCAT score is required.

Were tests required? MCAT and CASPer required.

Are tests expected next year? Yes.

Postgraduate Training Match Rate: 98.3% (2021)

USMLE First-Time Pass Rate
Step 1: N/A
Step 2 CK: N/A
Step 2 CS: N/A

Other: Accelerated MD program (3 years) available. For more information, visit:http://njms.rutgers.edu/admissions/programs_accelerated_md.cfm

7-year BA/MD program available to high school applicants. For more information, visit:http://njms.rutgers.edu/admissions/programs_7_8_year.cfm

RUTGERS, ROBERT WOOD JOHNSON MEDICAL SCHOOL

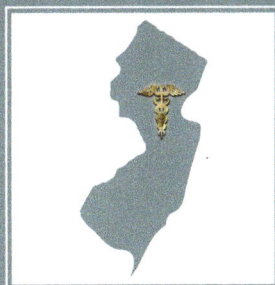

Address: One Robert Wood Johnson Place, New Brunswick, NJ 08901
Website: *http://rwjms.rutgers.edu/*
Contact: *https://rwjms.rutgers.edu/departments/medicine/contact-us*
Phone: (732) 235-7739

COST OF ATTENDANCE

In-State Tuition: $43,345
Fees & Expenses: $34,878
Total: $78,223

Out-of-State Tuition: $66,882
Fees & Expenses: $34,878
Total: $101,760

Financial Aid: https://financialaid.rutgers.edu/information-for-rbhs-students/

Percent Receiving Aid: 70%

ADDITIONAL INFORMATION

Interesting tidbit: Robert Wood Johnson Medical School offers a three-year accelerated primary care track - the Primary Accelerated Continuity Care Experience (PACCE). After completing this three-year curriculum, students move on to residency at one of the RWJMS affiliated Family Medicine Residency programs. Also, 2021 is the official launch of the 5 Cs Curriculum: Curiosity, Critical Thinking, Clinical Skills, Competence and Compassion.

What percent of students participate in global health experiences? 18%

What service learning opportunities exist? Homeless and Indigent Populations Health and Outreach Project. For more information, visit:http://rwjms.rutgers.edu/education/medical_education/research-and-community-experiences/community-health

What dual degree options exist? MD/PhD, MD/JD, MD/MPH, MD/MS in Clinical & Translational Science, and MD/MBA. For more information, visit:http://rwjms.rutgers.edu/education/medical_education/dual-degree-programs

Important Updates due to COVID-19: Accept pass/fail grades, for courses taken during the COVID pandemic.accept online courses undertaken to meet prerequisites. Require an MCAT score prior to offering an interview. Extend our interview schedule and slow our reviews so as to allow applicants more time to have their MCAT score available.

Were tests required? MCAT and CASPer required.

Are tests expected next year? Yes.

Postgraduate Training Match Rate: 95% (2021)

USMLE First-Time Pass Rate

Step 1: N/A

Step 2 CK: N/A

Step 2 CS: N/A

Other: BA/MD program available to Rutgers University students in their sophomore year. For more information, visit:https://hpo.rutgers.edu/special-programs/academic-programs/ba-md-rwj

CONNECTICUT

MAINE

MASSACHUSETTS

NEW HAMPSHIRE

NEW JERSEY

NEW YORK

PENNSYLVANIA

RHODE ISLAND

VERMONT

NORTHEAST

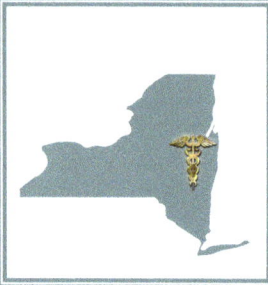

CONNECTICUT

MAINE

MASSACHUSETTS

NEW HAMPSHIRE

NEW JERSEY

NEW YORK

PENNSYLVANIA

RHODE ISLAND

VERMONT

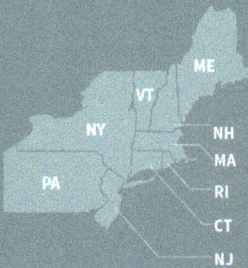

ALBANY MEDICAL COLLEGE

Address: 47 New Scotland Avenue, Albany, NY 12208
Website: *https://www.amc.edu/Academic/index.cfm*
Contact: *https://www.amc.edu/academic/undergraduate/Contact_Us.cfm*
Phone: (518) 262-5521

COST OF ATTENDANCE

In-State Tuition: $57,598
Fees & Expenses: $20,653
Total: $78,251

Out-of-State Tuition: $57,723
Fees & Expenses: $20,653
Total: $78,376

Financial Aid: https://www.amc.edu/academic/undergraduate/FinancialAid.cfm

Percent Receiving Aid: 82%

ADDITIONAL INFORMATION

Interesting tidbit: Albany Med is the only academic medical center within a 150-mile radius. It is committed to patient care, medical education, and biomedical research - ensuring access to medical and technological innovations for the region's 2.9 million people.

What percent of students participate in global health experiences? 10%

What service learning opportunities exist? Service learning is a requirement. For more information, visit:https://www.amc.edu/academic/undergraduate/LCME/service-learning.cfm

What dual degree options exist? MD/MPH, MD/MBA, and MD/PhD. For more information, visit:https://www.amc.edu/academic/Undergraduate_Admissions/special_programs.cfm

Important Updates due to COVID-19: For the spring 2020 semester, allow both pass/fail grades and on-line courses for pre-requisites. Secondary applications must be fully complete including MCAT score and supplemental application by December 15th, 2020.

Were tests required? MCAT required.

Are tests expected next year? Yes.

Postgraduate Training Match Rate: 99% (2021)

USMLE First-Time Pass Rate

Step 1: 98%

Step 2 CK: N/A

Step 2 CS: N/A

Other: BS/MD and other special programs available. For more information, visit:https://www.amc.edu/academic/Undergraduate_Admissions/special_programs.cfm

ALBERT EINSTEIN COLLEGE OF MEDICINE

Address: 1300 Morris Park Avenue, Bronx, NY 10461
Website: *https://www.einstein.yu.edu/*
Contact: *http://www.einstein.yu.edu/about/contact-us.asp*
Phone: (718) 430-2106

COST OF ATTENDANCE

In-State Tuition: $55,052
Fees & Expenses: $32,872
Total: $87,924

Financial Aid: https://www.einstein.yu.edu/education/md-program/financial-aid/

Percent Receiving Aid: 80%

ADDITIONAL INFORMATION

Interesting tidbit: Albert Einstein College of Medicine's M.D. curriculum includes the professional development phase, which is approximately 18 months and affords students the opportunity to hone in on a specialty. This phase consists of two required Acting Internships, as well as several selectives and clinical or classroom electives that students take either at a local affiliate, across the United States, or around the world. In addition, every Einstein student writes a Scholarly Paper (SP) based on mentor-guided research as a requirement for graduation.

What percent of students participate in global health experiences? 29%

What service learning opportunities exist? Hoops for Health, Homeless Outreach Program at Einstein, Einstein Buddies, and more. For more information, visit:https://www.einstein.yu.edu/diversity/diversity-enhancement/

What dual degree options exist? MD/PhD:http://www.einstein.yu.edu/education/mstp/

MD/MPH: http://www.einstein.yu.edu/education/einstein-cuny-md-mph/

Important Updates due to COVID-19: Accept on-line or pass/fail for prerequisite science courses for the spring 2020 semester and the fall 2020 semester. Applications are not considered until MCAT scores are available.

Were tests required? MCAT required.

Are tests expected next year? Yes.

Postgraduate Training Match Rate: 99% (2020)

USMLE First-Time Pass Rate

Step 1: 97%

Step 2 CK: 99%

Step 2 CS: 97%

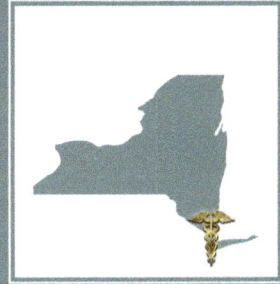

CONNECTICUT

MAINE

MASSACHUSETTS

NEW HAMPSHIRE

NEW JERSEY

NEW YORK

PENNSYLVANIA

RHODE ISLAND

VERMONT

NORTHEAST

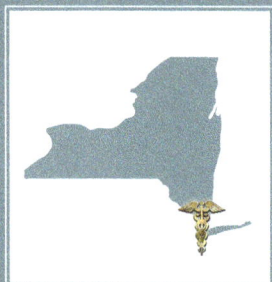

CONNECTICUT

MAINE

MASSACHUSETTS

NEW HAMPSHIRE

NEW JERSEY

NEW YORK

PENNSYLVANIA

RHODE ISLAND

VERMONT

COLUMBIA UNIVERSITY VAGELOS COLLEGE OF PHYSICIANS AND SURGEONS

Address: 630 West 168th Street, New York, NY 10032
Website: *https://www.ps.columbia.edu/*
Contact: *https://www.ps.columbia.edu/about-us/contact-vp-s*
Phone: (212) 305-3595

COST OF ATTENDANCE

Tuition: $66,814
Fees & Expenses: $33,246
Total: $100,060

Financial Aid: https://www.ps.columbia.edu/education/academic-programs/md-program/admissions/md-financial-aid

Percent Receiving Aid: 79%

ADDITIONAL INFORMATION

Interesting tidbit: The Columbia University Vagelos College of Physicians and Surgeons dates back more than 250 years to 1767 (then known as King's College). Columbia's medical school was the first in the American Colonies to grant the MD degree in 1770.

What percent of students participate in global health experiences? 35%

What service learning opportunities exist? Opportunities in Guatemala, Columbia Student Medical Outreach (CoSMO), etc. For more information, visit:https://www.ps.columbia.edu/education/academic-programs/programs-physical-therapy/doctor-physical-therapy/service-experiential

What dual degree options exist? MD/PhD, MD/OMFS, MD/MS in Biomedical Science, MD/MPH, MD/MBA, MD/MS in Biomedical Engineering, and MD/MA in Biomedical Informatics. For more information, visit:https://www.ps.columbia.edu/education/academic-programs/md-dual-degrees-and-special-programs

Important Updates due to COVID-19: Accept Pass/Fail grades for prerequisite courses taken at schools who decided to go Pass/Fail for the 2020 academic calendar and Spring/Summer 2021 semesters.

Were tests required? MCAT required.

Are tests expected next year? Yes.

Postgraduate Training Match Rate: N/A

USMLE First-Time Pass Rate

Step 1: N/A

Step 2 CK: N/A

Step 2 CS: N/A

Other: 3-year accelerated MD program available. For more information, visit:https://www.ps.columbia.edu/education/academic-programs/doctoral-degree-programs/3-year-phd-md-program

CUNY SCHOOL OF MEDICINE

Address: 160 Convent Ave., New York, NY 10031
Website: *https://www.ccny.cuny.edu/csom*
Contact: *https://www.ccny.cuny.edu/about/contact*
Phone: (212) 650-7718

COST OF ATTENDANCE

Tuition: $41,600
Fees & Expenses: $27,870
Total: $69,470

Financial Aid: https://www.ccny.cuny.edu/financialaid

Percent Receiving Aid: 83%

ADDITIONAL INFORMATION

Interesting tidbit: The Sophie Davis Biomedical Education Program at the CUNY School of Medicine is an accelerated combined degree program, where qualified students receive the Bachelor of Science (BS) degree after completing an integrated three-year education and then transition into the CUNY School of Medicine to earn their Doctor of Medicine (MD) degree.

What percent of students participate in global health experiences? 18%

What service learning opportunities exist? N/A

What dual degree options exist? CUNY SOM Sophie Davis only offers a BS/MD program.

Important Updates due to COVID-19: Implemented a temporary suspension of standardized admissions testing requirements, and therefore the ACT and SAT will not be considered for Fall 2021 admission.

Were tests required? No.

Are tests expected next year? Yes.

Postgraduate Training Match Rate: 100% (2020)

USMLE First-Time Pass Rate

Step 1: N/A

Step 2 CK: N/A

Step 2 CS: N/A

Note: CUNY SOM only offers a BS/MD program that is available to high school applicants. For more information, visit:https://www.ccny.cuny.edu/csom/bsmd

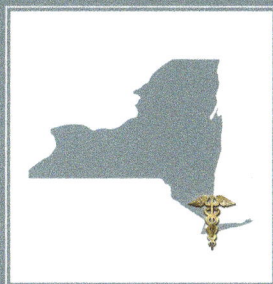

CONNECTICUT

MAINE

MASSACHUSETTS

NEW HAMPSHIRE

NEW JERSEY

NEW YORK

PENNSYLVANIA

RHODE ISLAND

VERMONT

NORTHEAST

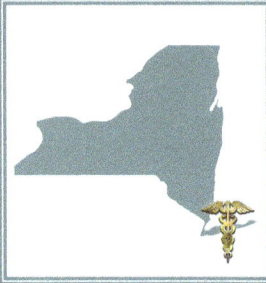

CONNECTICUT

MAINE

MASSACHUSETTS

NEW HAMPSHIRE

NEW JERSEY

NEW YORK

PENNSYLVANIA

RHODE ISLAND

VERMONT

DONALD AND BARBARA ZUCKER SCHOOL OF MEDICINE AT HOFSTRA/NORTHWELL

Address: 500 Hofstra University, Hempstead, NY 11549
Website: *https://medicine.hofstra.edu/*
Contact: *https://medicine.hofstra.edu/admission/md/contactus.html*
Phone: (516) 463-7516

COST OF ATTENDANCE

Tuition: $54,525
Fees & Expenses: $33,442
Total: $87,967

Financial Aid: https://medicine.hofstra.edu/financialaid/index.html

Percent Receiving Aid: 86%

ADDITIONAL INFORMATION

Interesting tidbit: Years 1 and 2 curriculum is organized around weekly themes anchored in our small group, problem/case-based learning program. Contact hours are limited each week to allow for ample self-directed learning time and opportunities for review and reinforcement.

What percent of students participate in global health experiences? 10%

What service learning opportunities exist? Student-run free clinic. For more information, visit:https://medicine.hofstra.edu/students/student-clinic.html

What dual degree options exist? MD/PhD, MD/MPH, and MD/MBA. For more information, visit:https://medicine.hofstra.edu/about/at-a-glance.html

Important Updates due to COVID-19: Accept pass/fail graded course for the spring semester of 2020 and online coursework and labs for the spring semester and summer session of 2020.

Were tests required? MCAT and CASPer required.

Are tests expected next year? Yes.

Postgraduate Training Match Rate: 100% (2021)

USMLE First-Time Pass Rate

Step 1: N/A

Step 2 CK: N/A

Step 2 CS: N/A

Other: 4+4 BS/MD Program available to high school applicants. For more information, visit:https://www.hofstra.edu/admission/adm_4plus4.html

ICAHN SCHOOL OF MEDICINE AT MOUNT SINAI

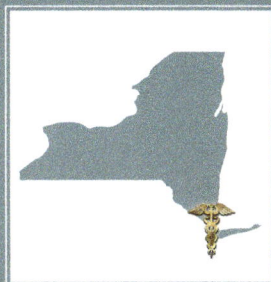

Address: One Gustave L. Levy Place, New York, NY 10029
Website: *https://icahn.mssm.edu/*
Contact: *https://icahn.mssm.edu/about/contact-us*
Phone: (212) 241-6696

COST OF ATTENDANCE

Tuition: $60,405
Fees & Expenses: $25,515
Total: $85,920

Financial Aid: https://icahn.mssm.edu/education/financial-aid

Percent Receiving Aid: 53%

ADDITIONAL INFORMATION

Interesting tidbit: The Icahn School of Medicine is the medical and graduate school of the Mount Sinai Health System—the largest healthcare network in New York City. ISM Medical School's MD program explicitly blurs the traditional distinction between pre-clinical and clinical years by integrating the basic sciences across courses as well-initiating students into the clinical environment from their first day of school.

What percent of students participate in global health experiences? 32%

What service learning opportunities exist? Student-run health clinic serving uninsured residents of East Harlem, Medical Mandarin, MedStart, etc. For more information, visit:https://icahn.mssm.edu/education/medical/engagement

What dual degree options exist? MD/PhD and MD/MPHD. For more information, visit:https://icahn.mssm.edu/education/dual-specialty

Important Updates due to COVID-19: Accept P/F grading for Spring 2020 courses and online coursework and labs for Spring 2020 and Summer 2020.

Were tests required? MCAT required.

Are tests expected next year? Yes.

Postgraduate Training Match Rate: N/A

USMLE First-Time Pass Rate

Step 1: N/A

Step 2 CK: N/A

Step 2 CS: N/A

Other: Early Assurance pathway for college undergraduate applicants. For more information, visit:https://icahn.mssm.edu/education/admissions/application/flexmed

CONNECTICUT

MAINE

MASSACHUSETTS

NEW HAMPSHIRE

NEW JERSEY

NEW YORK

PENNSYLVANIA

RHODE ISLAND

VERMONT

NORTHEAST

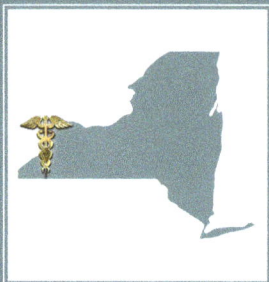

CONNECTICUT

MAINE

MASSACHUSETTS

NEW HAMPSHIRE

NEW JERSEY

NEW YORK

PENNSYLVANIA

RHODE ISLAND

VERMONT

JACOBS SCHOOL OF MEDICINE AND BIOMEDICAL SCIENCES AT THE UNIVERSITY AT BUFFALO

Address: 955 Main St, Buffalo, NY 14203
Website: *http://medicine.buffalo.edu/*
Contact: *http://medicine.buffalo.edu/about/contact_us.html*
Phone: (716) 829-3466

COST OF ATTENDANCE

In-State Tuition: $43,670
Fees & Expenses: $29,197
Total: $72,867

Out-of-State Tuition: $65,160
Fees & Expenses: $29,197
Total: $94,357

Financial Aid: http://medicine.buffalo.edu/education/md/about-the-program/financial-assistance.html

Percent Receiving Aid: 81%

ADDITIONAL INFORMATION

Interesting tidbit: UB MD offers an organ-based curriculum, which emphasizes self-directed learning and trains you to think critically and solve problems individually or as a team. Students' sustained clinical experience begins within their second month at UB.

What percent of students participate in global health experiences? 20%

What service learning opportunities exist? Lighthouse Free Medical Clinic, Prescription for Warmth, UB HEALS, etc. For more information, visit:http://medicine.buffalo.edu/about/community_outreach.html

What dual degree options exist? MD/PhD, MD/MPH, and MD/MBA. For more information, visit:http://medicine.buffalo.edu/education/md/about-the-program/joint-and-dual-degree-programs.html

Important Updates due to COVID-19: Accept online coursework from spring and summer 2020 semesters, and pass/fail grades without prejudice for spring 2020 without prejudice. Screen applications regardless of whether or not the MCAT score is submitted. However, all applicants must take the MCAT, by the end of January 2021, and report their score to apply for the 2020-21 admissions cycle.

Were tests required? MCAT required.

Are tests expected next year? Yes.

Postgraduate Training Match Rate: 100% (2021)

USMLE First-Time Pass Rate

Step 1: N/A

Step 2 CK: N/A

Step 2 CS: N/A

NEW YORK MEDICAL COLLEGE

Address: 40 Sunshine Cottage Road, Valhalla, NY 10595
Website: *https://www.nymc.edu/*
Contact: *https://www.nymc.edu/school-of-medicine-som/contact-som/*
Phone: (914) 594-4507

COST OF ATTENDANCE

Tuition: $55,670
Fees & Expenses: $28,019
Total: $83,689

Financial Aid: https://www.nymc.edu/school-of-medicine-som/admissions--financial-aid/

Percent Receiving Aid: 72%

ADDITIONAL INFORMATION

Interesting tidbit: New York Medical College accepted women as early as 1863 and graduated women of color beginning in 1870. It was also the first medical school in the U.S. to establish a scholarship program for minority students.

What percent of students participate in global health experiences? 8%

What service learning opportunities exist? Summer Service Learning Preceptorship and various volunteer opportunities. For more information, visit:https://www.nymc.edu/school-of-medicine-som/student-life/community-involvement-and-service-learning/

What dual degree options exist? MD/PhD and MD/MPH. For more information on the MD/MPH:https://www.nymc.edu/school-of-medicine-som/som-academics/dual-degree-programs/mdmph-program/

For more information on the MD/PhD:https://www.nymc.edu/school-of-medicine-som/som-academics/dual-degree-programs/mdphd-program/

Important Updates due to COVID-19: Due to the COVID-19 pandemic, we are extending our MCAT deadline to include tests offered through December 2020. We will be accepting Pass/Fail coursework for Winter & Spring 2020 and online & Lab coursework for Winter & Spring 2020, including prerequisite courses.

Were tests required? MCAT and CASPer required.

Are tests expected next year? Yes.

Postgraduate Training Match Rate: 99%

USMLE First-Time Pass Rate

Step 1: N/A

Step 2 CK: N/A

Step 2 CS: N/A

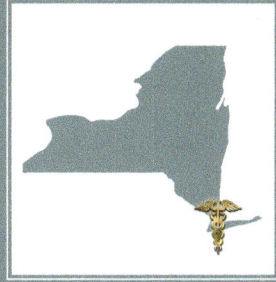

CONNECTICUT

MAINE

MASSACHUSETTS

NEW HAMPSHIRE

NEW JERSEY

NEW YORK

PENNSYLVANIA

RHODE ISLAND

VERMONT

NORTHEAST

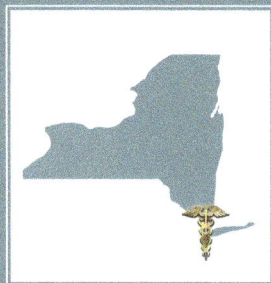

CONNECTICUT

MAINE

MASSACHUSETTS

NEW HAMPSHIRE

NEW JERSEY

NEW YORK

PENNSYLVANIA

RHODE ISLAND

VERMONT

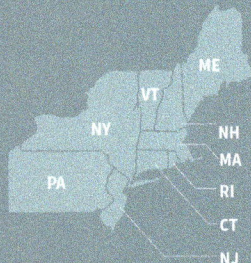

NEW YORK UNIVERSITY GROSSMAN SCHOOL OF MEDICINE

Address: 550 First Avenue New York, NY 10016
Website: *https://med.nyu.edu/our-community/about-us*
Contact: *https://med.nyu.edu/our-community/contact-us*
Phone: (212) 263-5290

COST OF ATTENDANCE

Tuition: $0*
Fees & Expenses: $30,110
Total: $30,110

*NYU Grossman SOM offers full-tuition scholarships ($58,226) to all current students and future matriculated students in the MD degree program, regardless of merit or financial need.

Financial Aid: https://med.nyu.edu/education/md-degree/md-affordability-financial-aid/types-financial-aid

Percent Receiving Aid: 100%

ADDITIONAL INFORMATION

Interesting tidbits: NYU Grossman School of Medicine's accelerated three-year MD degree pathway—the first of its kind at a nationally ranked academic medical center—allows students to earn the MD degree more quickly and at a significantly reduced cost. Upon meeting the academic and professional standards for graduation from medical school, students are ranked to match into an NYU Grossman SOM residency program.

What percent of students participate in global health experiences? 16%

What service learning opportunities exist? Service learning through rotations.

What dual degree options exist? MD/MPH, MD/MBA, MD/MS in Translational Research, MD/MA in Bioethics, and MD/PhD. For more information, visit:https://med.nyu.edu/education/md-degree/dual-md-masters-degrees

Important Updates due to COVID-19: Accept 2020 spring and summer courses graded on a pass/fail basis and online courses and labs for this period.

Were tests required? MCAT required.

Are tests expected next year? Yes.

Postgraduate Training Match Rate: N/A

USMLE First-Time Pass Rate

Step 1: N/A

Step 2 CK: N/A

Step 2 CS: N/A

Other: Accelerated three-year MD pathway. For more information, visit:https://med.nyu.edu/education/md-degree/accelerated-three-year-md

NEW YORK UNIVERSITY LONG ISLAND SCHOOL OF MEDICINE

Address: 259 1st St, Mineola, NY 11501
Website: *https://medli.nyu.edu/*
Contact: *Call or contact via email: medli.admissions@nyulangone.org*
Phone: (516) 240-7240

COST OF ATTENDANCE

Tuition: $0*
Fees & Expenses: $33,582
Total: $33,582

***Note:** Although this medical school is tuition-free, students are responsible to pay for their educational and living expenses.

Financial Aid: https://medli.nyu.edu/financial-aid

Percent Receiving Aid: 100%. This medical school offers full-tuition scholarships.

ADDITIONAL INFORMATION

Interesting tidbit: NYU Long Island School of Medicine's innovative three-year curriculum prepares physicians to become leaders in primary care.

What percent of students participate in global health experiences? N/A

What service learning opportunities exist? N/A

What dual degree options exist? No dual degree options.

Important Updates due to COVID-19: Accept accept pass/fail grading and online coursework, including labs.

Were tests required? MCAT required.

Are tests expected next year? Yes.

Postgraduate Training Match Rate: N/A*

USMLE First-Time Pass Rate*

Step 1: N/A

Step 2 CK: N/A

Step 2 CS: N/A

*This medical school opened in 2019. Therefore, there is no USMLE nor match rate data yet.

Note: This is a three-year MD program.

CONNECTICUT

MAINE

MASSACHUSETTS

NEW HAMPSHIRE

NEW JERSEY

NEW YORK

PENNSYLVANIA

RHODE ISLAND

VERMONT

NORTHEAST

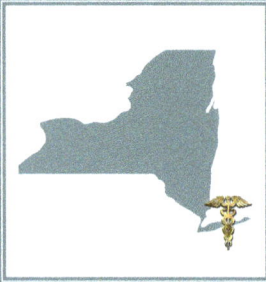

CONNECTICUT

MAINE

MASSACHUSETTS

NEW HAMPSHIRE

NEW JERSEY

NEW YORK

PENNSYLVANIA

RHODE ISLAND

VERMONT

RENAISSANCE SCHOOL OF MEDICINE AT STONY BROOK UNIVERSITY

Address: 101 Nicolls Road, Health Sciences Center, Stony Brook, NY 11794
Website: *https://renaissance.stonybrookmedicine.edu/*
Contact: *https://renaissance.stonybrookmedicine.edu/som/contact*
Phone: (631) 444-2113

COST OF ATTENDANCE

In-State Tuition: $43,670
Fees & Expenses: $30,700
Total: $74,370

Out-of-State Tuition: $66,160
Fees & Expenses: $30,700
Total: $96,860

Financial Aid: https://renaissance.stonybrookmedicine.edu/admissions/financial_info

Percent Receiving Aid: 73%

ADDITIONAL INFORMATION

Interesting tidbit: The Stony Brook University School of Medicine is #1 ranked public medical school in the State of New York (U.S. News & World Report).

What percent of students participate in global health experiences? 33%

What service learning opportunities exist? Global Health opportunities and service learning through student organizations.

What dual degree options exist? MD/PhD, MD/MPH, MD/MBA, and MD/MA. For more information, visit:https://renaissance.stonybrookmedicine.edu/admissions/special_programs

Important Updates due to COVID-19: Online courses and pass/fail grades will be accepted, without prejudice, for courses taken during the spring, summer and fall 2020, and spring 2021 semesters.

Were tests required? MCAT and CASPer required.

Are tests expected next year? Yes.

Postgraduate Training Match Rate: 98%

USMLE First-Time Pass Rate

Step 1: 100%

Step 2 CK: 98%

Step 2 CS: 94%

Note: 3-year Accelerated MD program available. For more information, visit:https://renaissance.stonybrookmedicine.edu/3YMD

Other: Scholars for Medicine BS-BA/MD Program (8-year) available to high school applicants. For more information, visit:https://renaissance.stonybrookmedicine.edu/admissions/scholars

STATE UNIVERSITY OF NEW YORK DOWNSTATE MEDICAL UNIVERSITY COLLEGE OF MEDICINE

Address: 450 Clarkson Ave., Brooklyn, NY 11203
Website: *https://www.downstate.edu/college-of-medicine/*
Contact: *https://sls.downstate.edu/admissions/*
Phone: (718) 270-2446

COST OF ATTENDANCE

In-State Tuition: $43,670
Fees & Expenses: $34,297
Total: $77,967

Out-of-State Tuition: $65,160
Fees & Expenses: $34,297
Total: $99,457

Financial Aid: https://sls.downstate.edu/financial_aid/index.html

Percent Receiving Aid: 74%

ADDITIONAL INFORMATION

Interesting tidbit: The SUNY Downstate College of Medicine was the first medical school founded within a hospital, making bedside training an integral part of students' education.

What percent of students participate in global health experiences? 10%

What service learning opportunities exist? Service learning through student organizations.

What dual degree options exist? MD/PhD and MD/MPH. For more information, visit:https://sls.downstate.edu/admissions/com/entry_pathways.html

Important Updates due to COVID-19: The Admissions Committee is flexible in its admission criteria including, but not limited to: Pass/Fail grades, on-line coursework, and/or discontinuation of activities.

Were tests required? MCAT required.

Are tests expected next year? Yes.

Postgraduate Training Match Rate: 97% (2021)

USMLE First-Time Pass Rate

Step 1: N/A

Step 2 CK: N/A

Step 2 CS: N/A

Other: BA/MD Program available to high school applicants. For more information, visit:https://sls.downstate.edu/admissions/com/entry_pathways.html

CONNECTICUT

MAINE

MASSACHUSETTS

NEW HAMPSHIRE

NEW JERSEY

NEW YORK

PENNSYLVANIA

RHODE ISLAND

VERMONT

NORTHEAST

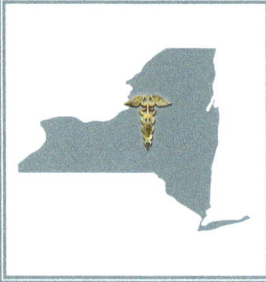

CONNECTICUT

MAINE

MASSACHUSETTS

NEW HAMPSHIRE

NEW JERSEY

NEW YORK

PENNSYLVANIA

RHODE ISLAND

VERMONT

STATE UNIVERSITY OF NEW YORK UPSTATE MEDICAL CENTER COLLEGE OF MEDICINE

Address: 766 Irving Avenue, Syracuse, NY 13210
Website: *https://www.upstate.edu/com/*
Contact: *https://www.upstate.edu/com/contact.php*
Phone: (315) 464-4570

COST OF ATTENDANCE

In-State Tuition: $43,020
Fees & Expenses: $23,251
Total: $66,271

Out-of-State Tuition: $65,160
Fees & Expenses: $23,251
Total: $88,411

Financial Aid: https://www.upstate.edu/financialaid/index.php
Percent Receiving Aid: 81%

ADDITIONAL INFORMATION

Interesting tidbit: In the 1890s, the SU College of Medicine was among the first in America (along with Johns Hopkins, Harvard, Penn, and a few others) to organize its curriculum according to the so-called "German model," with intense scientific and especially laboratory training for students in the first two years, and rigorous clinical training on rounds thereafter.

What percent of students participate in global health experiences? 14%

What service learning opportunities exist? Mentorship, educational programs, clinic volunteer work, etc. For more information, visit:https://www.upstate.edu/outreach/

What dual degree options exist? MD/MPH:https://www.upstate.edu/mph/admissions/md-mph-admissions.php

Important Updates due to COVID-19: Accept Pass/Fail coursework if applicant's school required the students. Accept online courses if they are offered by the school at which the candidate was already enrolled. If a candidate's school did not allow the students to complete the lab component, it will be considered on a case-by-case basis.

Were tests required? MCAT and CASPer required.

Are tests expected next year? Yes.

Postgraduate Training Match Rate: 97% (2021)

USMLE First-Time Pass Rate (2016)

Step 1: 99%

Step 2 CK: 99%

Step 2 CS: 99%

Other: Upstate Accelerated Scholars for high school applicants and the Early Assurance Program for college sophomores. For more information, visit:https://www.upstate.edu/com/admissions/options/index.php

Rural Medical Scholars Program (RMSP): https://www.upstate.edu/fmed/education/rmed/index.php

UNIVERSITY OF ROCHESTER SCHOOL OF MEDICINE AND DENTISTRY

Address: 601 Elmwood Ave, Rochester, NY 14642
Website: *https://www.urmc.rochester.edu/smd.aspx*
Contact: *https://www.urmc.rochester.edu/contact.aspx*
Phone: (585) 275-4539

COST OF ATTENDANCE

Tuition: $61,500
Fees & Expenses: $22,298
Total: $83,798

Financial Aid: https://www.urmc.rochester.edu/education/financial-aid-office.aspx

Percent Receiving Aid: 83%

ADDITIONAL INFORMATION

Interesting tidbit: The University of Rochester Medical Center is a private, coeducational, nonsectarian, and nonprofit research university. It has achieved top-15 rankings in NIH funding in neurology, oral biology, public health and musculoskeletal research.

What percent of students participate in global health experiences? 24%

What service learning opportunities exist? UR Well, art program for hospitalized children, Refugee Student Alliance, etc. For more information, visit:https://www.urmc.rochester.edu/education/md/outreach.aspx

What dual degree options exist? MD/MBA, MD/PhD, and MD/MS. For more information, visit:https://www.urmc.rochester.edu/education/md/admissions/your-journey/combined-dual-degrees.aspx

Important Updates due to COVID-19: Accept P/NP grades for Spring and Summer 2020 semesters, including on-line labs. Accept virtual prerequisite science classes and labs.

Were tests required? MCAT and CASPer required.

Are tests expected next year? Yes.

Postgraduate Training Match Rate: 99%

USMLE First-Time Pass Rate

Step 1: 99%

Step 2 CK: N/A

Step 2 CS: N/A

Other: Rochester Early Medical Scholars (REMS) BA-BS/MD program available to high school applicants. For more information, visit:https://enrollment.rochester.edu/combined-degree-programs/rems/

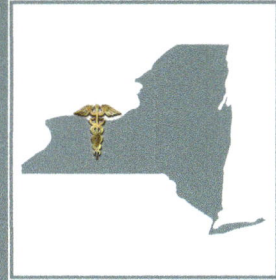

CONNECTICUT

MAINE

MASSACHUSETTS

NEW HAMPSHIRE

NEW JERSEY

NEW YORK

PENNSYLVANIA

RHODE ISLAND

VERMONT

NORTHEAST

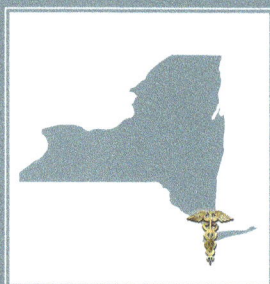

CONNECTICUT

MAINE

MASSACHUSETTS

NEW HAMPSHIRE

NEW JERSEY

NEW YORK

PENNSYLVANIA

RHODE ISLAND

VERMONT

WEILL CORNELL MEDICINE

Address: 1300 York Avenue, New York, NY 10065
Website: *https://weill.cornell.edu/*
Contact: *https://weill.cornell.edu/our-story/contact-weill-cornell-medicine*
Phone: (212) 746-1067

COST OF ATTENDANCE

Tuition: $61,110
Fees & Expenses: $28,020
Total: $89,130

Financial Aid: https://medicaleducation.weill.cornell.edu/admissions/costs-aid

Percent Receiving Aid: 79%

ADDITIONAL INFORMATION

Interesting tidbit: Weill Cornell Medical College offers an unparalleled breadth of research opportunities by virtue of the co-presence, on a single campus, of five renowned institutions - NewYork-Presbyterian Hospital (NYPH), Weill Cornell Medical College (WCMC), Memorial Sloan Kettering Cancer Center (MSKCC), Rockefeller University, and the Hospital for Special Surgery (HSS).

What percent of students participate in global health experiences? 28%

What service learning opportunities exist? Community Clinic, Music and Medicine, and more. For more information, visit:https://medicaleducation.weill.cornell.edu/admissions/opportunities-engagement

What dual degree options exist? MD/MBA:https://medicaleducation.weill.cornell.edu/medical-education/joint-degree-programs/md-mba MD/PhD:https://mdphd.weill.cornell.edu/

Important Updates due to COVID-19: Accept Pass/Fail prerequisite courses and online prerequisite courses and labs completed during the global health crisis.

Were tests required? MCAT required.

Are tests expected next year? Yes.

Postgraduate Training Match Rate: N/A

USMLE First-Time Pass Rate

Step 1: N/A

Step 2 CK: N/A

Step 2 CS: N/A

DREXEL UNIVERSITY COLLEGE OF MEDICINE

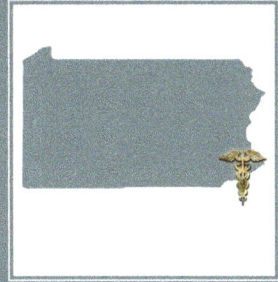

Address: 2900 W. Queen Lane, Philadelphia, PA 19129
Website: *https://drexel.edu/medicine/*
Contact: *https://drexel.edu/medicine/about/contact-information/*
Phone: (215) 991-8202
Other Locations: Classes also held at Center City campus

COST OF ATTENDANCE

Tuition: $58,978
Fees & Expenses: $24,295
Total: $83,273

Financial Aid: https://drexel.edu/medicine/academics/md-program/md-program-admissions/tuition-financial-aid/

Percent Receiving Aid: 79%

ADDITIONAL INFORMATION

Interesting tidbit: Drexel University College of Medicine represents the consolidation of two venerable medical schools with rich and intertwined histories: Hahnemann Medical College and Woman's Medical College of Pennsylvania. Woman's Medical College of PA was the first medical school for women in the world.

What percent of students participate in global health experiences? 10%

What service learning opportunities exist? Student-run health clinics, educational outreach, global health, etc. For more information, visit:https://drexel.edu/medicine/community-engagement/overview/

What dual degree options exist? MD/MPH, MD/MBA, MD/MS, and MD/PhD. For more information, visit:https://drexel.edu/medicine/academics/dual-degree-programs/

Important Updates due to COVID-19: N/A

Were tests required? MCAT and CASPer required.

Are tests expected next year? Yes.

Postgraduate Training Match Rate: 95.1% (2021)

USMLE First-Time Pass Rate

Step 1: 99%

Step 2 CK: 99%

Step 2 CS: 99%

Other: Early Assurance BA-BS/MD Program for high school applicants. For more information, visit:https://drexel.edu/medicine/academics/md-program/md-program-admissions/accelerated-early-linkage/

Various opportunities, such as additional year of focused study, research, or service projects (EDGE Program), Global Health Education, Spanish for Medical Professionals, and more. For more information, visit:https://drexel.edu/medicine/academics/md-program/additional-opportunities/

CONNECTICUT

MAINE

MASSACHUSETTS

NEW HAMPSHIRE

NEW JERSEY

NEW YORK

PENNSYLVANIA

RHODE ISLAND

VERMONT

NORTHEAST

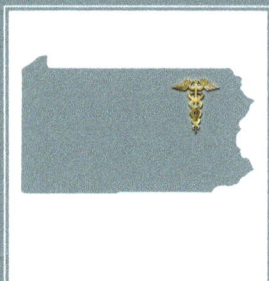

CONNECTICUT

MAINE

MASSACHUSETTS

NEW HAMPSHIRE

NEW JERSEY

NEW YORK

PENNSYLVANIA

RHODE ISLAND

VERMONT

GEISINGER COMMONWEALTH SCHOOL OF MEDICINE

Address: 525 Pine Street, Scranton, PA 18509
Website: *https://www.geisinger.edu/education*
Contact: *Contact via phone.*
Phone: (570) 504-9068

Other locations: Wilkes-Barre, PA; Sayre, PA; Danville, PA; Atlantic City, NJ

COST OF ATTENDANCE

In-State Tuition: $56,800
Fees & Expenses: $31,983
Total: $88,783

Out-of-State Tuition: $63,100
Fees & Expenses: $31,983
Total: $95,083

Financial Aid: https://www.geisinger.edu/education/admissions/financial-aid

Percent Receiving Aid: 88%

ADDITIONAL INFORMATION

Interesting tidbit: Through Abigail Geisinger Scholars Program, students will graduate without tuition debt and receive a $2,000 per month stipend. Upon completion of residency training, you'll become a Geisinger-employed physician (in family medicine, internal medicine, medicine-pediatrics or psychiatry).

What percent of students participate in global health experiences? 9%

What service learning opportunities exist? Students are required to volunteer for 100 hours. For more information, visit:https://www.geisinger.edu/education/community/office-of-community-engagement

What dual degree options exist? No dual degree options listed.

Important Updates due to COVID-19: accept pass/fail grades and online courses for the semesters impacted by COVID-19.

Were tests required? MCAT required.

Are tests expected next year? Yes.

Postgraduate Training Match Rate: N/A

USMLE First-Time Pass Rate

Step 1: 97%

Step 2 CK: N/A

Step 2 CS: N/A

Other: Geisinger Scholar Programs. For more information, visit:https://www.geisinger.edu/education/admissions/financial-aid/geisinger-scholar-programs

LEWIS KATZ SCHOOL OF MEDICINE AT TEMPLE UNIVERSITY

Address: 3500 N. Broad Street, Philadelphia, PA 19140
Website: *https://medicine.temple.edu/*
Contact: *https://medicine.temple.edu/education/md-program/contact-us*
Phone: (215) 707-3656

Other locations: Pittsburgh, PA; Bethlehem, PA; Danville, PA; Upland, PA

COST OF ATTENDANCE

In-State Tuition: $53,406
Fees & Expenses: $26,092
Total: $79,498

Out-of-State Tuition: $56,628
Fees & Expenses: $26,092
Total: $82,720

Financial Aid: https://medicine.temple.edu/education/md-program/how-apply/financial-aid

Percent Receiving Aid: 86%

ADDITIONAL INFORMATION

Interesting tidbit: The Lewis Katz School of Medicine wasfounded in 1901 as Pennsylvania's first co-educational medical school. It began as a night and weekend teaching venture to accommodate working-class citizens who sought to improve their lives — and the lives of others — through medical education.

What percent of students participate in global health experiences? 25%

What service learning opportunities exist? Pediatric Interest Group, laboratory science lessons at local elementary schools, work with homeless population, etc. For more information, visit:https://medicine.temple.edu/education/md-program/why-temple/community-engagement

What dual degree options exist? MD/MBA, MD/PhD, and MD/MA. For more information, visit:https://medicine.temple.edu/education/md-program/dual-degree-programs

Important Updates due to COVID-19: Accept online coursework and Pass/Fail grading for the spring 2020 semester.

Were tests required? MCAT and CASPer required.

Are tests expected next year? Yes.

Postgraduate Training Match Rate: N/A

USMLE First-Time Pass Rate

Step 1: N/A

Step 2 CK: N/A

Step 2 CS: N/A

Other: BA/MD program available to high school applicants. For more information, visit:https://medicine.temple.edu/education/md-program/how-apply/special-admissions-program

CONNECTICUT

MAINE

MASSACHUSETTS

NEW HAMPSHIRE

NEW JERSEY

NEW YORK

PENNSYLVANIA

RHODE ISLAND

VERMONT

NORTHEAST

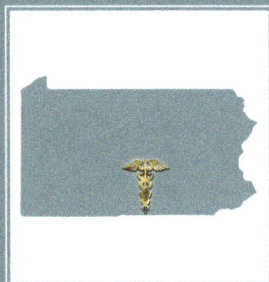

CONNECTICUT

MAINE

MASSACHUSETTS

NEW HAMPSHIRE

NEW JERSEY

NEW YORK

PENNSYLVANIA

RHODE ISLAND

VERMONT

PENN STATE COLLEGE OF MEDICINE

Address: 500 University Drive, Hershey, PA 17033
Website: *https://med.psu.edu/*
Contact: *https://med.psu.edu/contact*
Phone: (717) 531-8755

COST OF ATTENDANCE

Tuition: $50,960
Fees & Expenses: $24,812
Total: $75,772

Financial Aid: https://med.psu.edu/md/tuition

Percent Receiving Aid: 90%

ADDITIONAL INFORMATION

Interesting tidbit: Penn State College of Medicine offers three curriculum options (open to all enrolled MD students) - Hershey Curriculum, University Park Curriculum, and the Accelerated 3+ Pathways. Three curriculum options allow students to find the best fit for their learning and development.

What percent of students participate in global health experiences? 38%

What service learning opportunities exist? Big Brothers Big Sisters, Penn State Children's Hospital, AIDS Awareness, etc. For more information, visit:https://students.med.psu.edu/md-students/community-service/

What dual degree options exist? MD/MBA, MD/MPH, MD/M.Ed., and MD/PhD. For more information, visit:https://med.psu.edu/combined-programs

Important Updates due to COVID-19: Accept pass/fail grades for prerequisite courses and online laboratory credit through fall 2021. Require completion of the MCAT examination in order to apply to the College of Medicine.

Were tests required? MCAT anc CASPer required.

Are tests expected next year? Yes.

Postgraduate Training Match Rate: N/A

USMLE First-Time Pass Rate

Step 1: N/A

Step 2 CK: N/A

Step 2 CS: N/A

Other: Accelerated Pathways available. For more information, visit:https://med.psu.edu/md/accelerated

Early Assurance Opportunities available to Penn State undergraduates. For more information, visit:https://science.psu.edu/interdisciplinary-programs/premedicine/early-admission-to-professional-school

SIDNEY KIMMEL MEDICAL COLLEGE AT THOMAS JEFFERSON UNIVERSITY

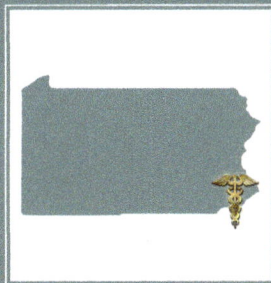

Address: 1015 Walnut Street, Philadelphia, PA 19107
Website: *https://www.jefferson.edu/university/skmc.html*
Contact: *https://www.jefferson.edu/university/skmc/contact.html*
Phone: (215) 955-6983

COST OF ATTENDANCE

Tuition: $60,314
Fees & Expenses: $26,561
Total: $86,875

Financial Aid: https://www.jefferson.edu/university/academic-affairs/tju/academic-services/financial_aid.html

Percent Receiving Aid: 73%

ADDITIONAL INFORMATION

Interesting tidbit: SK Medical College at Thomas Jefferson University is born out of a merger between Philadelphia University and Thomas Jefferson University. Thomas Jefferson University was founded in 1824 as Jefferson Medical College, and Philadelphia University was founded in 1884 as the Philadelphia Textile School. The new Jefferson was established on July 1, 2017 as a result of the merger of these two renowned universities.

What percent of students participate in global health experiences? 12%

What service learning opportunities exist? Service learning through student organizations.

What dual degree options exist? MD/MPH, MD/MBA-MHA and MD/PhD. For more information, visit:https://www.jefferson.edu/university/skmc/programs.html

Important Updates due to COVID-19: Accept Pass/Fail, online courses. Applications are held for review until the results of that MCAT have been received.

Were tests required? MCAT required.

Are tests expected next year? Yes.

Postgraduate Training Match Rate: N/A

USMLE First-Time Pass Rate

Step 1: N/A

Step 2 CK: N/A

Step 2 CS: N/A

Other: BS/MD Program (7-year) available to high school applicants. For more information, visit:https://www.jefferson.edu/university/skmc/programs/penn-state-accelerated.html

CONNECTICUT

MAINE

MASSACHUSETTS

NEW HAMPSHIRE

NEW JERSEY

NEW YORK

PENNSYLVANIA

RHODE ISLAND

VERMONT

NORTHEAST

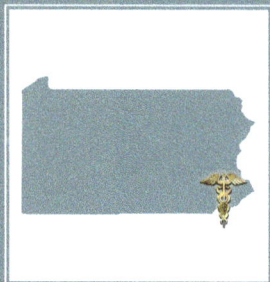

CONNECTICUT

MAINE

MASSACHUSETTS

NEW HAMPSHIRE

NEW JERSEY

NEW YORK

PENNSYLVANIA

RHODE ISLAND

VERMONT

THE RAYMOND AND RUTH PERELMAN SCHOOL OF MEDICINE AT THE UNIVERSITY OF PENNSYLVANIA

Address: 3400 Civic Center Boulevard, Building 421, Philadelphia, PA 19104
Website: *https://www.med.upenn.edu/*
Contact: *https://www.med.upenn.edu/psom/contact.html*
Phone: (215) 898-8001

COST OF ATTENDANCE

Tuition: $61,586
Fees & Expenses: $33,341
Total: $94,927

Financial Aid: https://www.med.upenn.edu/admissions/financial-aid.html

Percent Receiving Aid: 88%

ADDITIONAL INFORMATION

Interesting tidbit: With over 2,300 full-time members, Penn's faculty has an outstanding reputation. Sixty-five members of the Penn family have been elected to the Institute of Medicine, one of the highest honors in the fields of health and medicine. In the last year, Penn faculty members were awarded 83 patents for their research efforts.

What percent of students participate in global health experiences? 22%

What service learning opportunities exist? Partnerships with neighboring schools, running free clinics, conducting free AIDS testing, etc. For more information, visit:https://www.med.upenn.edu/psom/community.html

What dual degree options exist? MD/MBA, MD/JD, MD/MPH, MD/PhD and several other MD/Masters programs. For more information, visit:https://www.med.upenn.edu/educ_combdeg/

Important Updates due to COVID-19: Review applications, regardless of the grading policy under the current pandemic. Any PSOM applicant who was provided the option to continue with the typical grading system but elected P/F for courses that prerequisites for medical school entrance is required to provide a written explanation regarding the decision to elect P/F.

Were tests required? MCAT required.

Are tests expected next year? Yes.

Postgraduate Training Match Rate: 97% (2021)

USMLE First-Time Pass Rate

Step 1: N/A

Step 2 CK: N/A

Step 2 CS: N/A

UNIVERSITY OF PITTSBURGH SCHOOL OF MEDICINE

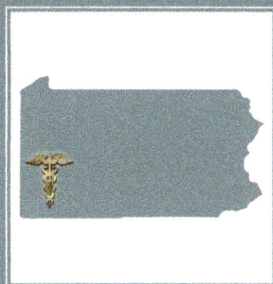

Address: 3550 Terrace Street, Pittsburgh, PA 15261
Website: *https://www.medschool.pitt.edu/*
Contact: *https://www.medschool.pitt.edu/about/contact-us*
Phone: (412) 648-8975

COST OF ATTENDANCE

In-State Tuition: $57,684
Fees & Expenses: $25,579
Total: $83,263

Out-of-State Tuition: $59,930
Fees & Expenses: $25,579
Total: $85,509

Financial Aid: https://www.medadmissions.pitt.edu/financial-aid-overview

Percent Receiving Aid: 81%

ADDITIONAL INFORMATION

Interesting tidbit: The current UPSOM curriculum was implemented in 2004, in which key subject matter is longitudinally integrated throughout the curriculum, building upon a foundation of prior learning while providing a level-appropriate and well-synchronized introduction of new content.

What percent of students participate in global health experiences? 17%

What service learning opportunities exist? Health Outreach Education Program (HOEP), Operation Safety Net (OSN), Oncology Patients and Loving Students (OPALS), etc. For more information, visit:https://www.medadmissions.pitt.edu/additional-links/student-enrichment-opportunities

What dual degree options exist? MD/MPH, and MD/MA. For more information on these programs, visit:https://www.medadmissions.pitt.edu/programs/other-opportunities

MD/PhD: https://www.mdphd.pitt.edu/

Important Updates due to COVID-19: Accept Pass/Fail (Pass/No Credit, Satisfactory/Unsatisfactory) prerequisites and online prerequisite coursework and lab. Review and extend interview invitations without a MCAT score but applicants need to submit a MCAT score before the application moves forward in the final decision making process.

Were tests required? MCAT required.

Are tests expected next year? Yes.

Postgraduate Training Match Rate: 96% (2021)

USMLE First-Time Pass Rate

Step 1: N/A

Step 2 CK: N/A

Step 2 CS: N/A

Other: Guaranteed Admit Program (GA) available to high school applicants. For more information, visit:https://www.medadmissions.pitt.edu/programs/guaranteed-admissions-program

CONNECTICUT

MAINE

MASSACHUSETTS

NEW HAMPSHIRE

NEW JERSEY

NEW YORK

PENNSYLVANIA

RHODE ISLAND

VERMONT

NORTHEAST

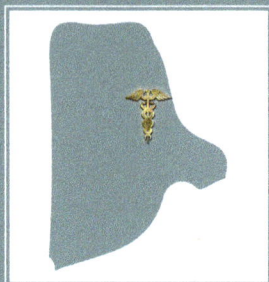

CONNECTICUT

MAINE

MASSACHUSETTS

NEW HAMPSHIRE

NEW JERSEY

NEW YORK

PENNSYLVANIA

RHODE ISLAND

VERMONT

WARREN ALPERT MEDICAL SCHOOL OF BROWN UNIVERSITY

Address: 222 Richmond Street, Providence, RI 02912
Website: *https://medical.brown.edu/*
Contact: *https://medical.brown.edu/contact-us*
Phone: (401) 863-2149

COST OF ATTENDANCE

In-State Tuition: $66,110
Fees & Expenses: $30,030
Total: $94,140

Financial Aid: https://medical.brown.edu/admission-aid/financial-aid

Percent Receiving Aid: 72%

ADDITIONAL INFORMATION

Interesting tidbit: There are four different routes of admission to the Brown AMS - AMCAS (standard), Early Identification Program, PLME and post-baccalaureate. Among the MD Class of 2023, 52% entered via AMCAS, 3% via Early Identification Program, 41% via PLME and 3% via post-baccalaureate.

What percent of students participate in global health experiences? 23%

What service learning opportunities exist? International exchange program and service learning through student organizations.

What dual degree options exist? MD/MPH, MD/PhD, and MD/MS in Population Medicine, Medical Science, and Medical Physics. For more information, visit:https://medical.brown.edu/education/degree-programs

Important Updates due to COVID-19: Accept pass/fail and on-line coursework taken in 2020, even for prerequisite courses.

Were tests required? MCAT required.

Are tests expected next year? Yes.

Postgraduate Training Match Rate: N/A

USMLE First-Time Pass Rate

Step 1: N/A

Step 2 CK: N/A

Step 2 CS: N/A

Other: BS/MD Program in Liberal Medical Education (PLME), 8-year program for high school applicants. For more information, visit:https://www.brown.edu/academics/medical/plme/

ME
VT
NY
NH
MA
PA
RI
CT
NJ

THE ROBERT LARNER, M.D. COLLEGE OF MEDICINE AT THE UNIVERSITY OF VERMONT

Address: 89 Beaumont Ave., Burlington, VT 05405
Website: *http://www.med.uvm.edu/*
Contact: *http://www.med.uvm.edu/com/contactus*
Phone: (802) 656-2156

COST OF ATTENDANCE

In-State Tuition: $37,070
Fees & Expenses: $24,888
Total: $61,958

Out-of-State Tuition: $64,170
Fees & Expenses: $25,506
Total: $89,676

Financial Aid: https://www.uvm.edu/studentfinancialservices/types_aid_and_how_apply

Percent Receiving Aid: 88%

ADDITIONAL INFORMATION

Interesting tidbit: The Vermont Integrated Curriculum (VIC) is divided into three levels of increasing complexity and breadth of study - Foundations, Clinical Clerkship, and Advanced Integration. Instruction progresses from being teacher-directed to being student-directed.

What percent of students participate in global health experiences? 22%

What service learning opportunities exist? Community medical school, global health program, etc. For more information, visit:http://www.med.uvm.edu/community/

What dual degree options exist? No dual degree options listed.

Important Updates due to COVID-19: Accept Pass/Fail grades for prerequisite courses and online courses and labs.

Were tests required? MCAT and CASPer required.

Are tests expected next year? Yes.

Postgraduate Training Match Rate: 107 students matched (2021)

USMLE First-Time Pass Rate

Step 1: "high 90's"

Step 2 CK: "high 90's"

Step 2 CS: "high 90's"

CONNECTICUT

MAINE

MASSACHUSETTS

NEW HAMPSHIRE

NEW JERSEY

NEW YORK

PENNSYLVANIA

RHODE ISLAND

VERMONT

ME
VT
NY
NH
MA
PA
RI
CT
NJ

NORTHEAST

ILLINOIS

INDIANA

IOWA

KANSAS

MICHIGAN

MINNESOTA

MISSOURI

NEBRASKA

NORTH DAKOTA

OHIO

SOUTH DAKOTA

WISCONSIN

CHAPTER 3

REGION TWO

MIDWEST

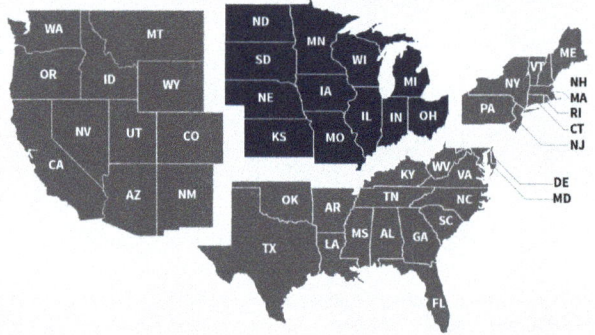

35 Programs | 12 States

MEDICAL PROGRAMS

Medical School	Ave. GPA & MCAT Early Decision (ED): Yes/No Int'l Students: Yes/No Reapps: Yes/No	Admissions Statistics	Science Req. Other than Gen Chem, OChem, Physics, Bio
Carle Illinois College of Medicine 807 S Wright St, Champaign, IL 61820	3.71 (overall) 3.64 (science) MCAT: 513 ED: No Int'l Student: Yes Reapps: N/A	**(2019)** Apps Received: 2350 Interview Received: N/A Number Enrolled: 32 Admitted Rate: 1.4% **(2020)** Apps Received: 2830 Interview Received: 0 Number Enrolled: 47 Admitted Rate: 1.7%	N/A See Chart. for rec
Chicago Medical School at Rosalind Franklin University of Medicine and Science 3333 Green Bay Road, North Chicago, IL 60064	3.74 (overall) 3.67 (science) MCAT: 513 ED: Yes Int'l Student: No Reapps: N/A	**(2019)** Apps Received: 15415 Interview Received: 761 Number Enrolled: 189 Admitted Rate: 1.2% **(2020)** Apps Received: 11893 Interview Received: 823 Number Enrolled: 189 Admitted Rate: 1.6%	Biochem.
Loyola University Chicago Stritch School of Medicine 2160 South First Avenue, Maywood, IL 60153	3.76 (overall) 3.70 (science) MCAT: 512 ED: No Int'l Student: No Reapps: N/A	**(2019)** Apps Received: 14905 Interview Received: 650 Number Enrolled: 170 Admitted Rate: 1.1% **(2020)** Apps Received: 14305 Interview Received: 540 Number Enrolled: 170 Admitted Rate: 1.2%	N/A See Chart.
Northwestern University Feinberg School of Medicine 420 E Superior St, Chicago, IL 60611	3.91 (overall) 3.90 (science) MCAT: 520 ED: Yes Int'l Student: Yes Reapps: N/A	**(2019)** Apps Received: 6878 Interview Received: 819 Number Enrolled: 159 Admitted Rate: 2.3% **(2020)** Apps Received: 7045 Interview Received: 801 Number Enrolled: 160 Admitted Rate: 2.3%	N/A See Chart.

MEDICAL PROGRAMS

Medical School	Ave. GPA & MCAT Early Decision (ED): Yes/No Int'l Students: Yes/No Reapps: Yes/No	Admissions Statistics	Science Req. Other than Gen Chem, OChem, Physics, Bio
Rush Medical College of Rush University Medical Center 600 S Paulina St Suite 524, Chicago, IL 60612	3.67 (overall) 3.58 (science) MCAT: 511 ED: No Int'l Student: No Reapps: N/A	**(2019)** Apps Received: 11297 Interview Received: 476 Number Enrolled: 144 Admitted Rate: 1.3% **(2020)** Apps Received: 11028 Interview Received: 509 Number Enrolled: 155 Admitted Rate: 1.4%	N/A See Chart.
Southern Illinois University 801 N Rutledge St, Springfield, IL 62702	3.81 (overall) 3.75 (science) MCAT: 506 ED: No Int'l Student: No Reapps: N/A	**(2019)** Apps Received: 1196 Interview Received: 314 Number Enrolled: 72 Admitted Rate: 6% **(2020)** Apps Received: 1152 Interview Received: 278 Number Enrolled: 80 Admitted Rate: 6.9%	N/A See Chart.
University of Chicago 924 E. 57th Street, Suite 104, Chicago, IL 60637	3.93 (overall) 3.92 (science) MCAT: 521 ED: No Int'l Student: Yes Reapps: N/A	**(2019)** Apps Received: 5683 Interview Received: 639 Number Enrolled: 90 Admitted Rate: 1.6% **(2020)** Apps Received: 6146 Interview Received: 631 Number Enrolled: 90 Admitted Rate: 1.5%	Biochem.

MIDWEST

MEDICAL PROGRAMS

Medical School	Ave. GPA & MCAT Early Decision (ED): Yes/No Int'l Students: Yes/No Reapps: Yes/No	Admissions Statistics	Science Req. Other than Gen Chem, OChem, Physics, Bio
University of Illinois 1853 W. Polk, Chicago, IL 60612	3.76 (overall) 3.71 (science) MCAT: 513 ED: Yes Int'l Student: Yes Reapps: N/A	**(2019)** Apps Received: 5722 Interview Received: 852 Number Enrolled: 291 Admitted Rate: 5% **(2020)** Apps Received: 5015 Interview Received: 686 Number Enrolled: 299 Admitted Rate: 6%	Biochem. Advanced Level Bio.
Indiana University 340 W 10th St., #6200, Indianapolis, IN 46202	3.84 (overall) 3.80 (science) MCAT: 512 ED: Yes Int'l Student: No Reapps: N/A	**(2019)** Apps Received: 6683 Interview Received: 1113 Number Enrolled: 365 Admitted Rate: 5.5% **(2020)** Apps Received: 5982 Interview Received: 1036 Number Enrolled: 365 Admitted Rate: 6.1%	N/A See Chart.
University of Iowa 451 Newton Road, 200 Medicine Administration Building, Iowa City, IA 52242	3.86 (overall) 3.84 (science) MCAT: 515 ED: No Int'l Student: No Reapps: N/A	**(2019)** Apps Received: 3878 Interview Received: 717 Number Enrolled: 152 Admitted Rate: 3.9% **(2020)** Apps Received: 4021 Interview Received: 723 Number Enrolled: 152 Admitted Rate: 3.8%	Biochem. Advanced Level Bio.
University of Kansas 3901 Rainbow Blvd, Kansas City, KS 66160	3.88 (overall) 3.86 (science) MCAT: 512 ED: Yes Int'l Student: No Reapps: N/A	**(2019)** Apps Received: 3207 Interview Received: 526 Number Enrolled: 211 Admitted Rate: 6.6% **(2020)** Apps Received: 3079 Interview Received: 544 Number Enrolled: 211 Admitted Rate: 6.9%	N/A See Chart.

Medical School	Ave. GPA & MCAT Early Decision (ED): Yes/No Int'l Students: Yes/No Reapps: Yes/No	Admissions Statistics	Science Req. Other than Gen Chem, OChem, Physics, Bio
Central Michigan University 1280 S. East Campus Dr., Mount Pleasant, MI 48859	3.69 (overall) 3.60 (science) MCAT: 508 ED: Yes Int'l Student: No Reapps: N/A	**(2019)** Apps Received: 7360 Interview Received: 432 Number Enrolled: 103 Admitted Rate: 1.4% **(2020)** Apps Received: 6475 Interview Received: 465 Number Enrolled: 103 Admitted Rate: 1.6%	N/A See Chart.
Michigan State University 804 Service Road, Suite A112, East Lansing, MI 48824	3.76 (overall) 3.68 (science) MCAT: 509 ED: No Int'l Student: No Reapps: N/A	**(2019)** Apps Received: 7994 Interview Received: 516 Number Enrolled: 190 Admitted Rate: 2.4% **(2020)** Apps Received: 8856 Interview Received: 531 Number Enrolled: 188 Admitted Rate: 2.1%	Biochem. Advanced Level Bio.
Oakland University 586 Pioneer Drive, Rochester, MI 48309	3.85 (overall) 3.81 (science) MCAT: 510 ED: No Int'l Student: No Reapps: N/A	**(2019)** Apps Received: 7550 Interview Received: 500 Number Enrolled: 125 Admitted Rate: 1.8% **(2020)** Apps Received: 6961 Interview Received: 550 Number Enrolled: 125 Admitted Rate: 1.8%	Biochem.

MIDWEST

MEDICAL PROGRAMS

Medical School	Ave. GPA & MCAT Early Decision (ED): Yes/No Int'l Students: Yes/No Reapps: Yes/No	Admissions Statistics	Science Req. Other than Gen Chem, OChem, Physics, Bio
University of Michigan 1301 Catherine Street, Ann Arbor, MI 48109	3.87 (overall) 3.84 (science) MCAT: 518 ED: No Int'l Student: No Reapps: N/A	**(2019)** Apps Received: 7896 Interview Received: 507 Number Enrolled: 177 Admitted Rate: 2.2% **(2020)** Apps Received: 8267 Interview Received: 468 Number Enrolled: 168 Admitted Rate: 2%	N/A See Chart.
Wayne State University 540 E. Canfield, Detroit, MI 48201	3.86 (overall) 3.84 (science) MCAT: 513 ED: Yes Int'l Student: Yes Reapps: N/A	**(2019)** Apps Received: 9993 Interview Received: 1102 Number Enrolled: 292 Admitted Rate: 2.9% **(2020)** Apps Received: 9516 Interview Received: 1184 Number Enrolled: 291 Admitted Rate: 3.1%	N/A See Chart.
Western Michigan University 300 Portage Street, Kalamazoo, MI 49007	3.79 (overall) 3.76 (science) MCAT: 516 ED: No Int'l Student: No Reapps: N/A	**(2019)** Apps Received: 4143 Interview Received: 420 Number Enrolled: 84 Admitted Rate: 2% **(2020)** Apps Received: 3558 Interview Received: 417 Number Enrolled: 84 Admitted Rate: 2.4%	N/A See Chart.
Mayo Clinic Alix School of Medicine 200 First Street SW, Rochester, MN 55905	3.94 (overall) 3.94 (science) MCAT: 520 ED: No Int'l Student: No Reapps: N/A	**(2019)** Apps Received: 7265 Interview Received: 816 Number Enrolled: 102 Admitted Rate: 1.4% **(2020)** Apps Received: 6327 Interview Received: 862 Number Enrolled: 105 Admitted Rate: 1.7%	Biochem.

Medical School	Ave. GPA & MCAT Early Decision (ED): Yes/No Int'l Students: Yes/No Reapps: Yes/No	Admissions Statistics	Science Req. Other than Gen Chem, OChem, Physics, Bio
University of Minnesota 420 Delaware St SE, Minneapolis, MN 55455	3.81 (overall) 3.73 (science) MCAT: 513 ED: No Int'l Student: No Reapps: N/A	**(2019)** Apps Received: 5561 Interview Received: 644 Number Enrolled: 240 Admitted Rate: 4.3% **(2020)** Apps Received: 4936 Interview Received: 648 Number Enrolled: 241 Admitted Rate: 4.9%	N/A See Chart.
Saint Louis University 1402 S. Grand Blvd., St. Louis, MO 63104	3.91 (overall) 3.90 (science) MCAT: 514 ED: Yes Int'l Student: Yes Reapps: N/A	**(2019)** Apps Received: 6834 Interview Received: 966 Number Enrolled: 180 Admitted Rate: 2.6% **(2020)** Apps Received: 5906 Interview Received: 1094 Number Enrolled: 183 Admitted Rate: 3.1%	N/A See Chart.
University of Missouri-Columbia 1 Hospital Dr, Columbia, MO 65212	3.86 (overall) 3.81 (science) MCAT: 509 ED: Yes Int'l Student: No Reapps: N/A	**(2019)** Apps Received: 3390 Interview Received: 405 Number Enrolled: 112 Admitted Rate: 3.3% **(2020)** Apps Received: 3069 Interview Received: 407 Number Enrolled: 128 Admitted Rate: 4.2%	N/A See Chart.

MIDWEST

MEDICAL PROGRAMS

Medical School	Ave. GPA & MCAT Early Decision (ED): Yes/No Int'l Students: Yes/No Reapps: Yes/No	Admissions Statistics	Science Req. Other than Gen Chem, OChem, Physics, Bio
University of Missouri-Kansas City 2411 Holmes Street, Kansas City, Missouri 64108	3.89 (overall) 3.87 (science) MCAT: 509 ED: No Int'l Student: No Reapps: N/A	**(2019)** Apps Received: 1303 Interview Received: 427 Number Enrolled: 115 Admitted Rate: 8.8% **(2020)** Apps Received: 1936 Interview Received: 127 Number Enrolled: 124 Admitted Rate: 6.4%	Biochem. Genetics
Washington University in St. Louis 660 S Euclid Ave, St. Louis, MO 63110	3.94 (overall) 3.94 (science) MCAT: 521 ED: No Int'l Student: Yes Reapps: N/A	**(2019)** Apps Received: 4766 Interview Received: 1087 Number Enrolled: 101 Admitted Rate: 2.1% **(2020)** Apps Received: 4547 Interview Received: 1140 Number Enrolled: 104 Admitted Rate: 2.3%	N/A See Chart.
Creighton University 2500 California Plaza, Omaha, NE 68178	3.84 (overall) 3.78 (science) MCAT: 513 ED: Yes Int'l Student: Yes (case by case) Reapps: N/A	**(2019)** Apps Received: 6375 Interview Received: 665 Number Enrolled: 166 Admitted Rate: 2.6% **(2020)** Apps Received: 6834 Interview Received: 685 Number Enrolled: 167 Admitted Rate: 2.4%	Biochem. Physio.

Medical School	Ave. GPA & MCAT / Early Decision (ED): Yes/No / Int'l Students: Yes/No / Reapps: Yes/No	Admissions Statistics	Science Req. Other than Gen Chem, OChem, Physics, Bio
University of Nebraska 42nd and Emile, Omaha, NE 68198	3.90 (overall) 3.87 (science) MCAT: 513 ED: Yes Int'l Student: Yes (case by case) Reapps: N/A	**(2019)** Apps Received: 1590 Interview Received: 374 Number Enrolled: 132 Admitted Rate: 8.3% **(2020)** Apps Received: 1655 Interview Received: 472 Number Enrolled: 131 Admitted Rate: 7.9%	Biochem. Genetics
University of North Dakota 1301 N Columbia Rd, Grand Forks, ND 58203	3.80 (overall) 3.74 (science) MCAT: 507 ED: Yes Int'l Student: No Reapps: Yes	**(2019)** Apps Received: 1718 Interview Received: 184 Number Enrolled: 77 Admitted Rate: 4.5% **(2020)** Apps Received: 1453 Interview Received: 192 Number Enrolled: 67 Admitted Rate: 4.6%	N/A See Chart.
Wright State University 3640 Colonel Glenn Hwy, Dayton, OH 45435	3.73 (overall) 3.63 (science) MCAT: 508 ED: Yes Int'l Student: No Reapps: N/A	**(2019)** Apps Received: 6119 Interview Received: 431 Number Enrolled: 119 Admitted Rate: 1.9% **(2020)** Apps Received: 7522 Interview Received: 393 Number Enrolled: 118 Admitted Rate: 1.6%	Biochem. w/ Lab

MIDWEST

MEDICAL PROGRAMS

Medical School	Ave. GPA & MCAT / Early Decision (ED): Yes/No / Int'l Students: Yes/No / Reapps: Yes/No	Admissions Statistics	Science Req. Other than Gen Chem, OChem, Physics, Bio
Case Western Reserve University 9501 Euclid Ave., Cleveland, OH 44106	3.86 (overall) 3.83 (science) MCAT: 519 ED: No Int'l Student: Yes Reapps: N/A	**(2019)** Apps Received: 7556 Interview Received: 1083 Number Enrolled: 214 Admitted Rate: 2.8% **(2020)** Apps Received: 8121 Interview Received: 1048 Number Enrolled: 214 Admitted Rate: 2.6%	Biochem.
Northeast Ohio Medical University 4209 State Route 44, Rootstown, OH 44272	3.76 (overall) 3.69 (science) MCAT: 507 ED: Yes Int'l Student: No Reapps: N/A	**(2019)** Apps Received: 4069 Interview Received: 389 Number Enrolled: 151 Admitted Rate: 3.7% **(2020)** Apps Received: 3990 Interview Received: 528 Number Enrolled: 151 Admitted Rate: 3.8%	Biochem.
The Ohio State University 370 W. 9th Avenue, Columbus, OH 43210	3.92 (overall) 3.91 (science) MCAT: 517 ED: No Int'l Student: No Reapps: N/A	**(2019)** Apps Received: 7725 Interview Received: 556 Number Enrolled: 209 Admitted Rate: 2.7% **(2020)** Apps Received: 7106 Interview Received: 576 Number Enrolled: 205 Admitted Rate: 2.9%	N/A See Chart.
University of Cincinnati 3230 Eden Ave, Cincinnati, OH 45267	3.84 (overall) 3.81 (science) MCAT: 517 ED: Yes Int'l Student: No Reapps: N/A	**(2019)** Apps Received: 4734 Interview Received: 634 Number Enrolled: 185 Admitted Rate: 3.9% **(2020)** Apps Received: 5114 Interview Received: 621 Number Enrolled: 182 Admitted Rate: 3.6%	N/A See Chart.

MEDICAL PROGRAMS

Medical School	Ave. GPA & MCAT Early Decision (ED): Yes/No Int'l Students: Yes/No Reapps: Yes/No	Admissions Statistics	Science Req. Other than Gen Chem, OChem, Physics, Bio
The University of Toledo 3000 Arlington Ave, Toledo, OH 43614	3.76 (overall) 3.66 (science) MCAT: 51 ED: No Int'l Student: No Reapps: N/A	**(2019)** Apps Received: 5411 Interview Received: 397 Number Enrolled: 175 Admitted Rate: 3.2% **(2020)** Apps Received: 6233 Interview Received: 381 Number Enrolled: 176 Admitted Rate: 2.8%	Biochem.
University of South Dakota 1400 W. 22nd St., Sioux Falls, SD 57105	3.87 (overall) 3.87 (science) MCAT: 508 ED: No Int'l Student: No Reapps: N/A	**(2019)** Apps Received: 836 Interview Received: 207 Number Enrolled: 70 Admitted Rate: 8.4% **(2020)** Apps Received: 744 Interview Received: 208 Number Enrolled: 69 Admitted Rate: 9.3%	Biochem.
Medical College of Wisconsin 8701 Watertown Plank Road, Milwaukee, WI 53226	3.73 (overall) 3.67 (science) MCAT: 511 ED: Yes Int'l Student: Yes (case by case) Reapps: N/A	**(2019)** Apps Received: 7936 Interview Received: 820 Number Enrolled: 252 Admitted Rate: 3.2% **(2020)** Apps Received: 9341 Interview Received: 818 Number Enrolled: 266 Admitted Rate: 2.8%	Advanced Bio. Biochem.

MIDWEST

MEDICAL PROGRAMS

Medical School	Ave. GPA & MCAT Early Decision (ED): Yes/No Int'l Students: Yes/No Reapps: Yes/No	Admissions Statistics	Science Req. Other than Gen Chem, OChem, Physics, Bio
University of Wisconsin 2130 Health Sciences Learning Center, Madison, WI 53705	3.80 (overall) 3.76 (science) MCAT: 513 ED: No Int'l Student: No Reapps: Yes	**(2019)** Apps Received: 4815 Interview Received: 565 Number Enrolled: 179 Admitted Rate: 3.7% **(2020)** Apps Received: 5075 Interview Received: 612 Number Enrolled: 171 Admitted Rate: 3.4%	Biochem.

ILLINOIS

INDIANA

IOWA

KANSAS

MICHIGAN

MINNESOTA

MISSOURI

NEBRASKA

NORTH DAKOTA

OHIO

SOUTH DAKOTA

WISCONSIN

CARLE ILLINOIS COLLEGE OF MEDICINE

Address: 807 S Wright St, Champaign, IL 61820
Website: *https://medicine.illinois.edu/*
Contact: *https://carleillinoiscollegeofmedicine.as.me/StudentAffairs*
Phone: (217) 300-5700

COST OF ATTENDANCE

In-State Tuition: $46,608
Fees & Expenses: $32,163
Total: $78,771

Out-of-State Tuition: $61,342
Fees & Expenses: $30,503
Total: $91,845

Financial Aid: https://medicine.illinois.edu/admissions/tuition-fees/

Percent Receiving Aid: 100%

ADDITIONAL INFORMATION

Interesting tidbit: The Carle Illinois College of Medicine at the University of Illinois at Urbana-Champaign is the world's first engineering-based medical school. The curriculum infuses basic sciences, clinical sciences, engineering and innovation, and medical humanities into all four years.

What percent of students participate in global health experiences? N/A

What service learning opportunities exist? Discovery learning course involves global opportunities, clinical immersion, research immersion, or self-designed study. For more information, visit:https://medicine.illinois.edu/education/discovery-learning/

What dual degree options exist? MD/PhD.

Important Updates due to COVID-19: Adopt a holistic approach in reviewing applications so pandemic-related disruption does not unduly influence the overall review of the application.

Were tests required? MCAT required.

Are tests expected next year? Yes.

Postgraduate Training Match Rate: N/A

USMLE First-Time Pass Rate

Step 1: N/A

Step 2 CK: N/A

Step 2 CS: N/A

CHICAGO MEDICAL SCHOOL AT ROSALIND FRANKLIN UNIVERSITY OF MEDICINE AND SCIENCE

Address: 3333 Green Bay Road, North Chicago, IL 60064
Website: *https://www.rosalindfranklin.edu/academics/chicago-medical-school/*
Contact: *https://www.rosalindfranklin.edu/admission-aid/contact-us/*
Phone: (847) 578-3204

COST OF ATTENDANCE

Tuition: $63,223
Fees & Expenses: $22,803
Total: $86,026

Financial Aid: https://www.rosalindfranklin.edu/admission-aid/financial-services/financial-aid/

Percent Receiving Aid: 95%

ADDITIONAL INFORMATION

Interesting tidbit: In March 2004, The school was renamed to the current Rosalind Franklin University of Medicine and Science, in honor of Rosalind Franklin, PhD, a pioneer in the field of DNA research.

What percent of students participate in global health experiences? 17%

What service learning opportunities exist? Service learning through student organizations.

What dual degree options exist? MD/PhD. For more information, visit:https://www.rosalindfranklin.edu/academics/school-of-graduate-and-postdoctoral-studies/degree-programs/

Important Updates due to COVID-19: Accept pass/no pass grades, without prejudice, for courses taken during the COVID-19 pandemic. Accept online coursework including labs recognized and verified by AMCAS, without prejudice for courses taken during the COVID-19 pandemic.

Were tests required? MCAT and CASPer required.

Are tests expected next year? Yes.

Postgraduate Training Match Rate: N/A

USMLE First-Time Pass Rate

Step 1: 94%

Step 2 CK: N/A

Step 2 CS: N/A

ILLINOIS

INDIANA

IOWA

KANSAS

MICHIGAN

MINNESOTA

MISSOURI

NEBRASKA

NORTH DAKOTA

OHIO

SOUTH DAKOTA

WISCONSIN

MIDWEST

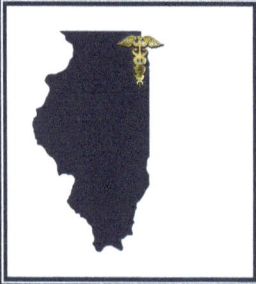

ILLINOIS

INDIANA

IOWA

KANSAS

MICHIGAN

MINNESOTA

MISSOURI

NEBRASKA

NORTH DAKOTA

OHIO

SOUTH DAKOTA

WISCONSIN

LOYOLA UNIVERSITY CHICAGO STRITCH SCHOOL OF MEDICINE

Address: 2160 South First Avenue, Maywood, IL 60153
Website: *https://ssom.luc.edu/*
Contact: *https://ssom.luc.edu/contact/*
Phone: (708) 216-3229

COST OF ATTENDANCE

Tuition: $61,000
Fees & Expenses: $26,105
Total: $87,105

Financial Aid: https://ssom.luc.edu/finaid/

Percent Receiving Aid: 83%

ADDITIONAL INFORMATION

Interesting tidbit: The Loyola University Chicago Stritch School of Medicine (SSOM) seeks to recruit and enroll students in full alignment with our Jesuit values who will uphold its Catholic heritage and Jesuit traditions.

What percent of students participate in global health experiences? 35%

What service learning opportunities exist? HPREP, Maywood Youth 4 Change, Housing Forward, etc. For more information, visit:https://ssom.luc.edu/diversity/community-outreach/

What dual degree options exist? MD/PhD, MD/MBA, MD/MPH, and MD/MA in Bioethics. For more information, visit:https://ssom.luc.edu/admissions/dualdegreeprograms/

Important Updates due to COVID-19: Accept Pass/Fail courses, as well as prerequisites completed online.

Were tests required? MCAT required.

Are tests expected next year? Yes.

Postgraduate Training Match Rate: N/A

USMLE First-Time Pass Rate

Step 1: N/A

Step 2 CK: N/A

Step 2 CS: N/A

NORTHWESTERN UNIVERSITY FEINBERG SCHOOL OF MEDICINE

Address: 420 E Superior St, Chicago, IL 60611
Website: *https://www.feinberg.northwestern.edu/*
Contact: *https://www.feinberg.northwestern.edu/about/contact/index.html*
Phone: (312) 503-8206

COST OF ATTENDANCE

Tuition: $64,262
Fees & Expenses: $30,116
Total: $94,378

Financial Aid: https://www.feinberg.northwestern.edu/admissions/how-to-apply/tuition.html

Percent Receiving Aid: 74%

ADDITIONAL INFORMATION

Interesting tidbit: In the Area of Scholarly Concentration (AOSC) program, one of the pillars of the curriculum leading to the MD degree, students perform a hypothesis-driven investigation or formal project in a individualized area of independent study within biomedical research or a medically-related field. Areas of investigation include clinical investigation, translational medicine, global health, community and family health, medical humanities and the medical social sciences.

What percent of students participate in global health experiences? 41%

What service learning opportunities exist? Global health training electives, homeless shelters, Alzheimer's Buddy Program, etc. For more information, visit:https://www.feinberg.northwestern.edu/sites/community-engagement/index.html

What dual degree options exist? MD/MBA, MD/MPH, MD/MS, and MD/PhD. For more information, visit:https://www.feinberg.northwestern.edu/admissions/md-education/

Important Updates due to COVID-19: Consider COVID-19–related disruptions in the review of applications (P/F, online coursework, delayed or cancelled MCAT, etc.) and review each candidate individually based on each candidate's unique circumstances.

Were tests required? MCAT required.

Are tests expected next year? Yes.

Postgraduate Training Match Rate: N/A

USMLE First-Time Pass Rate

Step 1: N/A

Step 2 CK: N/A

Step 2 CS: N/A

Other: BA/MD 7-year program available to high school applicants. For more information, visit:https://www.feinberg.northwestern.edu/sites/hpme/

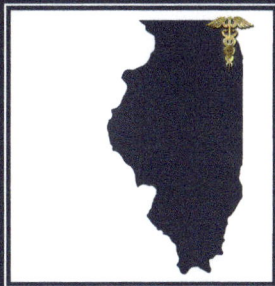

ILLINOIS

INDIANA

IOWA

KANSAS

MICHIGAN

MINNESOTA

MISSOURI

NEBRASKA

NORTH DAKOTA

OHIO

SOUTH DAKOTA

WISCONSIN

MIDWEST

ILLINOIS

INDIANA

IOWA

KANSAS

MICHIGAN

MINNESOTA

MISSOURI

NEBRASKA

NORTH DAKOTA

OHIO

SOUTH DAKOTA

WISCONSIN

RUSH MEDICAL COLLEGE OF RUSH UNIVERSITY MEDICAL CENTER

Address: 600 S Paulina St Suite 524, Chicago, IL 60612
Website: *https://www.rushu.rush.edu/rush-medical-college*
Contact: *https://www.rushu.rush.edu/about/university-contacts*
Phone: (312) 942-6915

COST OF ATTENDANCE

Tuition: $47,166
Fees & Expenses: $35,289
Total: $82,455

Financial Aid: https://www.rushu.rush.edu/rush-medical-college/doctor-medicine-md-program/admissions/tuition-and-financial-aid

Percent Receiving Aid: 83%

ADDITIONAL INFORMATION

Interesting tidbit: Beginning immediately in the M1 year, Rush Medical curriculum immerses you in early clinical experiences to guide you in learning about patient histories, physical examinations and other clinical skills.

What percent of students participate in global health experiences? 19%

What service learning opportunities exist? Health care to individuals in underserved communities, community education for disease prevention, and educating youth about health science opportunities. For more information, visit:https://www.rushu.rush.edu/rush-experience/rush-community-service-initiatives-program

What dual degree options exist? No dual degree options listed.

Important Updates due to COVID-19: Courses taken online or graded as Pass/Fail due to institutional responses to the pandemic are considered without prejudice.

Were tests required? MCAT required.

Are tests expected next year? Yes.

Postgraduate Training Match Rate: N/A

USMLE First-Time Pass Rate

Step 1: N/A

Step 2 CK: N/A

Step 2 CS: N/A

SOUTHERN ILLINOIS UNIVERSITY SCHOOL OF MEDICINE

Address: 801 N Rutledge St, Springfield, IL 62702
Website: *https://www.siumed.edu/*
Contact: *https://www.siumed.edu/contact-us*
Phone: (217) 545-6013

COST OF ATTENDANCE

Tuition: $33,474
Fees & Expenses: $22,287
Total: $55,761

Financial Aid: https://www.siumed.edu/studentaffairs/financial-aid.html

Percent Receiving Aid: 89%

ADDITIONAL INFORMATION

Interesting tidbit: SIU was the fifth pilot project to bring humanities into the clinical experience. The Medical Humanities department offers a comprehensive Doctoring curriculum allowing students to gain a greater understanding of the complex policy, legal, ethical, philosophical, psychosocial and spiritual issues affecting health care providers, patients and the community at large.

What percent of students participate in global health experiences? 15%

What service learning opportunities exist? Outreach sites in 90 Illinois communities and telehealth networks. Students are dedicated to serving the underserved. For more information, visit:http://www.siumed.edu/about-siu-school-medicine.html

What dual degree options exist? MD/MPH:https://www.siumed.edu/popscipolicy/mdmph-program.html

MD/JD:https://www.siumed.edu/medhum/mdjd-dual-degree-program.html

Important Updates due to COVID-19: N/A

Were tests required? MCAT required.

Are tests expected next year? Yes.

Postgraduate Training Match Rate: N/A

USMLE First-Time Pass Rate

Step 1: N/A

Step 2 CK: N/A

Step 2 CS: N/A

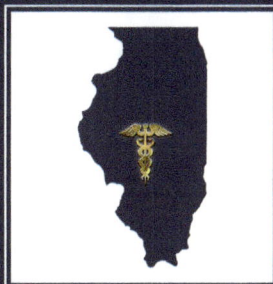

ILLINOIS

INDIANA

IOWA

KANSAS

MICHIGAN

MINNESOTA

MISSOURI

NEBRASKA

NORTH DAKOTA

OHIO

SOUTH DAKOTA

WISCONSIN

MIDWEST

ILLINOIS

INDIANA

IOWA

KANSAS

MICHIGAN

MINNESOTA

MISSOURI

NEBRASKA

NORTH DAKOTA

OHIO

SOUTH DAKOTA

WISCONSIN

UNIVERSITY OF CHICAGO DIVISION OF THE BIOLOGICAL SCIENCES, THE PRITZKER SCHOOL OF MEDICINE

Address: 924 E. 57th Street, Suite 104, Chicago, IL 60637
Website: *https://pritzker.uchicago.edu/*
Contact: *https://pritzker.uchicago.edu/about/contact-us*
Phone: (773) 702-1937

COST OF ATTENDANCE

Tuition: $57,681
Fees & Expenses: $30,484
Total: $88,165

Financial Aid: https://pritzker.uchicago.edu/admissions/financial-aid-incoming-students

Percent Receiving Aid: 90%

ADDITIONAL INFORMATION

Interesting tidbit: Pritzker is one of few medical schools to be located physically on its University campus. All medical education across the continuum—undergraduate medical education (medical school), graduate medical education (internship, residency, and fellowship), continuing medical education (faculty), and simulation is executed seamlessly on one campus.

What percent of students participate in global health experiences? 20%

What service learning opportunities exist? Student-run free clinics, volunteer events, and community organizations. For more information, visit:https://pritzker.uchicago.edu/community-service

What dual degree options exist? MD/PhD and MD/MBA:https://pritzker.uchicago.edu/academics

Important Updates due to COVID-19: Accept pass/fail grades for courses taken during the COVID-19 pandemic. Accept online and virtual courses and labs taken during the pandemic.

Were tests required? MCAT required.

Are tests expected next year? Yes.

Postgraduate Training Match Rate: N/A

USMLE First-Time Pass Rate

Step 1: N/A

Step 2 CK: N/A

Step 2 CS: N/A

Other: BS/MD program available to undergraduate students. For more information, visit:http://collegecatalog.uchicago.edu/thecollege/professionaloptionmedicine/

UNIVERSITY OF ILLINOIS COLLEGE OF MEDICINE

Address: 1853 W. Polk, Chicago, IL 60612
Website: *https://medicine.uic.edu/*
Contact: *https://medicine.uic.edu/about/contact-us/*
Phone: (312) 996-5636
Other locations: Peoria, IL; Rockford, IL; Urbana, IL

COST OF ATTENDANCE

In-State Tuition: $45,360
Fees & Expenses: $32,689
Total: $78,049
Out-of-State Tuition: $78,537

Fees & Expenses: $32,689
Total: $111,226

*Students are assigned to the Chicago campus, the Peoria campus, or the Rockford campus for the duration of the program. COA for Chicago campus: $78,049 (In-State) & $111,226 (Out-of-State); COA for Peoria/Rockford: $76,365 (In-State) & $109,542 (Out-of-State).

Financial Aid: https://medicine.uic.edu/education/md-admissions/tuition-and-financial-aid/

Percent Receiving Aid: 79%

ADDITIONAL INFORMATION

Interesting tidbit: University of Illinois College of Medicine is one of the largest medical schools in the country. The College of Medicine has four campuses located in Chicago, Peoria, Rockford, and Urbana, with specifics of the curriculum varying across campuses. Applicants will effectively be applying to all three of the campuses where the MD program is being offered to new applicants (Chicago, Peoria, and Rockford), and you will be asked upon acceptance for your site rank preference.

What percent of students participate in global health experiences? 8%

What service learning opportunities exist? Service learning through student organizations.

What dual degree options exist? MD/MBA, MD/MPH, MD/PhD, MD/MS in Bioengineering, and MD/MS in Clinical and Translational Science. For more information, visit:https://medicine.uic.edu/education/md-curriculum/curricular-programs/

Important Updates due to COVID-19: Accept courses evaluated as pass, satisfactory, or credit received.

Were tests required? MCAT and CASPer required.

Are tests expected next year? Yes.

Postgraduate Training Match Rate: N/A

USMLE First-Time Pass Rate

Step 1: N/A

Step 2 CK: N/A

Step 2 CS: N/A

Other: Guaranteed Professional Program Admissions (GPPA) Scholars Program available to high school applicants. For more information, visit:https://medicine.uic.edu/gppa/

ILLINOIS

INDIANA

IOWA

KANSAS

MICHIGAN

MINNESOTA

MISSOURI

NEBRASKA

NORTH DAKOTA

OHIO

SOUTH DAKOTA

WISCONSIN

MIDWEST

ILLINOIS

INDIANA

IOWA

KANSAS

MICHIGAN

MINNESOTA

MISSOURI

NEBRASKA

NORTH DAKOTA

OHIO

SOUTH DAKOTA

WISCONSIN

INDIANA UNIVERSITY SCHOOL OF MEDICINE

Address: 340 W 10th St., #6200, Indianapolis, IN 46202
Website: *https://medicine.iu.edu/*
Contact: *https://medicine.iu.edu/contacts*
Phone: (317) 274-3772

Other locations: Gary, IN; Notre Dame, IN; Evansville, IN; Fort Wayne, IN; Muncie, IN; Terre Haute, IN; W. Lafayette, IN; Bloomington, IN

COST OF ATTENDANCE

In-State Tuition: $35,000
Fees & Expenses: $29,468
Total: $64,468

Out-of-State Tuition: $60,000
Fees & Expenses: $29,851
Total: $89,851

Financial Aid: https://medicine.iu.edu/md/tuition/financial-aid

Percent Receiving Aid: 92%

ADDITIONAL INFORMATION

Interesting tidbit: Indiana University School of Medicine has nine campuses throughout the state with each location offering unique characteristics that are important to some students. After acceptance into the IU School of Medicine MD program, all applicants rank their campus preference and campus assignments are determined by computerized lottery based on applicant rankings and campus capacity.

What percent of students participate in global health experiences? 25%

What service learning opportunities exist? Global clinical care and IU Student Outreach Clinic. For more information, visit:https://medicine.iu.edu/md/service-learning

What dual degree options exist? MD/MPH, MD/MBA, MD/JD, MD/MA-MS, and MD/PhD. For more information, visit:https://medicine.iu.edu/dual-degrees

Important Updates due to COVID-19: Accept P/NP (no pass) or S/F grades as meeting requirements; may apply without an MCAT score but are encouraged to include a MCAT test date on the application.

Were tests required? MCAT and CASPer required.

Are tests expected next year? Yes.

Postgraduate Training Match Rate: N/A

USMLE First-Time Pass Rate

Step 1: N/A

Step 2 CK: N/A

Step 2 CS: N/A

UNIVERSITY OF IOWA ROY J. AND LUCILLE A. CARVER COLLEGE OF MEDICINE

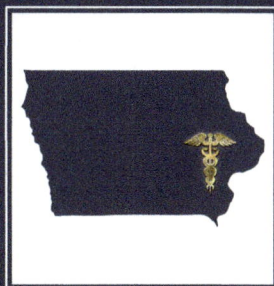

Address: 451 Newton Road, 200 Medicine Administration Building, Iowa City, IA 52242
Website: *https://medicine.uiowa.edu/*
Contact: *https://medicine.uiowa.edu/md/contact-md-program-form*
Phone: (319) 335-8052

Other locations: Des Moines, IA

COST OF ATTENDANCE

In-State Tuition: $37,769
Fees & Expenses: $22,895
Total: $60,664

Out-of-State Tuition: $58,544
Fees & Expenses: $22,895
Total: $81,439

Financial Aid: https://medicine.uiowa.edu/md/financial-aid

Percent Receiving Aid: 86%

ILLINOIS

INDIANA

IOWA

KANSAS

MICHIGAN

MINNESOTA

MISSOURI

NEBRASKA

NORTH DAKOTA

OHIO

SOUTH DAKOTA

WISCONSIN

ADDITIONAL INFORMATION

Interesting tidbit: The Carver College of Medicine's MD curriculum consists of a triple helix model composed of three strands that extend through all four years of medical school - Mechanisms of Health and Disease, Medicine and Society, and Clinical and Professional Skills. The strands are interwoven in a helical spiral that assures not only integration of their material but also affords the deliberate revisiting of material in a manner that promotes progressively deeper understanding and mastery.

What percent of students participate in global health experiences? 25%

What service learning opportunities exist? 2-year service learning elective available. For more information, visit:https://medicine.uiowa.edu/md/curriculum/community-health-outreach

What dual degree options exist? MD/MPH, MD/MBA, MD/JD, and MD/PhD. For more information, visit:https://medicine.uiowa.edu/md/student-support/registrar/combined-md-degree-programs

Important Updates due to COVID-19: Applicants should contact us if they do not receive letter grades for prerequisite courses, and we can review these on a case-by-case basis. Online lab courses will meet our pre-medical course requirements.

Were tests required? MCAT required.

Are tests expected next year? Yes.

Postgraduate Training Match Rate: 82% (2021)

USMLE First-Time Pass Rate

Step 1: 99%

Step 2 CK: 99%

Step 2 CS: 99%

MIDWEST

UNIVERSITY OF KANSAS SCHOOL OF MEDICINE

Address: 3901 Rainbow Blvd, Kansas City, KS 66160
Website: *http://www.kumc.edu/school-of-medicine.html*
Contact: *http://www.kumc.edu/school-of-medicine/education/admissions/contact-us.html*
Phone: (913) 588-5280

Other locations: Wichita, KS; Salina, KS

COST OF ATTENDANCE

In-State Tuition: $37,891
Fees & Expenses: $26,044
Total: $69,935

Out-of-State Tuition: $67,086
Fees & Expenses: $26,044
Total: $93,130

Financial Aid: http://www.kumc.edu/student-affairs/student-financial-aid.html

Percent Receiving Aid: 97%

ADDITIONAL INFORMATION

Interesting tidbit: KU School of Medicine has three campuses - Kansas City, Salina, and Wichita. While curricular requirements for years 3 and 4 will be the same on all three campuses, each campus has its own focus. The Salina campus focus is on delivery of health care in rural and secondary care centers. The Wichita campus focus is on primary-care medicine in community-based hospitals, and the Kansas City campus offers the full range of clinical opportunities available to students studying in an academic, tertiary health-care center.

What percent of students participate in global health experiences? 30%

What service learning opportunities exist? Global opportunities and community-based outreach. For more information, visit:http://www.kumc.edu/community-engagement.html

What dual degree options exist? MD/MPH, MD/MHSA, and MD/PhD. For more information, visit:http://www.kumc.edu/school-of-medicine/degree-programs.html

For information on the MD/MBA, visit:https://business.ku.edu/degrees/businessadmin/mba/full/dual

Important Updates due to COVID-19: Accept Pass/Fail and Credit/No Credit grades for course prerequisites and Online coursework and labs.

Were tests required? MCAT required.

Are tests expected next year? Yes.

Postgraduate Training Match Rate: N/A

USMLE First-Time Pass Rate

Step 1: N/A

Step 2 CK: N/A

Step 2 CS: N/A

CENTRAL MICHIGAN UNIVERSITY COLLEGE OF MEDICINE

Address: 1280 S. East Campus Dr., Mount Pleasant, MI 48859
Website: *https://www.cmich.edu/colleges/med/Pages/default.aspx*
Contact Email: *cmedadmit@cmich.edu*
Phone: (989) 774-7882

Other locations: Detroit, MI; Midland, MI; Saginaw, MI; Saint Joseph, MI

COST OF ATTENDANCE

In-State Tuition: $43,952
Fees & Expenses: $20,929
 Total: $64,881

Out-of-State Tuition: $64,062
Fees & Expenses: $20,929
Total: $74,991

Financial Aid: https://www.cmich.edu/colleges/med/Education/MD/Aid/Pages/default.aspx

Percent Receiving Aid: 82%

ADDITIONAL INFORMATION

Interesting tidbit: CMU College of Medicine focuses on recruiting students from Michigan who want to become doctors for Michigan. It is focused on growth with an emphasis on public health and clinical issues relevant to our region and state.

What percent of students participate in global health experiences? 13%

What service learning opportunities exist? Community partnerships and research. For more information, visit:https://www.cmich.edu/colleges/med/Impact/Initiatives/Pages/default.aspx

What dual degree options exist? MD/MBA. For more information, visit:https://www.cmich.edu/colleges/med/Education/MD/Curriculum/Pages/Dual.aspx

Important Updates due to COVID-19: Accept pass/fail or credit/no credit grades for any coursework taken during the impacted time frame, including prerequisite coursework.

Were tests required? MCAT required.

Are tests expected next year? Yes.

Postgraduate Training Match Rate: N/A

USMLE First-Time Pass Rate

Step 1: N/A

Step 2 CK: N/A

Step 2 CS: N/A

ILLINOIS

INDIANA

IOWA

KANSAS

MICHIGAN

MINNESOTA

MISSOURI

NEBRASKA

NORTH DAKOTA

OHIO

SOUTH DAKOTA

WISCONSIN

MIDWEST

MICHIGAN STATE UNIVERSITY COLLEGE OF HUMAN MEDICINE

Address: 804 Service Road, Suite A112, East Lansing, MI 48824
Website: *http://humanmedicine.msu.edu/*
Contact: *http://humanmedicine.msu.edu/Contact/Contact.htm*
Phone: (517) 353-9620

Other locations: Grand Rapids, MI; Flint, MI; Marquette, MI; Lansing, MI; Traverse City, MI; Midland, MI; Southfield, MI

COST OF ATTENDANCE

In-State Tuition: $32,252
Fees & Expenses: $23,070
Total: $55,322

Out-of-State Tuition: $59,808
Fees & Expenses: $30,503
Total: $82,076

Financial Aid: https://finaid.msu.edu/med/default.asp

Percent Receiving Aid: 93%

ADDITIONAL INFORMATION

Interesting tidbit: Three pillar communities provide the college's foundation for research and clinical services. Grand Rapids, the college's headquarters, is home to centers for excellence in women's health research and Parkinson's disease research. Lansing is the central location for clinical services through the university's health team and Flint offers programs and research in public health.

What percent of students participate in global health experiences? 31%

What service learning opportunities exist? Students are required to complete 40+ hours of service-learning for graduation. For more information, visit:http://humanmedicine.msu.edu/Medical_Education/Assets/Service_Learning.htm

What dual degree options exist? MD/MPH:https://mdadmissions.msu.edu/programs/md_mph.html

MD/MBA: https://mdadmissions.msu.edu/programs/md_mba.html

MD/PhD: https://mdadmissions.msu.edu/programs/md_phd.html

Important Updates due to COVID-19: Accept P/F grading for any courses from winter/spring 2020 through spring 2021, including prerequisites. Accept scores from any extended exam date that was subsequently added.

Were tests required? MCAT and CASPer required.

Are tests expected next year? Yes.

Postgraduate Training Match Rate: 99%

USMLE First-Time Pass Rate

Step 1: 95%

Step 2 CK: 97%

Step 2 CS: 94%

ILLINOIS

INDIANA

IOWA

KANSAS

MICHIGAN

MINNESOTA

MISSOURI

NEBRASKA

NORTH DAKOTA

OHIO

SOUTH DAKOTA

WISCONSIN

OAKLAND UNIVERSITY WILLIAM BEAUMONT SCHOOL OF MEDICINE

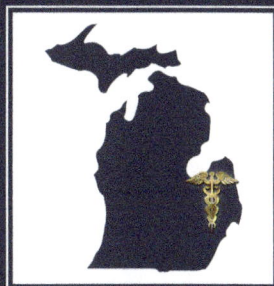

Address: 586 Pioneer Drive, Rochester, MI48309
Website: *https://oakland.edu/medicine/*
Contact Email: *medadmit@oakland.edu*
Phone: (248) 370-2769

COST OF ATTENDANCE

Tuition: $58,218
Fees & Expenses: $30,078
Total: $88,296

Financial Aid: https://oakland.edu/medicine/financial-services/

Percent Receiving Aid: 87%

ADDITIONAL INFORMATION

Interesting tidbit: A four-year-long research program requires each student to move beyond competency requirements and contribute to the advancement of medicine and healthcare by undertaking a scholarly project.

What percent of students participate in global health experiences? 8%

What service learning opportunities exist? Mentoring programs, MLK Day of Service, Make a Difference Day, etc. For more information, visit:https://oakland.edu/medicine/service-and-engagement-programs/compass/

What dual degree options exist? No dual degree options listed.

Important Updates due to COVID-19: Accept Pass/Fail grades and online courses completed at a regionally accredited university, preferably at a four-year institution.

Were tests required? MCAT required.

Are tests expected next year? Yes.

Postgraduate Training Match Rate: 97% (2021)

USMLE First-Time Pass Rate

Step 1: N/A

Step 2 CK: N/A

Step 2 CS: N/A

ILLINOIS

INDIANA

IOWA

KANSAS

MICHIGAN

MINNESOTA

MISSOURI

NEBRASKA

NORTH DAKOTA

OHIO

SOUTH DAKOTA

WISCONSIN

MIDWEST

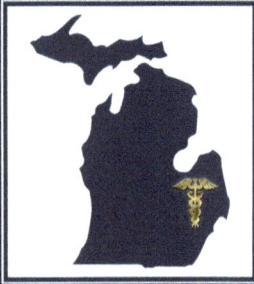

ILLINOIS

INDIANA

IOWA

KANSAS

MICHIGAN

MINNESOTA

MISSOURI

NEBRASKA

NORTH DAKOTA

OHIO

SOUTH DAKOTA

WISCONSIN

UNIVERSITY OF MICHIGAN MEDICAL SCHOOL

Address: 1301 Catherine Street, Ann Arbor, MI 48109
Website: *https://medicine.umich.edu/medschool/home*
Contact Email: *https://medicine.umich.edu/medschool/education/md-program/md-admissions/contact-us*
Phone: (734) 764-6317

COST OF ATTENDANCE

In-State Tuition: $42,282
Fees & Expenses: $26,500
Total: $68,782

Out-of-State Tuition: $61,680
Fees & Expenses: $27,250*
Total: $88,930

*Transportation fee for non-resident is $750 higher.

Financial Aid: https://medicine.umich.edu/medschool/education/md-program/financial-aid

Percent Receiving Aid: 82%

ADDITIONAL INFORMATION

Interesting tidbit: The Medical School was the University's first professional school. Its first graduating class of six students in 1851 paid a mere $5 for two years of medical education.

What percent of students participate in global health experiences? 19%

What service learning opportunities exist? Service learning through student organizations. For more information, visit:https://medicine.umich.edu/medschool/student-orgs

What dual degree options exist? MD/MPH, MD/MBA, MD/JD, and MD/PhD. For more information, visit:https://medicine.umich.edu/medschool/education/md-program/opportunities/dual-degrees

Important Updates due to COVID-19: More liberally accept pass/fail grades for the 2021-22 application cycle and online coursework.

Were tests required? MCAT required.

Are tests expected next year? Yes.

Postgraduate Training Match Rate: 98.2% (2021)

USMLE First-Time Pass Rate

Step 1: N/A

Step 2 CK: N/A

Step 2 CS: N/A

WAYNE STATE UNIVERSITY SCHOOL OF MEDICINE

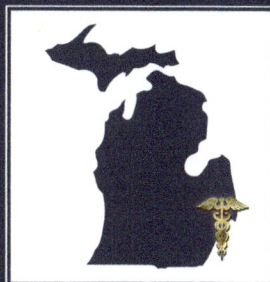

Address: 540 E. Canfield, Detroit, MI 48201
Website: *https://www.med.wayne.edu/*
Contact Email: *mdadmissions@wayne.edu*
Phone: (313) 577-1466

COST OF ATTENDANCE

In-State Tuition: $39,280
Fees & Expenses: $22,371
Total: $61,651

Out-of-State Tuition: $67,479
Fees & Expenses: $22,371
Total: $89,850

Financial Aid: https://wayne.edu/financial-aid/medicine

Percent Receiving Aid: 83%

ADDITIONAL INFORMATION

Interesting tidbit: Warrior M.D. Ambassadors welcomes students and community members to the Wayne State University School of Medicine. With their insider's knowledge about life as a Wayne State medical student, they are a great resource for all your questions.

What percent of students participate in global health experiences? 23%

What service learning opportunities exist? Mentoring, community education, research, etc. For more information, visit:https://www.med.wayne.edu/community

What dual degree options exist? MD/MPH and MD/PhD. For more information, visit:https://www.med.wayne.edu/admissions/application/degree-programs

Important Updates due to COVID-19: If no in-person courses are available and will accept courses from other 4-year colleges & universities with preference given to your home institution. Accept pass/fail coursework to fulfill prerequisites if taken during or after the Winter 2020 term.

Were tests required? MCAT required.

Are tests expected next year? Yes.

Postgraduate Training Match Rate: 97%

USMLE First-Time Pass Rate

Step 1: N/A

Step 2 CK: N/A

Step 2 CS: N/A

ILLINOIS

INDIANA

IOWA

KANSAS

MICHIGAN

MINNESOTA

MISSOURI

NEBRASKA

NORTH DAKOTA

OHIO

SOUTH DAKOTA

WISCONSIN

MIDWEST

ILLINOIS

INDIANA

IOWA

KANSAS

MICHIGAN

MINNESOTA

MISSOURI

NEBRASKA

NORTH DAKOTA

OHIO

SOUTH DAKOTA

WISCONSIN

WESTERN MICHIGAN UNIVERSITY HOMER STRYKER M.D. SCHOOL OF MEDICINE

Address: 300 Portage Street, Kalamazoo, MI 49007
Website: *https://med.wmich.edu/*
Contact: *https://med.wmich.edu/node/341*
Phone: (269) 337-6100

COST OF ATTENDANCE

Tuition: $63,500
Fees & Expenses: $24,428*
Total: $87,928

*Health insurance costs will be added upon request.

Financial Aid: https://med.wmich.edu/financial-aid

Percent Receiving Aid: 85%

ADDITIONAL INFORMATION

Interesting tidbit: WMed MD curriculum is decompressed, which means that it took the long summer break between years one and two and broke it into one-week intervals that are spread throughout the first two years of medical school.

What percent of students participate in global health experiences? 21%

What service learning opportunities exist? Active Citizenship rotation and service learning through student organizations. For more information, visit:https://med.wmich.edu/node/317

What dual degree options exist? MD/MBA:https://med.wmich.edu/node/221

MD/PhD: https://med.wmich.edu/node/267

Important Updates due to COVID-19: Consider, without prejudice, pass/fail, credit/no-credit, or virtual learning.

Were tests required? MCAT required.

Are tests expected next year? Yes.

Postgraduate Training Match Rate: N/A

USMLE First-Time Pass Rate

Step 1: N/A

Step 2 CK: N/A

Step 2 CS: N/A

MAYO CLINIC ALIX SCHOOL OF MEDICINE

Address: 200 First Street SW, Rochester, MN 55905
Website: *https://college.mayo.edu/academics/school-of-medicine/*
Contact: *https://college.mayo.edu/academics/school-of-medicine/contact/*
Phone: (507) 266-5568

COST OF ATTENDANCE

Tuition: $58,900
Fees & Expenses: $36,296
Total: $95,196

Financial Aid: https://college.mayo.edu/admissions-and-tuition/financial-aid/

Percent Receiving Aid: 92%

ADDITIONAL INFORMATION

Interesting tidbit: Mayo Clinic Alix School of Medicine is a national medical school that offers unique experiences at three different campus locations in Arizona, Florida, and Minnesota. Each campus offers a different personality as well as unique amenities and experiences. On the secondary application, applicants will have the opportunity to select and rank up to four campus track options.

What percent of students participate in global health experiences? 56%

What service learning opportunities exist? Mentorship programs, community health clinics, etc. For more information, visit:https://college.mayo.edu/academics/school-of-medicine/md-program/student-life/

What dual degree options exist? MD/PhD. For more information, visit:https://college.mayo.edu/academics/school-of-medicine/md-program/how-to-apply/

Important Updates due to COVID-19: Accept Pass/Fail grades and online courses and labs.

Were tests required? MCAT required.

Are tests expected next year? Yes.

Postgraduate Training Match Rate: N/A

USMLE First-Time Pass Rate

Step 1: N/A

Step 2 CK: N/A

Step 2 CS: N/A

ILLINOIS

INDIANA

IOWA

KANSAS

MICHIGAN

MINNESOTA

MISSOURI

NEBRASKA

NORTH DAKOTA

OHIO

SOUTH DAKOTA

WISCONSIN

MIDWEST

ILLINOIS

INDIANA

IOWA

KANSAS

MICHIGAN

MINNESOTA

MISSOURI

NEBRASKA

NORTH DAKOTA

OHIO

SOUTH DAKOTA

WISCONSIN

UNIVERSITY OF MINNESOTA MEDICAL SCHOOL

Address: 420 Delaware St SE, Minneapolis, MN 55455
Website: *https://med.umn.edu/*
Contact: *https://med.umn.edu/about/contact*
Phone: (612) 625-7077

COST OF ATTENDANCE

Twin Cities MD Program
In-State Tuition: $26,794
Fees & Expenses: $21,798
Total: $48,592

Out-of-State Tuition: $38,452
Fees & Expenses: $21,798
 Total: $60,250

Duluth MD Program
In-State Tuition: $26,794
Fees & Expenses: $18,196
Total: $44,990

Out-of-State Tuition: $38,452
Fees & Expenses: $18,736
Total: $57,188

Note: Medical students from South Dakota are able to apply for tuition reciprocity.

Financial Aid: https://med.umn.edu/md-students/financial-aid

Percent Receiving Aid: 89%

ADDITIONAL INFORMATION

Interesting tidbit: The U of M Medical School has two campuses: Twin Cities and Duluth. You can apply to one or both campuses and your choice will determine which supplemental application(s) you'll receive. Selection criteria is unique to each campus because the Twin Cities campus and the Duluth regional campus missions differ.

What percent of students participate in global health experiences? 15%

What service learning opportunities exist? Free clinic and service activities through the university and student organizations. For more information, visit:https://med.umn.edu/admissions/student-life

What dual degree options exist? MD/MPH, MD/MBA, MD/JD, MD/MHI, MD/MS in Biomedical Engineering, and MD/PhD. For more information, visit:https://med.umn.edu/education-training/degrees-offered

Important Updates due to COVID-19: Accept P/F grades for courses taken in the Spring and Summer of 2020 including prerequisites.

Were tests required? MCAT required.

Note: The University of Minnesota Medical School Twin Cities MD program is encouraging all applicants to complete an online situational judgment test administered by the Association of American Medical Colleges (AAMC) as part of their application for the 2021 cycle.

Are tests expected next year? Yes.

Postgraduate Training Match Rate: N/A

USMLE First-Time Pass Rate

Step 1: N/A

Step 2 CK: N/A

Step 2 CS: N/A

Other: BA/MD program available to high school applicants. For more information, visit:https://med.umn.edu/admissions/pre-med-student-opportunities/ba-md-scholars-program

SAINT LOUIS UNIVERSITY SCHOOL OF MEDICINE

Address: 1402 S. Grand Blvd., St. Louis, MO 63104
Website: *https://www.slu.edu/medicine/index.php*
Contact: *https://www.slu.edu/medicine/contact.php*
Phone: (314) 977-9875

COST OF ATTENDANCE

Tuition: $60,360
Fees & Expenses: $23,998
Total: $84,358

Financial Aid: https://www.slu.edu/medicine/about/student-resources/financial-aid/index.php

Percent Receiving Aid: 81%

ADDITIONAL INFORMATION

Interesting tidbit: Saint Louis University School of Medicine is a leading center of research in five key areas: cancer, infectious disease, liver disease, aging and brain disorders, and heart/lung disease. It is one of only nine NIH-funded vaccine research institutions.

What percent of students participate in global health experiences? 17%

What service learning opportunities exist? Volunteer at Casa de Salud, the Chinese Clinic, and engage in Adventures in Medicine and Science (AIMS) – a youth community outreach program. For more information, visit:https://www.slu.edu/medicine/clinics-community/index.php

What dual degree options exist? MD/PhD, MD/MPH, and MD/MBA. For more information, visit:https://www.slu.edu/medicine/medical-education/index.php

Important Updates due to COVID-19: Give full consideration to pass/fail grades for any lecture or laboratory courses taken during the Spring 2020 semester.

Were tests required? MCAT required.

Are tests expected next year? Yes.

Postgraduate Training Match Rate: N/A

USMLE First-Time Pass Rate

Step 1: N/A

Step 2 CK: N/A

Step 2 CS: N/A

Other: Medical Scholars Program (BS/MD) available to high school applicants. For more information, visit:https://www.slu.edu/scholars/medical-scholars/index.php

ILLINOIS

INDIANA

IOWA

KANSAS

MICHIGAN

MINNESOTA

MISSOURI

NEBRASKA

NORTH DAKOTA

OHIO

SOUTH DAKOTA

WISCONSIN

MIDWEST

ILLINOIS

INDIANA

IOWA

KANSAS

MICHIGAN

MINNESOTA

MISSOURI

NEBRASKA

NORTH DAKOTA

OHIO

SOUTH DAKOTA

WISCONSIN

UNIVERSITY OF MISSOURI-COLUMBIA SCHOOL OF MEDICINE

Address: 1 Hospital Dr, Columbia, MO 65212
Website: *https://medicine.missouri.edu/*
Contact: *https://medicine.missouri.edu/contact*
Phone: (573) 882-9219

Other locations: Springfield, MO

COST OF ATTENDANCE

In-State Tuition: $36,688
Fees & Expenses: $22,113
Total: $58,801

Out-of-State Tuition: $70,977
Fees & Expenses: $22,113
Total: $93,090

Financial Aid:https://medicine.missouri.edu/offices-programs/financial-aid

Percent Receiving Aid: 94%

ADDITIONAL INFORMATION

Interesting tidbit: The University of Missouri School of Medicine has expanded its medical school class size from 96 to 128 students to address a critical shortage of physicians in Missouri and the nation, and opened a second MU clinical campus in Springfield in June 2016.

What percent of students participate in global health experiences? 26%

What service learning opportunities exist? Global Health Scholars Program, Legacy Teachers, MedZou Community Health Clinic, etc. For more information, visit:https://medicine.missouri.edu/education/medical-education-curriculum/learning-experiences

What dual degree options exist? MD/PhD. For more information, visit:https://medicine.missouri.edu/education/md-phd-program

Important Updates due to COVID-19: Applicants not penalized for taking our required coursework as pass/fail for the Spring 2021 semester only.

Were tests required? MCAT required.

Are tests expected next year? Yes.

Postgraduate Training Match Rate: 97% (2021)

USMLE First-Time Pass Rate

Step 1: N/A

Step 2 CK: N/A

Step 2 CS: N/A

UNIVERSITY OF MISSOURI-KANSAS CITY SCHOOL OF MEDICINE

Address: 2411 Holmes Street, Kansas City, Missouri 64108
Website: *https://med.umkc.edu/*
Contact: *https://med.umkc.edu/directories/*
Phone: (816) 235-1870

COST OF ATTENDANCE

In-State Tuition: $34,583
Fees & Expenses: $17,728*
Total: $52,311

Out-of-State Tuition: $67,037**
Fees & Expenses: $17,728
Total: $84,765

*Additional fees may apply, fees associated with transportation, immunizations, the United States Medical Licensing Examination and other miscellaneous fees.

**Students who are residents of Kansas, Oklahoma, Nebraska, Arkansas or Illinois qualify for the regional tuition rate of $50,813. Financial Aid:https://med.umkc.edu/sa/finance/som_scholarships/
Percent Receiving Aid: 99%

ADDITIONAL INFORMATION

Interesting tidbit: Students join a group of 10 to 12 fellow medical students, called a docent team. Early and continued contact with a team of clinical physicians, known as docents, builds student capacity for clinical judgment. Docent teams include a docent, a clinical pharmacologist, a clinical medical librarian, an Education Team Coordinator and other health care professionals.

What percent of students participate in global health experiences? 19%

What service learning opportunities exist? Service learning through student organizations.

What dual degree options exist? No dual degree options listed.

Important Updates due to COVID-19: Accept pass/fail for the Spring 2021 semester only.

Were tests required? MCAT required.

Are tests expected next year? Yes.

Postgraduate Training Match Rate: N/A

USMLE First-Time Pass Rate

Step 1: N/A

Step 2 CK: N/A

Step 2 CS: N/A

Other: BA/MD (6-year) program available to high school applicants. For more information, visit: https://med.umkc.edu/bamd/

ILLINOIS

INDIANA

IOWA

KANSAS

MICHIGAN

MINNESOTA

MISSOURI

NEBRASKA

NORTH DAKOTA

OHIO

SOUTH DAKOTA

WISCONSIN

MIDWEST

ILLINOIS

INDIANA

IOWA

KANSAS

MICHIGAN

MINNESOTA

MISSOURI

NEBRASKA

NORTH DAKOTA

OHIO

SOUTH DAKOTA

WISCONSIN

WASHINGTON UNIVERSITY IN ST. LOUIS SCHOOL OF MEDICINE

Address: 660 S Euclid Ave, St. Louis, MO 63110
Website: *https://medicine.wustl.edu/*
Contact: *https://mdadmissions.wustl.edu/contact-us/*
Phone: (314) 362-6858

COST OF ATTENDANCE

Tuition: $65,001
Fees & Expenses: $25,029
Total: $90,030

Financial Aid: https://medicine.wustl.edu/education/financial-support/

Percent Receiving Aid: 84%

ADDITIONAL INFORMATION

Interesting tidbit: 20 years since last curriculum renewal, WashU Med recently implemented a new Gateway Curriculum, beginning with the entering class of 2020.

What percent of students participate in global health experiences? 27%

What service learning opportunities exist? Service learning through student organizations at the local, national, and global levels. For more information, visit:https://mdadmissions.wustl.edu/education/service-learning/

What dual degree options exist? MD/MBA, MD/MPH, MD/MS in Clinical Investigation, MD/MPHS, and MD/PhD. For more information, visit:https://medicine.wustl.edu/education/admissions/#medical-education

Important Updates due to COVID-19: Accept Pass/Fail grades and online coursework and labs from Winter/Spring 2020, Summer 2020, Fall 2020, and/or Winter/Spring 2021

Were tests required? MCAT required.

Are tests expected next year? Yes.

Postgraduate Training Match Rate: N/A

USMLE First-Time Pass Rate

Step 1: N/A

Step 2 CK: N/A

Step 2 CS: N/A

CREIGHTON UNIVERSITY SCHOOL OF MEDICINE

Address: 2500 California Plaza, Omaha, NE 68178
Website: *https://medschool.creighton.edu/*
Contact: *https://medschool.creighton.edu/about/contact*
Phone: (800) 325-4405

Other locations: Phoenix, AZ

COST OF ATTENDANCE

Tuition: $61,696
Fees & Expenses: $25,000
Total: $86,696

Financial Aid: https://medschool.creighton.edu/future-students/md-program/financial-information

Percent Receiving Aid: 83%

ADDITIONAL INFORMATION

Interesting tidbit: The Creighton University School of Medicine Is committed to educating physicians in the Jesuit, Catholic tradition.

What percent of students participate in global health experiences? 31%

What service learning opportunities exist? Magis Clinic, Project CURA, the Institute for Latin American Concern (ILAC), etc. For more information, visit:https://medschool.creighton.edu/current-students/service-opportunities

What dual degree options exist? MD/MBA and MD/PhD. For more information, visit:https://medschool.creighton.edu/future-students/dual-degree-programs

Important Updates due to COVID-19: Accept all non-prerequisite courses as pass/fail or satisfactory/unsatisfactory during this time of the COVID-19 pandemic. For prerequisite courses, consider Pass/Fail on a case-by-case basis.

Were tests required? MCAT required.

Are tests expected next year? Yes.

Postgraduate Training Match Rate: > 90% (2021)

USMLE First-Time Pass Rate

Step 1: N/A

Step 2 CK: N/A

Step 2 CS: N/A

ILLINOIS

INDIANA

IOWA

KANSAS

MICHIGAN

MINNESOTA

MISSOURI

NEBRASKA

NORTH DAKOTA

OHIO

SOUTH DAKOTA

WISCONSIN

MIDWEST

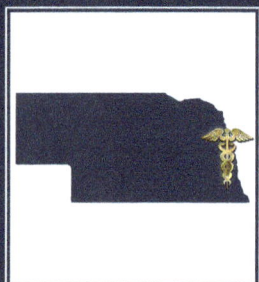

ILLINOIS

INDIANA

IOWA

KANSAS

MICHIGAN

MINNESOTA

MISSOURI

NEBRASKA

NORTH DAKOTA

OHIO

SOUTH DAKOTA

WISCONSIN

UNIVERSITY OF NEBRASKA COLLEGE OF MEDICINE

Address: 42nd and Emile, Omaha, NE 68198
Website: *https://www.unmc.edu/com/*
Contact: *https://www.unmc.edu/com/admissions/contact-information.html*
Phone: (402) 559-2259

COST OF ATTENDANCE

In-State Tuition: $35,360
Fees & Expenses: $28,045
Total: $63,405

Out-of-State Tuition: $57,290
Fees & Expenses: $28,975
Total: $86,265

Financial Aid: https://www.unmc.edu/financialaid/

Percent Receiving Aid: 94%

ADDITIONAL INFORMATION

Interesting tidbit: UNMC College of Medicine curriculum is divided into three phases - Foundations of Medicine (18 months), Clinical Applications (12 months) and Career Preparation (13 months). Phase 3 begins earlier than the fourth year of most traditional medical curricula, allowing students to explore career opportunities prior to residency application.

What percent of students participate in global health experiences? 34%

What service learning opportunities exist? Legacy Projects and SHARING Clinics. For more information, visit:https://www.unmc.edu/oce/engagement/index.html

What dual degree options exist? MD/MBA, MD/MPH, and MD/PhD. For more information, visit:https://www.unmc.edu/com/education/md-enrichment/dual-degree/index.html

Important Updates due to COVID-19: Accept Pass/No Credit grades for courses taken during the COVID-19 pandemic without conditions. Online coursework, including laboratory courses, will continue to be accepted in fulfillment of some prerequisites.

Were tests required? MCAT required.

Are tests expected next year? Yes.

Postgraduate Training Match Rate: N/A

USMLE First-Time Pass Rate

Step 1: N/A

Step 2 CK: N/A

Step 2 CS: N/A

UNIVERSITY OF NORTH DAKOTA SCHOOL OF MEDICINE AND HEALTH SCIENCES

Address: 1301 N Columbia Rd, Grand Forks, ND 58203
Website: *https://med.und.edu/*
Contact: *https://med.und.edu/admissions/index.html*
Phone: (701) 777-4221

COST OF ATTENDANCE

In-State Tuition: $34,762
Fees & Expenses: $23,168
Total: $57,930

Out-of-State Tuition: $61,630
Fees & Expenses: $23,168
Total: $86,033

Note: Minnesota residents pay a reduced out-of-state tuition at $38,063.

Financial Aid: https://med.und.edu/student-affairs-admissions/financial-aid/index.html

Percent Receiving Aid: 91%

ADDITIONAL INFORMATION

Interesting tidbit: Of its 78 admissions annually, seven students are part of its Indians into Medicine (INMED) Program. INMED is created to assist American Indian/Alaska Native students preparing for health careers. Sixty seats are reserved for students who are residents of North Dakota or have significant ties to the state. Eleven seats are reserved for residents of Minnesota and participating WICHE (Western Interstate Commission for Higher Education) states.

What percent of students participate in global health experiences? 16%

What service learning opportunities exist? Fetal Alcohol Syndrome Center, Rural Surgery Support Program, Center for Family Medicine, etc. For more information, visit:https://med.und.edu/service/index.html

What dual degree options exist? MD/MPH and MD/PhD. For more information, visit:https://med.und.edu/md-phd/

Important Updates due to COVID-19: Accept pass/fail grades, without prejudice, for courses taken during the COVID-19 pandemic.

Were tests required? MCAT required.

Are tests expected next year? Yes.

Postgraduate Training Match Rate: N/A

USMLE First-Time Pass Rate

Step 1: N/A

Step 2 CK: N/A

Step 2 CS: N/A

ILLINOIS

INDIANA

IOWA

KANSAS

MICHIGAN

MINNESOTA

MISSOURI

NEBRASKA

NORTH DAKOTA

OHIO

SOUTH DAKOTA

WISCONSIN

MIDWEST

ILLINOIS

INDIANA

IOWA

KANSAS

MICHIGAN

MINNESOTA

MISSOURI

NEBRASKA

NORTH DAKOTA

OHIO

SOUTH DAKOTA

WISCONSIN

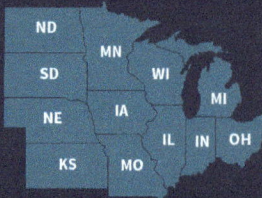

BOONSHOFT SCHOOL OF MEDICINE
WRIGHT STATE UNIVERSITY

Address: 3640 Colonel Glenn Hwy, Dayton, OH 45435
Website: *https://medicine.wright.edu/*
Contact: *https://medicine.wright.edu/about/directory-of-all-offices-and-departments*
Phone: (937) 775-2934

COST OF ATTENDANCE

In-State Tuition: $35,464
Fees & Expenses: $27,287
Total: $62,751

Out-of-State Tuition: $54,342
Fees & Expenses: $27,287
Total: $81,629

Financial Aid: https://medicine.wright.edu/admissions/financial-aid

Percent Receiving Aid: 92%

ADDITIONAL INFORMATION

Interesting tidbit: The Boonshoft School of Medicine was the first medical school in the nation to implement Team-Based Learning™, giving students real-world experience by working closely in small groups to master material, applying their knowledge to clinical cases and defending their diagnosis and treatment plans.

What percent of students participate in global health experiences? 40%

What service learning opportunities exist? Reach Out of Montgomery County, Student to Student, NOLA Service Trip, etc. For more information, visit:https://medicine.wright.edu/community/student-service-in-the-community

What dual degree options exist? MD/MBA, MD/MPH, and MD/PhD. For more information, visit:https://medicine.wright.edu/admissions/dual-degree-programs

Important Updates due to COVID-19: Pass/Fail is accepted for all coursework including prerequisites. Online coursework and labs will be accepted through the Summer 2021 term. MCAT will be required for matriculation but applications may be submitted without MCAT.

Were tests required? MCAT required.

Are tests expected next year? Yes.

Postgraduate Training Match Rate: N/A

USMLE First-Time Pass Rate

Step 1: N/A

Step 2 CK: N/A

Step 2 CS: N/A

CASE WESTERN RESERVE UNIVERSITY SCHOOL OF MEDICINE

Address: 9501 Euclid Ave., Cleveland, OH 44106
Website: *https://case.edu/medicine/*
Contact: *https://case.edu/medicine/admissions-programs/md-programs/contact-md-programs*
Phone: (216) 368-3450

COST OF ATTENDANCE

Tuition: $67,440
Fees & Expenses: $25,497
Total: $92,937

Financial Aid: https://case.edu/medicine/students/financial-aid

Percent Receiving Aid: 76%

ADDITIONAL INFORMATION

Interesting tidbit: CWRU School of Medicine boasts many "firsts". It instituted the first MD/PhD dual degree program in the country, upon which the NIH and others modeled their programs and the first DMD/MD dual degree program in the country. It is the third institution in history to receive the best possible score from LCME.

What percent of students participate in global health experiences? 22%

What service learning opportunities exist? Volunteer opportunities through Case Western and student-run organizations.

What dual degree options exist? MD/MBA, MD/MPH, MD/JD, MD/MA in Bioethics, MD/MS in Applied Anatomy, MD/MS in Biomedical Engineering, MD/MS in Biomedical Investigation, MD/MA in Anthropology, and MD/PhD. For more information, visit:https://case.edu/medicine/admissions-programs/md-programs/dual-degrees

Important Updates due to COVID-19: Accept Pass/No Pass grading for prerequisite courses and online laboratory credit for the winter/spring and summer 2020 semesters.

Were tests required? MCAT required.

Are tests expected next year? Yes.

Postgraduate Training Match Rate: N/A

USMLE First-Time Pass Rate

Step 1: N/A

Step 2 CK: N/A

Step 2 CS: N/A

Other: BA/MD 8-year program available to high school applicants. For more information, visit:https://case.edu/admission/academics/pre-professional-programs

ILLINOIS

INDIANA

IOWA

KANSAS

MICHIGAN

MINNESOTA

MISSOURI

NEBRASKA

NORTH DAKOTA

OHIO

SOUTH DAKOTA

WISCONSIN

MIDWEST

ILLINOIS

INDIANA

IOWA

KANSAS

MICHIGAN

MINNESOTA

MISSOURI

NEBRASKA

NORTH DAKOTA

OHIO

SOUTH DAKOTA

WISCONSIN

NORTHEAST OHIO MEDICAL UNIVERSITY COLLEGE OF MEDICINE

Address: 4209 State Route 44, Rootstown, OH 44272
Website: *https://www.neomed.edu/*
Contact: *https://www.neomed.edu/contact/*
Phone: (330) 325-6266

COST OF ATTENDANCE

In-State Tuition: $44,204
Fees & Expenses: $29,697
Total: $73,901

Out-of-State Tuition: $83,674
Fees & Expenses: $31,368
Total: $115,042

Financial Aid: https://www.neomed.edu/financialaid/

Percent Receiving Aid: 73%

ADDITIONAL INFORMATION

Interesting tidbit: The College of Medicine curriculum is undergoing a transformation. The academic calendar will be replaced with a new calendar that has 16-week semesters, a summer semester and a "Maymester" term. The summer semester will start the new academic year. The complete transition will occur over a period of several years.

What percent of students participate in global health experiences? 12%

What service learning opportunities exist? Alternative Spring Breaks, Make a Difference Day, MLK Day of Service, etc. For more information, visit:https://www.neomed.edu/community/service/

What dual degree options exist? No dual degree options listed.

Important Updates due to COVID-19: N/A

Were tests required? MCAT and CASPer required.

Are tests expected next year? Yes.

Postgraduate Training Match Rate: 98%

USMLE First-Time Pass Rate

Step 1: 96%

Step 2 CK: 98%

Step 2 CS: 95%

Other: NEOMED no longer offers combined degree programs nor the BS/MD program. However, they do offer Early Assurance pathways with seven partner institutions. For more information, visit:https://www.neomed.edu/medicine/admissions/paths/early-assurance/

THE OHIO STATE UNIVERSITY COLLEGE OF MEDICINE

Address: 370 W. 9th Avenue, Columbus, OH 43210
Website: *https://medicine.osu.edu/*
Contact: *https://medicine.osu.edu/contact-us*
Phone: (614) 685-3053

COST OF ATTENDANCE

In-State Tuition: $30,636
Fees & Expenses: $25,488
Total: $56,124

Out-of-State Tuition: $55,556
Fees & Expenses: $25,488
Total: $81,044

Financial Aid: https://medicine.osu.edu/student-resources/cost

Percent Receiving Aid: 92%

ADDITIONAL INFORMATION

Interesting tidbit: In addition to the traditional 4-year MD program, the Ohio State College of Medicine offers the accelerated 3-year Primary Care Track (PCT) for students who are committed to family medicine as their specialty of choice. Students who successfully graduate from the Primary Care Track program are ranked to match into the Ohio State Family Medicine Residency Program.

What percent of students participate in global health experiences? 38%

What service learning opportunities exist? Local specialty clinics, Healthy Community Day at the Wexner Medical Center, Global Health, etc. For more information, visit:https://medicine.osu.edu/why-choose-us/campus-life/community-service

What dual degree options exist? MD/JD, MD/MBA, MD/MPH, MD/MHA, and MD/PhD. For more information, visit:https://medicine.osu.edu/education/dual-degree

Important Updates due to COVID-19: Pass/Fail are allowed for all coursework taken during the Spring 2020 term, including prerequisites. Online labs are accepted for the Spring 2020 and Summer 2020 term. A valid MCAT score is required to receive a secondary at The Ohio State University College of Medicine.

Were tests required? MCAT required.

Are tests expected next year? Yes.

Postgraduate Training Match Rate: 98% (on average)

USMLE First-Time Pass Rate

Step 1: N/A

Step 2 CK: N/A

Step 2 CS: N/A

ILLINOIS

INDIANA

IOWA

KANSAS

MICHIGAN

MINNESOTA

MISSOURI

NEBRASKA

NORTH DAKOTA

OHIO

SOUTH DAKOTA

WISCONSIN

MIDWEST

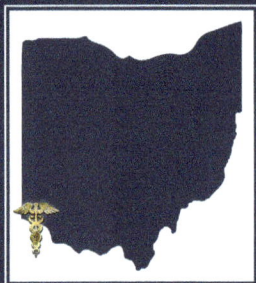

ILLINOIS

INDIANA

IOWA

KANSAS

MICHIGAN

MINNESOTA

MISSOURI

NEBRASKA

NORTH DAKOTA

OHIO

SOUTH DAKOTA

WISCONSIN

UNIVERSITY OF CINCINNATI COLLEGE OF MEDICINE

Address: 3230 Eden Ave, Cincinnati, OH 45267
Website: *https://www.med.uc.edu/*
Contact: *https://www.med.uc.edu/medicalstudentadmissions/ contact-us-staff*
Phone: (513) 558-7314

COST OF ATTENDANCE

In-State Tuition: $32,980
Fees & Expenses: $23,537
Total: $56,517

Out-of-State Tuition: $51,244
Fees & Expenses: $23,537
Total: $74,781

Financial Aid: https://www.med.uc.edu/financialservices/applying/ newstudents

Percent Receiving Aid: 80%

ADDITIONAL INFORMATION

Interesting tidbit: The University of Cincinnati College of Medicine is the second-oldest public college of medicine in the United States. The UC Academic Health Center is probably best known for the development of the first live, attenuated polio vaccine.

What percent of students participate in global health experiences? 11%

What service learning opportunities exist? Service learning through student organizations.

What dual degree options exist? MD/MPH available as a joint degree.

MD/MBA:https://www.med.uc.edu/MDMBA/requirements

MD/PhD:https://www.med.uc.edu/MSTP/applicationprocess/apply

Important Updates due to COVID-19: Pass-Fail grades are only accepted for coursework completed in the college setting for the winter/spring /summer of 2020, not after summer 2020. All on-line courses are accepted if completed between spring 2020 and summer 2021.

Were tests required? MCAT required.

Are tests expected next year? Yes.

Postgraduate Training Match Rate: 100% (2021)

USMLE First-Time Pass Rate

Step 1: N/A

Step 2 CK: N/A

Step 2 CS: N/A

Other: BS/MD 8-year program available to high school applicants. For more information, visit:https://www.med.uc.edu/connections

THE UNIVERSITY OF TOLEDO COLLEGE OF MEDICINE AND LIFE SCIENCES

Address: 3000 Arlington Ave, Toledo, OH 43614
Website: *https://www.utoledo.edu/med/*
Contact Email: *medadmissions@utoledo.edu*
Phone: (419) 383-4229

COST OF ATTENDANCE

In-State Tuition: $32,925
Fees & Expenses: $22,700
Total: $55,625

Out-of-State Tuition: $64,771
Fees & Expenses: $22,700
Total: $87,472

Financial Aid: https://www.utoledo.edu/med/md/admissions/scholarships/

Percent Receiving Aid: 84%

ADDITIONAL INFORMATION

Interesting tidbit: Beginning with the incoming class of 2017, The University of Toledo College of Medicine and Life Sciences implemented a redesigned curriculum. Officially called "Rocket Medicine," this major curriculum change puts an emphasis on a competency-based curriculum with early clinical experience and seamless integration of foundational and clinical sciences.

What percent of students participate in global health experiences? 22%

What service learning opportunities exist? Service learning through student organizations.

What dual degree options exist? MD/MBA, MD/JD, MD/MSBS, and MD/PhD. For more information, visit:https://www.utoledo.edu/med/admission/

For information on the MD/MPH, visit:https://www.utoledo.edu/med/gme/em/MD.%20MPH%20Program.html

Important Updates due to COVID-19: Accept online coursework, non-letter grading, online lab for prerequisites. Waive the requirement of a posted MCAT score for eligibility for a UToledo Secondary Application.

Were tests required? MCAT required.

Are tests expected next year? Yes.

Postgraduate Training Match Rate: N/A

USMLE First-Time Pass Rate

Step 1: N/A

Step 2 CK: N/A

Step 2 CS: N/A

Other: BACC2MD program available to high school applicants. For more information, visit:https://www.utoledo.edu/success/pre-health-advising/bacc2md.html

ILLINOIS

INDIANA

IOWA

KANSAS

MICHIGAN

MINNESOTA

MISSOURI

NEBRASKA

NORTH DAKOTA

OHIO

SOUTH DAKOTA

WISCONSIN

MIDWEST

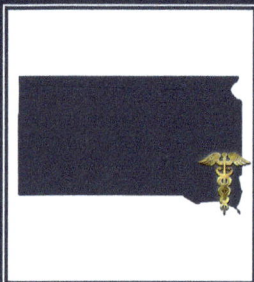

ILLINOIS

INDIANA

IOWA

KANSAS

MICHIGAN

MINNESOTA

MISSOURI

NEBRASKA

NORTH DAKOTA

OHIO

SOUTH DAKOTA

WISCONSIN

UNIVERSITY OF SOUTH DAKOTA SANFORD SCHOOL OF MEDICINE

Address: 1400 W. 22nd St., Sioux Falls, SD 57105
Website: *https://www.usd.edu/medicine*
Contact: *https://www.usd.edu/medicine/contact-us*
Phone: (605) 658-6302

Other locations: Rapid City, SD; Yankton, SD; Vermillion, SD; Spearfish, SD; Pierre, SD

COST OF ATTENDANCE

In-State Tuition: $31,787
Fees & Expenses: $26,561
Total: $58,348

Out-of-State Tuition: $76,173
Fees & Expenses: $26,561
Total: $102,734

Financial Aid: https://www.usd.edu/financial-aid

Percent Receiving Aid: 99%

ADDITIONAL INFORMATION

Interesting tidbit: In 2019, the University of South Dakota Sanford School of Medicine began incorporating "kindness" into its medical education, culture and strategy, identifying and elevating kindness as a fundamental component of healing and happiness. Kindness became a unifying focus of the medical school and an intentional part of the school's culture and curriculum.

What percent of students participate in global health experiences? 24%

What service learning opportunities exist? Coyote Clinic, international health care, cultural immersion project at Indian reservations, etc. For more information, visit:https://www.usd.edu/medicine/service

What dual degree options exist? MD/PhD. For more information, visit:https://www.usd.edu/medicine/mdphd-program

Important Updates due to COVID-19: Accept Pass/Fail grades for the prerequisite courses taken during the 2020 Spring/Summer/Fall semesters. As always, accept online coursework from any accredited institution.

Were tests required? MCAT required.

Are tests expected next year? Yes.

Postgraduate Training Match Rate: N/A

USMLE First-Time Pass Rate

Step 1: N/A

Step 2 CK: N/A

Step 2 CS: N/A

MEDICAL COLLEGE OF WISCONSIN

Address: 8701 Watertown Plank Road, Milwaukee, WI 53226
Website: *https://www.mcw.edu/*
Contact: *https://www.mcw.edu/contact-us*
Phone: (414) 955-8246

Other locations: De Pere, WI; Wausau, WI

COST OF ATTENDANCE

In-State Tuition: $53,080
Fees & Expenses: $20,485
Total: $73,565

Out-of-State Tuition: $56,780
Fees &Expenses: $20,485
Total: $77,265

Financial Aid: https://www.mcw.edu/education/academic-and-student-services/financial-aid-and-tuition

Percent Receiving Aid: 83%

ADDITIONAL INFORMATION

Interesting tidbit: MCW has three campuses - Milwaukee (flagship; 4-yr curriculum), Green Bay (3-yr curriculum), and Central Wisconsin (3-yr curriculum to train primary care physicians and psychiatrists). On the MCW Secondary Application, applicants will designate your campus preferences. There is only one secondary application and one application fee, regardless of campus preferences.

What percent of students participate in global health experiences? 13%

What service learning opportunities exist? Service learning through student organizations.

What dual degree options exist? MD/MPH, MD/MS in Clinical and Translational Science, and MD/PhD. For more information, visit:https://www.mcw.edu/education/medical-school

Important Updates due to COVID-19: Accept pass/fail grades for coursework, including prerequisites, taken during the COVID-19 pandemic (currently including January 2020 – present). Etend application deadline to February 25, 2021 and interview season to March.

Were tests required? MCAT and CASPer required.

Are tests expected next year? Yes.

Postgraduate Training Match Rate: N/A

USMLE First-Time Pass Rate

Step 1: N/A

Step 2 CK: N/A

Step 2 CS: N/A

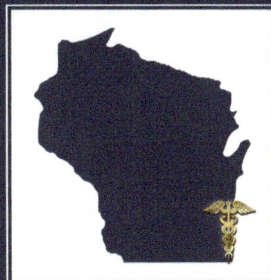

ILLINOIS

INDIANA

IOWA

KANSAS

MICHIGAN

MINNESOTA

MISSOURI

NEBRASKA

NORTH DAKOTA

OHIO

SOUTH DAKOTA

WISCONSIN

MIDWEST

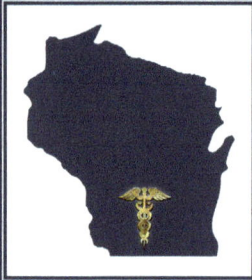

ILLINOIS

INDIANA

IOWA

KANSAS

MICHIGAN

MINNESOTA

MISSOURI

NEBRASKA

NORTH DAKOTA

OHIO

SOUTH DAKOTA

WISCONSIN

UNIVERSITY OF WISCONSIN SCHOOL OF MEDICINE AND PUBLIC HEALTH

Address: 2130 Health Sciences Learning Center, Madison, WI 53705
Website: *https://www.med.wisc.edu/*
Contact: *https://www.med.wisc.edu/contact/*
Phone: (608) 263-4925

COST OF ATTENDANCE

In-State Tuition: $39,636
Fees & Expenses: $27,680
Total: $67,316

Out-of-State Tuition: $55,812
Fees & Expenses: $27,680
Total: $83,492

Financial Aid: https://www.med.wisc.edu/education/md-program/admissions/scholarships-and-financial-aid/

Percent Receiving Aid: 91%

ADDITIONAL INFORMATION

Interesting tidbit: The ForWard Curriculum replaces the traditional model of medical education — two years of basic science followed by two years of clinical experiences — with a three-phase model that fully integrates basic, public health and clinical sciences throughout our medical students' education. Phase 3, the last 16 months, is dedicated to career exploration and internship preparation.

What percent of students participate in global health experiences? 28%

What service learning opportunities exist? Community education programs, patient care to underserved populations, etc. For more information, visit:https://www.med.wisc.edu/service/

What dual degree options exist? MD/MPH:https://www.med.wisc.edu/education/md-mph-program/

MD/PhD:https://www.med.wisc.edu/education/md-phd/

Important Updates due to COVID-19: Accept pass/fail (or equivalent) grades for coursework completed during the duration of the pandemic. Accept online courses including online lab courses taken at accredited institutions beginning in the spring 2020 term.

Were tests required? MCAT required.

Are tests expected next year? Yes.

Postgraduate Training Match Rate: 100% (2021)

USMLE First-Time Pass Rate

Step 1: N/A

Step 2 CK: N/A

112

ALABAMA

ARKANSAS

DELAWARE

DISTRICT OF
COLUMBIA

FLORIDA

GEORGIA

KENTUCKY

LOUISIANA

MARYLAND

MISSISSIPPI

NORTH CAROLINA

OKLAHOMA

SOUTH CAROLINA

TENNESSEE

TEXAS

VIRGINIA

WEST VIRGINIA

CHAPTER 4

REGION THREE

SOUTH

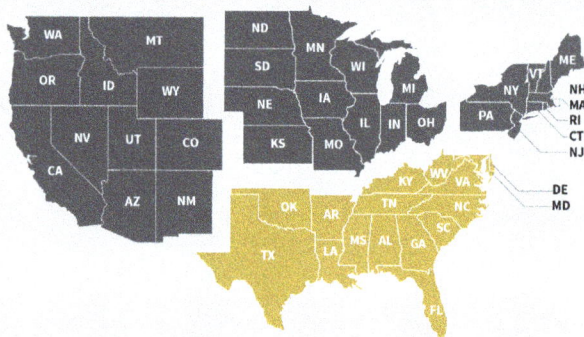

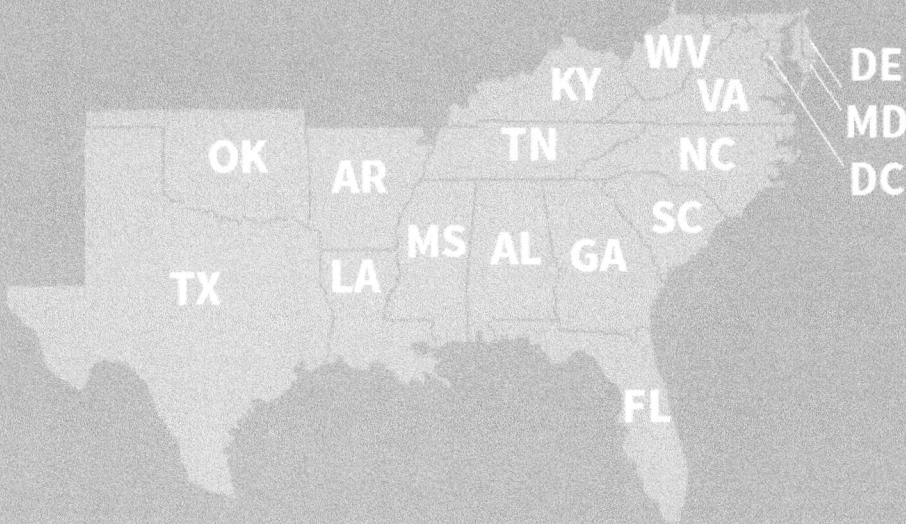

57 Programs | 16 States

MEDICAL PROGRAMS

Medical School	Ave. GPA & DAT / Early Decision (ED) : Yes/No / Int'l Students: Yes/No / Reapps: Yes/No	Admissions Statistics	Science Req. Other than Gen Chem, OChem, Physics, Bio
University of Alabama School of Medicine 1670 University Blvd, Birmingham, AL 35233	3.86 (overall) 3.84 (science) MCAT: 510 ED: Yes Int'l Student: No Reapps: N/A	**(2019)** Apps Received: 4,373 Interview Received: 469 Number Enrolled: 186 Admitted Rate: 4.3% **(2020)** Apps Received: 4,614 Interview Received: 485 Number Enrolled: 186 Admitted Rate: 4%	Biochem.
University of South Alabama 5795 USA Drive North, Mobile, AL 36688	3.91 (overall) 3.90 (science) MCAT: 511 ED: Yes Int'l Student: No Reapps: N/A	**(2019)** Apps Received: 1,554 Interview Received: 198 Number Enrolled: 74 Admitted Rate: 4.8% **(2020)** Apps Received: 1,433 Interview Received: 238 Number Enrolled: 74 Admitted Rate: 5.2%	N/A See Chart.
University of Arkansas 4301 W. Markham, #550,, Little Rock, AR 72205	3.85 (overall) 3.78 (science) MCAT: 508 ED: No Int'l Student: Nos Reapps: N/A	**(2019)** Apps Received: 2,556 Interview Received: 374 Number Enrolled: 172 Admitted Rate: 6.7% **(2020)** Apps Received: 2,189 Interview Received: 408 Number Enrolled: 173 Admitted Rate: 7.9%	Biochem.
Georgetown University 3900 Reservoir Road, NW Washington, DC 20007	3.79 (overall) 3.76 (science) MCAT: 513 ED: No Int'l Student: Yes Reapps: N/A	**(2019)** Apps Received: 13,149 Interview Received: 1,029 Number Enrolled: 203 Admitted Rate: 1.5% **(2020)** Apps Received: 14,455 Interview Received: 1,029 Number Enrolled: 203 Admitted Rate: 1.4%	N/A See Chart.

MEDICAL PROGRAMS

Medical School	Ave. GPA & DAT Early Decision (ED) : Yes/No Int'l Students: Yes/No Reapps: Yes/No	Admissions Statistics	Science Req. Other than Gen Chem, OChem, Physics, Bio
Howard University 520 W St, NW Washington, DC 20059	3.53 (overall) 3.41 (science) MCAT: 505 ED: No Int'l Student: Yes Reapps: N/A	**(2019)** Apps Received: 9,093 Interview Received: 348 Number Enrolled: 119 Admitted Rate: 1.3% **(2020)** Apps Received: 8,758 Interview Received: 364 Number Enrolled: 118 Admitted Rate: 1.3%	Biochem.
The George Washington University 2300 Eye Street, NW Washington, DC 20037	3.78 (overall) 3.73 (science) MCAT: 513 ED: Yes Int'l Student: Yes (case by case) Reapps: Yes	**(2019)** Apps Received: 14,997 Interview Received: 1,141 Number Enrolled: 184 Admitted Rate: 1.2% **(2020)** Apps Received: 14,611 Interview Received: 1,149 Number Enrolled: 178 Admitted Rate: 1.2%	N/A See Chart.
Florida Atlantic University 777 Glades Road, Boca Raton, FL 33431	3.80 (overall) 3.78 (science) MCAT: 513 ED: No Int'l Student: No Reapps: N/A	**(2019)** Apps Received: 3,586 Interview Received: 362 Number Enrolled: 66 Admitted Rate: 1.8% **(2020)** Apps Received: 3,748 Interview Received: 322 Number Enrolled: 65 Admitted Rate: 1.7%	N/A See Chart.

SOUTH

MEDICAL PROGRAMS

Medical School	Ave. GPA & DAT Early Decision (ED) : Yes/No Int'l Students: Yes/No Reapps: Yes/No	Admissions Statistics	Science Req. Other than Gen Chem, OChem, Physics, Bio
Florida International University Herbert Wertheim College of Medicine 11200 SW 8th Street, Miami, FL 33199	3.79 (overall) 3.75 (science) MCAT: 511 ED: No Int'l Student: No Reapps: N/A	**(2019)** Apps Received: 4,672 Interview Received: 553 Number Enrolled: 122 Admitted Rate: 2.6% **(2020)** Apps Received: 4,871 Interview Received: 512 Number Enrolled: 120 Admitted Rate: 2.5%	N/A See Chart.
Nova Southeastern University 3200 South University Drive, Davie, FL 33328	3.72 (overall) 3.67 (science) MCAT: 512 ED: No Int'l Student: No Reapps: N/A	**(2019)** Apps Received: 5,120 Interview Received: 274 Number Enrolled: 51 Admitted Rate: 1% **(2020)** Apps Received: 5,388 Interview Received: 321 Number Enrolled: 50 Admitted Rate: 0.9%	N/A See Chart.
The Florida State University 1115 West Call Street, Tallahassee, FL 32304	3.76 (overall) 3.69 (science) MCAT: 508 ED: Yes Int'l Student: No Reapps: N/A	**(2019)** Apps Received: 7,313 Interview Received: 300 Number Enrolled: 120 Admitted Rate: 1.6% **(2020)** Apps Received: 7,146 Interview Received: 272 Number Enrolled: 120 Admitted Rate: 1.7%	Biochem.

MEDICAL PROGRAMS

Medical School	Ave. GPA & DAT Early Decision (ED) : Yes/No Int'l Students: Yes/No Reapps: Yes/No	Admissions Statistics	Science Req. Other than Gen Chem, OChem, Physics, Bio
University of Central Florida 6850 Lake Nona Blvd., Orlando, FL 32827	3.88 (overall) 3.86 (science) MCAT: 514 ED: Yes Int'l Student: No Reapps: N/A	**(2019)** Apps Received: 5,120 Interview Received: 456 Number Enrolled: 120 Admitted Rate: 2.3% **(2020)** Apps Received: 4,676 Interview Received: 467 Number Enrolled: 120 Admitted Rate: 2.6%	N/A See Chart.
University of Florida 1600 SW Archer Rd, Gainesville, FL 32610	3.90 (overall) 3.87 (science) MCAT: 515 ED: No Int'l Student: No Reapps: Yes	**(2019)** Apps Received: 4,499 Interview Received: 355 Number Enrolled: 137 Admitted Rate: 3% **(2020)** Apps Received: 4,446 Interview Received: 358 Number Enrolled: 135 Admitted Rate: 3%	Biochem.
University of Miami Miller School of Medicine, Miami, FL 33136	3.78 (overall) 3.70 (science) MCAT: 514 ED: No Int'l Student: No Reapps: Yes	**(2019)** Apps Received: 9,175 Interview Received: 636 Number Enrolled: 207 Admitted Rate: 2.3% **(2020)** Apps Received: 8,779 Interview Received: 610 Number Enrolled: 204 Admitted Rate: 2.3%	Biochem.

SOUTH

MEDICAL PROGRAMS

Medical School	Ave. GPA & DAT Early Decision (ED) : Yes/No Int'l Students: Yes/No Reapps: Yes/No	Admissions Statistics	Science Req. Other than Gen Chem, OChem, Physics, Bio
USF Health Morsani College of Medicine 12901 Bruce B. Downs Blvd., Tampa, FL 33612	3.83 (overall) 3.80 (science) MCAT: 517 ED: Yes Int'l Student: No Reapps: N/A	**(2019)** Apps Received: 5,574 Interview Received: 627 Number Enrolled: 182 Admitted Rate: 3.3% **(2020)** Apps Received: 5,385 Interview Received: 690 Number Enrolled: 189 Admitted Rate: 3.5%	Biochem.
Emory University 100 Woodruff Circle, Atlanta, GA 30322	3.80 (overall) 3.78 (science) MCAT: 517 ED: No Int'l Student: Yes Reapps: N/A	**(2019)** Apps Received: 10,382 Interview Received: 668 Number Enrolled: 138 Admitted Rate: 1.3% **(2020)** Apps Received: 11,679 Interview Received: 661 Number Enrolled: 136 Admitted Rate: 1.2%	N/A See Chart.
Medical College of Georgia at Augusta University 1120 15th Street, Augusta, GA 30912	3.82 (overall) 3.80 (science) MCAT: 513 ED: Yes Int'l Student: No Reapps: Yes	**(2019)** Apps Received: 3,100 Interview Received: 539 Number Enrolled: 230 Admitted Rate: 7.4% **(2020)** Apps Received: 2,767 Interview Received: 608 Number Enrolled: 240 Admitted Rate: 8.7%	Biochem.
Mercer University 1550 College St, Macon, GA 31207	3.73 (overall) 3.67 (science) MCAT: 504 ED: Yes Int'l Student: No Reapps: N/A	**(2019)** Apps Received: 1,122 Interview Received: 400 Number Enrolled: 120 Admitted Rate: 10.7% **(2020)** Apps Received: 1,251 Interview Received: 400 Number Enrolled: 125 Admitted Rate: 10%	N/A See Chart.

Medical School	Ave. GPA & DAT / Early Decision (ED) : Yes/No / Int'l Students: Yes/No / Reapps: Yes/No	Admissions Statistics	Science Req. Other than Gen Chem, OChem, Physics, Bio
Morehouse School of Medicine 720 Westview Drive, S.W., Atlanta, GA 30310	63 (overall) 3.54 (science) MCAT: 504 ED: Yes Int'l Student: Yes Reapps: N/A	**(2019)** Apps Received: 7,316 Interview Received: 415 Number Enrolled: 100 Admitted Rate: 1.4% **(2020)** Apps Received: 6,648 Interview Received: 462 Number Enrolled: 105 Admitted Rate: 1.6%	N/A See Chart.
University of Kentucky College of Medicine 800 Rose Street MN 150, Lexington, KY 40506	3.81 (overall) 3.76 (science) MCAT: 508 ED: Yes Int'l Student: Yes (case by case) Reapps: N/A	**(2019)** Apps Received: 2,394 Interview Received: 508 Number Enrolled: 203 Admitted Rate: 8.5% **(2020)** Apps Received: 2,775 Interview Received: 520 Number Enrolled: 205 Admitted Rate: 7.4%	Biochem.
University of Louisville 323 East Chestnut, Louisville, KY 40202	3.77 (overall) 3.71 (science) MCAT: 509 ED: Yes Int'l Student: Yes (case by case) Reapps: N/A	**(2019)** Apps Received: 3,848 Interview Received: 452 Number Enrolled: 162 Admitted Rate: 4.2% **(2020)** Apps Received: 4,598 Interview Received: 475 Number Enrolled: 159 Admitted Rate:3.5%	N/A See Chart.

SOUTH

MEDICAL PROGRAMS

Medical School	Ave. GPA & DAT / Early Decision (ED) : Yes/No / Int'l Students: Yes/No / Reapps: Yes/No	Admissions Statistics	Science Req. Other than Gen Chem, OChem, Physics, Bio
Louisiana State University School of Medicine in Shreveport 1501 Kings Highway, Shreveport, LA 71130	3.77 (overall) 3.71 (science) MCAT: 506 ED: Yes Int'l Student: No Reapps: N/A	**(2019)** Apps Received: 2,866 Interview Received: 282 Number Enrolled: 150 Admitted Rate: 5.2% **(2020)** Apps Received: 3,893 Interview Received: 304 Number Enrolled: 148 Admitted Rate: 3.8%	Biochem.
LSU Health Sciences Center School of Medicine in New Orleans 2020 Gravier Street, 5th Floor, New Orleans, LA 70112	3.82 (overall) 3.77 (science) MCAT: 509 ED: Yes Int'l Student: No Reapps: N/A	**(2019)** Apps Received: 3,827 Interview Received: 520 Number Enrolled: 198 Admitted Rate: 5.2% **(2020)** Apps Received: 3,987 Interview Received: 458 Number Enrolled: 196 Admitted Rate: 4.9%	Biochem.
Tulane University 1430 Tulane Ave., New Orleans, LA 70112	3.63 (overall) 3.51 (science) MCAT: 511 ED: Yes Int'l Student: Yes Reapps: N/A	**(2019)** Apps Received: 12,982 Interview Received: 588 Number Enrolled: 190 Admitted Rate: 1.5% **(2020)** Apps Received: 12,752 Interview Received: 600 Number Enrolled: 190 Admitted Rate: 1.5%	N/A See Chart.
Johns Hopkins University 733 N Broadway, Baltimore, MD 21205	3.95 (overall) 3.96 (science) MCAT: 521 ED: No Int'l Student: Yes Reapps: N/A	**(2019)** Apps Received: 6,016 Interview Received: 657 Number Enrolled: 120 Admitted Rate: 2% **(2020)** Apps Received: 5,603 Interview Received: 664 Number Enrolled: 121 Admitted Rate: 2.2%	Biochem.

MEDICAL PROGRAMS

Medical School	Ave. GPA & DAT Early Decision (ED) : Yes/No Int'l Students: Yes/No Reapps: Yes/No	Admissions Statistics	Science Req. Other than Gen Chem, OChem, Physics, Bio
Uniformed Services University 4301 Jones Bridge Rd., Bethesda, MD 20814	3.76 (overall) 3.72 (science) MCAT: 510 ED: No Int'l Student: No Reapps: N/A	**(2019)** Apps Received: 3,096 Interview Received: 543 Number Enrolled: 175 Admitted Rate: 5.7% **(2020)** Apps Received: 3,114 Interview Received: 600 Number Enrolled: 169 Admitted Rate: 5.4%	N/A See Chart.
University of Maryland School of Medicine 655 W Baltimore St S, Baltimore, MD 21201	3.83 (overall) 3.79 (science) MCAT: 514 ED: Yes Int'l Student: No Reapps: N/A	**(2019)** Apps Received: 5,185 Interview Received: 589 Number Enrolled: 148 Admitted Rate: 2.9% **(2020)** Apps Received: 4,883 Interview Received: 546 Number Enrolled: 152 Admitted Rate: 3.1%	N/A See Chart.
University of Mississippi School of Medicine 2500 North State Street, Jackson, MS 39216	3.86 (overall) 3.82 (science) MCAT: 505 ED: Yes Int'l Student: No Reapps: N/A	**(2019)** Apps Received: 428 Interview Received: 279 Number Enrolled: 165 Admitted Rate: 38.6% **(2020)** Apps Received: 409 Interview Received: 261 Number Enrolled: 165 Admitted Rate: 40.3%	Biochem.

SOUTH

MEDICAL PROGRAMS

Medical School	Ave. GPA & DAT / Early Decision (ED) : Yes/No / Int'l Students: Yes/No / Reapps: Yes/No	Admissions Statistics	Science Req. Other than Gen Chem, OChem, Physics, Bio
Duke University School of Medicine DUMC 3710, Durham, NC 27710	3.89 (overall) 3.87 (science) MCAT: 519 ED: No Int'l Student: Yes Reapps: N/A	**(2019)** Apps Received: 6,951 Interview Received: 704 Number Enrolled: 121 Admitted Rate: 1.7% **(2020)** Apps Received: 7,620 Interview Received: 674 Number Enrolled: 121 Admitted Rate: 1.6%	N/A See Chart.
The Brody School of Medicine at East Carolina University 600 Moye Blvd., Greenville, NC 27834	3.71 (overall) 3.62 (science) MCAT: 509 ED: Yes Int'l Student: No Reapps: N/A	**(2019)** Apps Received: 1,075 Interview Received: 451 Number Enrolled: 86 Admitted Rate: 8% **(2020)** Apps Received: 1,025 Interview Received: 434 Number Enrolled: 86 Admitted Rate: 8.4%	Biochem.
University of North Carolina School of Medicine 321 S. Columbia Street, Chapel Hill, NC 27599	3.78 (overall) 3.72 (science) MCAT: 515 ED: No Int'l Student: Yes Reapps: Yes	**(2019)** Apps Received: 7,389 Interview Received: 597 Number Enrolled: 190 Admitted Rate: 2.3% **(2020)** Apps Received: 6,281 Interview Received: 629 Number Enrolled: 193 Admitted Rate: 3.1%	Biochem.
Wake Forest School of Medicine 475 Vine St., 1st Floor, Winston-Salem, NC 27101	3.76 (overall) 3.70 (science) MCAT: 513 ED: Yes Int'l Student: No Reapps: N/A	**(2019)** Apps Received: 10,703 Interview Received: 504 Number Enrolled: 145 Admitted Rate: 1.4% **(2020)** Apps Received: 9,246 Interview Received: 476 Number Enrolled: 145 Admitted Rate: 1.6%	N/A See Chart.

Medical School	Ave. GPA & DAT Early Decision (ED) : Yes/No Int'l Students: Yes/No Reapps: Yes/No	Admissions Statistics	Science Req. Other than Gen Chem, OChem, Physics, Bio
University of Oklahoma 800 Stanton L Young Blvd, Oklahoma City, OK 73117	3.85 (overall) 3.81 (science) MCAT: 511 ED: No Int'l Student: No Reapps: N/A	**(2019)** Apps Received: 2,662 Interview Received: 306 Number Enrolled: 165 Admitted Rate: 6.2% **(2020)** Apps Received: 2,760 Interview Received: 309 Number Enrolled: 164 Admitted Rate: 5.9%	Genetics, Cell Bio., or Molecular Bio.
Medical University of South Carolina College of Medicine 96 Johnathan Lucas St., Ste. 601, Charleston, SC 29425	3.83 (overall) 3.80 (science) MCAT: 510 ED: Yes Int'l Student: No Reapps: N/A	**(2019)** Apps Received: 4,088 Interview Received: 367 Number Enrolled: 171 Admitted Rate: 4.2% **(2020)** Apps Received: 3,707 Interview Received: 375 Number Enrolled: 173 Admitted Rate: 4.7%	N/A See Chart.
University of South Carolina, Columbia 6311 Garners Ferry Road, Columbia, SC 29209	3.79 (overall) 3.74 (science) MCAT: 508 ED: Yes Int'l Student: No Reapps: N/A	**(2019)** Apps Received: 3,006 Interview Received: 387 Number Enrolled: 97 Admitted Rate: 3.2% **(2020)** Apps Received: 2,969 Interview Received: 340 Number Enrolled: 99 Admitted Rate: 3.3%	N/A See Chart.

SOUTH

MEDICAL PROGRAMS

Medical School	Ave. GPA & DAT Early Decision (ED) : Yes/No Int'l Students: Yes/No Reapps: Yes/No	Admissions Statistics	Science Req. Other than Gen Chem, OChem, Physics, Bio
University of South Carolina, Greenville 607 Grove Road, Greenville, SC 29605	3.81 (overall) 3.76 (science) MCAT: 509 ED: Yes Int'l Student: No Reapps: N/A	**(2019)** Apps Received: 3,582 Interview Received: 355 Number Enrolled: 105 Admitted Rate: 2.9% **(2020)** Apps Received: 3,859 Interview Received: 360 Number Enrolled: 108 Admitted Rate: 2.8%	Biochem.
East Tennessee State University East Tennessee State University, Johnson City, TN 37614	3.81 (overall) 3.72 (science) MCAT: 508 ED: Yes Int'l Student: No Reapps: N/A	**(2019)** Apps Received: 2,386 Interview Received: 263 Number Enrolled: 72 Admitted Rate: 3% **(2020)** Apps Received: 2,433 Interview Received: 318 Number Enrolled: 72 Admitted Rate: 3%	N/A See Chart.
Meharry Medical College School of Medicine 1005 Dr. D. B. Todd Jr. Boulevard, Nashville, TN 37208	3.52 (overall) 3.40 (science) MCAT: 503 ED: Yes Int'l Student: No Reapps: N/A	**(2019)** Apps Received: 7,381 Interview Received: 339 Number Enrolled: 114 Admitted Rate: 1.5% **(2020)** Apps Received: 7,115 Interview Received: 379 Number Enrolled: 115 Admitted Rate: 1.6%	Biochem.
University of Tennessee Health Science Center 910 Madison Avenue, Ste 1031, Memphis, Tennessee 38163	3.82 (overall) 3.81 (science) MCAT: 513 ED: No Int'l Student: No Reapps: Yes	**(2019)** Apps Received: 2,207 Interview Received: 462 Number Enrolled: 170 Admitted Rate: 7.7% **(2020)** Apps Received: 2,065 Interview Received: 527 Number Enrolled: 170 Admitted Rate: 8.2%	N/A See Chart.

MEDICAL PROGRAMS

Medical School	Ave. GPA & DAT / Early Decision (ED) : Yes/No / Int'l Students: Yes/No / Reapps: Yes/No	Admissions Statistics	Science Req. Other than Gen Chem, OChem, Physics, Bio
Vanderbilt University 2209 Garland Drive, Nashville, TN 37240	3.94 (overall) 3.94 (science) MCAT: 521 ED: No Int'l Student: Yes Reapps: N/A	**(2019)** Apps Received: 5,982 Interview Received: 645 Number Enrolled: 97 Admitted Rate: 1.6% **(2020)** Apps Received: 5,880 Interview Received: 633 Number Enrolled: 94 Admitted Rate: 1.6%	N/A See Chart.
Baylor College of Medicine One Baylor Plaza, Houston, TX 77030	3.93 (overall) 3.91 (science) MCAT: 518 ED: Yes Int'l Student: Yes (case by case) Reapps: N/A	**(2019)** Apps Received: 6,688 Interview Received: 840 Number Enrolled: 186 Admitted Rate: 2.8% **(2020)** Apps Received: 6,260 Interview Received: 840 Number Enrolled: 186 Admitted Rate: 3%	Advanced Bio. Biochem.
The University of Texas Health Science Center at Houston 6431 Fannin Street, Houston, Texas 77030	3.88 (overall) 3.85 (science) MCAT: 513 ED: No Int'l Student: Yes Reapps: N/A	**(2019)** Apps Received: 5,451 Interview Received: 933 Number Enrolled: 240 Admitted Rate: 4.4% **(2020)** Apps Received: 5,471 Interview Received: 902 Number Enrolled: 240 Admitted Rate: 4.4%	N/A See Chart.

SOUTH

MEDICAL PROGRAMS

Medical School	Ave. GPA & DAT Early Decision (ED) : Yes/No Int'l Students: Yes/No Reapps: Yes/No	Admissions Statistics	Science Req. Other than Gen Chem, OChem, Physics, Bio
Paul L. Foster School of Medicine Texas Tech University Health Sciences Center 5001 El Paso Drive, El Paso, TX 79905	3.89 (overall) 3.88 (science) MCAT: 512 ED: No Int'l Student: No Reapps: N/A	**(2019)** Apps Received: 4,424 Interview Received: 602 Number Enrolled: 104 Admitted Rate: 2.4% **(2020)** Apps Received: 4,570 Interview Received: 649 Number Enrolled: 110 Admitted Rate: 2.4%	Biochem.
TCU and UNTHSC School of Medicine 3430 Camp Bowie Boulevard, Fort Worth, TX 76107	3.71 (overall) 3.63 (science) MCAT: 510 ED: No Int'l Student: No Reapps: N/A	**(2019)** Apps Received: 1,393 Interview Received: 272 Number Enrolled: 60 Admitted Rate: 4.3% **(2020)** Apps Received: 4,008 Interview Received: 247 Number Enrolled: 60 Admitted Rate: 1.5%	Biochem. Genetics Physio.
Texas A&M University Health Science Center College of Medicine 8447 Riverside Pkwy, Bryan, TX 77807	3.84 (overall) 3.83 (science) MCAT: 513 ED: No Int'l Student: Yes (case by case) Reapps: Yes	**(2019)** Apps Received: 5,151 Interview Received: 684 Number Enrolled: 120 Admitted Rate: 2.3% **(2020)** Apps Received: 5,203 Interview Received: 667 Number Enrolled: 175 Admitted Rate: 3.4%	Biochem.
Texas Tech University Health Sciences Center School of Medicine 3601 4th Street, Lubbock, TX 79430	3.87 (overall) 3.83 (science) MCAT: 510 ED: Yes Int'l Student: No Reapps: N/A	**(2019)** Apps Received: 4,882 Interview Received: 1,031 Number Enrolled: 180 Admitted Rate: 3.7% **(2020)** Apps Received: 4,910 Interview Received: 850 Number Enrolled: 180 Admitted Rate: 3.7%	Biochem.

MEDICAL PROGRAMS

Medical School	Ave. GPA & DAT Early Decision (ED) : Yes/No Int'l Students: Yes/No Reapps: Yes/No	Admissions Statistics	Science Req. Other than Gen Chem, OChem, Physics, Bio
The University of Texas at Austin Dell Medical School 1501 Red River St, Austin, TX 78712	3.92 (overall) 3.88 (science) MCAT: 515 ED: No Int'l Student: No Reapps: N/A	**(2019)** Apps Received: 5,078 Interview Received: 388 Number Enrolled: 50 Admitted Rate: 1% **(2020)** Apps Received: 5,116 Interview Received: 365 Number Enrolled: 50 Admitted Rate: 1%	Biochem.
The University of Texas Health Science Center at San Antonio Joe R. and Teresa Lozano Long School of Medicine 7703 Floyd Curl. San Antonio, TX 78229	(overall) 3.86 (science) MCAT: 517 ED: No Int'l Student: No Reapps: N/A	**(2019)** Apps Received: 5,299 Interview Received: 1,126 Number Enrolled: 211 Admitted Rate: 4% **(2020)** Apps Received: 5,421 Interview Received: 1,054 Number Enrolled: 212 Admitted Rate: 3.9%	Biochem.
The University of Texas Medical Branch at Galveston School of Medicine 301 University Boulevard, Galveston, TX 77555	3.88 (overall) 3.85 (science) MCAT: 511 ED: No Int'l Student: No Reapps: N/A	**(2019)** Apps Received: 5,220 Interview Received: 1,137 Number Enrolled: 230 Admitted Rate: 4.4% **(2020)** Apps Received: 5,150 Interview Received: 1,136 Number Enrolled: 230 Admitted Rate: 4.5%	N/A See Chart.

SOUTH

MEDICAL PROGRAMS

Medical School	Ave. GPA & DAT Early Decision (ED) : Yes/No Int'l Students: Yes/No Reapps: Yes/No	Admissions Statistics	Science Req. Other than Gen Chem, OChem, Physics, Bio
The University of Texas Rio Grande Valley School of Medicine 1201 W University Dr., Edinburg, TX 78539	3.72 (overall) 3.63 (science) MCAT: 510 ED: Yes Int'l Student: No Reapps: N/A	**(2019)** Apps Received: 4,368 Interview Received: 407 Number Enrolled: 55 Admitted Rate: 1.3% **(2020)** Apps Received: 4,410 Interview Received: 511 Number Enrolled: 55 Admitted Rate: 1.2%	Biochem.
The University of Texas Southwestern Medical School 5323 Harry Hines Boulevard, Dallas, TX 75390	3.90 (overall) 3.88 (science) MCAT: 518 ED: No Int'l Student: No Reapps: N/A	**(2019)** Apps Received: 5,401 Interview Received: 799 Number Enrolled: 220 Admitted Rate: 4% **(2020)** Apps Received: 5,405 Interview Received: 771 Number Enrolled: 228 Admitted Rate: 4.2%	Biochem.
University of Houston College of Medicine 4849 Calhoun Road, Houston, Texas 77204	3.66 (overall) 3.49 (science) MCAT: 505 ED: No Int'l Student: No Reapps: N/A	**(2019)** Apps Received: N/A Interview Received: N/A Number Enrolled: 30 Admitted Rate: N/A **(2020)** Apps Received: 2,216 Interview Received: 170 Number Enrolled: 30 Admitted Rate: 1.4%	Advanced Bio. Biochem. *This medical school welcomed its inaugural class in 2020.

MEDICAL PROGRAMS

Medical School	Ave. GPA & DAT Early Decision (ED) : Yes/No Int'l Students: Yes/No Reapps: Yes/No	Admissions Statistics	Science Req. Other than Gen Chem, OChem, Physics, Bio
Eastern Virginia Medical School 700 W. Olney Road, Norfolk, VA 23507	3.71 (overall) 3.66 (science) MCAT: 513 ED: Yes Int'l Student: No Reapps: N/A	**(2019)** Apps Received: 6,389 Interview Received: 750 Number Enrolled: 151 Admitted Rate: 2.4% **(2020)** Apps Received: 6,846 Interview Received: 799 Number Enrolled: 151 Admitted Rate: 2.2%	N/A See Chart.
University of Virginia 200 Jeanette Lancaster Way, Charlottesville, VA 22903	3.93 (overall) 3.91 (science) MCAT: 520 ED: No Int'l Student: Yes Reapps: N/A	**(2019)** Apps Received: 4,790 Interview Received: 581 Number Enrolled: 156 Admitted Rate: 3.3% **(2020)** Apps Received: 4,894 Interview Received: 584 Number Enrolled: 155 Admitted Rate: 3.2%	N/A See Chart.
Virginia Commonwealth University 1201 E Marshall St #4-100, Richmond, VA 23298	3.82 (overall) 3.79 (science) MCAT: 513 ED: Yes Int'l Student: Yes (case by case) Reapps: Yes	**(2019)** Apps Received: 7,998 Interview Received: 703 Number Enrolled: 184 Admitted Rate: 2.3% **(2020)** Apps Received: 7,258 Interview Received: 694 Number Enrolled: 186 Admitted Rate: 2.6%	N/A See Chart.

SOUTH

MEDICAL PROGRAMS

Medical School	Ave. GPA & DAT / Early Decision (ED) : Yes/No / Int'l Students: Yes/No / Reapps: Yes/No	Admissions Statistics	Science Req. Other than Gen Chem, OChem, Physics, Bio
Virginia Tech 2 Riverside Circle, Roanoke, VA 24016	3.57 (overall) 3.49 (science) MCAT: 512 ED: No Int'l Student: No Reapps: Yes	**(2019)** Apps Received: 4,483 Interview Received: 319 Number Enrolled: 43 Admitted Rate: 1% **(2020)** Apps Received: 4,294 Interview Received: 280 Number Enrolled: 48 Admitted Rate: 1.1%	N/A See Chart.
Marshall University 1600 Medical Center Drive, Suite 1400, Huntington, WV, 25701	3.70 (overall) 3.61 (science) MCAT: 502 ED: No Int'l Student: No Reapps: N/A	**(2019)** Apps Received: 2,205 Interview Received: 190 Number Enrolled: 80 Admitted Rate: 3.6% **(2020)** Apps Received: 2,131 Interview Received: 202 Number Enrolled: 80 Admitted Rate: 3.8%	Biochem.
West Virginia University 64 Medical Center Dr, Morgantown, WV 26506	3.88 (overall) 3.85 (science) MCAT: 509 ED: Yes Int'l Student: Yes (case by case) Reapps: N/A	**(2019)** Apps Received: 5,559 Interview Received: 622 Number Enrolled: 112 Admitted Rate: 2% **(2020)** Apps Received: 5,053 Interview Received: 611 Number Enrolled: 112 Admitted Rate: 2.2%	N/A See Chart.

ALABAMA

ARKANSAS

DELAWARE

DISTRICT OF
COLUMBIA

FLORIDA

GEORGIA

KENTUCKY

LOUISIANA

MARYLAND

MISSISSIPPI

NORTH CAROLINA

OKLAHOMA

SOUTH CAROLINA

TENNESSEE

TEXAS

VIRGINIA

WEST VIRGINIA

UNIVERSITY OF ALABAMA SCHOOL OF MEDICINE

Address: 1670 University Blvd, Birmingham, AL 35233
Website: *https://www.uab.edu/medicine/home/*
Contact: *https://www.uab.edu/medicine/home/contact-us*
Phone: (205) 934-2433

Other locations: Tuscaloosa, AL; Huntsville, AL; Montgomery, AL

COST OF ATTENDANCE

In-State Tuition: $33,067
Fees & Expenses: $28,968
Total: $78,771

Out-of-State Tuition: $66,079
Fees & Expenses: $28,968
Total: $95,047

Financial Aid: https://www.uab.edu/medicine/home/future-students/admissions/tuition-financial-aid-scholarships

Percent Receiving Aid: 82%

ADDITIONAL INFORMATION

Interesting tidbit: In the predoctoral medical education program, the first two basic science years are taught on the main campus of the University of Alabama School of Medicine at Birmingham; the last two clinical years are divided among the main campus and the three branch campuses in Huntsville, Montgomery and Tuscaloosa.

What percent of students participate in global health experiences? 27%

What service learning opportunities exist? Service learning through student organizations. For more information, visit:https://www.uab.edu/medicine/diversity/for-students-0/student-organizations

What dual degree options exist? MD/MPH:https://www.uab.edu/soph/home/graduate/programs/coordinated-degrees

MD/MBA:https://www.uab.edu/business/home/mba/md-mba-dual-degrees

MD/PhD:https://www.uab.edu/medicine/mstp/

Important Updates due to COVID-19: Accept pass or satisfactory grades during semesters impacted by COVID-19 and online coursework for all prerequisite lecture-based courses

Were tests required? MCAT and SJT required.

Are tests expected next year? Yes.

Postgraduate Training Match Rate: 100% (2021)

USMLE First-Time Pass Rate

Step 1: N/A

Step 2 CK: N/A

Step 2 CS: N/A

Other: Early Medical School Acceptance Program (EMSAP) is a BS/MD program available to undergraduate applicants. For more information, visit:https://www.uab.edu/students/academics/emsap

UNIVERSITY OF SOUTH ALABAMA COLLEGE OF MEDICINE

Address: 5795 USA Drive North, Mobile, AL 36688
Website: *https://www.southalabama.edu/colleges/com/*
Contact: *https://www.southalabama.edu/contactusa/*
Phone: (251) 460-7176

COST OF ATTENDANCE

In-State Tuition: $31,860
Fees & Expenses: $26,116
Total: $57,976

Out-of-State Tuition: $62,864
Fees & Expenses: $26,116
Total: $88,980

Financial Aid: https://www.southalabama.edu/colleges/com/futurestudents/scholarships.html

Percent Receiving Aid: 82%

ADDITIONAL INFORMATION

Interesting tidbit: The last two years of medical school are held in USA Health hospitals and care centers, as well as in offices of community physicians, and expand the students' education in the surroundings of full-time patient care. Service learning, a required component of undergraduate medical education, offers medical students opportunities to serve the community in Mobile and the surrounding area.

What percent of students participate in global health experiences? 35%

What service learning opportunities exist? At least 4 hours of volunteer work is required per semester for the first two years of medical school. Anatomy Outreach, BELONG, Buddy Ball at West Side Park, etc. For more information, visit:https://www.southalabama.edu/colleges/com/currentstudents/communityserviceandlearning.html

What dual degree options exist? MD/MBA. For more information, visit:https://www.southalabama.edu/colleges/mcob/mba/healthcare/

Important Updates due to COVID-19: Accept Pass/Fail grading for prerequisite coursework completed in the Spring semester of 2020. Accept online coursework for prerequisite courses completed in the Spring, Summer, and Fall semesters of 2020. Consider online course work completed in the Spring semester of 2021 on a case by case basis. MCAT taken at any time during 2020 accepted.

Were tests required? MCAT required.

Are tests expected next year? Yes.

Postgraduate Training Match Rate: 100% (2021)

USMLE First-Time Pass Rate

Step 1: N/A

Step 2 CK: N/A

Step 2 CS: N/A

ALABAMA

ARKANSAS

DELAWARE

DISTRICT OF COLUMBIA

FLORIDA

GEORGIA

KENTUCKY

LOUISIANA

MARYLAND

MISSISSIPPI

NORTH CAROLINA

OKLAHOMA

SOUTH CAROLINA

TENNESSEE

TEXAS

VIRGINIA

WEST VIRGINIA

SOUTH

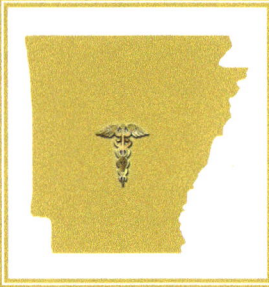

UNIVERSITY OF ARKANSAS FOR MEDICAL SCIENCES COLLEGE OF MEDICINE

Address: 4301 W. Markham, #550,, Little Rock, AR 72205
Website: *https://medicine.uams.edu/*
Contact: *https://web.uams.edu/about/contact-information/*
Phone: (501) 686-5354

Other locations: Fayetteville, AR

COST OF ATTENDANCE

In-State Tuition: $33,010
Fees & Expenses: $30,911
Total: $63,921

Out-of-State Tuition: $65,180
Fees & Expenses: $30,911
Total: $96,091

Financial Aid: https://medicine.uams.edu/for-medical-students/financial-aid/

Percent Receiving Aid: 87%

ADDITIONAL INFORMATION

Interesting tidbit: Rural Practice Scholarship Program, whose purpose is to increase the number of physicians practicing medicine in rural communities in Arkansas, awards $12,000 per year up to four years (while in medical school at UAMS). Participants agree to repay your loan by practicing full-time Primary Care in a qualifying Rural Community in Arkansas.

What percent of students participate in global health experiences? 13%

What service learning opportunities exist? Summer service learning projects and volunteer work through student organizations.

What dual degree options exist? MD/MPH:https://medicine.uams.edu/for-medical-school-applicants/md-mph-program/

MD/PhD:https://medicine.uams.edu/for-medical-school-applicants/md-phd-program/

Important Updates due to COVID-19: Continue to accept P/F grading for courses taken in the Fall 2020 semester;. Accept online courses and online labs.

Were tests required? MCAT required.

Are tests expected next year? Yes.

Postgraduate Training Match Rate: 91% (2021)

USMLE First-Time Pass Rate

Step 1: N/A

Step 2 CK: N/A

Step 2 CS: N/A

GEORGETOWN UNIVERSITY SCHOOL OF MEDICINE

Address: 3900 Reservoir Road, NW Washington, DC 20007
Website: *https://som.georgetown.edu/*
Contact Email: *medicaladmissions@georgetown.edu*
Phone: (202) 687-1154

COST OF ATTENDANCE

Tuition: $55,586
Fees & Expenses: $40,549
Total: $97,135

Financial Aid: https://som.georgetown.edu/admissions/financial-aid/

Percent Receiving Aid: 76%

ADDITIONAL INFORMATION

Interesting tidbit: Georgetown University School of Medicine is an institution rooted in the Catholic, Jesuit ideal of cura personalis, care of the whole person.

What percent of students participate in global health experiences? 17%

What service learning opportunities exist? Medical students must complete 20+ hours of community service prior to graduation. Camp Discovery, Little Friends for Peace, volunteer work at various elementary schools, etc. For more information, visit:https://som.georgetown.edu/medicaleducation/service/

What dual degree options exist? MD/MPH, MD/MBA, MD/MS, MD/MALS, and MD/PhD. For more information, visit:https://som.georgetown.edu/admissions/degrees-and-admissions/dualdegree/

Important Updates due to COVID-19: Consider Pass/Fail and Credit/No Credit courses, as well as prerequisites completed online.

Were tests required? MCAT required.

Are tests expected next year? Yes.

Postgraduate Training Match Rate: N/A

USMLE First-Time Pass Rate

Step 1: N/A

Step 2 CK: N/A

Step 2 CS: N/A

Other: Early Assurance Program (EAP) available to current Georgetown undergraduates. For more information, visit:https://som.georgetown.edu/admissions/degrees-and-admissions/md/early-assurance/

ALABAMA
ARKANSAS
DELAWARE
DISTRICT OF COLUMBIA
FLORIDA
GEORGIA
KENTUCKY
LOUISIANA
MARYLAND
MISSISSIPPI
NORTH CAROLINA
OKLAHOMA
SOUTH CAROLINA
TENNESSEE
TEXAS
VIRGINIA
WEST VIRGINIA

SOUTH

ALABAMA

ARKANSAS

DELAWARE

DISTRICT OF
COLUMBIA

FLORIDA

GEORGIA

KENTUCKY

LOUISIANA

MARYLAND

MISSISSIPPI

NORTH CAROLINA

OKLAHOMA

SOUTH CAROLINA

TENNESSEE

TEXAS

VIRGINIA

WEST VIRGINIA

HOWARD UNIVERSITY COLLEGE OF MEDICINE

Address: 520 W St, NW Washington, DC 20059
Website: *https://medicine.howard.edu/*
Contact: *https://medicine.howard.edu/contact-us*
Phone: (202) 806-6279

COST OF ATTENDANCE

Tuition: $46,610
Fees & Expenses: $32,168
Total: $78,778

Financial Aid: https://medicine.howard.edu/about-us/office-financial-aid

Percent Receiving Aid: 97%

ADDITIONAL INFORMATION

Interesting tidbit: Due to this unique origin of Howard University as an institution, Howard University College of Medicine's particular focus is on the education of disadvantaged students for careers in medicine and addressing the special health care needs of medically underserved communities

What percent of students participate in global health experiences? 19%

What service learning opportunities exist? Service learning through student organizations.

What dual degree options exist? MD/MBA and MD/PhD. For more information, visit:https://medicine.howard.edu/education/dual-degree-programs

Important Updates due to COVID-19: Accept P/F grades for courses taken during the COVID-19 pandemic. Accept online coursework taken at a regionally accredited institution, including labs taken during the pandemic.

Were tests required? MCAT and CASPer required.

Are tests expected next year? Yes.

Postgraduate Training Match Rate: N/A

USMLE First-Time Pass Rate

Step 1: N/A

Step 2 CK: N/A

Step 2 CS: N/A

Other: BS/MD 6-year program available to high school applicants. For more information, visit:https://medicine.howard.edu/education/dual-degree-programs

THE GEORGE WASHINGTON UNIVERSITY SCHOOL OF MEDICINE AND HEALTH SCIENCES

Address: 2300 Eye Street, NW Washington, DC 20037
Website: *https://smhs.gwu.edu/*
Contact: *https://smhs.gwu.edu/about/content/contact-smhs*
Phone: (202) 994-3506

COST OF ATTENDANCE

In-State Tuition: $63,920
Fees & Expenses: $23,939
Total: $87,859

Financial Aid: https://smhs.gwu.edu/fin-aid/

Percent Receiving Aid: 76%

ADDITIONAL INFORMATION

Interesting tidbit: The GW School of Medicine and Health Sciences (SMHS) is the first medical school in the nation's capital. Students and residents enjoy unmatched opportunities to engage with nearby government, non-governmental, and non-profit organizations -- many of these opportunities are due to the school's prime location in the nation's capital.

What percent of students participate in global health experiences? 17%

What service learning opportunities exist? ISCOPES, GW Healing Clinic, global opportunities, etc. For more information, visit:https://smhs.gwu.edu/academics/md-program/opportunities-students/service-community

What dual degree options exist? MD/MPH. For more information, visit:https://smhs.gwu.edu/academics/md-program/curriculum/clinical-public-health/combined-mdpublic-health-degree-programs

Important Updates due to COVID-19: Accept Pass/Fail for Spring 2020. will accept online courses for the Summer /Fall 2020 terms.

Were tests required? MCAT required.

Are tests expected next year? Yes.

Postgraduate Training Match Rate: N/A

USMLE First-Time Pass Rate

Step 1: N/A

Step 2 CK: N/A

Step 2 CS: N/A

Other: BS/MD 7-year/8-year program available to high school applicants. For more information, visit:https://smhs.gwu.edu/academics/md-program/admissions/joint-programs

ALABAMA

ARKANSAS

DELAWARE

DISTRICT OF COLUMBIA

FLORIDA

GEORGIA

KENTUCKY

LOUISIANA

MARYLAND

MISSISSIPPI

NORTH CAROLINA

OKLAHOMA

SOUTH CAROLINA

TENNESSEE

TEXAS

VIRGINIA

WEST VIRGINIA

SOUTH

CHARLES E. SCHMIDT COLLEGE OF MEDICINE AT FLORIDA ATLANTIC UNIVERSITY

Address: 777 Glades Road, Boca Raton, FL 33431
Website: http://med.fau.edu/
Contact: http://www.fau.edu/about/contact/
Phone: (561) 297-0440

COST OF ATTENDANCE

In-State Tuition: $28,111
Fees & Expenses: $32,841
Total: $60,952

Out-of-State Tuition: $62,532
Fees & Expenses: $32,841
Total: $97,094

Financial Aid: http://med.fau.edu/students/financialaid/index.php

Percent Receiving Aid: 79%

ADDITIONAL INFORMATION

Interesting tidbit: The Integrated Patient Focused Curriculum at FAU's Charles E. Schmidt College of Medicine features an early introduction to the patient and the community. Starting in the spring semester in year 1, students develop doctor/patient relationships with patients under the supervision of their physician preceptors in the community and at clinics that provide care to the under-served in Palm Beach County.

What percent of students participate in global health experiences? 18%

What service learning opportunities exist? Service learning projects. Students volunteer in K-12 settings, with one of the partner organizations, or delivering educational curricula for outreach programs. For more information, visit:http://med.fau.edu/home/diversity/community.php

What dual degree options exist? MD/MBA and MD/MHA. For more information, visit:http://med.fau.edu/admissions/dual-degrees.php

Important Updates due to COVID-19: N/A

Were tests required? MCAT and CASPer required.

Are tests expected next year? Yes.

Postgraduate Training Match Rate: 100%

USMLE First-Time Pass Rate

Step 1: N/A

Step 2 CK: N/A

Step 2 CS: N/A

Other: BS/MD program available to high school applicants. For more information, visit:http://med.fau.edu/admissions/pipeline.php

FLORIDA INTERNATIONAL UNIVERSITY HERBERT WERTHEIM COLLEGE OF MEDICINE

Address: 11200 SW 8th Street, Miami, FL 33199
Website: *https://medicine.fiu.edu/*
Contact Email: *med.admissions@fiu.edu*
Phone: (305) 348-0644

COST OF ATTENDANCE

In-State Tuition: $32,739
Fees & Expenses: $41,382
Total: $74,121

Out-of-State Tuition: $62,739
Fees & Expenses: $42,887
Total: $105,626

Financial Aid: https://medicine.fiu.edu/academics/degrees-and-programs/doctor-of-medicine/financial-assistance/index.html
Percent Receiving Aid: 90%

ADDITIONAL INFORMATION

Interesting tidbit: Through its innovative Neighborhood Health Education Learning Program (NeighborhoodHELP™), medical students perform longitudinal household visits to patients within medically underserved areas of Miami-Dade County. These visits of interprofessional teams, that include FIU nursing and social work students (and education and law students as household needs are identified) allow the students to learn, first-hand, how social factors critically impact health and disease.

What percent of students participate in global health experiences? 21%

What service learning opportunities exist? MedSWISH (Medical Students Working to Improve Society & Health), Green Family Foundation Neighborhood HELP, etc. For more information, visit:https://medicine.fiu.edu/about/community-engagement/index.html

What dual degree options exist? MD/MBA:https://medicine.fiu.edu/academics/degrees-and-programs/combined-md-and-professional-mba-degree-in-healthcare-management/index.html

MD/MPH:https://medicine.fiu.edu/academics/degrees-and-programs/combined-md-and-mph-degree/index.html

Important Updates due to COVID-19: N/A

Were tests required? MCAT required.

Are tests expected next year? Yes.

Postgraduate Training Match Rate: N/A

USMLE First-Time Pass Rate

Step 1: N/A

Step 2 CK: N/A

Step 2 CS: N/Λ

ALABAMA
ARKANSAS
DELAWARE
DISTRICT OF COLUMBIA
FLORIDA
GEORGIA
KENTUCKY
LOUISIANA
MARYLAND
MISSISSIPPI
NORTH CAROLINA
OKLAHOMA
SOUTH CAROLINA
TENNESSEE
TEXAS
VIRGINIA
WEST VIRGINIA

SOUTH

ALABAMA

ARKANSAS

DELAWARE

DISTRICT OF
COLUMBIA

FLORIDA

GEORGIA

KENTUCKY

LOUISIANA

MARYLAND

MISSISSIPPI

NORTH CAROLINA

OKLAHOMA

SOUTH CAROLINA

TENNESSEE

TEXAS

VIRGINIA

WEST VIRGINIA

NOVA SOUTHEASTERN UNIVERSITY DR. KIRAN C. PATEL COLLEGE OF ALLOPATHIC MEDICINE

Address: 3200 South University Drive, Davie, FL 33328
Website: *https://md.nova.edu/index.html*
Contact: *https://md.nova.edu/contact/index.html*
Phone: (954) 262-1535

COST OF ATTENDANCE

In-State Tuition: $55,671
Fees & Expenses: $47,730
Total: $103,401

Out-of-State Tuition: $62,390
Fees & Expenses: $47,730
Total: $110,120

Financial Aid: https://md.nova.edu/admissions/financial-aid-scholarships.html

Percent Receiving Aid: 91%

ADDITIONAL INFORMATION

Interesting tidbit: At NSU College of Allopathic Medicine, students will learn alongside others training as pharmacists, nurses, speech-language pathologists, physical therapists, occupational therapists and other health care specialists.

What percent of students participate in global health experiences? N/A

What service learning opportunities exist? Service learning through student organizations and community health partnerships. For more information, visit:https://md.nova.edu/about/community.html

What dual degree options exist? No dual degree options listed.

Important Updates due to COVID-19: N/A

Were tests required? MCAT required.

Are tests expected next year? Yes.

Postgraduate Training Match Rate: N/A

USMLE First-Time Pass Rate

Step 1: N/A

Step 2 CK: N/A

Step 2 CS: N/A

THE FLORIDA STATE UNIVERSITY COLLEGE OF MEDICINE

Address: 1115 West Call Street, Tallahassee, FL 32304
Website: *https://med.fsu.edu/*
Contact: *https://med.fsu.edu/comaboutus/contact-us*
Phone: (850) 644-7904

Other locations: Daytona Beach, FL; Fort Pierce, FL; Orlando, FL; Pensacola, FL; Sarasota, FL; Tallahassee, FL

COST OF ATTENDANCE

In-State Tuition: $19,696
Fees & Expenses: $21,064
Total: $40,760

Out-of-State Tuition: $45,733
Fees & Expenses: $21,064
Total: $66,797

Financial Aid: https://med.fsu.edu/financialaid/home

Percent Receiving Aid: 89%

ADDITIONAL INFORMATION

Interesting tidbit: The students spend their first two years taking basic science courses on the FSU campus in Tallahassee and are then assigned to one of six regional medical school campuses for their third- and fourth-year clinical training. Because Florida State University does not (or will not) own a teaching hospital, the FSU clinical faculty will draw heavily on the pool of local and regional community physicians.

What percent of students participate in global health experiences? 30%

What service learning opportunities exist? Service trips both locally and internationally. For more information, visit:https://med.fsu.edu/fsucares/service-learning-trips

What dual degree options exist? No dual degree options listed.

Important Updates due to COVID-19: N/A

Were tests required? MCAT required.

Are tests expected next year? Yes.

Postgraduate Training Match Rate: N/A

USMLE First-Time Pass Rate

Step 1: N/A

Step 2 CK: N/A

Step 2 CS: N/A

ALABAMA
ARKANSAS
DELAWARE
DISTRICT OF COLUMBIA
FLORIDA
GEORGIA
KENTUCKY
LOUISIANA
MARYLAND
MISSISSIPPI
NORTH CAROLINA
OKLAHOMA
SOUTH CAROLINA
TENNESSEE
TEXAS
VIRGINIA
WEST VIRGINIA

SOUTH

ALABAMA

ARKANSAS

DELAWARE

DISTRICT OF
COLUMBIA

FLORIDA

GEORGIA

KENTUCKY

LOUISIANA

MARYLAND

MISSISSIPPI

NORTH CAROLINA

OKLAHOMA

SOUTH CAROLINA

TENNESSEE

TEXAS

VIRGINIA

WEST VIRGINIA

UNIVERSITY OF CENTRAL FLORIDA
COLLEGE OF MEDICINE

Address: 6850 Lake Nona Blvd., Orlando, FL 32827
Website: *https://med.ucf.edu/*
Contact:
Phone: (407) 266-1350

COST OF ATTENDANCE

In-State Tuition: $29,680
Fees & Expenses: $25,821
Total: $55,501

Out-of-State Tuition: $56,554
Fees & Expenses: $25,821
Total: $82,375

Financial Aid: https://med.ucf.edu/student-affairs/financial-services/

Percent Receiving Aid: 100%

ADDITIONAL INFORMATION

Interesting tidbit: The UCF College of Medicine is a research-based medical school, where 100% of students are involved in research. Also, starting in the first year of medical education, students work with community preceptors in a variety of settings to practice skills and to apply the concepts mastered in the integrated basic science curriculum to real patients.

What percent of students participate in global health experiences? 27%

What service learning opportunities exist? Community-based and global service learning projects. For more information, visit:https://med.ucf.edu/academics/md-program/service-learning/

What dual degree options exist? MD/MBA, MD/MS in Biomedical Engineering, and MD/PhD. For more information, visit:https://med.ucf.edu/academics/md-program/dual-joint-degrees/

Important Updates due to COVID-19: Accept P/F grades issued during the COVID-19 crisis as well as online courses.

Were tests required? MCAT required.

Are tests expected next year? Yes.

Postgraduate Training Match Rate: 98.3%

USMLE First-Time Pass Rate

Step 1: N/A

Step 2 CK: N/A

Step 2 CS: N/A

Other: Burnett Medical Scholars BS/MD program available to high school applicants. For more information, visit:https://honors.ucf.edu/admissions/burnett-medical-scholars/

UNIVERSITY OF FLORIDA COLLEGE OF MEDICINE

Address: 1600 SW Archer Rd, Gainesville, FL 32610
Website: *https://med.ufl.edu/*
Contact: *https://med.ufl.edu/contact-information/*
Phone: (352) 273-7990

Other locations: Jacksonville, FL

COST OF ATTENDANCE

In-State Tuition: $37,130
Fees & Expenses: $20,580
Total: $57,710

Out-of-State Tuition: $49,390
Fees & Expenses: $20,580
Total: $69,970

Financial Aid: https://finaid.med.ufl.edu/

Percent Receiving Aid: 90%

ADDITIONAL INFORMATION

Interesting tidbit: The College of Medicine is the largest of six colleges at the University of Florida Academic Health Center. The college's Gainesville campus is comprised of 28 clinical and basic science departments. The Jacksonville campus delivers medical care in an urban setting, and performs research and educates medical students and residents.

What percent of students participate in global health experiences? 38%

What service learning opportunities exist? Service learning through student organizations.

What dual degree options exist? MD/MBA, MD/MPH, MD/JD, and MD/PhD. For more information, visit:https://admissions.med.ufl.edu/admission-requirements/dual-degrees/

Important Updates due to COVID-19: Prerequisite lectures and labs are acceptable regardless of in-person, online or hybrid format. Accept MCAT scores earned as early as 2017.

Were tests required? MCAT required.

Are tests expected next year? Yes.

Postgraduate Training Match Rate: N/A

USMLE First-Time Pass Rate

Step 1: N/A

Step 2 CK: N/A

Step 2 CS: N/A

Other: The Medical Honors Program (MHP) is a 7-year BS/MD program available to second-year undergraduate students. For more information, visit:https://mhp.med.ufl.edu/

ALABAMA
ARKANSAS
DELAWARE
DISTRICT OF COLUMBIA
FLORIDA
GEORGIA
KENTUCKY
LOUISIANA
MARYLAND
MISSISSIPPI
NORTH CAROLINA
OKLAHOMA
SOUTH CAROLINA
TENNESSEE
TEXAS
VIRGINIA
WEST VIRGINIA

SOUTH

ALABAMA

ARKANSAS

DELAWARE

DISTRICT OF
COLUMBIA

FLORIDA

GEORGIA

KENTUCKY

LOUISIANA

MARYLAND

MISSISSIPPI

NORTH CAROLINA

OKLAHOMA

SOUTH CAROLINA

TENNESSEE

TEXAS

VIRGINIA

WEST VIRGINIA

UNIVERSITY OF MIAMI LEONARD M. MILLER SCHOOL OF MEDICINE

Address: Miller School of Medicine, Miami, FL 33136
Website: *https://med.miami.edu/*
Contact: *https://med.miami.edu/admissions/contact-us*
Phone: (305) 243-3234

COST OF ATTENDANCE

Tuition: $48,663
Fees & Expenses: $32,470
Total: $81,133

Financial Aid: https://med.miami.edu/medical-education/divisions/student-financial-assistance

Percent Receiving Aid: 74%

ADDITIONAL INFORMATION

Interesting tidbit: Since the Miller School is no longer subsidized by the State of Florida, Florida residents are not given preference in admissions decisions. The Miller School has made a significant commitment to enroll more students from outside the state of Florida.

What percent of students participate in global health experiences? 39%

What service learning opportunities exist? Department of Community Service (DOCS), IDEA Exchange, Shop Docs, etc. For more information, visit:https://med.miami.edu/en/about-us/community-outreach

What dual degree options exist? MD/MPH, MD/MBA, MD/JD, MD/MS in Genomic Medicine, and MD/PhD. For more information, visit:https://med.miami.edu/medical-programs

Important Updates due to COVID-19: Accept Pass/Fail and online coursework. Waive laboratory requirements. Allow official transcripts to be submitted after the deadline.

Were tests required? MCAT and CASPer required.

Are tests expected next year? Yes.

Postgraduate Training Match Rate: N/A

USMLE First-Time Pass Rate

Step 1: N/A

Step 2 CK: N/A

Step 2 CS: N/A

Other: Health Professions Mentoring Program (HPM), previously the Honors Program in Medical Education (HPME), is a BS/MD program. For more information, visit:http://admissions.med.miami.edu/md-programs/dual-degree-program-in-medicine

In addition, the Medical Scholars Program is a BS/MD program available to University of Miami undergraduate students. For more information, visit:http://admissions.med.miami.edu/md-programs/medical-scholars-program

USF HEALTH MORSANI COLLEGE OF MEDICINE

Address: 12901 Bruce B. Downs Blvd., Tampa, FL 33612
Website: *https://health.usf.edu/medicine*
Contact Email: *md-admissions@health.usf.edu*
Phone: (813) 974-2229

Other locations: Allentown, PA

COST OF ATTENDANCE

In-State Tuition: $33,726
Fees & Expenses: $24,508
Total: $58,234

Out-of-State Tuition: $54,916
Fees & Expenses: $24,508
Total: $79,424

Financial Aid: https://health.usf.edu/well/financial-aid

Percent Receiving Aid: 79%

ADDITIONAL INFORMATION

Interesting tidbit: The USF College of Medicine has led USF's aggressive drive to achieve the fastest growth of federally-sponsored research in the nation. The college is home to one of the largest freestanding Alzheimer's centers, and a USF Diabetes Center is internationally recognized for more than $400 million in diabetes and autoimmune research.

What percent of students participate in global health experiences? 42%

What service learning opportunities exist? Service learning through student organizations and student-run clinic (BRIDGE). For more information, visit:https://health.usf.edu/bridge

What dual degree options exist? MD/PhD, MD/MBA, and MD/MPH. For more information, visit:https://health.usf.edu/medicine/mdprogram/combined

Important Updates due to COVID-19: Accept Pass/Fail grading for courses taken the spring and summer 2020 semesters, including laboratory credit taken online.

Were tests required? MCAT required.

Are tests expected next year? Yes.

Postgraduate Training Match Rate: 100%

USMLE First-Time Pass Rate

Step 1: N/A

Step 2 CK: N/A

Step 2 CS: N/A

Other: BS/MD 7-year program available to first-year undergraduate students. For more information, visit:https://www.usf.edu/honors/prospective-students/7-year-med.aspx

ALABAMA
ARKANSAS
DELAWARE
DISTRICT OF COLUMBIA
FLORIDA
GEORGIA
KENTUCKY
LOUISIANA
MARYLAND
MISSISSIPPI
NORTH CAROLINA
OKLAHOMA
SOUTH CAROLINA
TENNESSEE
TEXAS
VIRGINIA
WEST VIRGINIA

SOUTH

ALABAMA

ARKANSAS

DELAWARE

DISTRICT OF
COLUMBIA

FLORIDA

GEORGIA

KENTUCKY

LOUISIANA

MARYLAND

MISSISSIPPI

NORTH CAROLINA

OKLAHOMA

SOUTH CAROLINA

TENNESSEE

TEXAS

VIRGINIA

WEST VIRGINIA

EMORY UNIVERSITY SCHOOL OF MEDICINE

Address: 100 Woodruff Circle, Atlanta, GA 30322
Website: *https://www.med.emory.edu/*
Contact: *https://www.med.emory.edu/about/contact-us.html*
Phone: (404) 727-5660

COST OF ATTENDANCE

Tuition: $52,000
Fees & Expenses: $38,590
Total: $90,590

Financial Aid: https://www.med.emory.edu/education/programs/md/md-financial-aid/index.html

Percent Receiving Aid: 68%

ADDITIONAL INFORMATION

Interesting tidbit: Emory MD program's clinical training begins the very first week, with rotations starting halfway through the second year. This grants valuable hands-on exposure to a range of specialties and subspecialties, giving students experience in 14 disciplines in both hospital and outpatient settings before they begin applying to residency programs.

What percent of students participate in global health experiences? 22%

What service learning opportunities exist? Heel to Heal 5k, Art for a Cause, Emory Farmworker Project, etc. For more information, visit:https://www.med.emory.edu/clinical-experience/community-learning/index.html

What dual degree options exist? MD/MPH, MD/MBA, MD/MA in Bioethics, MD/MS in Clinical Research, and MD/PhD. For more information, visit:https://www.med.emory.edu/education/programs/md/index.html

Important Updates due to COVID-19: Accept pass/fail courses, as well as online courses, toward the course requirements. Must meet our MCAT prescreening criteria in order to receive an invitation to complete the Emory Supplemental Application.

Were tests required? MCAT required.

Are tests expected next year? Yes.

Postgraduate Training Match Rate: N/A

USMLE First-Time Pass Rate

Step 1: N/A

Step 2 CK: N/A

Step 2 CS: N/A

MEDICAL COLLEGE OF GEORGIA AT AUGUSTA UNIVERSITY

Address: 1120 15th Street, Augusta, GA 30912
Website: *https://www.augusta.edu/mcg/*
Contact: *https://www.augusta.edu/mcg/medicine/contactus.php*
Phone: (706) 721-3186

Other locations: Athens, GA

COST OF ATTENDANCE

In-State Tuition: $28,926
Fees & Expenses: $30,845
Total: $59,771

Out-of-State Tuition: $57,850
Fees & Expenses: $30,945
Total: $88,695

Financial Aid: https://www.augusta.edu/mcg/admissions/
financialoverview.php

Percent Receiving Aid: 82%

ADDITIONAL INFORMATION

Interesting tidbit: MCG at Augusta University is Georgia's only public medical school. It is one of the nation's largest medical schools with the main campus in Augusta and regional clinical campuses for third- and fourth-year students across the state and a second four-year campus in Athens in partnership with the University of Georgia.

What percent of students participate in global health experiences? 25%

What service learning opportunities exist? Service learning is required. Types of activities include student-run free clinics, student organizations, etc. For more information, visit:https://www.augusta.edu/mcg/students/volunteering.php

What dual degree options exist? MD/MPH and MD/MBA:https://www.augusta.edu/mcg/coffice/degree-programs.php

MD/PhD: https://www.augusta.edu/mcg/mdphd/

Important Updates due to COVID-19: Accept pass/fail and online coursework from Spring Semester 2020- Spring Semester 2021.

Were tests required? MCAT and CASPer required.

Are tests expected next year? Yes.

Postgraduate Training Match Rate: 99% (2021)

USMLE First-Time Pass Rate

Step 1: N/A

Step 2 CK: N/A

Step 2 CS: N/A

Other: Professional Scholars Program (BS/MD) is a 7-year program available to high school applicants. For more information, visit:https://www.augusta.edu/admissions/professionalscholars.php

ALABAMA
ARKANSAS
DELAWARE
DISTRICT OF COLUMBIA
FLORIDA
GEORGIA
KENTUCKY
LOUISIANA
MARYLAND
MISSISSIPPI
NORTH CAROLINA
OKLAHOMA
SOUTH CAROLINA
TENNESSEE
TEXAS
VIRGINIA
WEST VIRGINIA

SOUTH

MERCER UNIVERSITY SCHOOL OF MEDICINE

Address: 1550 College St, Macon, GA 31207
Website: *https://medicine.mercer.edu/*
Contact: *https://www.mercer.edu/contacts/*
Phone: (478) 301-5425

Other locations: Savannah, GA; Columbus, GA

COST OF ATTENDANCE

Tuition: $42,586
Fees & Expenses: $24,324
Total: $66,910

Financial Aid: https://medicine.mercer.edu/student-affairs-and-services/financial-planning/

Percent Receiving Aid: 88%

ADDITIONAL INFORMATION

Interesting tidbit: The full four-year M.D. program is offered in the Macon and Savannah campuses and Years 3 and 4 of the M.D. programs are additionally offered at the Columbus campus.

What percent of students participate in global health experiences? 28%

What service learning opportunities exist? Service learning through student organizations.

What dual degree options exist? No dual degree options listed.

Important Updates due to COVID-19: Accept pass/fail grades and online coursework, including labs from the Spring and Summer semesters of the 2019-2020 academic year and the Fall, Spring, and Summer semesters of the 2020-2021 academic year.

Were tests required? MCAT and CASPer required.

Are tests expected next year? Yes.

Postgraduate Training Match Rate: 100% (2021)

USMLE First-Time Pass Rate

Step 1: N/A

Step 2 CK: N/A

Step 2 CS: N/A

MOREHOUSE SCHOOL OF MEDICINE

Address: 720 Westview Drive, S.W., Atlanta, GA 30310
Website: *https://www.msm.edu/*
Contact: *https://www.msm.edu/about_us/facts/facts_contactus.php*
Phone: (404) 752-1650

COST OF ATTENDANCE

Tuition: $45,208
Fees & Expenses: $37,836
Total: $83,044

Financial Aid: https://www.msm.edu/FinancialAid/index.php

Percent Receiving Aid: 93%

ADDITIONAL INFORMATION

Interesting tidbit: Morehouse School of Medicine is an integrated member of the largest consortium of Historically Black Colleges and Universities in the world - Atlanta University Center.

What percent of students participate in global health experiences? 30%

What service learning opportunities exist? Community Engagement Day, H.E.A.L. Clinic, community health course within the curriculum, etc. For more information, visit:https://www.msm.edu/Community/index.php

What dual degree options exist? MD/MPH, MD/MSCR, and MD/PhD. For more information, visit:https://www.msm.edu/Admissions/dualdegreeprograms.php

For information on the MD/MBA, visit:https://www.msm.edu/Education/md-mba/

Important Updates due to COVID-19: Accept P/F and online course credits for Spring, Summer and Fall 2020 only. Will not consider online prerequisite courses taken during Spring 2020.

Were tests required? MCAT and SJT required.

Are tests expected next year? Yes.

Postgraduate Training Match Rate: 98% (2020)

USMLE First-Time Pass Rate

Step 1: N/A

Step 2 CK: N/A

Step 2 CS: N/A

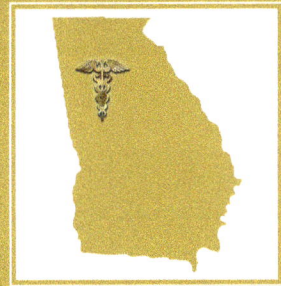

ALABAMA
ARKANSAS
DELAWARE
DISTRICT OF COLUMBIA
FLORIDA
GEORGIA
KENTUCKY
LOUISIANA
MARYLAND
MISSISSIPPI
NORTH CAROLINA
OKLAHOMA
SOUTH CAROLINA
TENNESSEE
TEXAS
VIRGINIA
WEST VIRGINIA

SOUTH

UNIVERSITY OF KENTUCKY COLLEGE OF MEDICINE

Address: 800 Rose Street MN 150, Lexington, KY 40506
Website: https://med.uky.edu/
Contact via phone
Phone: (859) 562-2507

Other locations: Lexington, KY; Bowling Green, KY; Morehead, KY

COST OF ATTENDANCE

In-State Tuition: $38,920
Fees & Expenses: $26,837
Total: $65,757

Out-of-State Tuition: $71,400
Fees & Expenses: $26,837
Total: $98,241

Financial Aid: http://meded.med.uky.edu/financial-aid

Percent Receiving Aid: 90%

ADDITIONAL INFORMATION

Interesting tidbit: University of Kentucky is one of few universities to have all six health science colleges (Medicine, Nursing, Dentistry, Pharmacy, Public Health, and Health Sciences) all on the same university campus making it well-positioned for interprofessional health care education and collaborative research. Currently, the UK College of Medicine has 276,555 square feet of research space.

What percent of students participate in global health experiences? 16%

What service learning opportunities exist? Rotations and volunteer opportunities through UK Center of Excellence in Rural Health, Area Health Education Center Program, Kentucky Ambulatory Network, etc. For more information, visit:https://med.uky.edu/outreach

What dual degree options exist? MD/MPH:https://meded.med.uky.edu/mdmph-program

MD/MBA: https://meded.med.uky.edu/mdmba-program

MD/PhD: http://mdphd.med.uky.edu/

Important Updates due to COVID-19: Accept P/F grading for prerequisite coursework for Spring Semester 2020.

Were tests required? MCAT required.

Are tests expected next year? Yes.

Postgraduate Training Match Rate: N/A

USMLE First-Time Pass Rate

Step 1: N/A

Step 2 CK: N/A

Step 2 CS: N/A

Other: Early Assurance Program available to applicants interested in practicing in Kentucky. Students in their second semester of sophomore year in college may apply. For more information, visit:https://meded.med.uky.edu/medical-education-early-assurance-program-lexington-campus

ALABAMA

ARKANSAS

DELAWARE

DISTRICT OF COLUMBIA

FLORIDA

GEORGIA

KENTUCKY

LOUISIANA

MARYLAND

MISSISSIPPI

NORTH CAROLINA

OKLAHOMA

SOUTH CAROLINA

TENNESSEE

TEXAS

VIRGINIA

WEST VIRGINIA

UNIVERSITY OF LOUISVILLE SCHOOL OF MEDICINE

Address: 323 East Chestnut, Louisville, KY 40202
Website: *http://louisville.edu/medicine*
Contact: *http://louisville.edu/medicine/contact*
Phone: (502) 852-5193

COST OF ATTENDANCE

In-State Tuition: $41,778
Fees & Expenses: $26,116
Total: $67,894

Out-of-State Tuition: $63,530
Fees & Expenses: $26,116
Total: $89,646

Financial Aid: http://louisville.edu/medicine/financialaid

Percent Receiving Aid: 86%

ADDITIONAL INFORMATION

Interesting tidbit: The University of Louisville School of Medicine introduced the Advisory College Program in the fall of 2011. This program is designed to develop and foster relationships between classmates, as well as promote vertical relationships between students from other classes. Upon matriculation, each incoming student is assigned to one of six Advisory Colleges.

What percent of students participate in global health experiences? 25%

What service learning opportunities exist? Service learning through student organizations, free clinics, community partnerships, etc. For more information, visit:http://louisville.edu/medicine/outreach

What dual degree options exist? MD/MBA, MD/MA in Bioethics and Medical Humanities, and MD/PhD. For more information, visit:http://louisville.edu/medicine/degrees/dualdegree

Important Updates due to COVID-19: Accept P/F grading for Spring 2020 courses only. Standard practice gives no preference online or in-person as long as the courses are completed at an accredited institution.

Were tests required? MCAT required.

Are tests expected next year? Yes.

Postgraduate Training Match Rate: N/A

USMLE First-Time Pass Rate

Step 1: N/A

Step 2 CK: N/A

Step 2 CS: N/A

ALABAMA
ARKANSAS
DELAWARE
DISTRICT OF COLUMBIA
FLORIDA
GEORGIA
KENTUCKY
LOUISIANA
MARYLAND
MISSISSIPPI
NORTH CAROLINA
OKLAHOMA
SOUTH CAROLINA
TENNESSEE
TEXAS
VIRGINIA
WEST VIRGINIA

SOUTH

LOUISIANA STATE UNIVERSITY SCHOOL OF MEDICINE IN SHREVEPORT

Address: 1501 Kings Highway, Shreveport, LA 71130
Website: *https://www.lsuhs.edu/our-schools/school-of-medicine*
Contact: *https://lsuhealthshreveport.formstack.com/forms/website_contact_us_main*
Phone: (318) 675-5190

COST OF ATTENDANCE

In-State Tuition: $29,343
Fees & Expenses: $26,830
Total: $56,173

Out-of-State Tuition: $61,165
Fees & Expenses: $26,830
Total: $87,995

Financial Aid: https://www.lsuhs.edu/admissions/student-financial-services/student-financial-aid

Percent Receiving Aid: 84%

ADDITIONAL INFORMATION

Interesting tidbit: Medical students interact with patients from their very first semester and learn from a combination of lectures, small groups, standardized patient exercises and clinical skills throughout their training. Those with a heightened interest in research can opt to enroll in the Research Distinction Track.

What percent of students participate in global health experiences? 15%

What service learning opportunities exist? After school programs, helping elder adults, assisting individuals experiencing homelessness, etc. For more information, visit:https://www.lsuhs.edu/our-schools/school-of-medicine/student-affairs/student-involvement

What dual degree options exist? MD/PhD. For more information, visit:https://www.lsuhs.edu/our-schools/school-of-medicine/admissions/combined

Important Updates due to COVID-19: Allow both pass/fail grades and online courses for prerequisites taken during the spring 2020, fall 2020, and spring 2021 semesters. Letters of Recommendation for the 2020-2021 cycle are optional.

Were tests required? MCAT required.

Are tests expected next year? Yes.

Postgraduate Training Match Rate: N/A

USMLE First-Time Pass Rate

Step 1: N/A

Step 2 CK: N/A

Step 2 CS: N/A

LSU HEALTH SCIENCES CENTER SCHOOL OF MEDICINE IN NEW ORLEANS

Address: 2020 Gravier Street, 5th Floor, New Orleans, LA 70112
Website: https://www.medschool.lsuhsc.edu/
Contact: https://www.lsuhsc.edu/ContactUs/
Phone: (504) 568-8501

Other locations: Baton Rouge, LA; Lafayette, LA

COST OF ATTENDANCE

In-State Tuition: $32,937
Fees & Expenses: $30,752
Total: $63,669

Out-of-State Tuition: $61,114
Fees & Expenses: $30,752
Total: $91,866

Financial Aid: https://www.medschool.lsuhsc.edu/admissions/Aid.aspx

Percent Receiving Aid: 81%

ADDITIONAL INFORMATION

Interesting tidbit: The Honors Program is in addition to the regular curriculum and is designed to challenge the exceptional student while stimulating the interest of the individual. It entails an independent research program encompassing both the basic and clinical sciences. Students who have maintained high academic standards during their first semester in the School of Medicine are eligible for consideration.

What percent of students participate in global health experiences? 19%

What service learning opportunities exist? Service learning through student organizations.

What dual degree options exist? MD/MPH:https://publichealth.lsuhsc.edu/

MD/PhD: https://graduatestudies.lsuhsc.edu/md_phd/

Important Updates due to COVID-19: Accept P/F grades instead of letter grades (even for prerequisites). Accept online coursework including lab for both prerequisite and upper level science courses from accredited schools.

Were tests required? MCAT required.

Are tests expected next year? Yes.

Postgraduate Training Match Rate: N/A

USMLE First-Time Pass Rate

Step 1: N/A

Step 2 CK: N/A

Step 2 CS: N/A

ALABAMA

ARKANSAS

DELAWARE

DISTRICT OF COLUMBIA

FLORIDA

GEORGIA

KENTUCKY

LOUISIANA

MARYLAND

MISSISSIPPI

NORTH CAROLINA

OKLAHOMA

SOUTH CAROLINA

TENNESSEE

TEXAS

VIRGINIA

WEST VIRGINIA

SOUTH

ALABAMA

ARKANSAS

DELAWARE

DISTRICT OF COLUMBIA

FLORIDA

GEORGIA

KENTUCKY

LOUISIANA

MARYLAND

MISSISSIPPI

NORTH CAROLINA

OKLAHOMA

SOUTH CAROLINA

TENNESSEE

TEXAS

VIRGINIA

WEST VIRGINIA

TULANE UNIVERSITY SCHOOL OF MEDICINE

Address: 1430 Tulane Avenue, New Orleans, LA 70112
Website: *https://medicine.tulane.edu/*
Contact: *https://medicine.tulane.edu/admissions/contact-us*
Phone: (504) 988-5331

COST OF ATTENDANCE

Tuition: $69,308
Fees & Expenses: $29,644
Total: $98,952

Financial Aid: https://financialaid.tulane.edu/

Percent Receiving Aid: 78%

ADDITIONAL INFORMATION

Interesting tidbit: In the aftermath of Hurricane Katrina, Tulane School of Medicine evacuated to Baylor College of Medicine in Texas, where medical students resumed their studies. Tulane medical school administrators coordinated the school's return to New Orleans, which began in November 2005.

What percent of students participate in global health experiences? 19%

What service learning opportunities exist? Service learning through student organizations and student-run free clinics. For more information, visit:https://medicine.tulane.edu/admissions/student-run-clinics

What dual degree options exist? MD/MBA, MD/MPH, and MD/PhD. For more information, visit:https://medicine.tulane.edu/education/combined-degrees

Important Updates due to COVID-19: Accept online courses.

Were tests required? MCAT required. CASPer Test encouraged.

Are tests expected next year? Yes.

Postgraduate Training Match Rate: N/A

USMLE First-Time Pass Rate

Step 1: N/A

Step 2 CK: N/A

Step 2 CS: N/A

Other: Tulane Accelerated Physician Training Program (TAP-TP) is a 7-year BS/MD program available to Tulane University undergraduates. For more information, visit:https://advising.tulane.edu/pre-health/path/special-programs/tap-tp

JOHNS HOPKINS UNIVERSITY SCHOOL OF MEDICINE

Address: 733 N Broadway, Baltimore, MD 21205
Website: *https://www.hopkinsmedicine.org/som/*
Contact: *https://www.hopkinsmedicine.org/som/contact/*
Phone: (410) 955-3182

COST OF ATTENDANCE

Tuition: $58,000
Fees & Expenses: $32,126
Total: $89,126

Financial Aid: https://www.hopkinsmedicine.org/som/offices/finaid/

Percent Receiving Aid: 79%

ADDITIONAL INFORMATION

Interesting tidbit: the Johns Hopkins Genes to Society curriculum departs from the traditional a dichotomous view of "normal human biology (health)" and "abnormal physiology (disease)." It presents a model of health grounded in what we've learned from the Human Genome Project about human variability, risk and the ability to modulate disease presentation and outcomes.

What percent of students participate in global health experiences? 23%

What service learning opportunities exist? Service learning through student organizations.

What dual degree options exist? MD/PhD, MD/MBA, and MD/MSHCM. For more information, visit:https://www.hopkinsmedicine.org/som/education-programs/md-program/curriculum-and-degrees/combined-degree-programs.html

MD/MPH: https://www.jhsph.edu/academics/degree-programs/master-of-public-health/

Important Updates due to COVID-19: Accept online prerequisite courses completed at an accredited college or university. Accept P/F grades reported as such due to the pandemic.

Were tests required? MCAT required.

Are tests expected next year? Yes.

Postgraduate Training Match Rate: N/A

USMLE First-Time Pass Rate

Step 1: N/A

Step 2 CK: N/A

Step 2 CS: N/A

ALABAMA
ARKANSAS
DELAWARE
DISTRICT OF COLUMBIA
FLORIDA
GEORGIA
KENTUCKY
LOUISIANA
MARYLAND
MISSISSIPPI
NORTH CAROLINA
OKLAHOMA
SOUTH CAROLINA
TENNESSEE
TEXAS
VIRGINIA
WEST VIRGINIA

SOUTH

ALABAMA

ARKANSAS

DELAWARE

DISTRICT OF COLUMBIA

FLORIDA

GEORGIA

KENTUCKY

LOUISIANA

MARYLAND

MISSISSIPPI

NORTH CAROLINA

OKLAHOMA

SOUTH CAROLINA

TENNESSEE

TEXAS

VIRGINIA

WEST VIRGINIA

UNIFORMED SERVICES UNIVERSITY OF THE HEALTH SCIENCES, F. EDWARD HÉBERT SCHOOL OF MEDICINE

Address: 4301 Jones Bridge Rd., Bethesda, MD 20814
Website: *https://www.usuhs.edu/medschool*
Contact: *https://www.usuhs.edu/contactus*
Phone: (301) 295-3101

COST OF ATTENDANCE

Tuition: $0
Fees & Expenses: $0
Total: $0

Financial Aid: Accepted students are commissioned as Second Lieutenants in one of the four uniformed services. Students pay no tuition or fees and, in fact, receive the full salary and benefits of a uniformed officer throughout their four years at the university in exchange for active duty service commitment. Upon graduation, students are promoted to the rank of Captain in the Air Force or Army or the rank of Lieutenant in the Navy or Public Health Service and are obligated to serve as medical officers for a minimum of 7 years.

Percent Receiving Aid: N/A

ADDITIONAL INFORMATION

Interesting tidbit: the Uniformed Services University of the Health Sciences (USU) was established in 1972 to assure that the Army, Navy, Air Force, and U.S. Public Health Service would have a steady supply of physician-leaders to provide the backbone for their medical corps. Each student will be sworn in as an officer in the military before they arrive for their first semester (commission as officers into one of the four uniformed services before beginning classes). Active duty service commitment is seven years for the Army, Navy, and Air Force, and ten years for the Public Health Service.

What percent of students participate in global health experiences? 20%

What service learning opportunities exist? Clinical training across the country, global service learning opportunities, etc.

What dual degree options exist? MD/PhD. For more information, visit:https://www.usuhs.edu/graded/application.html

Important Updates due to COVID-19: Accept online and pass/fail grades, without prejudice, for courses taken during the COVID-19 pandemic. Community college, online and hybrid courses are accepted as long as it is a U.S. accredited university or college. This includes science labs.

Were tests required? MCAT required.

Are tests expected next year? Yes.

Postgraduate Training Match Rate: N/A

USMLE First-Time Pass Rate

Step 1: N/A

Step 2 CK: N/A

Step 2 CS: N/A

UNIVERSITY OF MARYLAND SCHOOL OF MEDICINE

Address: 655 W Baltimore St S, Baltimore, MD 21201
Website: *https://www.medschool.umaryland.edu/*
Contact: *https://www.medschool.umaryland.edu/admissions/Contact-Us/*
Phone: (410) 706-7478

COST OF ATTENDANCE

In-State Tuition: $37,810
Fees & Expenses: $39,337
Total: $77,147

Out-of-State Tuition: $66,905
Fees & Expenses: $40,537
Total: $107,442

Financial Aid: https://www.umaryland.edu/fin/

Percent Receiving Aid: 72%

ADDITIONAL INFORMATION

Interesting tidbit: University of Maryland School of Medicine was chartered in 1807 as the first public medical school in the United States. The School of Medicine faculty is an innovator in translational medicine with 600 active patents and 24 start-up companies.

What percent of students participate in global health experiences? 20%

What service learning opportunities exist? Community outreach in clinics, homeless shelters, local schools, hospitals, etc. For more information, visit:https://www.medschool.umaryland.edu/about/Community-Engagement/

What dual degree options exist? MD/MPH and MD/PhD. For more information, visit:https://www.medschool.umaryland.edu/education/Graduate-Education/Combined-Degrees/

Important Updates due to COVID-19: Accept online coursework for any course (including course requirements) from the Spring 2020 semester through the Summer 2021 semester. Accept P/F grading from Spring 2020 through Spring 2021 semesters.

Were tests required? MCAT required.

Are tests expected next year? Yes.

Postgraduate Training Match Rate: N/A

USMLE First-Time Pass Rate

Step 1: N/A

Step 2 CK: N/A

Step 2 CS: N/A

ALABAMA
ARKANSAS
DELAWARE
DISTRICT OF COLUMBIA
FLORIDA
GEORGIA
KENTUCKY
LOUISIANA
MARYLAND
MISSISSIPPI
NORTH CAROLINA
OKLAHOMA
SOUTH CAROLINA
TENNESSEE
TEXAS
VIRGINIA
WEST VIRGINIA

SOUTH

ALABAMA

ARKANSAS

DELAWARE

DISTRICT OF
COLUMBIA

FLORIDA

GEORGIA

KENTUCKY

LOUISIANA

MARYLAND

MISSISSIPPI

NORTH CAROLINA

OKLAHOMA

SOUTH CAROLINA

TENNESSEE

TEXAS

VIRGINIA

WEST VIRGINIA

UNIVERSITY OF MISSISSIPPI SCHOOL OF MEDICINE

Address: 2500 North State Street, Jackson, MS 39216
Website: *https://www.umc.edu/som/SOM_Home.html*
Contact Email: *AdmitMD@umc.edu*
Phone: (601) 984-5010

COST OF ATTENDANCE

Tuition: $31,197
Fees & Expenses: $28,933
Total: $60,190

Financial Aid: https://www.umc.edu/Office%20of%20 Academic%20Affairs/For-Students/Student%20Financial%20Aid/ Student-Financial-Aid.html

Percent Receiving Aid: 89%

ADDITIONAL INFORMATION

Interesting tidbit: The University of Mississippi Medical Center, located in Jackson, is the state's only academic health science center. UMMC has expanded its School of Medicine to help train more physicians for our state, with the goal of helping create a healthier Mississippi.

What percent of students participate in global health experiences? 24%

What service learning opportunities exist? Service learning through community partnerships and student organizations. For more information, visit:https://www.umc.edu/Office%20 of%20Academic%20Affairs/For-Students/Office%20for%20 Community%20Engagement%20and%20Service%20Learning/ Office%20for%20Community%20Engagement%20and%20 Service%20Learning.html

What dual degree options exist? MD/PhD. For more information, visit:https://www.umc.edu/graduateschool/Degree-Programs/MD-PhD/MD-PhD-Overview.html

Important Updates due to COVID-19: Accept pass grades for coursework for the spring 2020 semester; Accept online or hybrid coursework for lectures and labs for summer 2020, fall 2020, and spring 2021 but online courses must be taken at one and not multiple institutions.

Were tests required? MCAT required.

Are tests expected next year? Yes.

Postgraduate Training Match Rate: N/A

USMLE First-Time Pass Rate

Step 1: N/A

Step 2 CK: N/A

Step 2 CS: N/A

DUKE UNIVERSITY SCHOOL OF MEDICINE

Address: DUMC 3710, Durham, NC 27710
Website: *https://medschool.duke.edu/*
Contact: *https://medschool.duke.edu/about-us/contact-us*
Phone: 919) 684-2985

COST OF ATTENDANCE

Tuition: $63,310
Fees & Expenses: $31,168
Total: $94,478

Financial Aid: https://medschool.duke.edu/education/student-services/office-financial-aid

Percent Receiving Aid: 74%

ADDITIONAL INFORMATION

Interesting tidbit: A unique curriculum for MD students allows students to study the core basic sciences for one year instead of two, giving them the opportunity to devote their entire third year to a scholarly research project. Students care for patients during their second year, a full year earlier than their peers.

What percent of students participate in global health experiences? 17%

What service learning opportunities exist? Service learning through student organizations.

What dual degree options exist? MD/PhD, MD/JD, MD/MALS, MD/MBA, MD/MPP, MD/MA in Bioethics and Science Policy, and MD/MPH. For more information, visit:https://medschool.duke.edu/education/degree-programs-and-admissions/third-year-program/dual-degree-programs

Important Updates due to COVID-19: Accept letter grades, P/F grades, S/U grades, withdraws, etc. Accept online courses for semesters during COVID-19. Application can be reviewed and an applicant can be invited for an interview without score but the MCAT test is required for acceptance consideration.

Were tests required? MCAT required.

Are tests expected next year? Yes.

Postgraduate Training Match Rate: N/A

USMLE First-Time Pass Rate

Step 1: N/A

Step 2 CK: N/A

Step 2 CS: N/A

ALABAMA
ARKANSAS
DELAWARE
DISTRICT OF COLUMBIA
FLORIDA
GEORGIA
KENTUCKY
LOUISIANA
MARYLAND
MISSISSIPPI
NORTH CAROLINA
OKLAHOMA
SOUTH CAROLINA
TENNESSEE
TEXAS
VIRGINIA
WEST VIRGINIA

SOUTH

THE BRODY SCHOOL OF MEDICINE AT EAST CAROLINA UNIVERSITY

Address: 600 Moye Blvd Greenville, NC 27834
Website: *https://medicine.ecu.edu/*
Contact: *https://medicine.ecu.edu/contact-us/*
Phone: (252) 744-2202

COST OF ATTENDANCE

Tuition: $23,134
Fees & Expenses: $26,122
Total: $49,256

Financial Aid: https://medicine.ecu.edu/studentaffairs/financial-aid/

Percent Receiving Aid: 89%

ADDITIONAL INFORMATION

Interesting tidbit: Brody School of Medicine at East Carolina University was established with a strong primary care orientation. One of its framing missions is to increase the supply of primary care physicians to serve the state.

What percent of students participate in global health experiences? 27%

What service learning opportunities exist? Community outreach through student organizations. In addition, a Service Learning Distinction Track is available. For more information, visit:https://medicine.ecu.edu/medicaleducation/service-learning/

What dual degree options exist? MD/MBA, MD/MPH, and MD/PhD. For more information, visit:https://medicine.ecu.edu/dual-degree/

Important Updates due to COVID-19: Accept P/F grading.

Were tests required? MCAT required.

Are tests expected next year? Yes.

Postgraduate Training Match Rate: N/A

USMLE First-Time Pass Rate

Step 1: N/A

Step 2 CK: N/A

Step 2 CS: N/A

Other: Early Assurance Program available to first-year East Carolina University undergraduates. For more information, visit:https://medicine.ecu.edu/admissions/early-assurance-program/

ALABAMA

ARKANSAS

DELAWARE

DISTRICT OF COLUMBIA

FLORIDA

GEORGIA

KENTUCKY

LOUISIANA

MARYLAND

MISSISSIPPI

NORTH CAROLINA

OKLAHOMA

SOUTH CAROLINA

TENNESSEE

TEXAS

VIRGINIA

WEST VIRGINIA

UNIVERSITY OF NORTH CAROLINA SCHOOL OF MEDICINE

Address: 321 S. Columbia Street Chapel Hill, NC 27599
Website: *https://www.med.unc.edu/*
Contact: *https://www.med.unc.edu/md/administration/contact-information/*
Phone: (919) 962-8331

Other locations: Wilmington, NC; Charlotte, NC; Asheville, NC

COST OF ATTENDANCE

In-State Tuition: $34,932
Fees & Expenses: $35,968
Total: $70,990

Out-of-State Tuition: $62,325
Fees & Expenses: $35,969
Total: $99,239

Financial Aid: https://www.med.unc.edu/ome/finaid/

Percent Receiving Aid: 87%

ADDITIONAL INFORMATION

Interesting tidbit: The School of Medicine launched its new curriculum, Translational Education at Carolina (TEC), in August 2014. It offers earlier clinical opportunities in specialty fields to better inform residency program decisions. In the Individualization Phase, students will take electives and seek out research opportunities.

What percent of students participate in global health experiences? 30%

What service learning opportunities exist? Rural Health elective, global health opportunities, and various community service programs. For more information, visit:https://www.med.unc.edu/ome/studentaffairs/research-service-and-international-opportunities/community-and-service-learning-opportunities/

What dual degree options exist? MD/MPH, MD/MBA, and MD/PhD. For more information, visit:https://www.med.unc.edu/education/combined-programs/

Important Updates due to COVID-19: Online instruction is acceptable during the pandemic. However, if your school is only offering P/F for a required course, we may require additional documentation from your school.

Were tests required? MCAT required.

Are tests expected next year? Yes.

Postgraduate Training Match Rate: 96% (2021)

USMLE First-Time Pass Rate

Step 1: N/A

Step 2 CK: N/A

Step 2 CS: N/A

ALABAMA
ARKANSAS
DELAWARE
DISTRICT OF COLUMBIA
FLORIDA
GEORGIA
KENTUCKY
LOUISIANA
MARYLAND
MISSISSIPPI
NORTH CAROLINA
OKLAHOMA
SOUTH CAROLINA
TENNESSEE
TEXAS
VIRGINIA
WEST VIRGINIA

SOUTH

ALABAMA

ARKANSAS

DELAWARE

DISTRICT OF
COLUMBIA

FLORIDA

GEORGIA

KENTUCKY

LOUISIANA

MARYLAND

MISSISSIPPI

NORTH CAROLINA

OKLAHOMA

SOUTH CAROLINA

TENNESSEE

TEXAS

VIRGINIA

WEST VIRGINIA

WAKE FOREST SCHOOL OF MEDICINE

Address: 475 Vine St., 1st Floor, Winston-Salem, NC 27101
Website: *https://school.wakehealth.edu/*
Contact Email: *medadmit@wakehealth.edu*
Phone: (336) 716-4264

COST OF ATTENDANCE

Tuition: $61,200
Fees & Expenses: $28,092
Total: $89,292

Financial Aid: https://school.wakehealth.edu/Education-and-Training/MD-Program/Costs-and-Financial-Aid

Percent Receiving Aid: 79%

ADDITIONAL INFORMATION

Interesting tidbit: Like many other schools, Wake Forest School of Medicine revamped its curriculum to move away from the traditional 2 preclinical + 2 clinical years. The "Wake Ready!" curriculum is comprised of Foundations (preclinical), Immersion (clinical) and Individualization (clinical). The Individualization phase allows students significant flexibility in adapting their training to meet the demands and expectations of their career path.

What percent of students participate in global health experiences? 35%

What service learning opportunities exist? Service learning through student organizations. For more information, visit:https://school.wakehealth.edu/Education-and-Training/Student-Affairs/Student-groups

What dual degree options exist? MD/MS in Clinical Population and Translational Science, MD/MA in Bioethics, and MD/PhD. For more information, visit:https://school.wakehealth.edu/Education-and-Training/Joint-Degree-Programs

Important Updates due to COVID-19: It is standard practice that Wake Forest School of Medicine does not require specific coursework for application.

Were tests required? MCAT and CASPer required.

Are tests expected next year? Yes.

Postgraduate Training Match Rate: 100% (2021)

USMLE First-Time Pass Rate

Step 1: N/A

Step 2 CK: N/A

Step 2 CS: N/A

UNIVERSITY OF OKLAHOMA COLLEGE OF MEDICINE

Address: 800 Stanton L Young Blvd, Oklahoma City, OK 73117
Website: *https://medicine.ouhsc.edu/*
Contact: *https://medicine.ouhsc.edu/Prospective-Students/ Admissions/Contact-Us*
Phone: (405) 271-2331

Other locations: Tulsa, OK

COST OF ATTENDANCE

In-State Tuition: $31,082
Fees & Expenses: $27,947
Total: $59,029

Out-of-State Tuition: $65,410
Fees & Expenses: $27,947
Total: $93,357

Financial Aid: https://financialservices.ouhsc.edu/Departments/ Student-Financial-Aid

Percent Receiving Aid: 80%

ADDITIONAL INFORMATION

Interesting tidbit: Anatomical Donor Luncheon pairs first-year medical students with the families of the donor body they will encounter in anatomy lab. Students learn about the donor's life and are reminded of the selfless act of the donation for their education.

What percent of students participate in global health experiences? 15%

What service learning opportunities exist? Service learning through student organizations.

What dual degree options exist? MD/PhD. For more information, visit:https://mdphd.ouhsc.edu/

Important Updates due to COVID-19: Accept Pass/Fail grades for courses (including prerequisites) taken Spring semester 2020.

Were tests required? MCAT required.

Are tests expected next year? Yes.

Postgraduate Training Match Rate: N/A

USMLE First-Time Pass Rate

Step 1: N/A

Step 2 CK: N/A

Step 2 CS: N/A

ALABAMA

ARKANSAS

DELAWARE

DISTRICT OF COLUMBIA

FLORIDA

GEORGIA

KENTUCKY

LOUISIANA

MARYLAND

MISSISSIPPI

NORTH CAROLINA

OKLAHOMA

SOUTH CAROLINA

TENNESSEE

TEXAS

VIRGINIA

WEST VIRGINIA

SOUTH

MEDICAL UNIVERSITY OF SOUTH CAROLINA COLLEGE OF MEDICINE

Address: 96 Johnathan Lucas St., Ste. 601, Charleston, SC 29425
Website: *https://medicine.musc.edu/*
Contact: *https://web.musc.edu/about/contact*
Phone: (843) 792-2536
Other locations: Anderson, SC

COST OF ATTENDANCE

In-State Tuition: $31,001
Fees & Expenses: $29,662
Total: $60,663

Out-of-State Tuition: $53,001
Fees & Expenses: $29,662
Total: $82,663

Financial Aid: https://education.musc.edu/students/enrollment/financial-aid

Percent Receiving Aid: 85%

ADDITIONAL INFORMATION

Interesting tidbit: An accelerated track offers a select number of eligible students the opportunity to complete their degree in three years and join one of the participating residency programs at MUSC. A parallel clinical track at the MUSC-AnMed Health Clinical Campus offers accepted students the opportunity to complete a comparable, primary-care focused clinical curriculum (year 3 and year 4) in a community-based setting.

What percent of students participate in global health experiences? 20%

What service learning opportunities exist? Service learning through student organizations. Additionally, various tracks available: Research, Health Humanities, Global Health, and Physician as Teacher. For more information, visit:https://medicine.musc.edu/education/medical-students/student-affairs/msrp/flex-phase/com-service-learning

What dual degree options exist? MD/PhD. For more information, visit:https://gradstudies.musc.edu/programs/dual-degree/mstp

Important Updates due to COVID-19: Accept Pass/No Pass grading for Spring 2020, Fall 2020, Spring 2021 and Fall 2021 coursework. Online courses from an accredited college or university may be acceptable. However, applicants who have successfully completed science coursework in a formal classroom setting will be deemed more competitive in the selection process than students who completed these courses in online programs.

Were tests required? MCAT required.

Are tests expected next year? Yes.

Postgraduate Training Match Rate: 97.7% (2021)

USMLE First-Time Pass Rate

Step 1: N/A

Step 2 CK: N/A

Step 2 CS: N/A

ALABAMA

ARKANSAS

DELAWARE

DISTRICT OF COLUMBIA

FLORIDA

GEORGIA

KENTUCKY

LOUISIANA

MARYLAND

MISSISSIPPI

NORTH CAROLINA

OKLAHOMA

SOUTH CAROLINA

TENNESSEE

TEXAS

VIRGINIA

WEST VIRGINIA

UNIVERSITY OF SOUTH CAROLINA SCHOOL OF MEDICINE, COLUMBIA

Address: 6311 Garners Ferry Road, Columbia, SC 29209
Website: *https://www.sc.edu/study/colleges_schools/medicine/index.php*
Contact: *https://www.sc.edu/study/colleges_schools/medicine/about_the_school/contact/index.php*
Phone: (803) 216-3625

Other locations: Florence, SC

COST OF ATTENDANCE

In-State Tuition: $42,888
Fees & Expenses: $25,995
Total: $68,883

Out-of-State Tuition: $87,150
Fees & Expenses: $25,995
Total: $113,145

Financial Aid: https://www.sc.edu/study/colleges_schools/medicine/education/student_career_services/financial_aid/index.php

Percent Receiving Aid: 89%

ADDITIONAL INFORMATION

Interesting tidbit: UofSC School of Medicine Columbia's partnerships with technology leaders like General Electric give them access to the latest equipment, sometimes before it even hits the market.

What percent of students participate in global health experiences? 15%

What service learning opportunities exist? Service learning through student organizations.

What dual degree options exist? MD/PhD. For more information, visit:https://www.sc.edu/study/colleges_schools/medicine/education/md_program/md_phd/index.php

Important Updates due to COVID-19: accept pass/fail courses and online labs during the Spring 2020/2021, Summer 2020/2021 and/or Fall 2020/2021 semesters.

Were tests required? MCAT required.

Are tests expected next year? Yes.

Postgraduate Training Match Rate: 100% (2021)

USMLE First-Time Pass Rate

Step 1: N/A

Step 2 CK: N/A

Step 2 CS: N/A

Other: BA/MD program (the "BARSC-MD") is available to incoming honors freshmen. For more information, visit:https://sc.edu/study/colleges_schools/honors_college/internal/courses_requirements/build_your_own_major_barsc/index.php

ALABAMA
ARKANSAS
DELAWARE
DISTRICT OF COLUMBIA
FLORIDA
GEORGIA
KENTUCKY
LOUISIANA
MARYLAND
MISSISSIPPI
NORTH CAROLINA
OKLAHOMA
SOUTH CAROLINA
TENNESSEE
TEXAS
VIRGINIA
WEST VIRGINIA

SOUTH

ALABAMA

ARKANSAS

DELAWARE

DISTRICT OF
COLUMBIA

FLORIDA

GEORGIA

KENTUCKY

LOUISIANA

MARYLAND

MISSISSIPPI

NORTH CAROLINA

OKLAHOMA

SOUTH CAROLINA

TENNESSEE

TEXAS

VIRGINIA

WEST VIRGINIA

UNIVERSITY OF SOUTH CAROLINA SCHOOL OF MEDICINE, GREENVILLE

Address: 607 Grove Road, Greenville, SC 29605
Website: *https://www.sc.edu/study/colleges_schools/medicine_greenville/index.php*
Contact: *https://www.sc.edu/study/colleges_schools/medicine_greenville/contact/index.php*
Phone: (864) 455-8201

COST OF ATTENDANCE

In-State Tuition: $44,612
Fees & Expenses: $22,623
Total: $67,235

Out-of-State Tuition: $88,874
Fees & Expenses: $22,623
Total: $111,497

Financial Aid: https://www.sc.edu/study/colleges_schools/medicine_greenville/financialaid/index.php

Percent Receiving Aid: 89%

ADDITIONAL INFORMATION

Interesting tidbit: The University of South Carolina School of Medicine Greenville is a four-year medical program developed as a partnership between the University of South Carolina, the state's largest university and the Greenville Health System, the state's largest public hospital. The UofSC School of Medicine Greenville requires first-year medical students to complete an emergency medical technician training course to certification.

What percent of students participate in global health experiences? 13%

What service learning opportunities exist? Service learning through student organizations.

What dual degree options exist? No dual degree options listed.

Important Updates due to COVID-19: accept prerequisites as pass/fail courses and online labs to meet the requirements if they were taken during a semester when your University offered online-only schedules for health and safety reasons.

Were tests required? MCAT required.

Are tests expected next year? Yes.

Postgraduate Training Match Rate: 99% (2021)

USMLE First-Time Pass Rate

Step 1: N/A

Step 2 CK: N/A

Step 2 CS: N/A

EAST TENNESSEE STATE UNIVERSITY
JAMES H. QUILLEN COLLEGE OF MEDICINE

Address: East Tennessee State University, Johnson City, TN 37614
Website: *https://www.etsu.edu/com/*
Contact: *https://www.etsu.edu/com/contactus.php*
Phone: (423) 439-2033

COST OF ATTENDANCE

In-State Tuition: $32,834
Fees & Expenses: $26,522
Total: $59,356

Out-of-State Tuition: $42,684
Fees & Expenses: $26,522
Total: $69,206

Financial Aid: https://www.etsu.edu/com/sa/comfinaid/

Percent Receiving Aid: 92%

ADDITIONAL INFORMATION

Interesting tidbit: Quillen College of Medicine is a major health care provider for East Tennessee. In view of this responsibility, the college emphasizes primary care as the focus of medical practice and training programs. The primary mission of the Quillen College of Medicine is to educate future physicians, especially those with an interest in primary care, to practice in underserved rural communities.

What percent of students participate in global health experiences? 50%

What service learning opportunities exist? Service learning built into the curriculum. Students demonstrate service to various agencies and organizations (e.g., Coalition for Kids, Habitat for Humanity, the Salvation Army, etc.). For more information, visit:https://www.etsu.edu/coe/chs/servicelearning/

What dual degree options exist? MD/MPH. For more information, visit:https://www.etsu.edu/com/sa/admissions/mdmph.php

Important Updates due to COVID-19: Accept pass/fail grades, without prejudice, for courses taken during the COVID-19 pandemic.

Were tests required? MCAT and CASPer required.

Are tests expected next year? Yes.

Postgraduate Training Match Rate: 96% (2021)

USMLE First-Time Pass Rate

Step 1: N/A

Step 2 CK: N/A

Step 2 CS: N/A

ALABAMA
ARKANSAS
DELAWARE
DISTRICT OF COLUMBIA
FLORIDA
GEORGIA
KENTUCKY
LOUISIANA
MARYLAND
MISSISSIPPI
NORTH CAROLINA
OKLAHOMA
SOUTH CAROLINA
TENNESSEE
TEXAS
VIRGINIA
WEST VIRGINIA

SOUTH

ALABAMA

ARKANSAS

DELAWARE

DISTRICT OF
COLUMBIA

FLORIDA

GEORGIA

KENTUCKY

LOUISIANA

MARYLAND

MISSISSIPPI

NORTH CAROLINA

OKLAHOMA

SOUTH CAROLINA

TENNESSEE

TEXAS

VIRGINIA

WEST VIRGINIA

MEHARRY MEDICAL COLLEGE SCHOOL OF MEDICINE

Address: 1005 Dr. D. B. Todd Jr. Boulevard, Nashville, TN 37208
Website: *https://home.mmc.edu/*
Contact Email: *admissions@mmc.edu*
Phone: (615) 327-6998

COST OF ATTENDANCE

Tuition: $52,617
Fees & Expenses: $37,803
Total: $90,420
Financial Aid: https://home.mmc.edu/financial-aid/

Percent Receiving Aid: 92%

ADDITIONAL INFORMATION

Interesting tidbit: Meharry Medical College is the first medical school in the South for African Americans, It was founded in 1876 by Samuel Meharry and his four brothers in response to an Act of Kindness he had received on a Kentucky road one rainy night—a chance meeting now known as The Salt Wagon Story. It has become one of the nation's oldest and largest historically black academic health science centers.

What percent of students participate in global health experiences? 13%

What service learning opportunities exist? Service learning through student organizations.

What dual degree options exist? MD/MPH and MD/PhD. For more information, visit:https://www.mmc.edu/education/sogsr/academicprograms/

Important Updates due to COVID-19: N/A

Were tests required? MCAT and CASPer required.

Are tests expected next year? Yes.

Postgraduate Training Match Rate: N/A

USMLE First-Time Pass Rate

Step 1: 82%

Step 2 CK: 91%

Step 2 CS: 81%

Other: BS/MD program available for first-year undergraduate applicants. Meharry Medical College has partnerships with several undergraduate institutions. For more information, visit:https://home.mmc.edu/education/center-of-excellence/

UNIVERSITY OF TENNESSEE HEALTH SCIENCE CENTER COLLEGE OF MEDICINE

Address: 910 Madison Avenue, Ste 1031, Memphis, Tennessee 38163
Website: https://www.uthsc.edu/medicine/
Contact: https://www.uthsc.edu/contacts/
Phone: (901) 448-5561

Other locations: Chattanooga, TN; Knoxville, TN; Nashville, TN

COST OF ATTENDANCE

In-State Tuition: $36,566
Fees & Expenses: $25,976
Total: $60,542

Out-of-State Tuition: $60,489
Fees & Expenses: $30,503
Total: $86,465

Financial Aid: https://www.uthsc.edu/medicine/admissions/financial-aid.php

Percent Receiving Aid: 89%

ADDITIONAL INFORMATION

Interesting tidbit: UTHSC College of Medicine has three campuses - the Memphis Campus, the Knoxville campus, and the Chattanooga campus. Medical Students from the College of Medicine spend their first two years on the Memphis Campus and then rotate on all three Campuses for clinical training.

What percent of students participate in global health experiences? 6%

What service learning opportunities exist? Street Medicine, Clinica Esperanza, Refugee Empowerment Program, etc. For more information, visit:https://www.uthsc.edu/medicine/medical-education/service-learning.php

What dual degree options exist? MD/PhD

Important Updates due to COVID-19: Accept pass/fail grades for courses as well as online and/or virtual coursework (including labs) taken during the COVID-19 pandemic

Were tests required? MCAT required.

Are tests expected next year? Yes.

Postgraduate Training Match Rate: N/A

USMLE First-Time Pass Rate

Step 1: N/A

Step 2 CK: N/A

Step 2 CS: N/A

ALABAMA
ARKANSAS
DELAWARE
DISTRICT OF COLUMBIA
FLORIDA
GEORGIA
KENTUCKY
LOUISIANA
MARYLAND
MISSISSIPPI
NORTH CAROLINA
OKLAHOMA
SOUTH CAROLINA
TENNESSEE
TEXAS
VIRGINIA
WEST VIRGINIA

SOUTH

ALABAMA

ARKANSAS

DELAWARE

DISTRICT OF COLUMBIA

FLORIDA

GEORGIA

KENTUCKY

LOUISIANA

MARYLAND

MISSISSIPPI

NORTH CAROLINA

OKLAHOMA

SOUTH CAROLINA

TENNESSEE

TEXAS

VIRGINIA

WEST VIRGINIA

VANDERBILT UNIVERSITY SCHOOL OF MEDICINE

Address: 2209 Garland Drive, Nashville, TN 37240
Website: *https://medschool.vanderbilt.edu/*
Contact: *https://medschool.vanderbilt.edu/contact-information/*
Phone: (615) 322-2145

COST OF ATTENDANCE

Tuition: $63,610
Fees & Expenses: $36,328
Total: $99,938

Financial Aid: https://medschool.vanderbilt.edu/financial-aid/

Percent Receiving Aid: 78%

ADDITIONAL INFORMATION

Interesting tidbit: Health care is rapidly evolving and Vanderbilt School of Medicine's innovative curriculum ("Curriculum 2.0") prepares students to succeed in the future by focusing on how to learn. Curriculum 2.0 includes an enhanced focus on communication skills, individualized learning plans, and cultural competencies to meet the changing needs of health care.

What percent of students participate in global health experiences? 35%

What service learning opportunities exist? Service learning built into the curriculum. Students may also engage in community service through student organizations.

What dual degree options exist? MD/MPH:https://medschool.vanderbilt.edu/mph/md-mph-dual-degree/

MD/MBA: https://business.vanderbilt.edu/mba/curriculum/joint-degrees/

MD/JD: https://law.vanderbilt.edu/prospective-students/dual-degree-programs.php

MD/PhD: https://medschool.vanderbilt.edu/mstp/

Important Updates due to COVID-19: Accept P/F grading and online coursework.

Were tests required? MCAT required.

Are tests expected next year? Yes.

Postgraduate Training Match Rate: N/A

USMLE First-Time Pass Rate

Step 1: N/A

Step 2 CK: N/A

Step 2 CS: N/A

BAYLOR COLLEGE OF MEDICINE

Address: One Baylor Plaza, Houston, TX 77030
Website: *https://www.bcm.edu/*
Contact: *https://www.bcm.edu/contact-us*
Phone: (713) 798-4842

COST OF ATTENDANCE

In-State Tuition: $19,425
Fees & Expenses: $32,211*
Total: $51,636

Out-of-State Tuition: $32,525
Fees& Expenses: $32,211
Total: $64,376

*Living expenses are calculated using a monthly estimate of $2,163 for 11 months.

Financial Aid: https://www.bcm.edu/education/financial-aid

Percent Receiving Aid: 70%

ADDITIONAL INFORMATION

Interesting tidbit: Learning in the Texas Medical Center - the world's largest medical complex - students will have access to the diverse care settings and patient populations you need to be prepared wherever your career path leads.

What percent of students participate in global health experiences? 12%

What service learning opportunities exist? Serving underserved populations, global opportunities, and educational outreach. For more information, visit:https://www.bcm.edu/community

What dual degree options exist? MD/MPH, MD/MBA, MD/JD, and MD/PhD. For more information, visit:https://www.bcm.edu/education/school-of-medicine/m-d-program/dual-degrees

Important Updates due to COVID-19: Accept pass/fail grading for prerequisites courses taken in Spring 2020 semester. Permits online prerequisite coursework and labs are not required for Biochemistry and Organic Chemistry.

Were tests required? MCAT and CASPer required.

Are tests expected next year? Yes.

Postgraduate Training Match Rate: N/A

USMLE First-Time Pass Rate

Step 1: N/A

Step 2 CK: N/A

Step 2 CS: N/A

Other: Baylor2 Medical Track is an 8-year BA-BS/MD program available to high school applicants. For more information, visit:https://www.baylor.edu/admissions/index.php?id=872132

ALABAMA

ARKANSAS

DELAWARE

DISTRICT OF COLUMBIA

FLORIDA

GEORGIA

KENTUCKY

LOUISIANA

MARYLAND

MISSISSIPPI

NORTH CAROLINA

OKLAHOMA

SOUTH CAROLINA

TENNESSEE

TEXAS

VIRGINIA

WEST VIRGINIA

SOUTH

ALABAMA

ARKANSAS

DELAWARE

DISTRICT OF COLUMBIA

FLORIDA

GEORGIA

KENTUCKY

LOUISIANA

MARYLAND

MISSISSIPPI

NORTH CAROLINA

OKLAHOMA

SOUTH CAROLINA

TENNESSEE

TEXAS

VIRGINIA

WEST VIRGINIA

MCGOVERN MEDICAL SCHOOL AT THE UNIVERSITY OF TEXAS HEALTH SCIENCE CENTER AT HOUSTON

Address: 6431 Fannin Street, Houston, Texas 77030
Website: *https://med.uth.edu/*
Contact Email: *ms.admissions@uth.tmc.edu*
Phone: (713) 500-5116

COST OF ATTENDANCE

In-State Tuition: $18,604
Fees & Expenses: $32,143
Total: $50,747

Out-of-State Tuition: $26,125
Fees & Expenses: $32,143
Total: $58,268

Financial Aid: https://www.uth.edu/sfs/financial-aid/

Percent Receiving Aid: 67%

ADDITIONAL INFORMATION

Interesting tidbit: McGovern Medical School is the eighth-largest medical school in the United States. With more than 900 accredited residency and fellowship positions in specialty and subspecialties, it offers an incredible breadth of clinical training programs.

What percent of students participate in global health experiences? 18%

What service learning opportunities exist? Service learning through student organizations. For more information, visithttps://med.uth.edu/admissions/student-affairs/student-organizations/

What dual degree options exist? MD/MBA, MD/MPH, MD/OMFS, MD/MBE, MD/MS in Biomedical Informatics, and MD/PhD. For more information, visit:https://med.uth.edu/dualdegreeprograms/

Important Updates due to COVID-19: accept P/F grades and online coursework during the Spring 2020 or Winter 2020 semester from accredited institutions.

Were tests required? MCAT and CASPer required.

Are tests expected next year? Yes.

Postgraduate Training Match Rate: N/A

USMLE First-Time Pass Rate

Step 1: N/A

Step 2 CK: N/A

Step 2 CS: N/A

PAUL L. FOSTER SCHOOL OF MEDICINE TEXAS TECH UNIVERSITY HEALTH SCIENCES CENTER

Address: 5001 El Paso Drive, El Paso, TX 79905
Website: *https://elpaso.ttuhsc.edu/som/*
Contact Email: *fostersom.admissions@ttuhsc.edu*
Phone: (915) 215-4410

COST OF ATTENDANCE

In-State Tuition: $18,378
Fees & Expenses: $31,212
Total: $50,590

Out-of-State Tuition: $31,478
Fees & Expenses: $31,212
Total: $63,693

Financial Aid: https://elpaso.ttuhsc.edu/som/admissions/expenses.aspx

Percent Receiving Aid: 85%

ADDITIONAL INFORMATION

Interesting tidbit: As part of its curriculum, the PLFSOM requires all students to learn medical Spanish language skills. The PLFSOM is the only medical school in the U.S. with this requirement.

What percent of students participate in global health experiences? 19%

What service learning opportunities exist? Service learning through student organizations.

What dual degree options exist? MD/MPH. For more information, visit:https://elpaso.ttuhsc.edu/som/admissions/MPHOption.aspx

Important Updates due to COVID-19: Accept P/F grading and online prerequisite courses during the COVID 19 pandemic.

Were tests required? MCAT and CASPer required.

Are tests expected next year? Yes.

Postgraduate Training Match Rate: 100% (2021)

USMLE First-Time Pass Rate

Step 1: N/A

Step 2 CK: N/A

Step 2 CS: N/A

ALABAMA
ARKANSAS
DELAWARE
DISTRICT OF COLUMBIA
FLORIDA
GEORGIA
KENTUCKY
LOUISIANA
MARYLAND
MISSISSIPPI
NORTH CAROLINA
OKLAHOMA
SOUTH CAROLINA
TENNESSEE
TEXAS
VIRGINIA
WEST VIRGINIA

SOUTH

TCU AND UNTHSC SCHOOL OF MEDICINE

Address: 3430 Camp Bowie Boulevard, Fort Worth, TX 76107
Website: *https://mdschool.tcu.edu/*
Contact: *https://mdschool.tcu.edu/contact/*
Phone: (817) 735-7766

COST OF ATTENDANCE

Tuition: $60,318
Fees & Expenses: $29,578
Total: $89,896

Financial Aid: https://mdschool.tcu.edu/admissions/financial-aid/

Percent Receiving Aid: 100%

ADDITIONAL INFORMATION

Interesting tidbit: The Scholarly Pursuit and Thesis (SPT) course is integrated longitudinally throughout the School of Medicine four-year curriculum. The students will work closely with mentors they choose, course directors, and faculty to utilize these skills to develop a scholarly research prospectus. By the end of the SPT course, students will each write a capstone thesis and present their projects to the community at a research symposium showcasing their findings and innovative ideas for the future of medical research and patient care.

What percent of students participate in global health experiences? N/A

What service learning opportunities exist? Service learning through student organizations.

What dual degree options exist? No dual degree options listed.

Important Updates due to COVID-19: Accept online prerequisite courses. P/F grades considered on a case-by-case basis.

Were tests required? MCAT required.

Are tests expected next year? Yes.

Postgraduate Training Match Rate: N/A*

USMLE First-Time Pass Rate*

Step 1: N/A

Step 2 CK: N/A

Step 2 CS: N/A

***Note:** The inaugural class started in 2019, thus no USMLE nor match rate data yet.

TEXAS A&M UNIVERSITY HEALTH SCIENCE CENTER COLLEGE OF MEDICINE

Address: 8447 Riverside Pkwy, Bryan, TX 77807
Website: *https://medicine.tamu.edu/*
Contact Email: *admissions@medicine.tamhsc.edu*
Phone: (979) 436-0237

Other locations: Temple, TX; Round Rock, TX; Dallas, TX; Houston, TX; Corpus Christi, TX

COST OF ATTENDANCE

In-State Tuition: $21,760
Fees & Expenses: $30,750
Total: $52,510

Out-of-State Tuition: $34,860
Fees & Expenses: $31,156
Total: $66,016

Financial Aid: https://medicine.tamu.edu/financial-aid/index.html

Percent Receiving Aid: 80%

ADDITIONAL INFORMATION

Interesting tidbit: Texas A&M was established in 1876 as a military institution. Texas A&M College of Medicine honors Texas A&M University's rich military legacy. As part of the Cadet to Medicine program, current medical students serve as mentors to Corps of Cadets students.

What percent of students participate in global health experiences? 27%

What service learning opportunities exist? Service learning through student organizations. For more information, visit:https://medicine.tamu.edu/academics/students/organizations/index.html

What dual degree options exist? MD/MBA, MD/MPH, MD/MS in EDHP, and MD/MS in Medical Science. For more information, visit:https://medicine.tamu.edu/degrees/md-plus.html

MD/PhD: https://medicine.tamu.edu/degrees/md-phd.html

Important Updates due to COVID-19: Accept P/F grading and online prerequisite coursework and lab spring 2020 (including the winter 2020 quarter term) and summer 2020 terms.

Were tests required? MCAT and CASPer required.

Are tests expected next year? Yes.

Postgraduate Training Match Rate: N/A

USMLE First-Time Pass Rate

Step 1: N/A

Step 2 CK: N/A

Step 2 CS: N/A

ALABAMA
ARKANSAS
DELAWARE
DISTRICT OF COLUMBIA
FLORIDA
GEORGIA
KENTUCKY
LOUISIANA
MARYLAND
MISSISSIPPI
NORTH CAROLINA
OKLAHOMA
SOUTH CAROLINA
TENNESSEE
TEXAS
VIRGINIA
WEST VIRGINIA

SOUTH

ALABAMA

ARKANSAS

DELAWARE

DISTRICT OF
COLUMBIA

FLORIDA

GEORGIA

KENTUCKY

LOUISIANA

MARYLAND

MISSISSIPPI

NORTH CAROLINA

OKLAHOMA

SOUTH CAROLINA

TENNESSEE

TEXAS

VIRGINIA

WEST VIRGINIA

TEXAS TECH UNIVERSITY HEALTH SCIENCES CENTER SCHOOL OF MEDICINE

Address: 3601 4th Street, Lubbock, TX 79430
Website: *https://www.ttuhsc.edu/medicine/default.aspx*
Contact: *https://www.ttuhsc.edu/medicine/contact.aspx*
Phone: (806) 743-2297

Other locations: Amarillo, TX; Odessa, TX; Lubbock, TX

COST OF ATTENDANCE

Tuition: $17,411
Fees & Expenses: $33,792
Total: $51,203

Financial Aid: https://www.ttuhsc.edu/medicine/admissions/scholarship-information.aspx

Percent Receiving Aid: 84%

ADDITIONAL INFORMATION

Interesting tidbit: TTUHSC SOM pioneered the nation's first accelerated Family Medicine program, which remains one of its signature offerings. Students pursuing a career in Family Medicine can apply for this three-year program during their first year of medical school.

What percent of students participate in global health experiences? 25%

What service learning opportunities exist? Free Clinic, global health opportunities, and more. For more information, visit:https://www.ttuhsc.edu/student-affairs/free-clinic/

What dual degree options exist? MD/MPH:https://www.ttuhsc.edu/medicine/admissions/mdmph.aspx

MD/MBA:https://www.ttuhsc.edu/medicine/admissions/mdmba.aspx

MD/JD: https://www.ttuhsc.edu/medicine/admissions/mdjd.aspx

MD/PhD: https://www.ttuhsc.edu/biomedical-sciences/program/md-phd.aspx

Important Updates due to COVID-19: Accept online coursework & P/F courses.

Were tests required? MCAT and CASPer required.

Are tests expected next year? Yes.

Postgraduate Training Match Rate: N/A

USMLE First-Time Pass Rate

Step 1: N/A

Step 2 CK: N/A

Step 2 CS: N/A

THE UNIVERSITY OF TEXAS AT AUSTIN DELL MEDICAL SCHOOL

Address: 1501 Red River St, Austin, TX 78712
Website: *https://dellmed.utexas.edu/*
Contact: *https://dellmed.utexas.edu/about/contact-us*
Phone: (512) 495-5150

COST OF ATTENDANCE

In-State Tuition: $21,086
Fees & Expenses: $31,320
Total: $52,406

Out-of-State Tuition: $35,406
Fees & Expenses: $31,320
Total: $67,762

Financial Aid: https://dellmed.utexas.edu/education/student-resources/financial-aid

Percent Receiving Aid: 100%

ADDITIONAL INFORMATION

Interesting tidbit: Dell Med created a leading EDGE (Essentials, Delivery, Growth, and Exploration) curriculum. It begins with an accelerated pre-clinical curriculum (12 months) and leads to clerkships in the second year, a year earlier than most schools. The Growth "year" (nine-month block) provides students with the opportunity to gain experience in an area of personal interest and make progress toward individual goals. The Exploration year includes a capstone transition-to-residency experience.

What percent of students participate in global health experiences? 7%

What service learning opportunities exist? Service learning through student organizations.

What dual degree options exist? MD/MPH and MD/MBA. For more information, see "Dual Degree Options" at the bottom of this website:https://dellmed.utexas.edu/education/academics/undergraduate-medical-education/leading-edge-curriculum/year-3

Important Updates due to COVID-19: Accept P/F grading and online coursework for prerequisites.

Were tests required? MCAT required.

Are tests expected next year? Yes.

Postgraduate Training Match Rate: 100% (2021)

USMLE First-Time Pass Rate

Step 1: N/A

Step 2 CK: N/A

Step 2 CS: N/A

ALABAMA
ARKANSAS
DELAWARE
DISTRICT OF COLUMBIA
FLORIDA
GEORGIA
KENTUCKY
LOUISIANA
MARYLAND
MISSISSIPPI
NORTH CAROLINA
OKLAHOMA
SOUTH CAROLINA
TENNESSEE
TEXAS
VIRGINIA
WEST VIRGINIA

SOUTH

ALABAMA

ARKANSAS

DELAWARE

DISTRICT OF
COLUMBIA

FLORIDA

GEORGIA

KENTUCKY

LOUISIANA

MARYLAND

MISSISSIPPI

NORTH CAROLINA

OKLAHOMA

SOUTH CAROLINA

TENNESSEE

TEXAS

VIRGINIA

WEST VIRGINIA

THE UNIVERSITY OF TEXAS HEALTH SCIENCE CENTER AT SAN ANTONIO JOE R. AND TERESA LOZANO LONG SCHOOL OF MEDICINE

Address: 7703 Floyd Curl, San Antonio, TX 78229
Website: *http://som.uthscsa.edu/*
Contact Email: *LongSOM@uthscsa.edu*
Phone: (210) 567-6080

COST OF ATTENDANCE

In-State Tuition: $16,921
Fees & Expenses: $31,254
Total: $48,175

Out-of-State Tuition: $33,587
Fees & Expenses: $31,254
Total: $64,841

Financial Aid: https://oume.uthscsa.edu/admissions/fafsa-financial-aid-website/

Percent Receiving Aid: 84%

ADDITIONAL INFORMATION

Interesting tidbit: The Long School of Medicine does not have a secondary application.

What percent of students participate in global health experiences? 30%

What service learning opportunities exist? Service learning through student organizations.

What dual degree options exist? MD/MPH and MD/PhD. For more information, visit:https://oume.uthscsa.edu/curriculum/degree-programs/

Important Updates due to COVID-19: Accept P/F grading and online coursework for prerequisites

Were tests required? MCAT and CASPer required.

Are tests expected next year? Yes.

Postgraduate Training Match Rate: N/A

USMLE First-Time Pass Rate

Step 1: N/A

Step 2 CK: N/A

Step 2 CS: N/A

THE UNIVERSITY OF TEXAS MEDICAL BRANCH AT GALVESTON SCHOOL OF MEDICINE

Address: 301 University Boulevard, Galveston, TX 77555
Website: *https://som.utmb.edu/*
Contact: *https://www.utmb.edu/som/admissions-information/ welcome-meet-the-staff*
Phone: (409) 772-6958

COST OF ATTENDANCE

In-State Tuition: $20,271
Fees & Expenses: $34,390
Total: $54,580

Out-of-State Tuition: $34,981
Fees & Expenses: $34,390
Total: $69,291

Financial Aid: https://www.utmb.edu/enrollmentservices/ resources/financial-aid

Percent Receiving Aid: 71%

ADDITIONAL INFORMATION

Interesting tidbit: the University of Texas Medical Branch at Galveston (UTMB) School of Medicine encompasses thriving research and clinical enterprises across four campuses and seven hospitals. It is home to the Galveston National Laboratory, a level 4 federal biocontainment research facility, as well as clinical services and residency programs affiliated with NASA.

What percent of students participate in global health experiences? 21%

What service learning opportunities exist? Service learning through student organizations.

What dual degree options exist? MD/MBA, MD/MPH, MD/MS, and MD/PhD. For more information, visit:https://www.utmb.edu/som/ medical-education/degree-programs

Important Updates due to COVID-19: Accept P/F grading and online coursework for prerequisites

Were tests required? MCAT and CASPer required.

Are tests expected next year? Yes.

Postgraduate Training Match Rate: N/A

USMLE First-Time Pass Rate

Step 1: N/A

Step 2 CK: N/A

Step 2 CS: N/A

ALABAMA

ARKANSAS

DELAWARE

DISTRICT OF COLUMBIA

FLORIDA

GEORGIA

KENTUCKY

LOUISIANA

MARYLAND

MISSISSIPPI

NORTH CAROLINA

OKLAHOMA

SOUTH CAROLINA

TENNESSEE

TEXAS

VIRGINIA

WEST VIRGINIA

SOUTH

THE UNIVERSITY OF TEXAS RIO GRANDE VALLEY SCHOOL OF MEDICINE

Address: 1201 W University Dr, Edinburg, TX 78539
Website: *https://www.utrgv.edu/school-of-medicine/*
Contact: *https://www.utrgv.edu/school-of-medicine/contact/index.htm*
Phone: (956) 296-1600

COST OF ATTENDANCE

In-State Tuition: $19,639
Fees & Expenses: $28,317
Total: $47,956

Out-of-State Tuition: $32,739
Fees & Expenses: $28,317
Total: $61,056

Financial Aid: https://www.utrgv.edu/som/admissions/tuition-and-financial-aid/index.htm

Percent Receiving Aid: 100%

ADDITIONAL INFORMATION

Interesting tidbit: The UTRGV School of Medicine received preliminary accreditation from the LCME in October 2015, which allowed the School of Medicine to recruit for its first class. It is in the process of obtaining required provisional and full accreditation.

What percent of students participate in global health experiences? 12%

What service learning opportunities exist? UniMovil mobile health clinic, Area Health Education Centers (AHEC), student organizations, etc. For more information, visit:https://www.utrgv.edu/school-of-medicine/about/community/index.htm

What dual degree options exist? MD/MPH, MD/MS in Bioethics, and MD/MS in Biomedical Informatics. For more information, visit:https://www.utrgv.edu/som/admissions/som-programs/index.htm

Important Updates due to COVID-19: Accept P/F grading and online coursework for prerequisites.

Were tests required? MCAT required.

Are tests expected next year? Yes.

Postgraduate Training Match Rate: N/A

USMLE First-Time Pass Rate

Step 1: N/A

Step 2 CK: N/A

Step 2 CS: N/A

Other: Vaqueros MD, an Early Assurance Program (EAP), is available to South Texas high school applicants. For more information, visit:https://www.utrgv.edu/som/admissions/som-programs/index.htm

ALABAMA
ARKANSAS
DELAWARE
DISTRICT OF COLUMBIA
FLORIDA
GEORGIA
KENTUCKY
LOUISIANA
MARYLAND
MISSISSIPPI
NORTH CAROLINA
OKLAHOMA
SOUTH CAROLINA
TENNESSEE
TEXAS
VIRGINIA
WEST VIRGINIA

THE UNIVERSITY OF TEXAS SOUTHWESTERN MEDICAL SCHOOL

Address: 5323 Harry Hines Boulevard, Dallas, TX 75390
Website: *https://www.utsouthwestern.edu/education/medical-school/*
Contact: *https://www.utsouthwestern.edu/about-us/contact-us/*
Phone: (214) 648-5617

COST OF ATTENDANCE

In-State Tuition: $22,651
Fees & Expenses: $30,024
Total: $52,675

Out-of-State Tuition: $35,751
Fees & Expenses: $30,024
Total: $65,775

Financial Aid: https://www.utsouthwestern.edu/education/medical-school/admissions/cost-financial-aid.html

Percent Receiving Aid: 76%

ADDITIONAL INFORMATION

Interesting tidbit: Academic Colleges are small learning communities that bring together experienced faculty leaders with small groups of six students to observe and mirror the professional clinical skills, behaviors, and attitudes of a highly experienced physician. Students are assigned to one of the six Colleges on their first day of medical school and remain in their College for all four years of their education.

What percent of students participate in global health experiences? 24%

What service learning opportunities exist? Global health opportunities, volunteer service projects, student organizations, etc. For more information, visit:https://www.utsouthwestern.edu/education/students/community-service/

What dual degree options exist? MD/MPH, MD/MBA, and MD/PhD. For more information, visit:https://www.utsouthwestern.edu/education/medical-school/degrees-pathways/

Important Updates due to COVID-19: Accept P/F grading and online coursework for prerequisites.

Were tests required? MCAT and CASPer required.

Are tests expected next year? Yes.

Postgraduate Training Match Rate: N/A

USMLE First-Time Pass Rate

Step 1: N/A

Step 2 CK: N/A

Step 2 CS: N/A

ALABAMA
ARKANSAS
DELAWARE
DISTRICT OF COLUMBIA
FLORIDA
GEORGIA
KENTUCKY
LOUISIANA
MARYLAND
MISSISSIPPI
NORTH CAROLINA
OKLAHOMA
SOUTH CAROLINA
TENNESSEE
TEXAS
VIRGINIA
WEST VIRGINIA

SOUTH

ALABAMA

ARKANSAS

DELAWARE

DISTRICT OF COLUMBIA

FLORIDA

GEORGIA

KENTUCKY

LOUISIANA

MARYLAND

MISSISSIPPI

NORTH CAROLINA

OKLAHOMA

SOUTH CAROLINA

TENNESSEE

TEXAS

VIRGINIA

WEST VIRGINIA

UNIVERSITY OF HOUSTON COLLEGE OF MEDICINE

Address: 4849 Calhoun Road, Houston, Texas 77204
Website: *https://www.uh.edu/medicine/*
Contact: *https://www.uh.edu/medicine/contact-us/*
Phone: (713) 743-7047

COST OF ATTENDANCE

In-State Tuition: $24,264
Fees & Expenses: $25,598
Total: $47,862

Out-of-State Tuition: $37,361
Fees & Expenses: $25,598
Total: $60,960

Financial Aid: https://www.uh.edu/medicine/admissions/scholarship-financial-aid/

Percent Receiving Aid: N/A

ADDITIONAL INFORMATION

Interesting tidbit: Only applications submitted via TMDSAS will be accepted. Applicants cannot apply to the M.D. program through The American Medical College Application Service (AMCAS).

What percent of students participate in global health experiences? N/A*

What service learning opportunities exist? Household-Centered Care that focuses on health promotion activities and supporting individuals in households that face health disparities. For more information, visit: https://www.uh.edu/medicine/community-health/

What dual degree options exist? No dual degree options listed.

Important Updates due to COVID-19: Accept P/F grades for the terms impacted by COVID-19.

Were tests required? MCAT required.

Are tests expected next year? Yes.

Postgraduate Training Match Rate: N/A*

USMLE First-Time Pass Rate*

Step 1: N/A

Step 2 CK: N/A

Step 2 CS: N/A

*Note: This school will have its inaugural class start in 2020. No information on USMLE nor Match Rate.

EASTERN VIRGINIA MEDICAL SCHOOL

Address: 700 W. Olney Road, Norfolk, VA 23507
Website: *https://www.evms.edu/*
Contact: *https://www.evms.edu/contact_us/*
Phone: (757) 446-5812

COST OF ATTENDANCE

In-State Tuition: $33,105
Fees & Expenses: $28,377
Total: $61,482

Out-of-State Tuition: $56,382
Fees & Expenses: $28,377
Total: $84,759

Financial Aid: https://www.evms.edu/education/financial_aid/

Percent Receiving Aid: 87%

ADDITIONAL INFORMATION

Interesting tidbit: EVMS' new CareForward curriculum for MD students was one of only four winners of the Creating Value Challenge, a national competition. CareForward was honored as one of only two Teaching Value winners, focused on improving medical education curricula around delivering high-value care.

What percent of students participate in global health experiences? 16%

What service learning opportunities exist? Community-Engaged Learning initiative throughout four years of medical school. Students also become mentors to new medical students along their service learning journey. For more information, visit:https://www.evms.edu/education/resources/community-engaged_learning/

What dual degree options exist? MD/MBA and MD/MPH. For more information, visit:https://www.evms.edu/education/medical_programs/

Important Updates due to COVID-19: Accept pass/fail grades for the 2019-20 and 2020-21 academic school years.

Were tests required? MCAT required.

Are tests expected next year? Yes.

Postgraduate Training Match Rate: 98% (2020)

USMLE First-Time Pass Rate (2019/20)

Step 1: 99%

Step 2 CK: 100%

Step 2 CS: N/A

ALABAMA
ARKANSAS
DELAWARE
DISTRICT OF COLUMBIA
FLORIDA
GEORGIA
KENTUCKY
LOUISIANA
MARYLAND
MISSISSIPPI
NORTH CAROLINA
OKLAHOMA
SOUTH CAROLINA
TENNESSEE
TEXAS
VIRGINIA
WEST VIRGINIA

SOUTH

ALABAMA

ARKANSAS

DELAWARE

DISTRICT OF
COLUMBIA

FLORIDA

GEORGIA

KENTUCKY

LOUISIANA

MARYLAND

MISSISSIPPI

NORTH CAROLINA

OKLAHOMA

SOUTH CAROLINA

TENNESSEE

TEXAS

VIRGINIA

WEST VIRGINIA

UNIVERSITY OF VIRGINIA SCHOOL OF MEDICINE

Address: 200 Jeanette Lancaster Way, Charlottesville, VA 22903
Website: *https://med.virginia.edu/*
Contact: *https://med.virginia.edu/admissions/about/contact-us/*
Phone: (434) 924-5571

COST OF ATTENDANCE

In-State Tuition: $50,004
Fees & Expenses: $22,250
Total: $72,254

Out-of-State Tuition: $61,114
Fees & Expenses: $22,250
Total: $83,364

Financial Aid: https://med.virginia.edu/financial-aid/

Percent Receiving Aid: 81%

ADDITIONAL INFORMATION

Interesting tidbit: UVA School of Medicine's Patient Student Partnership (PSP) program is a longitudinal patient experience for UVA medical students. All students are assigned a chronically ill or elderly patient at the beginning of their first year that they follow throughout all four years of medical school.

What percent of students participate in global health experiences? 26%

What service learning opportunities exist? Service learning is embedded in the curriculum. A course, "Social Issues in Medicine" is required for first-year medical students. Students volunteer at various free clinics to help underserved populations. For more information, visit:https://med.virginia.edu/diversity/community/community-programs/programs-for-the-underserved/

What dual degree options exist? MD/MBA, MD/MPH, MD/JD, MD/MS in Clinical Research, MD/MS in Data Science, and MD/PhD. For more information, visit:https://med.virginia.edu/admissions/

Important Updates due to COVID-19: Honor any institutional policies regarding courses shifted to pass/fai. lEmploy a holistic admission review without prerequisites or specifications on lab work or online work.

Were tests required? MCAT required.

Are tests expected next year? Yes.

Postgraduate Training Match Rate: 99% (2018)

USMLE First-Time Pass Rate (2020)

Step 1: 99%

Step 2 CK: 99%

Step 2 CS: 98%

VIRGINIA COMMONWEALTH UNIVERSITY SCHOOL OF MEDICINE

Address: 1201 E Marshall St #4-100, Richmond, VA 23298
Website: *https://medschool.vcu.edu/*
Contact: see "MD Admissions Contacts": *https://medschool.vcu.edu/admissions/md/*
Phone: (804) 828-9630
Other locations: Falls Church, VA

COST OF ATTENDANCE

In-State Tuition: $33,751
Fees & Expenses: $37,442
Total: $71,193

Out-of-State Tuition: $56,577
Fees & Expenses: $38,132
Total: $94,709

Financial Aid: https://medschool.vcu.edu/about/deans-office/financial-aid/
Percent Receiving Aid: 72%

ADDITIONAL INFORMATION

Interesting tidbit: The Medical College of Virginia, precursor to VCU School of Medicine, was the first in the country to expand the medical school curriculum to four years. Today it has grown to serve as the area's only Level I Trauma Center as well as a major referral center for the Southeast.

What percent of students participate in global health experiences? 29%

What service learning opportunities exist? Service learning through student organizations and community-based partnerships.

What dual degree options exist? MD/PMHA, MD/MPH, and MD/PhD. For more information, visit:https://medschool.vcu.edu/admissions/combineddual-degree-opportunities-admissions/

Important Updates due to COVID-19: Accept courses that are pass/fail and online prerequisite coursework and laboratory courses for spring and summer 2021.

Were tests required? MCAT and CASPer required.

Are tests expected next year? Yes.

Postgraduate Training Match Rate: 94.1% (2021)

USMLE First-Time Pass Rate

Step 1: N/A

Step 2 CK: N/A

Step 2 CS: N/A

Other: VCU Guaranteed Admission Program (BS/MD) available to high school applicants. For more information, visit:https://honors.vcu.edu/admissions/guaranteed-admission/

ALABAMA
ARKANSAS
DELAWARE
DISTRICT OF COLUMBIA
FLORIDA
GEORGIA
KENTUCKY
LOUISIANA
MARYLAND
MISSISSIPPI
NORTH CAROLINA
OKLAHOMA
SOUTH CAROLINA
TENNESSEE
TEXAS
VIRGINIA
WEST VIRGINIA

SOUTH

VIRGINIA TECH CARILION SCHOOL OF MEDICINE

Address: 2 Riverside Circle, Roanoke, VA 24016
Website: *https://medicine.vtc.vt.edu/*
Contact: *https://medicine.vtc.vt.edu/about/contact.html*
Phone: (540) 526-2560

COST OF ATTENDANCE

Tuition: $54,653
Fees & Expenses: $27,675
Total: $82,328

Financial Aid: https://medicine.vtc.vt.edu/student-life/financial-aid.html

Percent Receiving Aid: 99%

ADDITIONAL INFORMATION

Interesting tidbit: The Virginia Tech Carilion School of Medicine is formed as a unique, public-private partnership between a cutting-edge research university (Virginia Tech) and a major health care institution (Carilion Clinic).

What percent of students participate in global health experiences? 10%

What service learning opportunities exist? Medicine and Health Day, Bradley Free Clinic, and a year-long service learning project requirement. For more information, visit:https://medicine.vtc.vt.edu/academics/distinctive-programs.html

What dual degree options exist? MD/MPH, MD/MBA, MD/MS in Translational Biology, Medicine, and Health, and MD/PhD. For more information, visit:https://medicine.vtc.vt.edu/academics/advanced-degree-opportunities.html

Important Updates due to COVID-19: Accept online coursework, labs, and pass/fail credits.

Were tests required? MCAT and CASPer required.

Are tests expected next year? Yes.

Postgraduate Training Match Rate: 100%

USMLE First-Time Pass Rate

Step 1: N/A

Step 2 CK: N/A

Step 2 CS: N/A

ALABAMA

ARKANSAS

DELAWARE

DISTRICT OF COLUMBIA

FLORIDA

GEORGIA

KENTUCKY

LOUISIANA

MARYLAND

MISSISSIPPI

NORTH CAROLINA

OKLAHOMA

SOUTH CAROLINA

TENNESSEE

TEXAS

VIRGINIA

WEST VIRGINIA

MARSHALL UNIVERSITY JOAN C. EDWARDS SCHOOL OF MEDICINE

Address: 1600 Medical Center Drive, Suite 1400, Huntington, WV, 25701
Website: *https://jcesom.marshall.edu/*
Contact: *https://jcesom.marshall.edu/admissions/contact-us/*
Phone: (800) 544-8514

COST OF ATTENDANCE

In-State Tuition: $23,094
Fees & Expenses: $21,495*
Total: $44,589

Out-of-State Tuition: $54,772
Fees & Expenses: $21,495*
Total: $76,267

*Health insurance costs to be added if elected.

Financial Aid: https://jcesom.marshall.edu/students/financial-assistance/

Percent Receiving Aid: 93%

ADDITIONAL INFORMATION

Interesting tidbit: Beginning with the 2022 Admissions Cycle (class entering in fall 2022) all applicants to Marshall University Joan C. Edwards School of Medicine will be required to complete a Situational Judgment Test (SJT) as part of the application for the Regular MD and MD/PhD programs.

What percent of students participate in global health experiences? 36%

What service learning opportunities exist? Service learning through student organizations. For more information, visit:https://jcesom.marshall.edu/students/community-service/

What dual degree options exist? MD/PhD. For more information, visit:https://jcesom.marshall.edu/research/office-of-research-and-graduate-education/graduate-education-programs/mdphd/

Important Updates due to COVID-19: Consider COVID-19–related disruptions in the review of applications (P/F, online coursework, delayed or cancelled MCAT, etc.) and review each candidate individually based on each candidate's unique circumstances.

Were tests required? MCAT and CASPer required.

Are tests expected next year? Yes (MCAT & SJT)

Postgraduate Training Match Rate: 100% (2021)

USMLE First-Time Pass Rate

Step 1: N/A

Step 2 CK: N/A

Step 2 CS: N/A

Other: BS/MD 7-year program available to West Virginia high school applicants. For more information, visit:https://jcesom.marshall.edu/students/bsmd-program/

ALABAMA
ARKANSAS
DELAWARE
DISTRICT OF COLUMBIA
FLORIDA
GEORGIA
KENTUCKY
LOUISIANA
MARYLAND
MISSISSIPPI
NORTH CAROLINA
OKLAHOMA
SOUTH CAROLINA
TENNESSEE
TEXAS
VIRGINIA
WEST VIRGINIA

SOUTH

WEST VIRGINIA UNIVERSITY SCHOOL OF MEDICINE

Address: 64 Medical Center Drive, Morgantown, WV 26506
Website: *https://medicine.hsc.wvu.edu/*
Contact: *https://medicine.hsc.wvu.edu/about/contact-us/*
Phone: (304) 293-2408

Other locations: Charleston, WV; Martinsburg, WV

COST OF ATTENDANCE

In-State Tuition: $20,124
Fees & Expenses: $12,587
Total: $32,771

Out-of-State Tuition: $40,824
Fees & Expenses: $17,487
Total: $58,311

Financial Aid: https://medicine.hsc.wvu.edu/md-admissions/tuition-and-aid/

Percent Receiving Aid: 86%

ADDITIONAL INFORMATION

Interesting tidbit: There are three campuses - Morgantown (main campus), Charleston, and Eastern. The main campus in Morgantown is located in the WVU Health Sciences Center. Most WVU medical students undergo a portion of their training at these off-campus sites where they learn the demands of rural health care first-hand.

What percent of students participate in global health experiences? 27%

What service learning opportunities exist? Service learning through student organizations.

What dual degree options exist? MD/PhD. For more information, visit:https://www.hsc.wvu.edu/resoff/graduate-education/phd-programs/mdphd-scholars-program/

Important Updates due to COVID-19: Online courses (including labs) and pass/fail grades are acceptable.

Were tests required? MCAT required. CASPer encouraged (testing for the 2022 cycle is optional).

Are tests expected next year? Yes.

Postgraduate Training Match Rate: N/A

USMLE First-Time Pass Rate

Step 1: N/A

Step 2 CK: N/A

Step 2 CS: N/A

CHAPTER 5

REGION FOUR
WEST

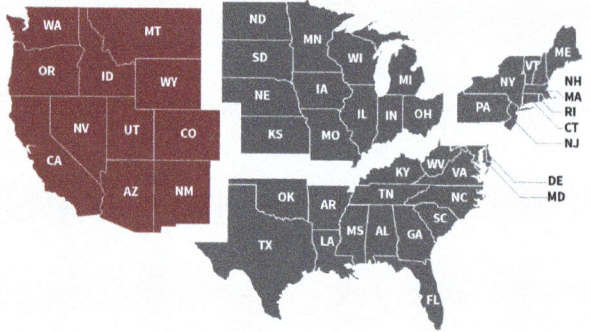

ALASKA

ARIZONA

CALIFORNIA

COLORADO

HAWAII

IDAHO

MONTANA

NEVADA

NEW MEXICO

OREGON

UTAH

WASHINGTON

WYOMING

23 *Programs* | 13 *States*

MEDICAL PROGRAMS

Medical School	Ave. GPA & MCAT / Early Decision (ED): Yes/No / Int'l Students: Yes/No / Reapps: Yes/No	Admissions Statistics	Science Req. Other than Gen Chem, OChem, Physics, Bio
The University of Arizona – Phoenix 475 North 5th Street, Phoenix, AZ 85004	3.84 (overall) 3.81 (science) MCAT: 515 ED: No Int'l Student: No Reapps: N/A	**(2019)** Apps Received: 5,835 Interview Received: 368 Number Enrolled: 80 Admitted Rate: 1.4% **(2020)** Apps Received: 6,079 Interview Received: 396 Number Enrolled: 100 Admitted Rate: 1.6%	Physio. Biochem.
The University of Arizona – Tucson 1501 N. Campbell Ave., Tucson, AZ 85724	3.79 (overall) 3.72 (science) MCAT: 510 ED: No Int'l Student: No Reapps: N/A	**(2019)** Apps Received: 9,940 Interview Received: 482 Number Enrolled: 119 Admitted Rate: 1.2% **(2020)** Apps Received: 9,563 Interview Received: 476 Number Enrolled: 117 Admitted Rate: 1.2%	Biochem. Cell Bio., Histology, Microbio., Pharmacology, Pathology, or Immunology Physio. Genetics. Molecular Bio. or Nucleic Acids
California Northstate University 9700 W. Taron Dr., Elk Grove, CA 95757	3.72 (overall) 3.64 (science) MCAT: 513 ED: Yes Int'l Student: Yes (case by case) Reapps: N/A	**(2019)** Apps Received: 4,184 Interview Received: 357 Number Enrolled: 96 Admitted Rate: 2.3% **(2020)** Apps Received: 4,427 Interview Received: 357 Number Enrolled: 101 Admitted Rate: 2.3%	Biochem.
California University of Science and Medicine 1501 Violet Street, Colton, CA 92324	3.68 (overall) 3.59 (science) MCAT: 512 ED: Yes Int'l Student: No Reapps: Yes	**(2019)** Apps Received: 5,494 Interview Received: 442 Number Enrolled: 98 Admitted Rate: 1.8% **(2020)** Apps Received: 5,383 Interview Received: 5453 Number Enrolled: 130, Admitted Rate: 2.4%	N/A See Chart.

Medical School	Ave. GPA & MCAT / Early Decision (ED): Yes/No / Int'l Students: Yes/No / Reapps: Yes/No	Admissions Statistics	Science Req. Other than Gen Chem, OChem, Physics, Bio
UCLA 885 Tiverton Drive, Los Angeles, CA 90095	3.84 (overall) 3.80 (science) MCAT: 516 ED: No Int'l Student: Yes Reapps: Yes	**(2019)** Apps Received: 13,101 Interview Received: 945 Number Enrolled: 180 Admitted Rate: 1.4% **(2020)** Apps Received: 11,778 Interview Received: 835 Number Enrolled: 175 Admitted Rate: 1.5%	N/A See Chart.
Kaiser Permanente School of Medicine 98 S. Los Robles Ave., Pasadena, CA 91101	3.87 (overall) 3.85 (science) MCAT: 516 ED: No Int'l Student: No Reapps: N/A	**(2019)** Apps Received: N/A Interview Received: N/A Number Enrolled: N/A Admitted Rate: N/A **(2020)** Apps Received: 10,478 Interview Received: 718 Number Enrolled: 50 Admitted Rate: 0.5%	N/A See Chart. *This medical school will have its inaugural class in 2020.
University of Southern California 1975 Zonal Ave., Los Angeles, CA 90033	3.76 (overall) 3.72 (science) MCAT: 517 ED: No Int'l Student: Yes (case by case) Reapps: Yes	**(2019)** Apps Received: 8,041 Interview Received: 736 Number Enrolled: 186 Admitted Rate: 2.3% **(2020)** Apps Received: 8,383 Interview Received: 721 Number Enrolled: 186 Admitted Rate: 2.2%	N/A See Chart.

WEST

MEDICAL PROGRAMS

Medical School	Ave. GPA & MCAT Early Decision (ED): Yes/No Int'l Students: Yes/No Reapps: Yes/No	Admissions Statistics	Science Req. Other than Gen Chem, OChem, Physics, Bio
Loma Linda University 11175 Campus St. Loma Linda, CA 92350	3.86 (overall) 3.82 (science) MCAT: 510 ED: Yes Int'l Student: Yes (case by case) Reapps: N/A	**(2019)** Apps Received: 6,318 Interview Received: 387 Number Enrolled: 168 Admitted Rate: 2.7% **(2020)** Apps Received: 6,192 Interview Received: 387 Number Enrolled: 168 Admitted Rate: 2.7%	Biochem.
Stanford University 291 Campus Drive, Li Ka Shing Building, Stanford, CA 94305	3.89 (overall) 3.88 (science) MCAT: 519 ED: No Int'l Student: Yes Reapps: N/A	**(2019)** Apps Received: 7,506 Interview Received: 480 Number Enrolled: 90 Admitted Rate: 1.2% **(2020)** Apps Received: 6,800 Interview Received: 469 Number Enrolled: 90 Admitted Rate: 1.3%	N/A See Chart.
University of California, Davis 4610 X Street, Sacramento, CA 95817	3.69 (overall) 3.64 (science) MCAT: 512 ED: No Int'l Student: Yes Reapps: N/A	**(2019)** Apps Received: 7,161 Interview Received: 482 Number Enrolled: 123 Admitted Rate: 1.7% **(2020)** Apps Received: 7,023 Interview Received: 485 Number Enrolled: 127 Admitted Rate: 1.8%	N/A See Chart.
University of California, Irvine 1001 Health Sciences Rd., Irvine, CA 92697	3.85 (overall) 3.83 (science) MCAT: 516 ED: No Int'l Student: No Reapps: N/A	**(2019)** Apps Received: 6,281 Interview Received: 600 Number Enrolled: 104 Admitted Rate: 1.7% **(2020)** Apps Received: 6,158 Interview Received: 558 Number Enrolled: 104 Admitted Rate: 1.7%	Biochem. Upper div. Bio.

Medical School	Ave. GPA & MCAT; Early Decision (ED): Yes/No; Int'l Students: Yes/No; Reapps: Yes/No	Admissions Statistics	Science Req. Other than Gen Chem, OChem, Physics, Bio
University of California, Riverside 900 University Ave., Riverside, CA 92521	3.59 (overall) 3.51 (science) MCAT: 508 ED: No Int'l Student: No Reapps: N/A	**(2019)** Apps Received: 5,902 Interview Received: 288 Number Enrolled: 77 Admitted Rate: 1.3% **(2020)** Apps Received: 5,669 Interview Received: 281 Number Enrolled: 78 Admitted Rate: 1.4%	Biochem.
University of California, San Diego 9500 Gilman Drive, La Jolla, CA 92093	3.83 (overall) 3.81 (science) MCAT: 517 ED: No Int'l Student: No Reapps: N/A	**(2019)** Apps Received: 7,398 Interview Received: 757 Number Enrolled: 134 Admitted Rate: 1.8% **(2020)** Apps Received: 7,741 Interview Received: 757 Number Enrolled: 133 Admitted Rate: 1.7%	N/A See Chart.
University of California, San Francisco 505 Parnassus Avenue, San Francisco, CA 94143	3.86 (overall) 3.86 (science) MCAT: 518 ED: No Int'l Student: No Reapps: N/A	**(2019)** Apps Received: 7,900 Interview Received: 468 Number Enrolled: 171 Admitted Rate: 2.2% **(2020)** Apps Received: 7,399 Interview Received: 507 Number Enrolled: 178 Admitted Rate: 2.4%	Biochem..

WEST

MEDICAL PROGRAMS

Medical School	Ave. GPA & MCAT / Early Decision (ED): Yes/No / Int'l Students: Yes/No / Reapps: Yes/No	Admissions Statistics	Science Req. Other than Gen Chem, OChem, Physics, Bio
University of Colorado 13001 E. 17th Place, Aurora, CO 80045	3.83 (overall) 3.80 (science) MCAT: 514 ED: No Int'l Student: Yes Reapps: N/A	**(2019)** Apps Received: 8,666 Interview Received: 654 Number Enrolled: 182 Admitted Rate: 2.1% **(2020)** Apps Received: 10,431 Interview Received: 706 Number Enrolled: 155 Admitted Rate: 1.5%	N/A See Chart.
The University of Hawaii at Manoa 651 Ilalo Street, Honolulu, HI 96813	3.84 (overall) 3.80 (science) MCAT: 513 ED: Yes Int'l Student: Yes Reapps: N/A	**(2019)** Apps Received: 1,980 Interview Received: 304 Number Enrolled: 77 Admitted Rate: 3.9% **(2020)** Apps Received: 2,175 Interview Received: 306 Number Enrolled: 77 Admitted Rate: 3.5%	Biochem.
University of Nevada, Las Vegas 2040 W. Charleston Blvd., 3rd Floor, Las Vegas, NV 89102	3.76 (overall) 3.68 (science) MCAT: 512 ED: Yes Int'l Student: No Reapps: N/A	**(2019)** Apps Received: 1,942 Interview Received: 304 Number Enrolled: 60 Admitted Rate: 3% **(2020)** Apps Received: 1,796 Interview Received: 308 Number Enrolled: 60 Admitted Rate: 3.3%	Biochem.
University of Nevada, Reno 1664 N. Virginia Street, Reno, NV 89557	3.82 (overall) 3.80 (science) MCAT: 509 ED: Yes Int'l Student: No Reapps: Yes	**(2019)** Apps Received: 1,484 Interview Received: 326 Number Enrolled: 68 Admitted Rate: 4.6% **(2020)** Apps Received: 1,643 Interview Received: 343 Number Enrolled: 70 Admitted Rate: 4.3%	Biochem. Upper Div. Science Biochem.

Medical School	Ave. GPA & MCAT Early Decision (ED): Yes/No Int'l Students: Yes/No Reapps: Yes/No	Admissions Statistics	Science Req. Other than Gen Chem, OChem, Physics, Bio
University of New Mexico 915 Camino de Salud, Albuquerque, NM 87106	3.80 (overall) 3.74 (science) MCAT: 505 ED: Yes Int'l Student: Yes (case by case) Reapps: N/A	**(2019)** Apps Received: 1,862 Interview Received: 231 Number Enrolled: 103 Admitted Rate: 5.5% **(2020)** Apps Received: 1,722 Interview Received: 250 Number Enrolled: 97 Admitted Rate: 5.6%	Biochem.
Oregon Health & Science University 2730 SW Moody Avenue, Portland, OR 97239	3.77 (overall) 3.72 (science) MCAT: 512 ED: No Int'l Student: Yes (case by case) Reapps: N/A	**(2019)** Apps Received: 6,209 Interview Received: 555 Number Enrolled: 160 Admitted Rate: 2.3% **(2020)** Apps Received: 6,555 Interview Received: 566 Number Enrolled: 150 Admitted Rate: 2.3%	N/A See Chart.
University of Utah 30 North 1900 East, Salt Lake City, UT 84132	3.82 (overall) 3.77 (science) MCAT: 513 ED: Yes Int'l Student: Yes Reapps: N/A 3.84	**(2019)** Apps Received: 3,850 Interview Received: 560 Number Enrolled: 125 Admitted Rate: 3.2% **(2020)** Apps Received: 3,406 Interview Received: 589 Number Enrolled: 125 Admitted Rate: 3.7%	Biochem. or Cell Bio.

WEST

MEDICAL PROGRAMS

Medical School	Ave. GPA & MCAT Early Decision (ED): Yes/No Int'l Students: Yes/No Reapps: Yes/No	Admissions Statistics	Science Req. Other than Gen Chem, OChem, Physics, Bio
University of Washington 1959 NE Pacific St., Seattle, WA 98195	3.74 (overall) 3.67 (science) MCAT: 512 ED: No Int'l Student: No Reapps: N/A	**(2019)** Apps Received: 8,190 Interview Received: 832 Number Enrolled: 270 Admitted Rate: 3.3% **(2020)** Apps Received: 7,572 Interview Received: 686 Number Enrolled: 270 Admitted Rate: 3.6%	N/A See Chart.
Washington State University 412 E. Spokane Falls Blvd., Spokane, WA 99202	3.67 (overall) 3.59 (science) MCAT: 510 ED: No Int'l Student: No Reapps: N/A	**(2019)** Apps Received: 1,554 Interview Received: 344 Number Enrolled: 80 Admitted Rate: 5.1% **(2020)** Apps Received: 1,444 Interview Received: 350 Number Enrolled: 80 Admitted Rate: 5.5%	N/A See Chart.

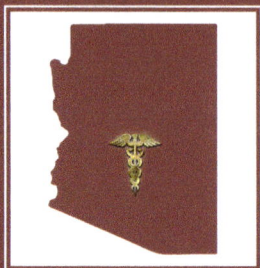

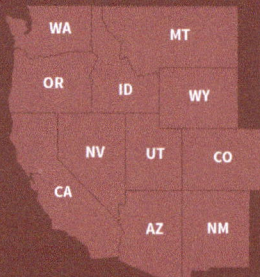

THE UNIVERSITY OF ARIZONA COLLEGE OF MEDICINE - PHOENIX

Address: 475 North 5th Street, Phoenix, AZ 85004
Website: *https://phoenixmed.arizona.edu/*
Contact: *https://phoenixmed.arizona.edu/contact*
Phone: (602) 827-2005

COST OF ATTENDANCE

In-State Tuition: $34,380
Fees & Expenses: $31,840
Total: $66,220

Out-of-State Tuition: $54,980
Fees & Expenses: $33,840
Total: $88,820

Financial Aid: https://phoenixmed.arizona.edu/financial-aid

Percent Receiving Aid: 92%

ADDITIONAL INFORMATION

Interesting tidbit: Every student at the College of Medicine-Phoenix designs and successfully completes a hypothesis-driven research Scholarly Project (SP). The college is one of only four medical schools in the country that requires every student to design and complete a four-year Scholarly Project.

What percent of students participate in global health experiences? 29%

What service-learning opportunities exist? Community Health Initiative – Phoenix (CHIP) is a student-run service-learning program that offers various opportunities for community service focused on uninsured and underserved individuals. For more information, visit:https://phoenixmed.arizona.edu/chip

What dual degree options exist? MD/MBA, MD/MPH, and MD/PhD. For more information, visit:https://phoenixmed.arizona.edu/education/dual-degrees

Important Updates due to COVID-19: Accept pass/fail graded courses taken during the COVID-19 pandemic regardless of whether you opted in or if pass/fail was implemented school-wide by your current university, and continue to accept online courses from regionally accredited institutions to meet any of our prerequisite course requirements.

Were tests required? MCAT required.

Are tests expected next year? Yes.

Postgraduate Training Match Rate: N/A

USMLE First-Time Pass Rate

Step 1: N/A

Step 2 CK: N/A

Step 2 CS: N/A

ALASKA

ARIZONA

CALIFORNIA

COLORADO

HAWAII

IDAHO

MONTANA

NEVADA

NEW MEXICO

OREGON

UTAH

WASHINGTON

WYOMING

THE UNIVERSITY OF ARIZONA COLLEGE OF MEDICINE – TUCSON

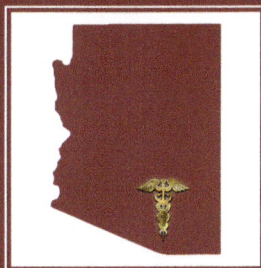

Address: 1501 N. Campbell Ave., Tucson, AZ 85724
Website: *https://medicine.arizona.edu/*
Contact: *https://medicine.arizona.edu/admissions/staff*
Phone: (520) 626-6214

COST OF ATTENDANCE

In-State Tuition: $34,910
Fees & Expenses: $27,400
Total: $62,314

Out-of-State Tuition: $55,514
Fees & Expenses: $27,400
Total: $82,914

Financial Aid: https://financial-aid.medicine.arizona.edu/

Percent Receiving Aid: 93%

ADDITIONAL INFORMATION

Interesting tidbit: The University of Arizona College of Medicine – Tucson, founded on the campus of the University of Arizona in 1967, was the state's first MD degree-granting college.

What percent of students participate in global health experiences? 22%

What service-learning opportunities exist? The Commitment to Underserved People (CUP) program is a student-run service-learning initiative. Students may also be in the community service distinction track. For more information, visit:https://medicine.arizona.edu/education/md-program/distinction-tracks/community-service

What dual degree options exist? MD/Ph.D. For more information, visit:https://mdphd.medicine.arizona.edu/

Important Updates due to COVID-19: Accept pass/fail grading for courses from Spring and Summer 2020.

Were tests required? MCAT required.

Are tests expected next year? Yes.

Postgraduate Training Match Rate: N/A

USMLE First-Time Pass Rate

Step 1: N/A

Step 2 CK: N/A

Step 2 CS: N/A

ALASKA

ARIZONA

CALIFORNIA

COLORADO

HAWAII

IDAHO

MONTANA

NEVADA

NEW MEXICO

OREGON

UTAH

WASHINGTON

WYOMING

WEST

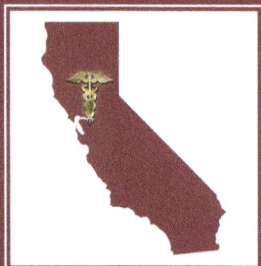

ALASKA

ARIZONA

CALIFORNIA

COLORADO

HAWAII

IDAHO

MONTANA

NEVADA

NEW MEXICO

OREGON

UTAH

WASHINGTON

WYOMING

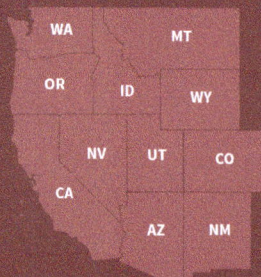

CALIFORNIA NORTHSTATE UNIVERSITY COLLEGE OF MEDICINE

Address: 9700 W. Taron Dr., Elk Grove, CA 95757
Website: *https://medicine.cnsu.edu/*
Contact: *https://medicine.cnsu.edu/contact/contact-us*
Phone: (916) 686-7300

COST OF ATTENDANCE

Tuition: $62,648
Fees & Expenses: $38,982
Total: $101,630

Financial Aid: http://www.cnsu.edu/student-financial-aid-office/student-financial-aid-officem

Percent Receiving Aid: 70%

ADDITIONAL INFORMATION

Interesting tidbit: California Northstate University College of Medicine is at Step 4, or "Accredited, Provisional Status," of a five-step accreditation process.

What percent of students participate in global health experiences? 15%

What service-learning opportunities exist? Students work with community organizations. For more information, visit:https://medicine.cnsu.edu/students-com/service-learning-activities/service-learning-activities

What dual degree options exist? No dual degree options listed.

Important Updates due to COVID-19: Distance-learning Science coursework and lab work with pass/fail grades will be taken into consideration for the fulfillment of prerequisites, case by case. Consider MCAT scores as soon as they are received.

Were tests required? MCAT required.

Are tests expected next year? Yes.

Postgraduate Training Match Rate: 98% (2021)

USMLE First-Time Pass Rate

Step 1: N/A

Step 2 CK: N/A

Step 2 CS: N/A

Other: BS/MD 6-year/7-year program available to high school applicants. For more information, visit:http://healthsciences.cnsu.edu/programs-offered/bs-md-combined-program/about

CALIFORNIA UNIVERSITY OF SCIENCE AND MEDICINE – SCHOOL OF MEDICINE

Address: 1501 Violet Street, Colton, CA 92324
Website: *https://www.cusm.org/*
Contact *Email: Admissions@cusm.org*
Phone: (909) 490-5910

COST OF ATTENDANCE

Tuition: $60,000
Fees & Expenses: $23,991
Total: $83,991

Financial Aid: https://www.cusm.org/school-of-medicine/financial-aid/getting-started.php

Percent Receiving Aid: 49%

ADDITIONAL INFORMATION

Interesting tidbit: CUSM-SOM was granted Preliminary Accreditation in February 2018.

What percent of students participate in global health experiences? N/A

What service-learning opportunities exist? service-learning through student organizations.

What dual degree options exist? No dual degree options listed.

Important Updates due to COVID-19: N/A

Were tests required? MCAT required.

Are tests expected next year? Yes.

Postgraduate Training Match Rate: N/A*

USMLE First-Time Pass Rate*

Step 1: N/A

Step 2 CK: N/A

Step 2 CS: N/A

*Note: This medical school welcomed its inaugural class in 2018. Thus, no USMLE nor match rate data yet.

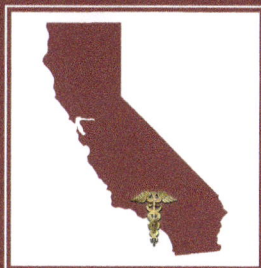

ALASKA

ARIZONA

CALIFORNIA

COLORADO

HAWAII

IDAHO

MONTANA

NEVADA

NEW MEXICO

OREGON

UTAH

WASHINGTON

WYOMING

WEST

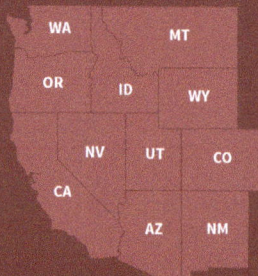

DAVID GEFFEN SCHOOL OF MEDICINE AT UCLA

Address: 885 Tiverton Drive, Los Angeles, CA 90095
Website: *https://medschool.ucla.edu/*
Contact: *https://medschool.ucla.edu/contact-us*
Phone: (310) 825-6081

COST OF ATTENDANCE

In-State Tuition: $43,726
Fees & Expenses: $34,320
Total: $78,046

Out-of-State Tuitio: $55,975
Fees & Expenses: $34,320
Total: $90,291

Financial Aid: https://medschool.ucla.edu/current-financial-aid-scholarships

Percent Receiving Aid: 90%

ADDITIONAL INFORMATION

Interesting tidbit: In just 60 years, the David Geffen School of Medicine at UCLA has joined the ranks of the nation's elite medical schools. Classes were initially held in what had been the reception lounge of the old Religious Conference Building on Le Conte Avenue.

What percent of students participate in global health experiences? 19%

What service-learning opportunities exist? Student-run homeless clinic, mobile clinic, Care Harbor clinic, etc. For more information, visit:https://medschool.ucla.edu/apply-service-opportunities

What dual degree options exist? MD/MBA, MD/MPH, MD/MPP, MD/DDS, and MD/PhD. For more information, visit:https://medschool.ucla.edu/current-articulated-concurrent

Important Updates due to COVID-19: Accept pass/fail grades, without prejudice, for courses taken during the COVID-19 pandemic. Online courses or courses moved to virtual delivery due to the COVID-19 pandemic will be acceptable for admissions consideration as long as these grades appear on your official transcript of grades from your accredited institution.

Were tests required? MCAT required.

Are tests expected next year? Yes.

Postgraduate Training Match Rate: N/A

USMLE First-Time Pass Rate

Step 1: N/A

Step 2 CK: N/A

Step 2 CS: N/A

KAISER PERMANENTE SCHOOL OF MEDICINE

Address: 98 S. Los Robles Ave., Pasadena, CA 91101
Website: *https://medschool.kp.org/*
Contact: *https://medschool.kp.org/about/offices-and-departments/office-of-admissions#OffAdmiss_Contact*
Phone: (888) 576-3348

COST OF ATTENDANCE

Tuition: $0
Fees & Expenses: $34,600
Total: $34,600

Financial Aid: Kaiser Permanente will waive all tuition and fees for classes entering in the fall of 2020 through 2024. Students enrolled in the first five cohorts at the school will receive a waiver for the cost of a health plan from Kaiser Permanente, unless they have an equivalent health plan. These first five cohorts of students are only responsible to pay for their living expenses. For more information, visit:https://medschool.kp.org/admissions/tuition-and-financial-aid

*Note: These figures reflect Kaiser Permanente's estimated student living expenses.

Percent Receiving Aid: N/A

ADDITIONAL INFORMATION

Interesting tidbit: Kaiser Permanente School of Medicine welcomed its inaugural class in 2020.

What percent of students participate in global health experiences? N/A

What service-learning opportunities exist? service-learning in the curriculum. Students volunteer at community health clinics, support health education in local schools, prepare meals for local homeless shelters, etc. For more information, visit:https://medschool.kp.org/student-life/service-learning

What dual degree options exist? MD/Ph.D. For more information, visit:https://medschool.kp.org/homepage

Important Updates due to COVID-19: Accept Pass/Fail grades, without prejudice, for courses taken by applicants during the COVID-19 pandemic.

Were tests required? MCAT required.

Are tests expected next year? Yes.

Postgraduate Training Match Rate: N/A*

USMLE First-Time Pass Rate

Step 1: N/A*

Step 2 CK: N/A*

Step 2 CS: N/A*

*Note: This medical school had its inaugural class in July 2020. Thus, no USMLE nor match rate data yet.

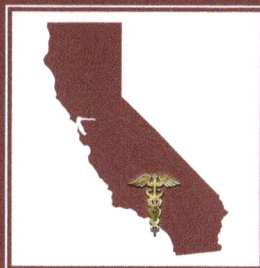

ALASKA

ARIZONA

CALIFORNIA

COLORADO

HAWAII

IDAHO

MONTANA

NEVADA

NEW MEXICO

OREGON

UTAH

WASHINGTON

WYOMING

WEST

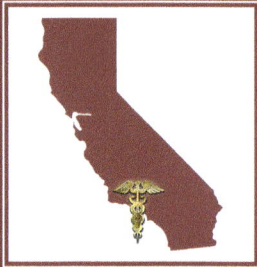

ALASKA

ARIZONA

CALIFORNIA

COLORADO

HAWAII

IDAHO

MONTANA

NEVADA

NEW MEXICO

OREGON

UTAH

WASHINGTON

WYOMING

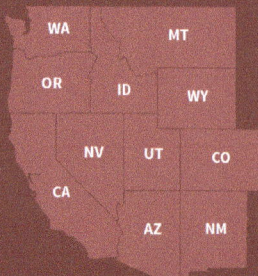

KECK SCHOOL OF MEDICINE OF THE UNIVERSITY OF SOUTHERN CALIFORNIA

Address: 1975 Zonal Ave., Los Angeles, CA 90033
Website: *https://keck.usc.edu/*
Contact: *https://keck.usc.edu/education/md-program/contact-us/*
Phone: (323) 442-2552

COST OF ATTENDANCE

Tuition: $66,150
Fees & Expenses: $32,006
Total: $98,156

Financial Aid: https://keck.usc.edu/education/md-program/financial-aid/

Percent Receiving Aid: 80%

ADDITIONAL INFORMATION

Interesting tidbit: All students train at the Los Angeles County + USC Medical Center, one of the largest medical teaching centers in the United States. Through affiliations with over a dozen other private and public hospitals, students receive a remarkably broad clinical training experience.

What percent of students participate in global health experiences? 18%

What service-learning opportunities exist? Education programs, USC student-run clinic, health science mentors, etc. For more information, visit:https://keck.usc.edu/community-engagement/

What dual degree options exist? MD/MPH, MD/MBA, and MD/Ph.D. For more information, visit:https://keck.usc.edu/education/md-program/combined-degrees/

Important Updates due to COVID-19: Accept pass/fail grades, without prejudice, for courses taken during the COVID-19 pandemic.

Were tests required? MCAT required.

Are tests expected next year? Yes.

Postgraduate Training Match Rate: 98% (2021)

USMLE First-Time Pass Rate

Step 1: N/A

Step 2 CK: N/A

Step 2 CS: N/A

LOMA LINDA UNIVERSITY SCHOOL OF MEDICINE

Address: 11175 Campus St. Loma Linda, CA 92350
Website: *https://medicine.llu.edu/*
Contact: *https://medicine.llu.edu/about/contact-us*
Phone: (909) 558-4467

COST OF ATTENDANCE

Tuition: $59,452
Fees & Expenses: $24,215
Total: $83,667

Financial Aid: https://medicine.llu.edu/admissions/medical-school-admissions/financial-aid

Percent Receiving Aid: 97%

ADDITIONAL INFORMATION

Interesting tidbit: Loma Linda University is a Seventh-day Adventist university, offering a unique learning environment through the integration of health, science, and faith.

What percent of students participate in global health experiences? 29%

What service-learning opportunities exist? Mission trips, Minority Introduction to the Health Sciences (MITHS), Healthy Neighborhoods Project, etc. For more information, visit:https://medicine.llu.edu/about/community-engagement-mission-trips

What dual degree options exist? MD/PhD. For more information, visit:https://medicine.llu.edu/research/graduate-programs/mdphd-program

Important Updates due to COVID-19: Pass/Fail grading accepted for coursework taken during the winter/spring 2020 academic terms only. Online coursework and labs for the prerequisites accepted.

Were tests required? MCAT required.

Are tests expected next year? Yes.

Postgraduate Training Match Rate: N/A

USMLE First-Time Pass Rate

Step 1: N/A

Step 2 CK: N/A

Step 2 CS: N/A

ALASKA

ARIZONA

CALIFORNIA

COLORADO

HAWAII

IDAHO

MONTANA

NEVADA

NEW MEXICO

OREGON

UTAH

WASHINGTON

WYOMING

WEST

ALASKA

ARIZONA

CALIFORNIA

COLORADO

HAWAII

IDAHO

MONTANA

NEVADA

NEW MEXICO

OREGON

UTAH

WASHINGTON

WYOMING

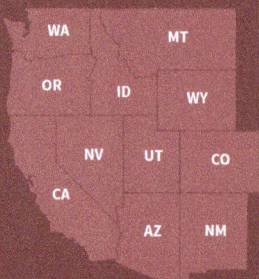

STANFORD UNIVERSITY SCHOOL OF MEDICINE

Address: 291 Campus Drive, Li Ka Shing Building, Stanford, CA 94305
Website: *http://med.stanford.edu/*
Contact: *https://med.stanford.edu/about/contacts.html*
Phone: (650) 723-4000

COST OF ATTENDANCE

Tuition: $82,924
Fees & Expenses: $48,936
Total: $131,860

Financial Aid: http://med.stanford.edu/md/financial-aid.html

!81%

ADDITIONAL INFORMATION

Interesting tidbit: Stanford University School of Medicine is a tobacco-free zone with no smoking or vaping allowed anywhere on its campus. This prohibition includes all leased or owned facilities off-campus as well.

What percent of students participate in global health experiences? 23%

What service-learning opportunities exist? Free clinics, global health initiatives, student organizations, etc. For more information, visit:http://med.stanford.edu/school/community-engagement.html

What dual degree options exist? MD/MPH, MD/MBA, MD/JD, MD/MS, MD/MPP, and MD/Ph.D. For more information, visit:http://med.stanford.edu/education/dual-degree-programs.html

Important Updates due to COVID-19: N/A

Were tests required? MCAT required.

Are tests expected next year? Yes.

Postgraduate Training Match Rate: N/A

USMLE First-Time Pass Rate

Step 1: N/A

Step 2 CK: N/A

Step 2 CS: N/A

THE UNIVERSITY OF CALIFORNIA, DAVIS SCHOOL OF MEDICINE

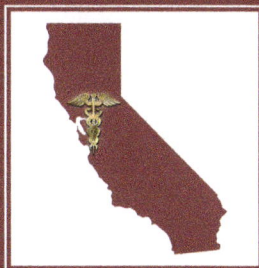

Address: 4610 X Street, Sacramento, CA 95817
Website: *https://health.ucdavis.edu/medschool/*
Contact: *https://health.ucdavis.edu/mdprogram/admissions/contactus.html*
Phone: (916) 734-4800

COST OF ATTENDANCE

In-State Tuition: $41,927
Fees & Expenses: $27,299
Total: $69,226

Out-of-State Tuition: $54,172
Fees & Expenses: $27,299
Total: $81,471

Financial Aid: https://health.ucdavis.edu/financialaid/index.html

Percent Receiving Aid: 91%

ADDITIONAL INFORMATION

Interesting tidbit: The UC Davis School of Medicine is one of the most diverse in the nation. It ranked #4 nationally in diversity and is the top-ranked medical school for diversity outside of the East Coast, according to U.S. News & World Report 2021.

What percent of students participate in global health experiences? 17%

What service-learning opportunities exist? Student-run clinics, student interest groups, global health, etc. For more information, visit:https://health.ucdavis.edu/mdprogram/service-learning-opportunities/index.html

What dual degree options exist? MD/MPH and MD/PhD. For more information, visit:https://health.ucdavis.edu/mdprogram/dual_degree_programs/index.html

Important Updates due to COVID-19: Accept pass/fail grades, without prejudice, for courses taken during the COVID pandemic. Accept online courses if they are offered by the school at which the candidate was enrolled prior to the pandemic.

Were tests required? MCAT required.

Are tests expected next year? Yes.

Postgraduate Training Match Rate: N/A

USMLE First-Time Pass Rate

Step 1: N/A

Step 2 CK: N/A

Step 2 CS: N/A

ALASKA

ARIZONA

CALIFORNIA

COLORADO

HAWAII

IDAHO

MONTANA

NEVADA

NEW MEXICO

OREGON

UTAH

WASHINGTON

WYOMING

WEST

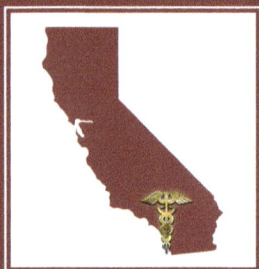

ALASKA

ARIZONA

CALIFORNIA

COLORADO

HAWAII

IDAHO

MONTANA

NEVADA

NEW MEXICO

OREGON

UTAH

WASHINGTON

WYOMING

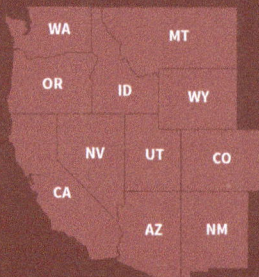

UNIVERSITY OF CALIFORNIA, IRVINE SCHOOL OF MEDICINE

Address: 1001 Health Sciences Rd., Irvine, CA 92697
Website: *https://www.som.uci.edu/*
Contact: *https://www.som.uci.edu/contact-us.asp*
Phone: (800) 824-5388

COST OF ATTENDANCE

In-State Tuition: $35,220
Fees & Expenses: $31,397
Total: $66,617

Out-of-State Tuitio: $47,465
Fees & Expenses: $31,397
Total: $78,862

Financial Aid: http://www.meded.uci.edu/Admissions/financial-aid.asp

Percent Receiving Aid: 87%

ADDITIONAL INFORMATION

Interesting tidbit: UCI Medical Center is the principal clinical facility for the UCI School of Medicine's teaching and research programs. For 18 consecutive years, the medical center has been rated among the nation's best hospitals by U.S. News & World Report.

What percent of students participate in global health experiences? 44%

What service-learning opportunities exist? service-learning through community service student organizations, student-run clinics, and community outreach partnerships. For more information, visit:https://www.meded.uci.edu/diversity/index.asp

What dual degree options exist? MD/MBA, MD/MPH, and MD/PhD. For more information, visit:https://www.meded.uci.edu/curricular-affairs/about-dual-degree-programs.asp

Important Updates due to COVID-19: Accept pass/fail grades, without prejudice, for courses taken during the COVID-19 pandemic.

Were tests required? MCAT required.

Are tests expected next year? Yes.

Postgraduate Training Match Rate: N/A

USMLE First-Time Pass Rate

Step 1: N/A

Step 2 CK: N/A

UNIVERSITY OF CALIFORNIA, RIVERSIDE SCHOOL OF MEDICINE

Address: 900 University Ave., Riverside, CA 92521
Website: *https://medschool.ucr.edu/*
Contact: *https://somsa.ucr.edu/admission-medical-school*
Phone: (951) 827-4353

COST OF ATTENDANCE

In-State Tuition: $42,537
Fees & Expenses: $34,906
*Total: $77,443

Out-of-State Tuitio: $53,652
Fees & Expenses: $34,906
*Total: $88,558

* Total for living off-campus. COA for living on-campus is $68,293 (In-State) & $79,408 (Out-of-State).

Financial Aid: https://somsa.ucr.edu/general-information-financial-aid

Percent Receiving Aid: 71%

ADDITIONAL INFORMATION

Interesting tidbit: UC Riverside began training physicians in partnership with UCLA David Geffen School of Medicine. In July 2008, the UC Board of Regents approve the establishment of the UCR School of Medicine and became an independent four-year program.

What percent of students participate in global health experiences? 24%

What service-learning opportunities exist? service-learning through student organizations. For more information, visit:https://somsa.ucr.edu/student-interest-groups

What dual degree options exist? MD/Ph.D.:https://biomed.ucr.edu/mdphd-combined-degree

MD/MPP: https://medschool.ucr.edu/mdmpp

Important Updates due to COVID-19: Accept prerequisite courses and/or labs completed as part of online or hybrid programs since March 2020.

Were tests required? MCAT required.

Are tests expected next year? Yes.

Postgraduate Training Match Rate: 97% (2021)

USMLE First-Time Pass Rate

Step 1: N/A

Step 2 CK: N/A

Step 2 CS: N/A

ALASKA

ARIZONA

CALIFORNIA

COLORADO

HAWAII

IDAHO

MONTANA

NEVADA

NEW MEXICO

OREGON

UTAH

WASHINGTON

WYOMING

WEST

ALASKA

ARIZONA

CALIFORNIA

COLORADO

HAWAII

IDAHO

MONTANA

NEVADA

NEW MEXICO

OREGON

UTAH

WASHINGTON

WYOMING

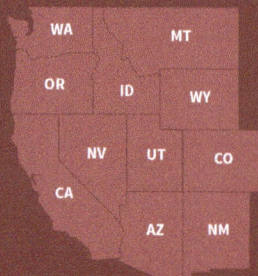

UNIVERSITY OF CALIFORNIA, SAN DIEGO SCHOOL OF MEDICINE

Address: 9500 Gilman Drive, La Jolla, CA 92093
Website: *https://medschool.ucsd.edu/Pages/default.aspx*
Contact: *https://medschool.ucsd.edu/admissions/Pages/Contact-Us.aspx*
Phone: (858) 534-3880

COST OF ATTENDANCE

In-State Tuition: $38,753
Fees & Expenses: $34,192
Total: $68,990

Out-of-State Tuitio: $50,998
Fees & Expenses: $34,192
Total: $85,190

Financial Aid: https://medschool.ucsd.edu/admissions/financial-aid/pages/default.aspx

Percent Receiving Aid: 78%

ADDITIONAL INFORMATION

Interesting tidbit: UC San Diego School of Medicine has long been at the forefront of translational — or "bench-to-bedside" — research, transforming patient care through discovery and innovation leading to new drugs and technologies. Translational research is carried out every day in the hundreds of clinical trials of promising new therapies offered through UC San Diego Health.

What percent of students participate in global health experiences? 24%

What service-learning opportunities exist? Student-run free clinic and various opportunities through student organizations. For more information, visit:https://medschool.ucsd.edu/som/fmph/education/freeclinic/pages/default.aspx

What dual degree options exist? MD/MPH:https://publichealth.sdsu.edu/programs/mph/mph-md/

MD/Ph.D.: https://medschool.ucsd.edu/education/mstp/pages/default.aspx

Important Updates due to COVID-19: Accept pass/fail grades, without prejudice, for courses taken during the COVID-19 pandemic. Accept applications from individuals who were unable to take the MCAT due to COVID-related test cancellations but require applicants to have taken the MCAT before the school makes admissions decisions for the Class of 2025.

Were tests required? MCAT required.

Are tests expected next year? Yes.

Postgraduate Training Match Rate: N/A

USMLE First-Time Pass Rate

Step 1: N/A

Step 2 CK: N/A

Step 2 CS: N/A

UNIVERSITY OF CALIFORNIA, SAN FRANCISCO SCHOOL OF MEDICINE

Address: 505 Parnassus Avenue, San Francisco, CA 94143
Website: *https://medschool.ucsf.edu/*
Contact Email: *admissions@medsch.ucsf.edu*
Phone: (415) 476-4044

COST OF ATTENDANCE

In-State Tuition: $35,214
Fees & Expenses: $38,472
Total: $73,686

Out-of-State Tuitio: $47,459
Fees & Expenses: $38,472
Total: $85,931

Financial Aid: https://finaid.ucsf.edu/application-process/student-budget

Percent Receiving Aid: 91%

ADDITIONAL INFORMATION

Interesting tidbit: The UCSF School of Medicine earns its greatest distinction from the quality of its students and its outstanding faculty -- including six Nobel laureates, 51 National Academy of Sciences members, 64 American Academy of Arts and Sciences members, 105 National Academy of Medicine members, and 17 Howard Hughes Medical Institute investigators.

What percent of students participate in global health experiences? 21%

What service-learning opportunities exist? Student-run clinics, student organizations, etc.

What dual degree options exist? MD/MPH, MD/MAS, MD/MS, and MD/Ph.D. For more information, visit:https://meded.ucsf.edu/md-program/prospective-students/admissions-md-program/degrees-and-programs/education-programs

Important Updates due to COVID-19: Accept applications without an MCAT score due to the COVID-19 pandemic. All candidates were screened and interview decisions were offered without the utilization of an MCAT score. Accept pass/fail grades, without prejudice, for courses taken during the COVID-19 pandemic. Accept online courses if they are offered by the school at which the candidate was enrolled prior to the current crisis.

Were tests required? MCAT required.

Are tests expected next year? Yes.

Postgraduate Training Match Rate: 100% (2021)

USMLE First-Time Pass Rate

Step 1: N/A

Step 2 CK: N/A

Step 2 CS: N/A

ALASKA

ARIZONA

CALIFORNIA

COLORADO

HAWAII

IDAHO

MONTANA

NEVADA

NEW MEXICO

OREGON

UTAH

WASHINGTON

WYOMING

WEST

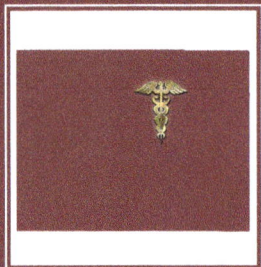

ALASKA

ARIZONA

CALIFORNIA

COLORADO

HAWAII

IDAHO

MONTANA

NEVADA

NEW MEXICO

OREGON

UTAH

WASHINGTON

WYOMING

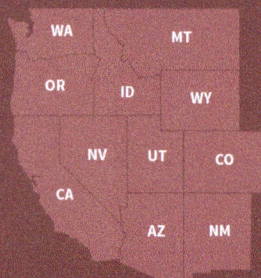

UNIVERSITY OF COLORADO SCHOOL OF MEDICINE

Address: 13001 E. 17th Place, Aurora, CO 80045
Website: *https://medschool.cuanschutz.edu/*
Contact: *http://www.ucdenver.edu/academics/colleges/ medicalschool/education/Admissions/contactinfo/Pages/Contact%20 Us.aspx*
Phone: (303) 724-5375

Other locations: Colorado Springs, CO

COST OF ATTENDANCE

In-State Tuition: $41,520
Fees & Expenses: $29,592
Total: $71,112

Out-of-State Tuitio: $77,474
Fees & Expenses: $29,592
Total: $107,066

Financial Aid: http://www.ucdenver.edu/anschutz/ studentresources/FASO/school-pages/Pages/medical-students.aspx

Percent Receiving Aid: 84%

ADDITIONAL INFORMATION

Interesting tidbit: The CU School of Medicine began humbly in 1883 with two students and two professors. Now, its total enrollment is 802 students.

What percent of students participate in global health experiences? 17%

What service-learning opportunities exist? service-learning through student organizations.

What dual degree options exist? MD/MPH:http://www.ucdenver. edu/academics/colleges/PublicHealth/admissionsandaid/ howtoapply/Pages/DualDegreeReqs.aspx

MD/Ph.D.: https://medschool.cuanschutz.edu/mstp

Important Updates due to COVID-19: Accept both pass/fail grades and online courses for the spring 2020 through summer 2021 semesters.

Were tests required? MCAT and CASPer required.

Are tests expected next year? Yes.

Postgraduate Training Match Rate: N/A

USMLE First-Time Pass Rate

Step 1: N/A

Step 2 CK: N/A

Step 2 CS: N/A

Other: BA-BS/MD program available to Colorado high school applicants. For more information, visit:https://clas.ucdenver.edu/ health-professions-programs/babs-md-program-information

JOHN A. BURNS SCHOOL OF MEDICINE
UNIVERSITY OF HAWAII AT MANOA

Address: 651 Ilalo Street, Honolulu, HI 96813
Website: *https://jabsom.hawaii.edu/*
Contact: *https://admissions.jabsom.hawaii.edu/contact-us/*
Phone: (808) 692-0892

COST OF ATTENDANCE

In-State Tuition: $36,672
Fees & Expenses: $33,804
Total: $70,476

Out-of-State Tuitio: $71,328
Fees & Expenses: $33,804
Total: $105,132

Financial Aid: https://admissions.jabsom.hawaii.edu/prospective-students/tuition-financial-support/

Percent Receiving Aid: 89%

ADDITIONAL INFORMATION

Interesting tidbit: In 2017, the John A. Burns School of Medicine (JABSOM)'s MD program received an eight year accreditation – the maximum possible – and in 2013, its Graduate Medical Education (Residency Training) program received the maximum 12 year accreditation.

What percent of students participate in global health experiences? 34%

What service-learning opportunities exist? service-learning through student organizations.

What dual degree options exist? No dual degree options listed.

Important Updates due to COVID-19: Accept online lab courses from Spring 2020 – Spring 2022

Were tests required? MCAT required.

Are tests expected next year? Yes.

Postgraduate Training Match Rate: N/A

USMLE First-Time Pass Rate

Step 1: N/A

Step 2 CK: N/A

Step 2 CS: N/A

ALASKA

ARIZONA

CALIFORNIA

COLORADO

HAWAII

IDAHO

MONTANA

NEVADA

NEW MEXICO

OREGON

UTAH

WASHINGTON

WYOMING

WEST

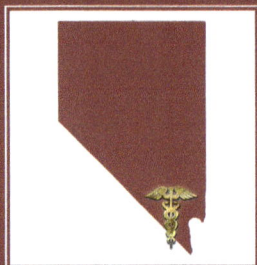

ALASKA

ARIZONA

CALIFORNIA

COLORADO

HAWAII

IDAHO

MONTANA

NEVADA

NEW MEXICO

OREGON

UTAH

WASHINGTON

WYOMING

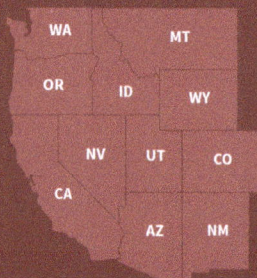

UNIVERSITY OF NEVADA, LAS VEGAS SCHOOL OF MEDICINE

Address: 2040 W. Charleston Blvd., 3rd Floor, Las Vegas, NV 89102
Website: *https://www.unlv.edu/medicine*
Contact: *https://www.unlv.edu/medicine/contact*
Phone: (702) 895-0325

COST OF ATTENDANCE

In-State Tuition: $27,000
Fees & Expenses: $41,746
Total: $68,746

Out-of-State Tuitio: $56,000
Fees & Expenses: $41,746
Total: $97,746

Financial Aid: https://www.unlv.edu/medicine/student-financial-services

Percent Receiving Aid: 100%

ADDITIONAL INFORMATION

Interesting tidbit: The UNLV School of Medicine begins operations in July 2017 with the charter class of 60 medical students. Four years later in February 2021, UNLV School of Medicine receives full accreditation by the LCME.

What percent of students participate in global health experiences? N/A

What service-learning opportunities exist? service-learning through student organizations and other opportunities. For more information, visit:https://www.unlv.edu/sll

What dual degree options exist? No dual degree options listed

Important Updates due to COVID-19: Accept P/F coursework from Spring 2020, Summer 2020, and Fall 2020 without prejudice, and online prerequisite coursework during Spring 2020, Summer 2020, Fall 2020 and Spring 2021.

Were tests required? MCAT required.

Are tests expected next year? Yes.

Postgraduate Training Match Rate: N/A

USMLE First-Time Pass Rate

Step 1: N/A

Step 2 CK: N/A

Step 2 CS: N/A

UNIVERSITY OF NEVADA, RENO SCHOOL OF MEDICINE

Address: 1664 N. Virginia Street, Reno, NV 89557
Website: *https://med.unr.edu/*
Contact: https://med.unr.edu/md-admissions/contact-us
Phone: (775) 784-6063

Other locations: Elko, NV

COST OF ATTENDANCE

In-State Tuition: $30,210
Fees & Expenses: $33,532
Total: $63,742

Out-of-State Tuitio: $57,704
Fees & Expenses: $33,532
Total: $91,236

Financial Aid: https://med.unr.edu/student-affairs/resources/
financial-planning/financial-aid

Percent Receiving Aid: 97%

ADDITIONAL INFORMATION

Interesting tidbit: University of Nevada, Reno among only 130
institutions to receive the R1 designation by Carnegie Classification
of Institutions of Higher Education. To reach the classification of
"R1," or "very high research activity," doctoral universities must
demonstrate uncommon productivity and output in the areas of
research and graduate education.

**What percent of students participate in global health
experiences?** 19%

What service-learning opportunities exist? Scholarly
Concentration in service-learning (SCISL) available. In addition,
opportunities through student organizations available. For more
information on the scholarly concentration, visit:https://med.unr.
edu/office-of-medical-research/scholarly-concentration/scholarly-
concentration-in-service-learning-(scisl)

What dual degree options exist? MD/MBA, MD/MPH, and MD/Ph.D.
For more information, visit:https://med.unr.edu/md-admissions/
combined-degree

Important Updates due to COVID-19: For applicants unable to
secure a clinical letter of evaluation written by an MD, DO, PA or NP
as a direct result of Covid-19, this requirement is waived and an
alternative letter of evaluation is accepted.

Were tests required? MCAT and CASPer required.

Are tests expected next year? Yes.

Postgraduate Training Match Rate: N/A

USMLE First-Time Pass Rate

Step 1: N/A

Step 2 CK: N/A

Step 2 CS: N/A

Other: BS/MD program available to Nevada
high school applicants. For more information,
visit:https://med.unr.edu/md-admissions/bs-
md-program

ALASKA

ARIZONA

CALIFORNIA

COLORADO

HAWAII

IDAHO

MONTANA

NEVADA

NEW MEXICO

OREGON

UTAH

WASHINGTON

WYOMING

WEST

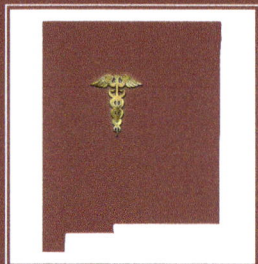

ALASKA

ARIZONA

CALIFORNIA

COLORADO

HAWAII

IDAHO

MONTANA

NEVADA

NEW MEXICO

OREGON

UTAH

WASHINGTON

WYOMING

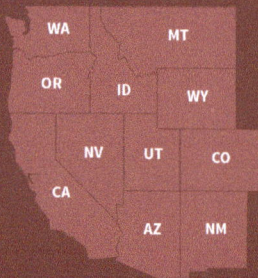

UNIVERSITY OF NEW MEXICO SCHOOL OF MEDICINE

Address: 915 Camino de Salud, Albuquerque, NM 87106
Website: *https://hsc.unm.edu/school-of-medicine/*
Contact: *https://hsc.unm.edu/contacts.html*
Phone: (505) 272-4766

COST OF ATTENDANCE

In-State Tuition: $15,946
Fees & Expenses: $35,356
Total: $51,302

Out-of-State Tuitio: $44,024
Fees & Expenses: $35,356
Total: $79,380

Financial Aid: https://hsc.unm.edu/academicaffairs/financialaid/

Percent Receiving Aid: 89%

ADDITIONAL INFORMATION

Interesting tidbit: UNM School of Medicine was born out of New Mexico's growing shortage of physicians and no medical school to train them. The first class of UNM MDs graduated in 1968.

What percent of students participate in global health experiences? 9%

What service-learning opportunities exist? service-learning through student organizations and global opportunities.

What dual degree options exist? MD/MPH:https://hsc.unm.edu/school-of-medicine/education/md/mdmph.html

MD/Ph.D.: https://hsc.unm.edu/research/brep/graduate/md-phd/

Important Updates due to COVID-19: Accept lectures and labs taken both online and in person and CR/NC coursework.

Were tests required? MCAT required.

Are tests expected next year? Yes.

Postgraduate Training Match Rate: N/A

USMLE First-Time Pass Rate

Step 1: N/A

Step 2 CK: N/A

Step 2 CS: N/A

Other: BA/MD program available to New Mexico high school applicants. For more information, visit:https://hsc.unm.edu/school-of-medicine/education/md/bamd/

OREGON HEALTH & SCIENCE UNIVERSITY SCHOOL OF MEDICINE

Address: 2730 SW Moody Avenue, Portland, OR 97239
Website: *https://www.ohsu.edu/school-of-medicine*
Contact: *https://www.ohsu.edu/school-of-medicine/contact-us-school-medicine-office-dean*
Phone: (503) 494-2998

COST OF ATTENDANCE

In-State Tuition: $46,752
Fees & Expenses: $30,690
Total: $77,442

Out-of-State Tuitio: $70,580
Fees & Expenses: $30,690
Total: $101,270

Financial Aid: https://www.ohsu.edu/school-of-medicine/md-program/scholarships-medical-students

Percent Receiving Aid: 99%

ADDITIONAL INFORMATION

Interesting tidbit: OHSU School of Medicine was awarded full accreditation from the LCME in late June 2020.

What percent of students participate in global health experiences? 14%

What service-learning opportunities exist? service-learning through student organizations.

What dual degree options exist? MD/MPH and MD/Ph.D. For more information, visit:https://www.ohsu.edu/school-of-medicine/md-program/degree-dual-degree-and-other-opportunities

Important Updates due to COVID-19: Interview decisions were made with or without an MCAT score assuming the application is otherwise complete.

Were tests required? MCAT and CASPer required.

Are tests expected next year? Yes.

Postgraduate Training Match Rate: 97% (2021)

USMLE First-Time Pass Rate

Step 1: N/A

Step 2 CK: N/A

Step 2 CS: N/A

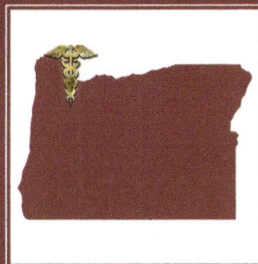

ALASKA

ARIZONA

CALIFORNIA

COLORADO

HAWAII

IDAHO

MONTANA

NEVADA

NEW MEXICO

OREGON

UTAH

WASHINGTON

WYOMING

WEST

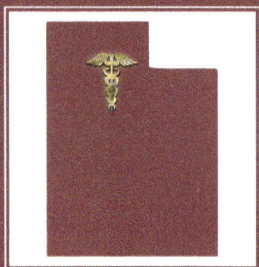

ALASKA

ARIZONA

CALIFORNIA

COLORADO

HAWAII

IDAHO

MONTANA

NEVADA

NEW MEXICO

OREGON

UTAH

WASHINGTON

WYOMING

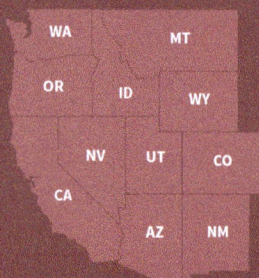

UNIVERSITY OF UTAH SCHOOL OF MEDICINE

Address: 30 North 1900 East, Salt Lake City, UT 84132
Website: *https://medicine.utah.edu/*
Contact: *https://medicine.utah.edu/students/current-students/contact.php*
Phone: (801) 581-7498

COST OF ATTENDANCE

In-State Tuition: $41,784
Fees & Expenses: $21,186
Total: $63,512

Out-of-State Tuitio: $77,991
Fees & Expenses: $21,186
Total: $99,177

Financial Aid: https://medicine.utah.edu/students/programs/financial-aid/

Percent Receiving Aid: 91%

ADDITIONAL INFORMATION

Interesting tidbit: The University of Utah School of Medicine serves as the only MD-granting institution in the state of Utah and as the only academic medical center in the Intermountain West.

What percent of students participate in global health experiences? 21%

What service-learning opportunities exist? service-learning required in the curriculum. Clinical opportunities, community outreach partnerships, K-12 education opportunities, etc. For more information, visit:https://medicine.utah.edu/outreach/med-students.php

What dual degree options exist? MD/MBA, MD/MPH, and MD/Ph.D. For more information, visit:https://medicine.utah.edu/students/programs/other/combined/

Important Updates due to COVID-19: Accept pass/fail grades and on-line courses for premedical coursework taken during the pandemic.

Were tests required? MCAT and SJT required.

Are tests expected next year? Yes.

Postgraduate Training Match Rate: 100%

USMLE First-Time Pass Rate

Step 1: N/A

Step 2 CK: N/A

Step 2 CS: N/A

UNIVERSITY OF WASHINGTON SCHOOL OF MEDICINE

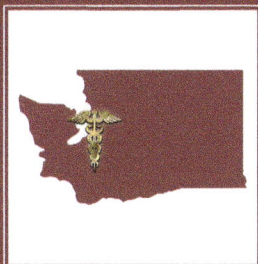

Address: 1959 NE Pacific St., Seattle, WA 98195
Website: *https://www.uwmedicine.org/school-of-medicine*
Contact: *https://www.uwmedicine.org/school-of-medicine/contact*
Phone: (206) 543-7212

Other locations: Moscow, ID; Laramie, WY; Bozeman, MT;
Anchorage, AK; Spokane, WA

COST OF ATTENDANCE

In-State Tuition: $39,012
Fees & Expenses: $23,696
Total: $62,708

Out-of-State Tuition: $69,444
Fees & Expenses: $23,696
Total: $93140

*Special tuition rates for residents of WWAMI states (Washington,
Wyoming, Alaska, Montana, or Idaho) Washing: $39,012; Wyoming:
$14,747; Alaska: $39,052; Montana: $8,972; Idaho: $38,610

Financial Aid: https://www.uwmedicine.org/school-of-medicine/
md-program/financial-aid

Percent Receiving Aid: 90%

ADDITIONAL INFORMATION

Interesting tidbit: In the early 1970s, the University of Washington
School of Medicine (UWSOM) formed a unique partnership with the
states of Washington, Alaska, Montana and Idaho, adding Wyoming
in 1996, to provide innovative and cost-effective medical education
to this region known as WWAMI.

**What percent of students participate in global health
experiences?** 13%

What service-learning opportunities exist? Health education,
advocacy, clinical services, etc. For more information, visit:https://
www.uwmedicine.org/school-of-medicine/md-program/service-
learning

What dual degree options exist? MD/MPH:https://depts.
washington.edu/hservmph/mdmph

MD/Ph.D.: http://mstp.washington.edu/

Important Updates due to COVID-19: Online coursework from
regionally accredited institutions accepted towards fulfilling
prerequisites. Pass/Fail courses also accepted towards fulfilling
prerequisites.

Were tests required? MCAT and CASPer required.

Are tests expected next year? Yes.

Postgraduate Training Match Rate: N/A

USMLE First-Time Pass Rate

Step 1: N/A

Step 2 CK: N/A

Step 2 CS: N/A

ALASKA

ARIZONA

CALIFORNIA

COLORADO

HAWAII

IDAHO

MONTANA

NEVADA

NEW MEXICO

OREGON

UTAH

WASHINGTON

WYOMING

WEST

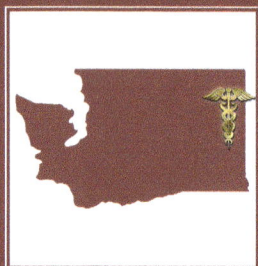

ALASKA

ARIZONA

CALIFORNIA

COLORADO

HAWAII

IDAHO

MONTANA

NEVADA

NEW MEXICO

OREGON

UTAH

WASHINGTON

WYOMING

WASHINGTON STATE UNIVERSITY ELSON S. FLOYD COLLEGE OF MEDICINE

Address: 412 E. Spokane Falls Blvd., Spokane, WA 99202
Website: *https://medicine.wsu.edu/*
Contact: *https://medicine.wsu.edu/contact/*
Phone: (509) 358-7944

Other locations: Everett, WA; Richland, WA; Vancouver, WA

COST OF ATTENDANCE

Tuition: $40,380
Fees & Expenses: $21,500
Total: $61,880

Financial Aid: https://medicine.wsu.edu/md-program/overview-applying-to-medical-school/financial-aid-and-estimated-cost-of-attendance/

Percent Receiving Aid: 95%

ADDITIONAL INFORMATION

Interesting tidbit: The Elson S. Floyd College of Medicine received provisional accreditation from the LCME in June 2019.

What percent of students participate in global health experiences? N/A

What service-learning opportunities exist? service-learning through student organizations.

What dual degree options exist? No dual degree options listed.

Important Updates due to COVID-19: Allow its 3 pre-req courses and the labs (physics, organic chemistry, biology) to be taken Pass/Fail in the semesters/quarters/terms of Spring, Summer, and Fall (if needed) in 2020. Have always allowed online coursework including the pre-reqs as long as coursework is taken at an accredited institution.

Were tests required? MCAT required.

Are tests expected next year? Yes.

Postgraduate Training Match Rate: 96% (2021)

USMLE First-Time Pass Rate

Step 1: N/A

Step 2 CK: N/A

Step 2 CS: N/A

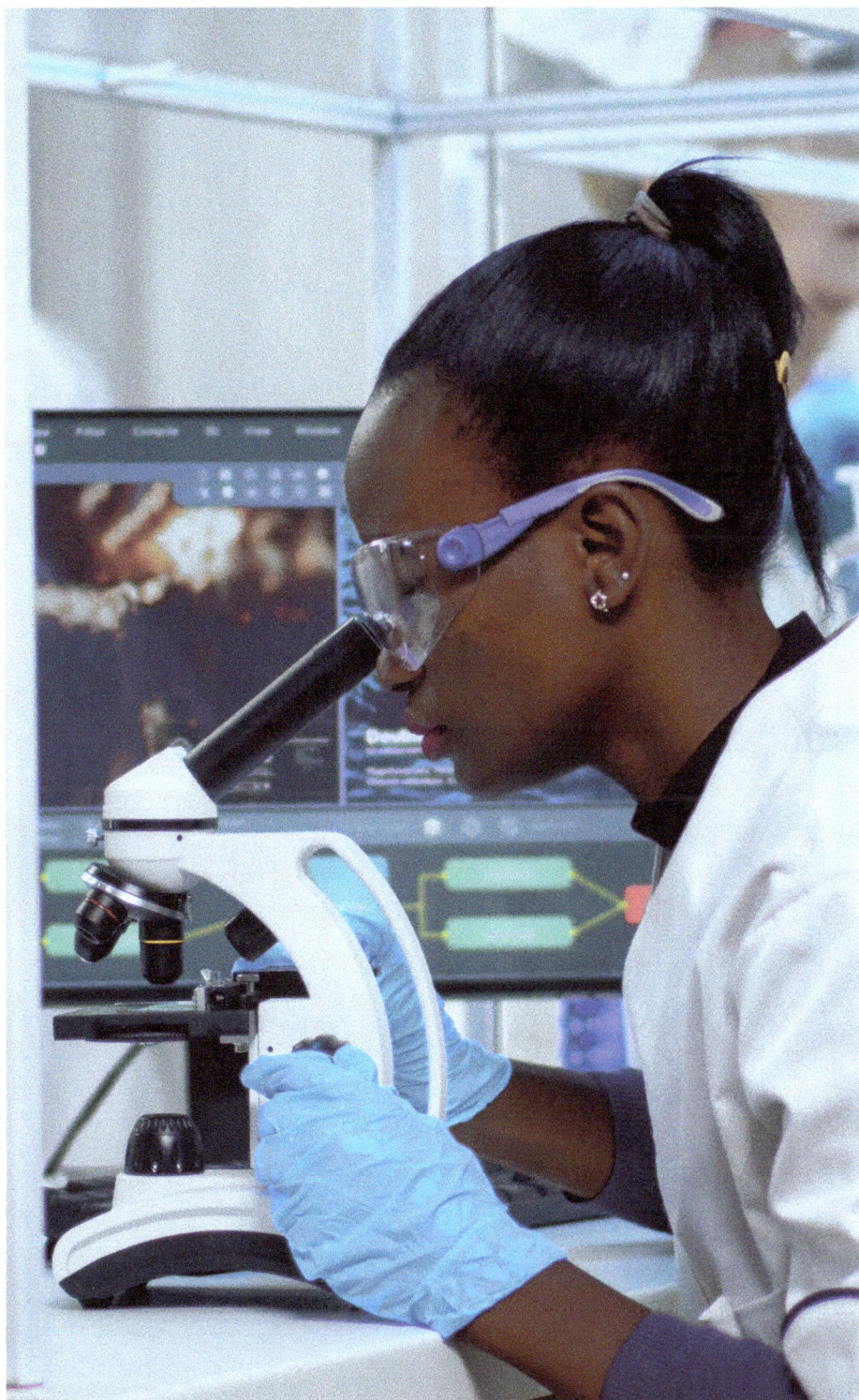

PUERTO RICO

CHAPTER 6
REGION FIVE
U.S TERRITORIES

4 *Programs* | **1** *Territory*

1. *PR – Ponce Health Sciences University School of Medicine*
2. *PR - San Juan Bautista School of Medicine*
3. *PR - Universidad Central del Caribe School of Medicine*
4. *PR - University of Puerto Rico School of Medicine*

MEDICAL PROGRAMS

Medical School	Ave. GPA & MCAT Early Decision (ED): Yes/No Int'l Students: Yes/No Reapps: Yes/No	Admissions Statistics	Science Req. Other than Gen Chem, OChem, Physics, Bio
Ponce Health Sciences University School of Medicine 388 Zona Industrial Reparada 2, Ponce, PR 00716, Puerto Rico	3.64 (overall) 3.50 (science) MCAT: 499 ED: YES Int'l Student: NO Reapps: N/A	**(2019)** Apps Received: 1525 Interview Received: 222 Number Enrolled: 100 Admitted Rate: 6.6% **(2020)** Apps Received: 1414 Interview Received: 352 Number Enrolled: 150 Admitted Rate: 10.6%	N/A See Chart.
San Juan Bautista School of Medicine Expreso Luis A. Ferré, Caguas, 00727, Puerto Rico	3.71 (overall) 3.62 (science) MCAT: 498 ED: Yes Int'l Student: Yes (case by case) Reapps: N/A	**(2019)** Apps Received: 1343 Interview Received: 239 Number Enrolled: 62 Admitted Rate: 4.6% **(2020)** Apps Received: 1261 Interview Received: 236 Number Enrolled: 63 Admitted Rate: 5%	N/A See Chart.
Universidad Central del Caribe School of Medicine Universidad Central del Caribe, Ave. Laurel, Santa Juanita, Bayamon, Puerto Rico, 00956	3.73 (overall) 3.64 (science) MCAT: 499 ED: No Int'l Student: Yes (case by case) Reapps: N/A	**(2019)** Apps Received: 1170 Interview Received: 186 Number Enrolled: 75 Admitted Rate: 6.4% **(2020)** Apps Received: 1006 Interview Received: 207 Number Enrolled: 75 Admitted Rate: 7.5%	N/A See Chart.
University of Puerto Rico School of Medicine Paseo Dr. Jose Celso Barbosa, San Juan, 00921, Puerto Rico, PR 00936	3.82 (overall) 3.74 (science) MCAT: 505 ED: No Int'l Student: No Reapps: N/A	**(2019)** Apps Received: 771 Interview Received: 160 Number Enrolled: 109 Admitted Rate: 14.1% **(2020)** Apps Received: 733 Interview Received: 165 Number Enrolled: 110 Admitted Rate: 15%	N/A See Chart.

PONCE HEALTH SCIENCES UNIVERSITY SCHOOL OF MEDICINE

Address: 388 Zona Industrial Reparada 2, Ponce, PR 00716, Puerto Rico
Website: *https://www.psm.edu/school-of-medicine/*
Contact: *https://www.psm.edu/contact/*
Phone: (787) 840-2575

COST OF ATTENDANCE

In-State Tuition: $39,218
Fees & Expenses: $19,862
Total: $59,080

Out-of-State Tuition: $62,400
Fees & Expenses: $19,862
Total: $82,262

Financial Aid: httpns://www.psm.edu/financial-aid-services/

Percent Receiving Aid: 91%

ADDITIONAL INFORMATION

Interesting tidbit: PHSU-SOM's mission is to train health care professionals in a bilingual (English-Spanish) academic environment that prepares them to serve both the Puerto Rican as well as the growing Hispanic population in the USA.

What percent of students participate in global health experiences? 17%

What service-learning opportunities exist? Service-learning through student organizations.

What dual degree options exist? No dual degree options listed.

Postgraduate Training Match Rate: N/A

Important Updates due to COVID-19: The Admissions Committee may, upon their discretion, recommend regular admission of a student who does not meet the admissions requirements to the institution as long as the conditions for the admission of said student are established. If the student fails to comply with any of the conditions, either academic or procedural (IE, documentation), the student will be suspended for non-compliance and their admission will not be extended.

Were tests required? MCAT required.

Are tests expected next year? Yes.

USMLE First-Time Pass Rate

Step 1: N/A

Step 2 CK: N/A

Step 2 CS: N/A

Other: The Binary Programs (BS/MD) are 6-year/7-year programs available for high school applicants in consortium with the Pontifical Catholic University of Puerto Rico and Interamerican University of PR at Ponce. For more information, visit:https://www.psm.edu/school-of-medicine/binary-program/

SAN JUAN BAUTISTA SCHOOL OF MEDICINE

Address: Expreso Luis A. Ferré, Caguas, 00727, Puerto Rico
Website: *https://www.sanjuanbautista.edu/*
Contact: *https://www.sanjuanbautista.edu/contactus.html*
Phone: (787) 743-3038

COST OF ATTENDANCE

In-State Tuition: $35,280
Fees & Expenses: $29,098
Total: $64,378

Out-of-State Tuition: $45,280
Fees & Expenses: $30,098
Total: $75,378

Financial Aid: https://www.sanjuanbautista.edu/financial-aid.html

Percent Receiving Aid: 84%

ADDITIONAL INFORMATION

Interesting tidbit: The San Juan Bautista School of Medicine (SJBSM)'s academic offers is comprised of four programs: Medical Doctor (MD), Master in Public Health (MPH evening program), and Bachelor in Science of Nursing (BSN).

What percent of students participate in global health experiences? 33%

What service-learning opportunities exist? Community Medicine Program, Early Disaster Responses, partnerships with community organizations, etc. For more information, visit:https://www.sanjuanbautista.edu/community-engagement/about-cmp.html

What dual degree options exist? No dual degree options listed.

Postgraduate Training Match Rate: N/A

Important Updates due to COVID-19: Accept pass grades for coursework and online coursework for lectures and will allow online labs during the COVID-19 pandemic.

Were tests required? MCAT and CASPer required.

Are tests expected next year? Yes.

USMLE First-Time Pass Rate

Step 1: N/A

Step 2 CK: N/A

Step 2 CS: N/A

PUERTO RICO

UNIVERSIDAD CENTRAL DEL CARIBE SCHOOL OF MEDICINE

Address: Universidad Central del Caribe, Ave. Laurel, Santa Juanita, Bayamon, Puerto Rico, 00956
Website: *http://www.uccaribe.edu/medicine/*
Contact: *http://www.uccaribe.edu/?page_id=392*
Phone: (787) 798-3001

COST OF ATTENDANCE

In-State Tuition: N/A
Fees & Expenses: N/A
Total: N/A

Out-of-State Tuition: N/A
Fees & Expenses: N/A
Total: N/A

Financial Aid: http://www.uccaribe.edu/admission/?page_id=1144

Percent Receiving Aid: 95%

ADDITIONAL INFORMATION

Interesting tidbit: Universidad Central del Caribe School of Medicine (UCC-SOM) was the first non-profit private medical school incorporate in Puerto Rico.

What percent of students participate in global health experiences? 20%

What service-learning opportunities exist? Orientation classes in public schools, health clinics for the homeless, etc. For more information, visit:http://www.uccaribe.edu/admission/?page_id=1764

What dual degree options exist? No dual degree options listed.

Postgraduate Training Match Rate: N/A

Important Updates due to COVID-19: Accept pass/fail graded courses taken during the COVID-19 pandemic regardless of whether you opted in or if pass/fail was implemented school-wide by your current university. Accept online coursework for prerequisite courses completed in both Spring and Summer semesters of 2020-2021.

Were tests required? MCAT and SJT required.

Are tests expected next year? Yes.

USMLE First-Time Pass Rate

Step 1: N/A

Step 2 CK: N/A

Step 2 CS: N/A

UNIVERSITY OF PUERTO RICO SCHOOL OF MEDICINE

Address: Paseo Dr. Jose Celso Barbosa, San Juan, 00921, Puerto Rico, PR 00936
Website: *https://md.rcm.upr.edu/md-program/*
Contact: *https://md.rcm.upr.edu/contact/*
Phone: (787) 758-2525

COST OF ATTENDANCE

Tuition: $16,000
Fees & Expenses: $28,631
Total: $44,631

Financial Aid: https://de.rcm.upr.edu/asistencia-economica

Percent Receiving Aid: 89%

ADDITIONAL INFORMATION

Interesting tidbit: Since the University of Puerto Rico – School of Medicine is a state-supported institution, preference will be given to qualified applicants who are legal residents of Puerto Rico. Out-of-state applicants are considered on a case-by-case basis.

What percent of students participate in global health experiences? 19%

What service-learning opportunities exist? Service-learning through student organizations.

What dual degree options exist? MD/JD. For more information, visit:http://derecho.uprrp.edu/grados-conjuntos/jd-y-md-universidad-de-puerto-rico/

Postgraduate Training Match Rate: N/A

Important Updates due to COVID-19: N/A

Were tests required? MCAT required.

Are tests expected next year? Yes.

USMLE First-Time Pass Rate

Step 1: 98%

Step 2 CK: N/A

Step 2 CS: N/A

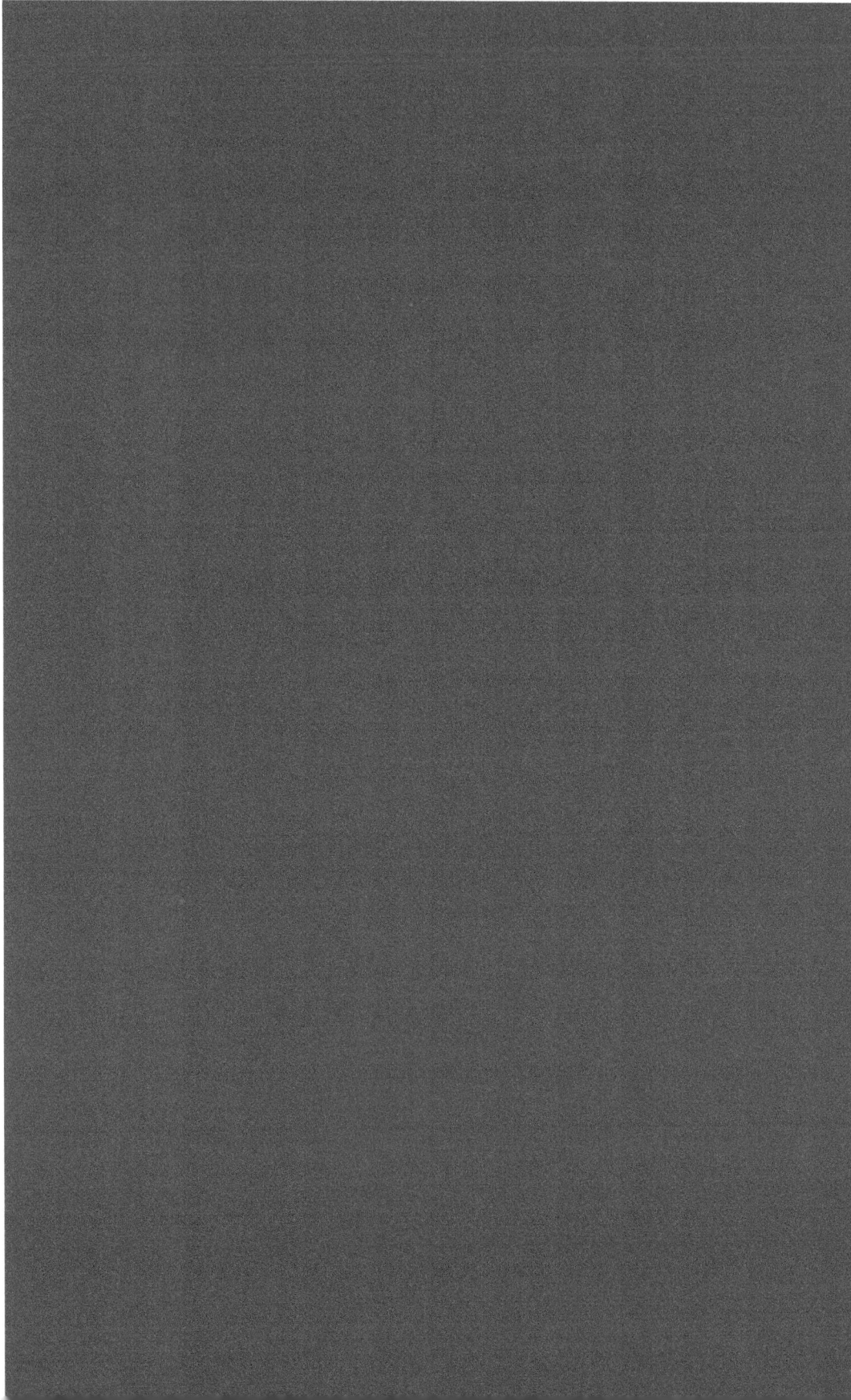

MEDICAL
SCHOOL LISTS

CHAPTER 7

MEDICAL SCHOOLS BY CITY/STATE

MD Schools	City	State	Website
University of Alabama School of Medicine	Birmingham	AL	https://www.uab.edu/medicine/home/
University of South Alabama College of Medicine	Mobile	AL	https://www.southalabama.edu/colleges/com/
University of Arkansas for Medical Sciences College of Medicine	Little Rock	AR	https://medicine.uams.edu/
The University of Arizona College of Medicine – Phoenix	Phoenix	AZ	https://phoenixmed.arizona.edu/
The University of Arizona College of Medicine – Tucson	Tucson	AZ	https://medicine.arizona.edu/
California University of Science and Medicine – School of Medicine	Colton	CA	https://www.cusm.org/
California Northstate University College of Medicine	Elk Grove	CA	https://medicine.cnsu.edu/
University of California, Irvine School of Medicine	Irvine	CA	https://www.som.uci.edu/
University of California, San Diego School of Medicine	La Jolla	CA	https://medschool.ucsd.edu/Pages/default.aspx
Loma Linda University School of Medicine	Loma Linda	CA	https://medicine.llu.edu/
David Geffen School of Medicine at UCLA	Los Angeles	CA	https://medschool.ucla.edu/
Keck School of Medicine of the University of Southern California	Los Angeles	CA	https://keck.usc.edu/
Kaiser Permanente School of Medicine	Pasadena	CA	https://medschool.kp.org/
University of California, Riverside School of Medicine	Riverside	CA	https://medschool.ucr.edu/

MD Schools	City	State	Website
University of California, Davis School of Medicine	Sacramento	CA	*https://health. ucdavis.edu/ medschool/*
University of California, San Francisco School of Medicine	San Francisco	CA	*https://medschool. ucsf.edu/*
Stanford University School of Medicine	Stanford	CA	*http://med.stanford. edu/*
University of Colorado School of Medicine	Aurora	CO	*https://medschool. cuanschutz.edu/*
University of Connecticut School of Medicine	Farmington	CT	*https://medicine. uconn.edu/*
Frank H. Netter MD School of Medicine at Quinnipiac University	Hamden	CT	*https://www.qu.edu/ schools/medicine. html*
Yale School of Medicine	New Haven	CT	*https://medicine. yale.edu/*
Georgetown University School of Medicine	Washington	DC	*https://som. georgetown.edu/*
Howard University College of Medicine	Washington	DC	*https://medicine. howard.edu/*
The George Washington University School of Medicine and Health Sciences	Washington	DC	*https://smhs.gwu. edu/*
Charles E. Schmidt College of Medicine at Florida Atlantic University	Boca Raton	FL	*http://med.fau.edu/*
Nova Southeastern University Dr. Kiran C. Patel College of Allopathic Medicine	Davie	FL	*https://md.nova.edu/ index.html*
University of Florida College of Medicine	Gainesville	FL	*https://med.ufl.edu/*

MD Schools	City	State	Website
Florida International University Herbert Wertheim College of Medicine	Miami	FL	https://medicine.fiu.edu/
University of Miami Leonard M. Miller School of Medicine	Miami	FL	https://med.miami.edu/
University of Central Florida College of Medicine	Orlando	FL	https://med.ucf.edu/
The Florida State University College of Medicine	Tallahassee	FL	https://med.fsu.edu/
USF Health Morsani College of Medicine	Tampa	FL	https://health.usf.edu/medicine
Emory University School of Medicine	Atlanta	GA	https://www.med.emory.edu/
Morehouse School of Medicine	Atlanta	GA	https://www.msm.edu/
Medical College of Georgia at Augusta University	Augusta	GA	https://www.augusta.edu/mcg/
Mercer University School of Medicine	Macon	GA	https://medicine.mercer.edu/
John A. Burns School of Medicine University of Hawaii at Manoa	Honolulu	HI	https://jabsom.hawaii.edu/
University of Iowa Roy J. and Lucille A. Carver College of Medicine	Iowa City	IA	https://medicine.uiowa.edu/
Carle Illinois College of Medicine	Champaign	IL	https://medicine.illinois.edu/
Northwestern University Feinberg School of Medicine	Chicago	IL	https://www.feinberg.northwestern.edu/
Rush Medical College of Rush University Medical Center	Chicago	IL	https://www.rushu.rush.edu/rush-medical-college

MD Schools	City	State	Website
University of Chicago Division of the Biological Sciences, The Pritzker School of Medicine	Chicago	IL	https://pritzker.uchicago.edu/
University of Illinois College of Medicine	Chicago	IL	https://medicine.uic.edu/
Loyola University Chicago Stritch School of Medicine	Maywood	IL	https://ssom.luc.edu/
Chicago Medical School at Rosalind Franklin University of Medicine and Science	North Chicago	IL	https://www.rosalindfranklin.edu/academics/chicago-medical-school/
Southern Illinois University School of Medicine	Springfield	IL	https://www.siumed.edu/
Indiana University School of Medicine	Indianapolis	IN	https://medicine.iu.edu/
University of Kansas School of Medicine	Kansas City	KS	http://www.kumc.edu/school-of-medicine.html
University of Kentucky College of Medicine	Lexington	KY	https://med.uky.edu/
University of Louisville School of Medicine	Louisville	KY	http://louisville.edu/medicine
LSU Health Sciences Center School of Medicine in New Orleans	New Orleans	LA	https://www.medschool.lsuhsc.edu/
Tulane University School of Medicine	New Orleans	LA	https://medicine.tulane.edu/
Louisiana State University School of Medicine in Shreveport	Shreveport	LA	https://www.lsuhs.edu/our-schools/school-of-medicine
Boston University School of Medicine	Boston	MA	https://www.bumc.bu.edu/busm/
Harvard Medical School	Boston	MA	https://hms.harvard.edu/

MD Schools	City	State	Website
Tufts University School of Medicine	Boston	MA	https://medicine.tufts.edu/
University of Massachusetts Medical School	North Worcester	MA	https://www.umassmed.edu/
Johns Hopkins University School of Medicine	Baltimore	MD	https://www.hopkinsmedicine.org/som/
University of Maryland School of Medicine	Baltimore	MD	https://www.medschool.umaryland.edu/
Uniformed Services University of the Health Sciences, F. Edward Hébert School of Medicine	Bethesda	MD	https://www.usuhs.edu/medschool
University of Michigan Medical School	Ann Arbor	MI	https://medicine.umich.edu/medschool/home
Wayne State University School of Medicine	Detroit	MI	https://www.med.wayne.edu/
Michigan State University College of Human Medicine	East Lansing	MI	http://humanmedicine.msu.edu/
Western Michigan University Homer Stryker M.D. School of Medicine	Kalamazoo	MI	https://med.wmich.edu/
Central Michigan University College of Medicine	Mt Pleasant	MI	https://www.cmich.edu/colleges/med/Pages/default.aspx
Oakland University William Beaumont School of Medicine	Rochester	MI	https://oakland.edu/medicine/
University of Minnesota Medical School	Minneapolis	MN	https://med.umn.edu/
Mayo Clinic Alix School of Medicine	Rochester	MN	https://college.mayo.edu/academics/school-of-medicine/
University of Missouri-Columbia School of Medicine	Columbia	MO	https://medicine.missouri.edu/

MD Schools	City	State	Website
University of Missouri-Kansas City School of Medicine	Kansas City	MO	https://med.umkc.edu/
Saint Louis University School of Medicine	St. Louis	MO	https://www.slu.edu/medicine/index.php
Washington University in St. Louis School of Medicine	St. Louis	MO	https://medicine.wustl.edu/
University of Mississippi School of Medicine	Jackson	MS	https://www.umc.edu/som/SOM_Home.html
University of North Carolina School of Medicine	Chapel Hill	NC	https://www.med.unc.edu/
Duke University School of Medicine	Durham	NC	https://medschool.duke.edu/
The Brody School of Medicine at East Carolina University	Greenville	NC	https://medicine.ecu.edu/
Wake Forest School of Medicine	Winston-Salem	NC	https://school.wakehealth.edu/
University of North Dakota School of Medicine and Health Sciences	Grand Forks	ND	https://med.und.edu/
Creighton University School of Medicine	Omaha	NE	https://medschool.creighton.edu/
University of Nebraska College of Medicine	Omaha	NE	https://www.unmc.edu/com/
Geisel School of Medicine at Dartmouth	Hanover	NH	https://geiselmed.dartmouth.edu/
Cooper Medical School of Rowan University	Camden	NJ	https://cmsru.rowan.edu/
Rutgers, Robert Wood Johnson Medical School	New Brunswick	NJ	http://rwjms.rutgers.edu/
Rutgers New Jersey Medical School	Newark	NJ	http://njms.rutgers.edu/

MD Schools	City	State	Website
Hackensack-Meridian School of Medicine at Seton Hall University	Nutley	NJ	https://www.shu.edu/medicine/
University of New Mexico School of Medicine	Albuquerque	NM	https://hsc.unm.edu/school-of-medicine/
University of Nevada, Las Vegas School of Medicine	Las Vegas	NV	https://www.unlv.edu/medicine
University of Nevada, Reno School of Medicine	Reno	NV	https://med.unr.edu/
Albany Medical College	Albany	NY	https://www.amc.edu/Academic/index.cfm
Albert Einstein College of Medicine	Bronx	NY	https://www.einstein.yu.edu/
State University of New York Downstate Medical Center College of Medicine	Brooklyn	NY	https://www.downstate.edu/college-of-medicine/
Jacobs School of Medicine and Biomedical Sciences at the University at Buffalo	Buffalo	NY	http://medicine.buffalo.edu/
New York University Long Island School of Medicine	Mineola	NY	https://medli.nyu.edu/
Columbia University Vagelos College of Physicians and Surgeons	New York	NY	https://www.ps.columbia.edu/
CUNY School of Medicine	New York	NY	https://www.ccny.cuny.edu/csom
Donald and Barbara Zucker School of Medicine at Hofstra/Northwell	New York	NY	https://medicine.hofstra.edu/
Icahn School of Medicine at Mount Sinai	New York	NY	https://icahn.mssm.edu/

MD Schools	City	State	Website
New York University Grossman School of Medicine	New York	NY	https://med.nyu.edu/our-community/about-us
Weill Cornell Medicine	New York	NY	https://weill.cornell.edu/
University of Rochester School of Medicine and Dentistry	Rochester	NY	https://www.urmc.rochester.edu/smd.aspx
Renaissance School of Medicine at Stony Brook University	Stony Brook	NY	https://renaissance.stonybrookmedicine.edu/
State University of New York Upstate Medical University College of Medicine	Syracuse	NY	https://www.upstate.edu/com/
New York Medical College	Valhalla	NY	https://www.nymc.edu/
University of Cincinnati College of Medicine	Cincinnati	OH	https://www.med.uc.edu/
Case Western Reserve University School of Medicine	Cleveland	OH	https://case.edu/medicine/
The Ohio State University College of Medicine	Columbus	OH	https://medicine.osu.edu/
Boonshoft School of Medicine Wright State University	Dayton	OH	https://medicine.wright.edu/
Northeast Ohio Medical University College of Medicine	Rootstown	OH	https://www.neomed.edu/
The University of Toledo College of Medicine and Life Sciences	Toledo	OH	https://www.utoledo.edu/med/
University of Oklahoma College of Medicine	Oklahoma City	OK	https://medicine.ouhsc.edu/
Oregon Health & Science University School of Medicine	Portland	OR	https://www.ohsu.edu/school-of-medicine

MD Schools	City	State	Website
Penn State College of Medicine	Hershey	PA	https://med.psu.edu/
Drexel University College of Medicine	Philadelphia	PA	https://drexel.edu/medicine/
Lewis Katz School of Medicine at Temple University	Philadelphia	PA	https://medicine.temple.edu/
Sidney Kimmel Medical College at Thomas Jefferson University	Philadelphia	PA	https://www.jefferson.edu/university/skmc.html
The Raymond and Ruth Perelman School of Medicine at the University of Pennsylvania	Philadelphia	PA	https://www.med.upenn.edu/
University of Pittsburgh School of Medicine	Pittsburgh	PA	https://www.medschool.pitt.edu/
Geisinger Commonwealth School of Medicine	Scranton	PA	https://www.geisinger.edu/education
Universidad Central del Caribe School of Medicine	Bayamon	PR	http://www.uccaribe.edu/medicine/
San Juan Bautista School of Medicine	Caguas	PR	https://www.sanjuanbautista.edu/
Ponce Health Sciences University School of Medicine	Ponce	PR	https://www.psm.edu/school-of-medicine/
University of Puerto Rico School of Medicine	San Juan	PR	https://md.rcm.upr.edu/md-program/
The Warren Alpert Medical School of Brown University	Providence	RI	https://medical.brown.edu/
Medical University of South Carolina College of Medicine	Charleston	SC	https://medicine.musc.edu/
University of South Carolina School of Medicine, Columbia	Columbia	SC	https://www.sc.edu/study/colleges_schools/medicine/index.php

MD Schools	City	State	Website
University of South Carolina School of Medicine, Greenville	Greenville	SC	https://www.sc.edu/study/colleges_schools/medicine_greenville/index.php
University of South Dakota Sanford School of Medicine	Sioux Falls	SD	https://www.usd.edu/medicine
East Tennessee State University James H. Quillen College of Medicine	Johnson City	TN	https://www.etsu.edu/com/
University of Tennessee Health Science Center College of Medicine	Memphis	TN	https://www.uthsc.edu/medicine/
Meharry Medical College School of Medicine	Nashville	TN	https://home.mmc.edu/
Vanderbilt University School of Medicine	Nashville	TN	https://medschool.vanderbilt.edu/
The University of Texas at Austin Dell Medical School	Austin	TX	https://dellmed.utexas.edu/
Texas A&M University Health Science Center College of Medicine	Bryan	TX	https://medicine.tamu.edu/
The University of Texas Southwestern Medical School	Dallas	TX	https://www.utsouthwestern.edu/education/medical-school/
The University of Texas Rio Grande Valley School of Medicine	Edinburg	TX	https://www.utrgv.edu/school-of-medicine/
Paul L. Foster School of Medicine Texas Tech University Health Sciences Center	El Paso	TX	https://elpaso.ttuhsc.edu/som/
TCU and UNTHSC School of Medicine	Fort Worth	TX	https://mdschool.tcu.edu/

MD Schools	City	State	Website
The University of Texas Medical Branch at Galveston School of Medicine	Galveston	TX	https://som.utmb.edu/
Baylor College of Medicine	Houston	TX	https://www.bcm.edu/
McGovern Medical School at The University of Texas Health Science Center at Houston	Houston	TX	https://med.uth.edu/
University of Houston College of Medicine	Houston	TX	https://www.uh.edu/medicine/
Texas Tech University Health Sciences Center School of Medicine	Lubbock	TX	https://www.ttuhsc.edu/medicine/default.aspx
The University of Texas Health Science Center at San Antonio Joe R. and Teresa Lozano Long School of Medicine	San Antonio	TX	http://som.uthscsa.edu/
University of Utah School of Medicine	Salt Lake City	UT	https://medicine.utah.edu/
University of Virginia School of Medicine	Charlottesville	VA	https://med.virginia.edu/
Eastern Virginia Medical School	Norfolk	VA	https://www.evms.edu/
Virginia Commonwealth University School of Medicine	Richmond	VA	https://medschool.vcu.edu/
Virginia Tech Carilion School of Medicine	Roanoke	VA	https://medicine.vtc.vt.edu/
The Robert Larner, M.D. College of Medicine at the University of Vermont	Burlington	VT	http://www.med.uvm.edu/
University of Washington School of Medicine	Seattle	WA	https://www.uwmedicine.org/school-of-medicine

MD Schools	City	State	Website
Washington State University Elson S. Floyd College of Medicine	Spokane	WA	*https://medicine.wsu.edu/*
University of Wisconsin School of Medicine and Public Health	Madison	WI	*https://www.med.wisc.edu/*
Medical College of Wisconsin	Milwaukee	WI	*https://www.mcw.edu/*
Marshall University Joan C. Edwards School of Medicine	Huntington	WV	https://jcesom.marshall.edu/
West Virginia University School of Medicine	Morgantown	WV	https://medicine.hsc.wvu.edu/

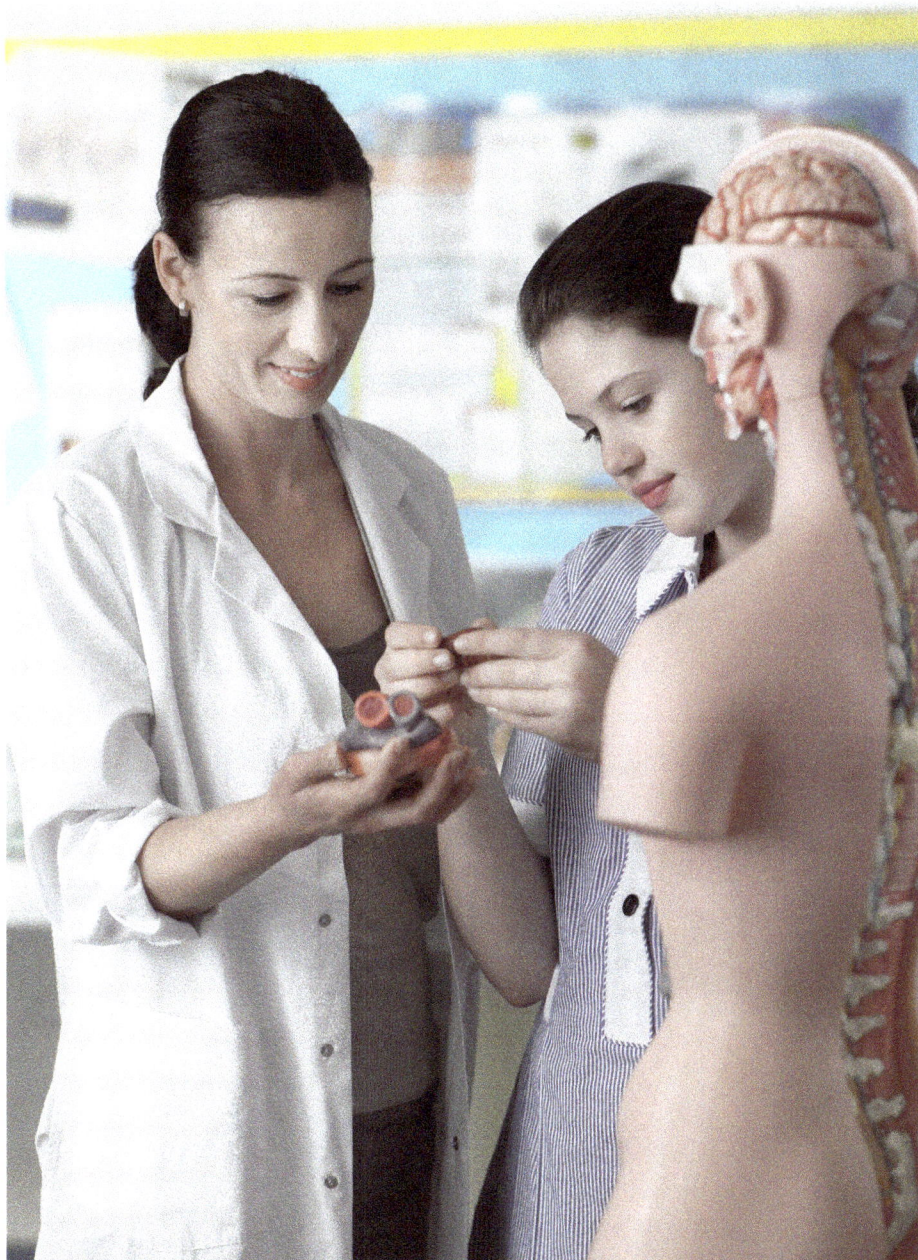

CHAPTER 8

MEDICAL SCHOOL PREREQUISITES

ALABAMA

School	Required	Recommended	Notes
UNIVERSITY OF ALABAMA SCHOOL OF MEDICINE	Behav. Sciences*, Biochem., Bio. w/ Lab, Engl.*, College Math* or Biostats., and Physics*.	N/A	AP credits accepted as long as they are listed on undergraduate transcript.
UNIVERSITY OF SOUTH ALABAMA COLLEGE OF MEDICINE	Bio. w/ Lab***, Engl.***, College Math***, Humanities***, Chem. w/ Lab***, OChem. w/ Lab***, and Physics w/ Lab***.	Biochem. is highly recommended.\n\nOther recommended courses: Genetics, Psych., and Comp. Science.	AP credits accepted as long as they are listed on undergraduate transcript.

ARIZONA

School	Required	Recommended	Notes
THE UNIVERSITY OF ARIZONA COLLEGE OF MEDICINE – PHOENIX	Chem., Biochem., Human or Mammalian Physio, additional Bio. course, Behav. Sciences, Writing-Intensive Course, Math (more advanced than College Algebra), and Humanities.	N/A	AP credits accepted as long as they are listed on undergraduate transcript.
THE UNIVERSITY OF ARIZONA COLLEGE OF MEDICINE – TUCSON	Physio., Biochem., Upper-division Molecular Bio., Social/Behav. Sciences, Stats., Upper Division Bio (choose: Cell Bio., Histology, Microbio., Pharmacology, Pathology, or Immunobiology), and Engl.	Biostats, For. Lang., and Labs recommended for all prerequisites when applicable.	AP credits accepted as long as they are listed on undergraduate transcript. If AP credits are used to satisfy prerequisite, students are expected to take upper-level coursework in that area.

For the number of hours required for prerequisite courses, and for the most up-to-date information, please refer to the individual school websites.

*A.P. credit satisfies the requirement.

** When A.P. credit is awarded, upper-level coursework in the same subject area is required.

*** A.P. credit may satisfy the requirement on a case by case basis.

ARKANSAS

School	Required	Recommended	Notes
UNIVERSITY OF ARKANSAS FOR MEDICAL SCIENCES COLLEGE OF MEDICINE	Behav. Sciences*, Biochem.***, Bio.*, Engl.*, Genetics*, Chem.*, OChem. w/ Lab, Physics*, and Stats.*.	Bio./Zoology, Comp. Science, Humanities, Psych., and Social Sciences*.	AP credits accepted as long as they are listed on undergraduate transcript.

CALIFORNIA

School	Required	Recommended	Notes
CALIFORNIA NORTHSTATE UNIVERSITY COLLEGE OF MEDICINE	Engl.*, Bio. w/ Lab, Chem. w/ Lab, OChem. w/ Lab, Physics, College Math (Stats./Calc. pref.), and Biochem.	Social Sciences, Behav. Sciences, For. Lang., Anatomy, Physio., Microbio., and Immunology.	AP credits accepted as long as they are listed on undergraduate transcript.
CALIFORNIA UNIVERSITY OF SCIENCE AND MEDICINE – SCHOOL OF MEDICINE	N/A	Behav. Sciences, Biochem., Bio. w/ Lab, Calc., Engl., Chem. w/ Lab, Molecular Bio., OChem. w/ Lab, and Physics w/ Lab.	No listed information on AP credits. Contact admissions.
DAVID GEFFEN SCHOOL OF MEDICINE AT UCLA	N/A	Behav. Sciences, Biochem., Calc., Engl., College Math, Engl., Genetics, Humanities, Chem. w/ Lab, OChem. w/ Lab, Physics w/ Lab, Psych., and Social Sciences.	AP credits accepted.
KAISER PERMANENTE SCHOOL OF MEDICINE	Behav. Sciences*, Bio. w/ Lab*, Humanities*, and Physics w/ Lab*.	OChem., Biochem., Calc., Stats., Epidemiology (or any public health course), and For. Lang.	AP credits accepted as long as they are listed on undergraduate transcript.

For the number of hours required for prerequisite courses, and for the most up-to-date information, please refer to the individual school websites.
*A.P. credit satisfies the requirement.
** When A.P. credit is awarded, upper-level coursework in the same subject area is required.
*** A.P. credit may satisfy the requirement on a case by case basis.

KECK SCHOOL OF MEDICINE OF THE UNIVERSITY OF SOUTHERN CALIFORNIA	N/A	Spanish and Stats. No other listed information.	No listed information on AP credits. Contact admissions.
LOMA LINDA UNIVERSITY SCHOOL OF MEDICINE	Biochem., Bio. w/ Lab, Chem. w/ Lab, OChem. w/ Lab, and Physics w/ Lab.	Behav. Sciences*, Calc.*, Engl.*, College Math*, Comp. Science*, Genetics, Humanities*, Psych.*, Social Sciences*, and Stats.*	AP credits for science prerequisites generally not accepted. If AP credit is held in required science areas, applicant must take advanced coursework in that area.
STANFORD UNIVERSITY SCHOOL OF MEDICINE	N/A	Behav. Sciences, Biochem., Bio., Engl., Genetics, Humanities, Chem., OChem., Physics, and Social Sciences.	No listed information on AP credits. Contact admissions.
UNIVERSITY OF CALIFORNIA, DAVIS SCHOOL OF MEDICINE	Bio.*, Chem.*, OChem.*, and Physics*.	Advanced Bio.*, Behav. Sciences, Biochem., Engl., College Math, Genetics, Human Physio., Humanities, and Social Sciences. Labs not required, but preferred.	AP credits accepted as long as they are listed on undergraduate transcript.
UNIVERSITY OF CALIFORNIA, IRVINE SCHOOL OF MEDICINE	Biochem., Bio., Upper-division Bio., Chem., OChem., and Physics.	Anatomy, Biostats., Bio. Lab, Chem. Lab, Cell Bio., Calc., Engl. Comp., Immunology, Microbio., Neuroscience, Psych. (Intro., Abnormal, and Developmental), and Spanish.	AP credits accepted for Chem. and Physics requirements. They must be listed on the undergraduate transcript.

For the number of hours required for prerequisite courses, and for the most up-to-date information, please refer to the individual school websites.

*A.P. credit satisfies the requirement.

** When A.P. credit is awarded, upper-level coursework in the same subject area is required.

*** A.P. credit may satisfy the requirement on a case by case basis.

UNIVERSITY OF CALIFORNIA, RIVERSIDE SCHOOL OF MEDICINE	Biochem. (lab rec.), Bio. (lab rec.)*, Calc./Stats.*, Engl.*, Chem. (lab rec.)*, OChem. (lab rec.), and Physics (lab rec.)*.	Engl. (Writing, Comp., Logic), Genetics, Humanities/Social Sciences, and Spanish.	AP credits with score of 3+ accepted.
UNIVERSITY OF CALIFORNIA, SAN DIEGO SCHOOL OF MEDICINE	N/A	Bio., Chem., OChem., Biochem., Physics, and Calc./Stats.	No listed information on AP credits. Contact admissions.
UNIVERSITY OF CALIFORNIA, SAN FRANCISCO SCHOOL OF MEDICINE	Bio. w/ Lab, Chem. w/ Lab*, OChem., Biochem., and Physics*.	Upper-level bio.	AP credits accepted for Chem. and Physics requirements. They must be listed on the undergraduate transcript.

COLORADO

School	Required	Recommended	Notes
UNIVERSITY OF COLORADO SCHOOL OF MEDICINE	N/A	Behav. Sciences, Biochem., Bio., Engl., College Math, Genetics, Chem., OChem., Psych., and Social Sciences.	AP credits accepted as long as they are listed on undergraduate transcript. If AP credits are used to satisfy science prerequisites, students are expected to take upper-level coursework in that area.

For the number of hours required for prerequisite courses, and for the most up-to-date information, please refer to the individual school websites.

*A.P. credit satisfies the requirement.

** When A.P. credit is awarded, upper-level coursework in the same subject area is required.

*** A.P. credit may satisfy the requirement on a case by case basis.

CONNECTICUT

School	Required	Recommended	Notes
FRANK H. NETTER MD SCHOOL OF MEDICINE AT QUINNIPIAC UNIVERSITY	Bio. w/ Lab, Chem. w/ Lab, OChem. w/ Lab, Biochem., Physics, Engl./ Writing Intensive, and College Math or Stats.	N/A	AP credits accepted.
UNIVERSITY OF CONNECTICUT SCHOOL OF MEDICINE	Chem. w/ Lab, OChem. w/ Lab, Physics w/ Lab, Bio./ Zoology w/ Lab, and Engl.	Biochem., Genetics, Physio., Engl. Comp. and Lit.	AP credits do not count towards prerequisite coursework. If AP credit is held in required area, applicant must take advanced coursework in that area.
YALE SCHOOL OF MEDICINE	Biochem. w/ Lab, Bio./Zoology w/ Lab, Chem. w/ Lab, OChem. w/ Lab, and Physics w/ Lab.	N/A	AP credits not accepted.

D.C.

School	Required	Recommended	Notes
GEORGETOWN UNIVERSITY SCHOOL OF MEDICINE	Bio. w/ Lab*, College Math*, Chem. w/ Lab*, OChem. w/ Lab*, and Physics w/ Lab*.	Microbio., Biochem.*, Calc.*, Engl.*, Psych.*, Comp. Science, Cellular Physio., Genetics*, Embryology, Biostats., Quantitative Analysis, Physical Chem., Humanities*, and Social/Behav. Sciences*.	AP credits accepted as long as they are listed on undergraduate transcript.

For the number of hours required for prerequisite courses, and for the most up-to-date information, please refer to the individual school websites.
*A.P. credit satisfies the requirement.
** When A.P. credit is awarded, upper-level coursework in the same subject area is required.
*** A.P. credit may satisfy the requirement on a case by case basis.

| HOWARD UNIVERSITY COLLEGE OF MEDICINE | Bio. w/ Lab, Chem. w/ Lab*, OChem. w/ Lab, Physics w/ Lab*, Math*/Stats., Engl.*, and Humanities coursework. | Anatomy & Physio., Cell Bio., Biochem., Developmental Bio. and Embryology, Genetics, Neuroscience, Psych.***, and Microbio. | AP credits accepted. |
| THE GEORGE WASHINGTON UNIVERSITY SCHOOL OF MEDICINE AND HEALTH SCIENCES | N/A | Bio. w/ Lab, Chem. w/ Lab, Physics w/ Lab, OChem. w/ Lab, Biochem. (if 2nd sem. of OChem. not taken), Stats./ Biostats/Probability, Engl., and Social/ Behav. Science. | AP credits not accepted. |

FLORIDA

School	Required	Recommended	Notes
CHARLES E. SCHMIDT COLLEGE OF MEDICINE AT FLORIDA ATLANTIC UNIVERSITY	Bio. w/ Lab*, Engl.*, College Math*, Chem. w/ Lab*, OChem. w/ Lab*, and Physics w/ Lab*.	Behav. Sciences*, Biochem. w/ Lab, Comp. Science*, Genetics w/ Lab*, Humanities*, Psych.*, and Social Sciences*.	AP credits accepted as long as they are listed on undergraduate transcript. If AP credits are used to satisfy prerequisites, students are expected to take upper-level coursework in that area.
FLORIDA INTERNATIONAL UNIVERSITY HERBERT WERTHEIM COLLEGE OF MEDICINE	Bio. w/ Lab*, Engl.*, College Math*, Chem. w/ Lab*, OChem. w/ Lab*, and Physics w/ Lab*.	Behav. Sciences*, Biochem. w/ Lab*, Cell Bio.*, For. Lang.*, Genetics*, Humanities*, Immunology*, Microbio.*, Social Sciences*, and Stats.	AP credits accepted.

For the number of hours required for prerequisite courses, and for the most up-to-date information, please refer to the individual school websites.

*A.P. credit satisfies the requirement.

** When A.P. credit is awarded, upper-level coursework in the same subject area is required.

*** A.P. credit may satisfy the requirement on a case by case basis.

NOVA SOUTHEASTERN UNIVERSITY DR. KIRAN C. PATEL COLLEGE OF ALLOPATHIC MEDICINE	Bio. w/ Lab*, Chem. w/ Lab*, OChem. w/ Lab* (Biochem. may substitute 2nd sem. of OChem.), Physics*, and College Math*.	Microbio., Cellular Physio., Genetics, Embryology, Biostats., Quantitative Analysis, Comp. Science, Physical Chem., Humanities, and Social/Behav. Sciences.	AP credits accepted as long as they are listed on undergraduate transcript.
THE FLORIDA STATE UNIVERSITY COLLEGE OF MEDICINE	Engl./Writing Intensive*, College Math*, Bio. w/ Lab*, OChem. w/ Lab*, Physics w/ Lab*, and Biochem.* (lab rec.).	Stats.*, Sociology*, Psych.*, Genetics*, and Spanish*.	AP credits accepted, although prerequisites taken at a four-year institution are preferred.
UNIVERSITY OF CENTRAL FLORIDA COLLEGE OF MEDICINE	Bio. w/ Lab*, Chem. w/ Lab*, OChem. w/ Lab*, Physics w/ Lab*, Engl.*, and College Math*.	Biochem., Genetics, Cell Bio., Stats., Comparative Anatomy, Calc. (strongly rec.), Humanities, Natural Sciences, and Communications Arts.	AP credits accepted. However, admissions expects that advanced-level undergraduate coursework is taken.
UNIVERSITY OF FLORIDA COLLEGE OF MEDICINE	Biochem., Bio. w/ Lab***, Chem. w/ Lab***, OChem. w/ Lab, and Physics w/ Lab***.	Stats., Genetics, Calc., Immunology, Physio., and Microbio.	AP credits accepted. However, if AP credit meets prerequisites, applicants are strongly encouraged to re-take coursework at undergraduate level or take advanced-level coursework in the same area.

For the number of hours required for prerequisite courses, and for the most up-to-date information, please refer to the individual school websites.
*A.P. credit satisfies the requirement.
** When A.P. credit is awarded, upper-level coursework in the same subject area is required.
*** A.P. credit may satisfy the requirement on a case by case basis.

UNIVERSITY OF MIAMI LEONARD M. MILLER SCHOOL OF MEDICINE	Behav. Sciences*, Biochem. (lab rec.), Bio. w/ Lab*, Engl.*, Chem. w/ Lab*, OChem. w/ Lab*, and Physics w/ Lab*.	Comp. Science***, Genetics***, Humanities***, Psych.***, Social Sciences***, Cell & Molecular Bio., Microbio., Physio., Immunology, Neuroscience, and Developmental Bio.	AP credits accepted as long as they are listed on undergraduate transcript.
USF HEALTH MORSANI COLLEGE OF MEDICINE	Bio. w/ Lab, Chem. w/ Lab, OChem. w/ Lab, Biochem., Physics w/ Lab, Math, and Engl.	Psych., Sociology, Arts, Humanities, and Ethics. Strongly encouraged: Molecular Bio., Genetics, and Microbio.	AP credits accepted. However, admissions expects that advanced-level undergraduate coursework is taken.

GEORGIA

School	Required	Recommended	Notes
EMORY UNIVERSITY SCHOOL OF MEDICINE	Physics w/ Lab*, Bio. w/ Lab*, Chem. w/ Lab*, OChem. w/ Lab*, Engl.*, and Humanities/Social Sciences*.	Behav. Sciences*, Biochem.*, Psych.*, and Social Sciences*.	AP credits accepted as long as they are listed on undergraduate transcript. However, admissions recommends that advanced-level undergraduate coursework is taken for science coursework.
MEDICAL COLLEGE OF GEORGIA AT AUGUSTA UNIVERSITY	Bio./Zoology w/ Lab**, Chem. w/ Lab**, OChem. w/ Lab, Biochem., Physics w/ Lab*, Engl.*, and Stats.*.	N/A	AP credits accepted as long as they are listed on undergraduate transcript.

For the number of hours required for prerequisite courses, and for the most up-to-date information, please refer to the individual school websites.

*A.P. credit satisfies the requirement.

** When A.P. credit is awarded, upper-level coursework in the same subject area is required.

*** A.P. credit may satisfy the requirement on a case by case basis.

MERCER UNIVERSITY SCHOOL OF MEDICINE	Bio. w/ Lab, Chem. w/ Lab, OChem. w/ Lab, and Physics w/ Lab*.	Behav. Sciences, Biochem., Engl.*, Calc.*, College Math*, Comp. Science*, Genetics*, Humanities*, Psych.*, and Social Sciences*.	AP credits accepted. However, if AP credit is taken for any science prerequisites (except Physics), one year of advanced science and lab in the same discipline is required.
MOREHOUSE SCHOOL OF MEDICINE	Bio. w/ Lab*, Engl.*, College Math*, Chem. w/ Lab*, OChem. w/ Lab*, and Physics w/ Lab*.	Behav. Sciences, Biochem. w/ Lab, Genetics*, Psych.*, and Stats.	AP credits accepted.

HAWAII

School	Required	Recommended	Notes
JOHN A. BURNS SCHOOL OF MEDICINE UNIVERSITY OF HAWAII AT MANOA	Bio. w/ Lab*, Physics w/ Lab*, Chem. w/ Lab*, OChem. w/ Lab*, and Biochem.*.	Anatomy, Behav. Sciences, Calc., Engl., Genetics, Humanities, Immunology, Microbio., Physio., Social Sciences, and Stats.	AP credits accepted as long as they are listed on undergraduate transcript.

For the number of hours required for prerequisite courses, and for the most up-to-date information, please refer to the individual school websites.

*A.P. credit satisfies the requirement.

** When A.P. credit is awarded, upper-level coursework in the same subject area is required.

*** A.P. credit may satisfy the requirement on a case by case basis.

ILLINOIS

School	Required	Recommended	Notes
CARLE ILLINOIS COLLEGE OF MEDICINE	N/A	Chem. w/ Lab, Biochem., Bio. w/ Lab, Physio./ Systems Bio./ Advanced Bio., Physics w/ Lab, Humanities/Social Sciences, Calc., Stats., Multivariable Calc., Differential Equations, and Linear Algebra.	AP credits not accepted unless succeeded by higher level courses at four-year institution.
CHICAGO MEDICAL SCHOOL AT ROSALIND FRANKLIN UNIVERSITY OF MEDICINE AND SCIENCE	Bio. w/ Lab**, Physics w/ Lab, Chem. w/ Lab**, OChem. w/ Lab**, Biochem. (lab rec.)*, and Behav./Social Sciences .	Stats., Advanced Bio. (Molecular and Cell Bio., Physio., Genetics, Microbio., Neurobio.), Engl. Comp., Humanities/ Social Sciences, Psych./Sociology, and Research Laboratory Course.	AP credits accepted. Admissions expects that advanced-level undergraduate coursework is taken.
LOYOLA UNIVERSITY CHICAGO STRITCH SCHOOL OF MEDICINE	Bio. w/ Lab***, Chem. w/ Lab***, and OChem.***.	Biochem., Genetics, Humanities, Molecular Bio., Physics*, and Physio.	AP credits accepted on a case-by-case basis.
NORTHWESTERN UNIVERSITY FEINBERG SCHOOL OF MEDICINE	Bio. w/ Lab**, Chem. w/ Lab**, OChem. w/ Lab**, Physics w/ Lab**.	Engl. Comp., Stats., Biochem., Genetics, Public Health, and Social Sciences.	AP credits accepted. Admissions expects that advanced-level undergraduate coursework is taken.
RUSH MEDICAL COLLEGE OF RUSH UNIVERSITY MEDICAL CENTER	N/A	Biochem., Cell Bio., Immunology, Molecular Bio., and Physio.	No listed information on AP credits. Contact admissions.

For the number of hours required for prerequisite courses, and for the most up-to-date information, please refer to the individual school websites.

*A.P. credit satisfies the requirement.

** When A.P. credit is awarded, upper-level coursework in the same subject area is required.

*** A.P. credit may satisfy the requirement on a case by case basis.

SOUTHERN ILLINOIS UNIVERSITY SCHOOL OF MEDICINE	N/A	Chem. w/ Lab, OChem. w/ Lab, Physics w/ Lab, Engl. Comp., Math, Stats., Bio. w/ Lab, and Biochem., Cell/ Molecular Bio., Physio., or Genetics.	No listed information on AP credits. Contact admissions.
UNIVERSITY OF CHICAGO DIVISION OF THE BIOLOGICAL SCIENCES, THE PRITZKER SCHOOL OF MEDICINE	Biochem.	Bio. w/ Lab***, College Engl., Genetics, Humanities, Chem. w/ Lab***, OChem. w/ Lab***, Physics***, Social Sciences, and Stats.	AP credits accepted on a case-by-case basis.
UNIVERSITY OF ILLINOIS COLLEGE OF MEDICINE	Advanced Level Bio.**, Biochem., Bio. w/ Lab***, Chem. w/ Lab***, OChem. w/ Lab***, Physics w/ Lab***, and Social/ Behav. Science*.	Behav. Sciences*, Genetics, Psych.*, and Social Sciences*.	AP credits accepted on a case-by-case basis.

INDIANA

School	Required	Recommended	Notes
INDIANA UNIVERSITY SCHOOL OF MEDICINE	Biochem.*, Bio. w/ Lab*, Chem. w/ Lab*, OChem. w/ Lab*, Physics w/ Lab*, Psych.*, and Social Sciences.	Behav. Sciences*, Bio./Zoology*, Calc.*, Engl.*, College Math*, Computer Science*, Genetics*, Humanities*, and Inorganic Chem. w/ Lab*.	AP credits accepted, however taking prerequisites at the college level is encouraged.

For the number of hours required for prerequisite courses, and for the most up-to-date information, please refer to the individual school websites.

*A.P. credit satisfies the requirement.

** When A.P. credit is awarded, upper-level coursework in the same subject area is required.

*** A.P. credit may satisfy the requirement on a case by case basis.

IOWA

School	Required	Recommended	Notes
UNIVERSITY OF IOWA ROY J. AND LUCILLE A. CARVER COLLEGE OF MEDICINE	Bio. w/ Lab, Advanced Bio., Chem. w/ Lab, OChem. w/ Lab, Physics w/ Lab, Biochem., Engl., Math/Stats., and Social/Behav. Sciences or Humanities.	Molecular and Cell Bio., Human Physio., Genetics, Microbio., Behav. Psych., Sociology, For. Lang., and non-science Writing Intensive Courses.	AP credits accepted as long as they are listed on undergraduate transcript.

KANSAS

School	Required	Recommended	Notes
UNIVERSITY OF KANSAS SCHOOL OF MEDICINE	Bio. w/ Lab*, Engl.*, Chem. w/ Lab*, OChem. w/ Lab*, and Physics w/ Lab*.	Immunology, Biochem., Genetics, Physio., Microbio., Natural Sciences, Behav./ Social Sciences, Humanities, Oral/Written Communications, and Social Determinants of Health (e.g., Cultural/Social Anthropology, Public or Population Health, Epidemiology, Environmental Health, Health Econ., Health Policy, History of Medicine/ Public Health, and Ethics related to Healthcare.)	AP credits accepted.

For the number of hours required for prerequisite courses, and for the most up-to-date information, please refer to the individual school websites.
*A.P. credit satisfies the requirement.
** When A.P. credit is awarded, upper-level coursework in the same subject area is required.
*** A.P. credit may satisfy the requirement on a case by case basis.

KENTUCKY

School	Required	Recommended	Notes
UNIVERSITY OF KENTUCKY COLLEGE OF MEDICINE	Biochem., Bio. (lab rec.)*, Engl., Chem. (lab rec.)*, OChem. (lab rec.)*, and Physics (lab rec.).	Behav. Sciences*, Genetics, Humanities, Psych.*, and Social Sciences*.	AP credits accepted.
UNIVERSITY OF LOUISVILLE SCHOOL OF MEDICINE	Biochem.*, Bio. w/ Lab, Engl.*, Chem. w/ Lab*, OChem.*, and Physics w/ Lab*.	Behav. Sciences, Genetics, Humanities, Physio., Psych., Social Sciences, and Stats.	AP credits accepted, except for Biology. In the case that AP Biology credit was awarded, applicant must take advanced level biology coursework.

LOUISIANA

School	Required	Recommended	Notes
LOUISIANA STATE UNIVERSITY SCHOOL OF MEDICINE IN SHREVEPORT	Bio., Chem., Biochem., Engl., and Humanities.	Cell Bio., Developmental Bio., Genetics, Histology, Immunology, Molecular Bio., Microbio., Neuroscience, and Physio.	AP credits accepted. LSU Shreveport strongly encourages taking coursework at a four-year institution.
LSU HEALTH SCIENCES CENTER SCHOOL OF MEDICINE IN NEW ORLEANS	Biochem., Bio. w/ Lab***, Engl., Chem. w/ Lab***, OChem. w/ Lab***, Physics w/ Lab***, and Stats.	Biochem., Cell Bio., Comparative Vertebrate Anatomy, Comp. Sciences, Embryology, Developmental Bio., Histology, Math., Microbio., Molecular Genetics, Physio., Stats., Epidemiology, Econ., Engl., Ethics, For. Lang., History, Philosophy, Psych., Public Speaking, and Sociology.	AP credits accepted on a case-by-case basis.

For the number of hours required for prerequisite courses, and for the most up-to-date information, please refer to the individual school websites.

*A.P. credit satisfies the requirement.

** When A.P. credit is awarded, upper-level coursework in the same subject area is required.

*** A.P. credit may satisfy the requirement on a case by case basis.

| TULANE UNIVERSITY SCHOOL OF MEDICINE | N/A | Behav. Sciences, Biochem., Bio. w/ Lab, Calc., Engl., Genetics, Chem. w/ Lab, OChem. w/ Lab, and Physics w/ Lab. | AP credits accepted. Admissions recommends that advanced-level undergraduate coursework is taken. |

MARYLAND

School	Required	Recommended	Notes
JOHNS HOPKINS UNIVERSITY SCHOOL OF MEDICINE	Biochem., Bio. w/ Lab*, Calc./Stats.*, Humanities/Social Sciences*, Chem. w/ Lab*, OChem. w/ Lab*, and Physics w/ Lab*.	Comp. Science and Genetics.	AP credits accepted as long as they are listed on undergraduate transcript.
UNIFORMED SERVICES UNIVERSITY OF THE HEALTH SCIENCES, F. EDWARD HÉBERT SCHOOL OF MEDICINE	Bio. w/ Lab*, Calc.*, Engl.*, Chem. w/ Lab*, OChem. w/ Lab, and Physics w/ Lab*.	Biochem., Humanities*, Psych.*, and Social Sciences*.	AP credits accepted. Admissions recommends that advanced-level undergraduate coursework is taken.
UNIVERSITY OF MARYLAND SCHOOL OF MEDICINE	Bio. w/ Lab*, Engl.*, Chem. w/ Lab*, OChem. w/ Lab*, and Physics w/ Lab*.	Behav. Sciences*, Biochem., Cell/ Molecular Bio., Genetics, Humanities*, Psych.*, Social Sciences*, and Stats.*.	AP credits accepted as long as they are listed on undergraduate transcript.

For the number of hours required for prerequisite courses, and for the most up-to-date information, please refer to the individual school websites.

*A.P. credit satisfies the requirement.

** When A.P. credit is awarded, upper-level coursework in the same subject area is required.

*** A.P. credit may satisfy the requirement on a case by case basis.

MASSACHUSETTS

School	Required	Recommended	Notes
BOSTON UNIVERSITY SCHOOL OF MEDICINE	Engl. Comp. or Lit., Humanities, Bio. w/ Lab, Chem. w/ Lab, OChem. w/ Lab, Physics, Stats., Biochem., Social and Behav. Sciences, and Genetics.	Molecular Bio. and Biostatistics and Epidemiology.	BU states that their prerequisite requirements are flexible. AP credits accepted on a case by case basis, however they discourage utilizing AP credits to fulfill prerequisites.
HARVARD MEDICAL SCHOOL	Pathways: Biol. w/ Lab (should include cellular and molecular aspects)**, Chem. w/ Lab**, OChem. w/ Lab, Biochem. w/ Lab, Physics**, Math (Calc and Stats, preferably Biostats.), and Writing. HST: Biol. w/ Lab (should include cellular and molecular aspects)**, Chem. w/ Lab**, OChem. w/ Lab, Biochem. w/ Lab, Physics (college-level), Math (Upper level math including differential equations and/or linear algebra and Stats. encouraged), and Writing.	Behav. Sciences, Physics Lab, Biostats., and Writing Intensive courses.	AP credits accepted for specific coursework.
TUFTS UNIVERSITY SCHOOL OF MEDICINE	Bio. w/ Lab, Chem. w/ Lab*, OChem., w/ Lab, and Physics w/ Lab.	Biochem.	AP credits accepted for specific coursework.

For the number of hours required for prerequisite courses, and for the most up-to-date information, please refer to the individual school websites.

*A.P. credit satisfies the requirement.

** When A.P. credit is awarded, upper-level coursework in the same subject area is required.

*** A.P. credit may satisfy the requirement on a case by case basis.

UNIVERSITY OF MASSACHUSETTS MEDICAL SCHOOL	Stats.**, Biochem., Chem. w/ Lab, OChem. w/ Lab, Calc., Engl., Physics w/ Lab, and Bio./ Zoology w/ Lab.	N/A	AP credits accepted as long as they are listed on undergraduate transcript.

MICHIGAN

School	Required	Recommended	Notes
CENTRAL MICHIGAN UNIVERSITY COLLEGE OF MEDICINE	Bio. w/ Lab and OChem. w/ Lab (or OChem. & Biochem. w/ Lab).	Biochem., Genetics, Human Anatomy, Human Physio., Math/Stats., OChem., Physics, and Social Sciences.	No listed information on AP credits. Contact admissions.
MICHIGAN STATE UNIVERSITY COLLEGE OF HUMAN MEDICINE	Biochem.*, Bio. w/ Lab*, College Math*, Chem. w/ Lab*, Upper-level Bio.*, OChem. w/ Lab*, Physics w/ Lab*, and Social Sciences*.	Behav. Sciences*, Engl.*, Comp. Science*, Genetics*, Humanities*, and Psych.*.	AP credits accepted as long as they are listed on undergraduate transcript.
OAKLAND UNIVERSITY WILLIAM BEAUMONT SCHOOL OF MEDICINE	Biochem., Stats., 1 Lab in Bio., Chem., or Physics, and Social/Behav. Sciences.	Philosophy, History, Lit., Language, Anthropology, Ethics, Theology, Psych., Sociology, Cultural Anthropology, Ecology, and Engl.	AP credits not accepted.
UNIVERSITY OF MICHIGAN MEDICAL SCHOOL	N/A	Biomedical & Social Sciences, Statistical Analysis & Epidemiology, Hypothesis Development & Investigation, and Analytical Thought & Problem-Solving Skills.	No listed information on AP credits. Contact admissions.

For the number of hours required for prerequisite courses, and for the most up-to-date information, please refer to the individual school websites.

*A.P. credit satisfies the requirement.

** When A.P. credit is awarded, upper-level coursework in the same subject area is required.

*** A.P. credit may satisfy the requirement on a case by case basis.

| WAYNE STATE UNIVERSITY SCHOOL OF MEDICINE | Bio. (lab rec.)*, College Writing/ Comp.*, Chem. (lab rec.)*, OChem. (lab rec.)*, and Physics (lab rec.)*. | Biochem., College Math, Medical Ethics, Social Sciences, and Stats. | AP credits accepted. |
| WESTERN MICHIGAN UNIVERSITY HOMER STRYKER M.D. SCHOOL OF MEDICINE | N/A | Biochem., Genetics, Human Anatomy, Human Physio., Immunology, and Stats. | No listed information on AP credits. Contact admissions. |

MINNESOTA

School	Required	Recommended	Notes
MAYO CLINIC ALIX SCHOOL OF MEDICINE	Bio. w/ Lab*, Chem. w/ Lab*, OChem. w/ Lab*, Physics w/ Lab*, and Biochem.*.	N/A	AP credits accepted as long as they are listed on undergraduate transcript. Students are encouraged to take higher level science courses.
UNIVERSITY OF MINNESOTA MEDICAL SCHOOL	Bio. w/ Lab, Chem. w/ Lab or OChem. w/ Lab, Upper Level Science, and Humanities or Social Sciences.	Biochem., Ethics, Genetics, Psych., Pharmacology, Stats., For. Lang., Independent Learning Coursework, Seminar Coursework, and Social/Behav. Sciences and Humanities.	AP credits not accepted. If AP credit has satisfied a prerequisite, student is required to take upper-level coursework in the same area.

For the number of hours required for prerequisite courses, and for the most up-to-date information, please refer to the individual school websites.

*A.P. credit satisfies the requirement.

** When A.P. credit is awarded, upper-level coursework in the same subject area is required.

*** A.P. credit may satisfy the requirement on a case by case basis.

MISSISSIPPI

School	Required	Recommended	Notes
UNIVERSITY OF MISSISSIPPI SCHOOL OF MEDICINE	2 Upper-Level Science Courses, Biochem. w/ Lab, and Physics w/ Lab.	Behav. Sciences, Bio. w/ Lab, Calc., Engl., College Math, Genetics, Humanities, OChem. w/ Lab, Psych., and Social Sciences.	AP credits not accepted. If AP credit has satisfied a prerequisite, student is required to take upper-level coursework in the same area.

MISSOURI

School	Required	Recommended	Notes
SAINT LOUIS UNIVERSITY SCHOOL OF MEDICINE	Bio./Zoology w/ Lab, Chem. w/ Lab, OChem. w/ Lab, Physics w/ Lab, Engl., and Humanities/Behav. Sciences.	Biochem., Psych., and Social Sciences.	AP credits accepted if listed on undergraduate transcript, however upper-level coursework is expected.
UNIVERSITY OF MISSOURI-COLUMBIA SCHOOL OF MEDICINE	Engl.*, Bio.*, College Math*, Chem.*, OChem.*, and Physics*.	Psych., Social Sciences, Humanities, Biochem., and Behav. Sciences.	AP credits accepted.
UNIVERSITY OF MISSOURI-KANSAS CITY SCHOOL OF MEDICINE	Biochem., Cell Bio.*, and Genetics.	Bio. w/ Lab*, Engl.*, College Math*, Chem. w/ Lab*, OChem. w/ Lab*, and Social Sciences.	AP credits accepted.
WASHINGTON UNIVERSITY IN ST. LOUIS SCHOOL OF MEDICINE	Bio.*, Calc.*, Chem.*, OChem.*, and Physics*.	Biochem.* and Stats.*.	AP credits accepted.

For the number of hours required for prerequisite courses, and for the most up-to-date information, please refer to the individual school websites.

*A.P. credit satisfies the requirement.

** When A.P. credit is awarded, upper-level coursework in the same subject area is required.

*** A.P. credit may satisfy the requirement on a case by case basis.

NEBRASKA

School	Required	Recommended	Notes
UNIVERSITY OF NEBRASKA COLLEGE OF MEDICINE	Biochem., Bio. w/ Lab***, Engl., Genetics, Humanities*, Chem. w/ Lab***, OChem. w/ Lab, and Physics w/ Lab***.	Behav. Sciences*, Bio./Zoology***, Calc., College Math, Psych.*, and Social Sciences*.	AP credits accepted on a case-by-case basis.

NEVADA

School	Required	Recommended	Notes
UNIVERSITY OF NEVADA, LAS VEGAS SCHOOL OF MEDICINE	Bio. w/ Lab, Biochem., Social & Behav. Sciences (Psych. or Sociology).	Genetics and Physics.	AP credits not accepted.
UNIVERSITY OF NEVADA, RENO SCHOOL OF MEDICINE	Behav. Sciences*, Biochem.*, Bio. w/ Lab*, Chem. w/ Lab*, OChem. w/ Lab*, Physics w/ Lab*, and Psych.	Microbio., Genetics, Calc., Stats., and Immunology.	AP credits accepted as long as they are listed on undergraduate transcript.

NEW HAMPSHIRE

School	Required	Recommended	Notes
GEISEL SCHOOL OF MEDICINE AT DARTMOUTH	Biochem., Bio. w/ Lab***, Chem. w/ Lab***, OChem. w/ Lab***, Calc./ Stats.***, and Physics***.	N/A	AP credits accepted on a case-by-case basis.

For the number of hours required for prerequisite courses, and for the most up-to-date information, please refer to the individual school websites.
*A.P. credit satisfies the requirement.
** When A.P. credit is awarded, upper-level coursework in the same subject area is required.
*** A.P. credit may satisfy the requirement on a case by case basis.

NEW JERSEY

School	Required	Recommended	Notes
COOPER MEDICAL SCHOOL OF ROWAN UNIVERSITY	Bio. w/ Lab, Chem. w/ Lab, and Engl.	Biochem., OChem. w/ Lab, Physics w/ Lab, Ethics, Behav. Science, Biostats., Humanities, and Spanish.	AP credits not accepted. If credit was given by undergraduate institution, student is expected to take upper level coursework in the area satisfied by AP credit.
HACKENSACK-MERIDIAN SCHOOL OF MEDICINE AT SETON HALL UNIVERSITY	Bio. w/ Lab*, Chem. w/ Lab*, Engl. Comp., Lit., Math, and 2 Sem. w/ Lab from the following: OChem., Biochem., Physics, Anatomy/ Physio., Zoology, or Botany.	Ethics, Spanish, Cell Bio., Ecology, Leadership, Econ., Political Science, Engineering, and Computer Sciences.	AP credits accepted as long as they are listed on undergraduate transcript.
RUTGERS NEW JERSEY MEDICAL SCHOOL	Bio. w/ Lab,* Chem. w/ Lab*, OChem. w/ Lab*, Physics w/ Lab*, and Engl./ Writing Intensive*.	Biochem., Calc., Genetics, and Stats.	AP credits accepted.
RUTGERS, ROBERT WOOD JOHNSON MEDICAL SCHOOL	Bio. or Zoology w/ Lab, Chem. w/ Lab, OChem. w/ Lab, Biochem., Physics w/ Lab, College Math, and Engl.	Cell Bio., Physio.*, Stats.*, and Molecular Bio.	AP credits accepted.

For the number of hours required for prerequisite courses, and for the most up-to-date information, please refer to the individual school websites.
*A.P. credit satisfies the requirement.
** When A.P. credit is awarded, upper-level coursework in the same subject area is required.
*** A.P. credit may satisfy the requirement on a case by case basis.

NEW MEXICO

School	Required	Recommended	Notes
UNIVERSITY OF NEW MEXICO SCHOOL OF MEDICINE	Biochem., Bio. w/ Lab*, Chem. w/ Lab*, OChem. w/ Lab*, and Physics*.	Anatomy & Physio. w/ Lab*, Molecular Genetics, Advanced Biochem., Developmental Bio., Psych./Sociology, Humanities, Immunology, and Microbio.	AP credits accepted.

NEW YORK

School	Required	Recommended	Notes
ALBANY MEDICAL COLLEGE	Bio. w/ Lab, Chem. w/ Lab, OChem. w/ Lab, and Physics.	N/A	AP credits accepted as long as they are listed on undergraduate transcript. If AP credits are used to satisfy prerequisite, students are expected to take upper-level coursework in that area.
ALBERT EINSTEIN COLLEGE OF MEDICINE	Behav. Sciences*, Bio. w/ Lab*, Chem. w/ Lab*, OChem. w/ Lab*, and Physics w/ Lab*.	Biochem. w/ Lab*, Calc., Engl.*, Math*, Computer Science*, Genetics w/ Lab, Humanities*, Psych.*, and Social Sciences*.	AP credits accepted.
COLUMBIA UNIVERSITY VAGELOS COLLEGE OF PHYSICIANS AND SURGEONS	Engl., Bio. w/ Lab, Physics w/ Lab, Chem. w/ Lab, and OChem. w/ Lab.	Biochem., Stats., and Biostats.	AP credits not accepted. If credit was given by undergraduate institution, student is expected to take upper level coursework in the area satisfied by AP credit.

For the number of hours required for prerequisite courses, and for the most up-to-date information, please refer to the individual school websites.
*A.P. credit satisfies the requirement.
** When A.P. credit is awarded, upper-level coursework in the same subject area is required.
*** A.P. credit may satisfy the requirement on a case by case basis.

CUNY SCHOOL OF MEDICINE	N/A	N/A	This university only offers a BS/MD program.
DONALD AND BARBARA ZUCKER SCHOOL OF MEDICINE AT HOFSTRA/ NORTHWELL	Technically, no required coursework.	Bio. w/ Lab, Chem. w/ Lab, OChem. w/ Lab, Biochem. w/ Lab, Stats., Calc., College Physics w/ Lab, and Engl. w/ Writing. Other recommended courses: Cell Bio., Embryology, Ethics, Genetics, Psych.*, Soc. Sciences*, and Molecular Bio.	AP credits accepted for certain coursework.
ICAHN SCHOOL OF MEDICINE AT MOUNT SINAI	Chem. w/ Lab**, OChem. w/ Lab**, Bio. w/ Lab**, Physics*, Stats., and Engl.	Second Language other than English, Integral Social Sciences (Political Science, Global Health, Psych., and Sociology).	AP credits accepted for certain coursework.
JACOBS SCHOOL OF MEDICINE AND BIOMEDICAL SCIENCES AT THE UNIVERSITY AT BUFFALO	Bio. w/ Lab*, College Engl.*, Chem. w/ Lab*, OChem. w/ Lab*, and Physics w/ Lab*.	Behav. Sciences*, Biochem.*, Computer Science*, Genetics*, Humanities*, Psych.*, Social Sciences*, and Stats.*	AP credits accepted.
NEW YORK MEDICAL COLLEGE	Engl., Bio. w/ Lab, Physics w/ Lab, Chem. w/ Lab, OChem. w/ Lab, and Biochem.	Upper-level science coursework.	No listed information on AP credits. Contact admissions.

For the number of hours required for prerequisite courses, and for the most up-to-date information, please refer to the individual school websites.
*A.P. credit satisfies the requirement.
** When A.P. credit is awarded, upper-level coursework in the same subject area is required.
*** A.P. credit may satisfy the requirement on a case by case basis.

NEW YORK UNIVERSITY GROSSMAN SCHOOL OF MEDICINE	N/A	Biochem.*, Bio. w/ Lab*, Engl.*, College Math*, Genetics*, Chem. w/ Lab*, OChem. w/ Lab*, Physics w/ Lab*, Psych.*, Social Sciences*, and Sociology*.	No strict requirements for pre-medical coursework.
NEW YORK UNIVERSITY LONG ISLAND SCHOOL OF MEDICINE	N/A	Behav. Sciences*, Biochem. w/ Lab*, Bio./Zoology w/ Lab*, Engl.*, College Math*, Genetics*, Humanities*, Chem. w/ Lab*, OChem. w/ Lab*, Physics w/ Lab*, Psych.*, and Social Sciences*.	No strict requirements for pre-medical coursework.
RENAISSANCE SCHOOL OF MEDICINE AT STONY BROOK UNIVERSITY	Bio. w/ Lab, Chem. w/ Lab, OChem. w/ Lab, Biochem., Engl., Physics w/ Lab, Social/Science/ Humanities, and Stats.	N/A	AP credits accepted for scores 4+.
STATE UNIVERSITY OF NEW YORK DOWNSTATE MEDICAL CENTER COLLEGE OF MEDICINE	Bio. w/ Lab*, Engl.*, Chem. w/ Lab*, OChem. w/ Lab*, and Physics w/ Lab*.	Biochem. w/ Lab*, Genetics w/ Lab*, Humanities, Psych., and Social Sciences.	AP credits accepted. Students are strongly encouraged to take upper level coursework in the area that AP credit satisfied prerequisites.
STATE UNIVERSITY OF NEW YORK UPSTATE MEDICAL UNIVERSITY COLLEGE OF MEDICINE	Bio. w/ Lab*, Chem. w/ Lab*, OChem. w/ Lab*, Biochem., Physics w/ Lab*, Stats.*, Engl. Elective, and Engl. Comp./Writing.	Genetics, Physio., Cell Bio., and Social Sciences*	N/A

For the number of hours required for prerequisite courses, and for the most up-to-date information, please refer to the individual school websites.

*A.P. credit satisfies the requirement.

** When A.P. credit is awarded, upper-level coursework in the same subject area is required.

*** A.P. credit may satisfy the requirement on a case by case basis.

UNIVERSITY OF ROCHESTER SCHOOL OF MEDICINE AND DENTISTRY	Bio. w/ Lab, Humanities, Chem. w/ Lab*, OChem. w/ Lab, Physics w/ Lab*, Biochem. w/ Lab (only req. if only 1 sem. of OChem is taken), Humanities/ Social Sciences, and Writing.	Chem., Stats., Biostats., Genetics, Physio., and Biochem.	AP credits accepted as long as they are listed on undergraduate transcript.
WEILL CORNELL MEDICINE	Bio. w/ Lab, Engl., Chem. w/ Lab, OChem. w/ Lab, and Physics w/ Lab*.	Behav. Sciences, Calc., Humanities, Psych., Social Sciences, and Stats.	AP credits accepted. Students are required to take upper level coursework in the area that AP credit satisfied prerequisites.

NORTH CAROLINA

School	Required	Recommended	Notes
DUKE UNIVERSITY SCHOOL OF MEDICINE	N/A	Behav. Sciences, Biochem., Cell Bio.***, Engl., Genetics, Chem.*, OChem.*, Physics, Psych., Social Sciences, Spanish, and Stats./ Biostats.***.	AP credits accepted as long as they are listed on undergraduate transcript.

For the number of hours required for prerequisite courses, and for the most up-to-date information, please refer to the individual school websites.

*A.P. credit satisfies the requirement.

** When A.P. credit is awarded, upper-level coursework in the same subject area is required.

*** A.P. credit may satisfy the requirement on a case by case basis.

THE BRODY SCHOOL OF MEDICINE AT EAST CAROLINA UNIVERSITY	Biochem., Bio. w/ Lab*, Engl.*, Humanities*, Chem. w/ Lab*, OChem. w/ Lab*, Physics w/ Lab*, Psych.*, Social Sciences*, and Stats./Biostats.*.	Genetics* and additional year of Engl.	AP credits accepted as long as they are listed on undergraduate transcript.
UNIVERSITY OF NORTH CAROLINA SCHOOL OF MEDICINE	Behav. Sciences, Bio. w/ Lab, Engl., Biochem., Humanities, Chem. w/ Lab, OChem. w/ Lab, Psych., Social Sciences, and Stats./ Biostats.	Genetics.	AP credits not accepted.
WAKE FOREST SCHOOL OF MEDICINE	N/A	Bio. w/ Lab, Chem. w/ Lab, OChem. w/ Lab, Physics w/ Lab, Molecular/ Cell Bio., Genetics, Anatomy, Physio., Neuroscience, Biochem., College Algebra, Stats., Psych., Behav. Psych., Abnormal Psych., Sociology, For. Lang. (especially Spanish), Philosophy, Medical Ethics, Literature, and coursework focused on health disparities.	AP credits accepted.

For the number of hours required for prerequisite courses, and for the most up-to-date information, please refer to the individual school websites.

*A.P. credit satisfies the requirement.

** When A.P. credit is awarded, upper-level coursework in the same subject area is required.

*** A.P. credit may satisfy the requirement on a case by case basis.

NORTH DAKOTA

School	Required	Recommended	Notes
UNIVERSITY OF NORTH DAKOTA SCHOOL OF MEDICINE AND HEALTH SCIENCES	N/A	Bio. w/ Lab*, Behav. Sciences*, Bio./Zoology w/ Lab*, Calc., Engl.*, College Math*, Comp. Science, Genetics, Humanities, Chem. w/ Lab*, OChem. w/ Lab*, Physics*, and Psych.*. Also strongly recommended: Upper-level Intensive Writing, Biochem.*, and 1-2 Upper-Level Bio. Courses.	AP credits accepted.

OHIO

School	Required	Recommended	Notes
BOONSHOFT SCHOOL OF MEDICINE WRIGHT STATE UNIVERSITY	Bio. w/ Lab, Chem. w/ Lab, OChem. w/ Lab, Physics w/ Lab, College Math, Engl., and Biochem.	N/A	AP credits accepted as long as they are listed on undergraduate transcript.
CASE WESTERN RESERVE UNIVERSITY SCHOOL OF MEDICINE	Chem. w/ Lab*, OChem. w/ Lab, Biochem., and Writing/College Engl.	Cellular Bio., Physics, Genetics, Biostats., Social/Behav. Sciences, and Research Experience.	AP credits accepted for Chem. only. Additional required coursework for MD/PhD.
NORTHEAST OHIO MEDICAL UNIVERSITY COLLEGE OF MEDICINE	OChem. w. Lab***, Physics w/ Lab***, Bio. w/ Lab***, and Biochem.***.	Anatomy, Calc.***, Cell Bio., Engl. Comp.***, Genetics, Immunology, Microbio., Molecular Bio., Physio., Psych.***, Sociology***, and Stats***.	AP credits accepted on a case-by-case basis.

For the number of hours required for prerequisite courses, and for the most up-to-date information, please refer to the individual school websites.

*A.P. credit satisfies the requirement.

** When A.P. credit is awarded, upper-level coursework in the same subject area is required.

*** A.P. credit may satisfy the requirement on a case by case basis.

THE OHIO STATE UNIVERSITY COLLEGE OF MEDICINE	Biochem.*, Bio.*, Chem. w/ Lab*, OChem. w/ Lab*, and Physics w/ Lab*.	Anatomy, Behav. Sciences*, Engl.*, Diversity/ Ethics*, Genetics*, Humanities*, Psych.*, and Social Sciences.	AP credits accepted.
THE UNIVERSITY OF TOLEDO COLLEGE OF MEDICINE AND LIFE SCIENCES	Biochem.*, Bio. w/ Lab*, Chem. w/ Lab*, OChem. w/ Lab*, and Physics*.	Anatomy*, Biostats.*, Engl.*, College Math*, Genetics*, Humanities*, Chem.*, Medical Terminology*, Physio.*, Psych.*, and Social Sciences.	AP credits accepted.
UNIVERSITY OF CINCINNATI COLLEGE OF MEDICINE	N/A	Anatomy & Physio. w/ Lab, Behav. Sciences*, Biochem., Bio.*, Engl.*, College Math*, Genetics, Histology, Humanities, Immunology, Chem.*, OChem. w/ Lab*, Physics w/ Lab*, Psych.*, and Social Sciences.	AP credits accepted.

OKLAHOMA

School	Required	Recommended	Notes
UNIVERSITY OF OKLAHOMA COLLEGE OF MEDICINE	Bio./Zoology w/ Lab*, Engl.*, Genetics/Cell Bio./ Molecular Bio., Humanities*, Chem.*, OChem.***, Physics***, Physics***, Psych*, and Social Sciences*.	Biochem. and a writing-intensive Engl. course.	AP credits accepted. However, students are required to take upper level coursework in the area that AP credit satisfied prerequisites.

For the number of hours required for prerequisite courses, and for the most up-to-date information, please refer to the individual school websites.

*A.P. credit satisfies the requirement.

** When A.P. credit is awarded, upper-level coursework in the same subject area is required.

*** A.P. credit may satisfy the requirement on a case by case basis.

OREGON

School	Required	Recommended	Notes
OREGON HEALTH & SCIENCE UNIVERSITY SCHOOL OF MEDICINE	N/A	Writing-Intensive, Stats., Calc., Comp. Science, Bio., Chem., OChem., Physics, Anatomy, Laboratory coursework, Psych., and Sociology.	AP credits accepted as long as they are listed on undergraduate transcript.

PENNSYLVANIA

School	Required	Recommended	Notes
DREXEL UNIVERSITY COLLEGE OF MEDICINE	N/A	Behav. Sciences*, Biochem.*, Bio.*, Engl.*, Genetics, Humanities*, Chem.*, Molecular Bio.*, OChem.*, Physics*, Psych.*, Social Sciences*, Biostats., and One year of lab experience (more than 1 recommended).	AP credits accepted. Students are strongly encouraged to take upper level coursework in the area that AP credit satisfied prerequisites.
GEISINGER COMMONWEALTH SCHOOL OF MEDICINE	Bio. w/ Lab, Chem. w/ Lab, OChem. w. Lab, Physics w/ Lab, and Engl./Engl. Comp.	N/A	AP credits accepted on a case-by-case basis.
LEWIS KATZ SCHOOL OF MEDICINE AT TEMPLE UNIVERSITY	N/A	Biochem., Bio. w/ Lab*, Humanities*, Chem. w/ Lab*, OChem. w/ Lab*, Physics w/ Lab*, and Psych.*.	AP credits accepted. Students are strongly encouraged to take upper level coursework in the area that AP credit satisfied prerequisites.

For the number of hours required for prerequisite courses, and for the most up-to-date information, please refer to the individual school websites.

*A.P. credit satisfies the requirement.

** When A.P. credit is awarded, upper-level coursework in the same subject area is required.

*** A.P. credit may satisfy the requirement on a case by case basis.

PENN STATE COLLEGE OF MEDICINE	N/A	Behav. Sciences*, Biochem.*, Bio. w/ Lab*, Calc.*, Engl.*, College Math*, Genetics, Chem. w/ Lab*, OChem. w/ Lab*, Physics w/ Lab*, Psych., and Social Sciences.	AP credits accepted. Students are strongly encouraged to take upper level coursework in the area that AP credit satisfied prerequisites.
SIDNEY KIMMEL MEDICAL COLLEGE AT THOMAS JEFFERSON UNIVERSITY	N/A	Behav. Sciences***, Biochem.***, Bio. w/ Lab***, Engl.***, College Math***, Genetics***, Humanities***, Chem. w/ Lab***, OChem. w/ Lab***, Physics w/ Lab***, Psych.***, and Social Sciences***.	AP credits accepted. Students are strongly encouraged to take upper level coursework in the area that AP credit satisfied prerequisites.
THE RAYMOND AND RUTH PERELMAN SCHOOL OF MEDICINE AT THE UNIVERSITY OF PENNSYLVANIA	N/A	Behav. Sciences*, Biochem.*, Bio. w/ Lab*, Engl.*, College Math*, Genetics*, Humanities*, Chem.*, OChem.*, Physics*, Psych.*, Social Sciences*, and Stats.*.	AP credits accepted as long as they are listed on undergraduate transcript.
UNIVERSITY OF PITTSBURGH SCHOOL OF MEDICINE	Bio. w/ Lab*, Chem. w/ Lab*, OChem. w/ Lab*, Physics w/ Lab*, Engl./Intensive Writing*, Biochem.*, and Stats*.	Psych.* and Biostats.*.	AP credits accepted as long as they are listed on undergraduate transcript.

For the number of hours required for prerequisite courses, and for the most up-to-date information, please refer to the individual school websites.
*A.P. credit satisfies the requirement.
** When A.P. credit is awarded, upper-level coursework in the same subject area is required.
*** A.P. credit may satisfy the requirement on a case by case basis.

PUERTO RICO

School	Required	Recommended	Notes
PONCE HEALTH SCIENCES UNIVERSITY SCHOOL OF MEDICINE	Behav. Sciences, Bio. w/ Lab, Chem. w/ Lab, Engl.***, College Math, OChem. w/ Lab, Physics w/ Lab, Social Sciences*, and Spanish*.	Biochem. and Psych.	AP credits accepted.
SAN JUAN BAUTISTA SCHOOL OF MEDICINE	Behav. Sciences, Bio. w/ Lab, Engl.*, Chem. w/ Lab, OChem. w/ Lab, Physics w/ Lab, and Spanish*.	Biochem., College Math, Comp. Science, Genetics, Humanities, Psych., and Social Sciences.	AP credits accepted.
UNIVERSIDAD CENTRAL DEL CARIBE SCHOOL OF MEDICINE	Behav. Sciences, Bio. w/ Lab, Engl.*, College Math*, Chem. w/ Lab, OChem. w/ Lab, Physics w/ Lab, and Spanish*.	Biochem., Comp. Science*, Genetics, Psych.*, and Social Sciences* (Sociology, Anthropology, and Econ rec.).	AP credits accepted.
UNIVERSITY OF PUERTO RICO SCHOOL OF MEDICINE	Behav. Sciences, Bio. w/ Lab, Engl., Chem. w/ Lab, OChem. w/ Lab, Physics w/ Lab, and Spanish.	Biochem., Comp. Science, and Humanities.	No listed information on AP credits. Contact admissions.

RHODE ISLAND

School	Required	Recommended	Notes
THE WARREN ALPERT MEDICAL SCHOOL OF BROWN UNIVERSITY	Biochem.*, Bio. w/ Lab**, Calc.*/Stats., Chem. w/ Lab*, OChem. w/ Lab*, and Physics*.	Behav. Sciences*, Engl., Genetics, Humanities, Social Sciences*, and Biostats.	AP credits accepted as long as they are listed on undergraduate transcript. 2 Biology courses must be taken in college.

For the number of hours required for prerequisite courses, and for the most up-to-date information, please refer to the individual school websites.

*A.P. credit satisfies the requirement.

** When A.P. credit is awarded, upper-level coursework in the same subject area is required.

*** A.P. credit may satisfy the requirement on a case by case basis.

SOUTH CAROLINA

School	Required	Recommended	Notes
MEDICAL UNIVERSITY OF SOUTH CAROLINA COLLEGE OF MEDICINE	N/A	Strongly recommend: Bio. w/ Lab*, Chem. w/ Lab*, OChem. w/ Lab,* and Physics w/ Lab*. Other recommended courses: Biochem.*, Anatomy*, Cell Bio.*, Embryology, Genetics*, Physio.*, Immunology, Stats., College Math, and Writing-Intensive coursework.	AP credits accepted as long as they are listed on undergraduate transcript.
UNIVERSITY OF SOUTH CAROLINA SCHOOL OF MEDICINE, COLUMBIA	N/A	Bio., Chem., OChem., Biochem., and advanced studies in the sciences.	No listed information on AP credits. Contact admissions.
UNIVERSITY OF SOUTH CAROLINA SCHOOL OF MEDICINE, GREENVILLE	Biochem.***, Bio. w/ Lab***, Engl.***, Chem. w/ Lab***, OChem. w/ Lab***, and Physics w/ Lab***.	Cell Bio.***, Genetics***, Psych.***, Social Sciences***, and Behav. Sciences***.	AP credits accepted as long as they are listed on undergraduate transcript. Students are strongly encouraged to take upper level coursework in the area that AP credit satisfied prerequisites.

SOUTH DAKOTA

School	Required	Recommended	Notes
UNIVERSITY OF SOUTH DAKOTA SANFORD SCHOOL OF MEDICINE	Biochem., Bio. w/ Lab*, College Math***, Chem. w/ Lab***, OChem. w/ Lab***, Physics w/ Lab***, and Stats.	Engl., Genetics, Microbio., Physio., Psych., and Social Sciences.	AP credits accepted on a case-by-case basis.

For the number of hours required for prerequisite courses, and for the most up-to-date information, please refer to the individual school websites.
*A.P. credit satisfies the requirement.
** When A.P. credit is awarded, upper-level coursework in the same subject area is required.
*** A.P. credit may satisfy the requirement on a case by case basis.

TENNESSEE

School	Required	Recommended	Notes
EAST TENNESSEE STATE UNIVERSITY JAMES H. QUILLEN COLLEGE OF MEDICINE	N/A	Behav. Sciences, Biochem. w/ Lab*, Bio. w/ Lab*, Calc., Engl.*, Communications*, Genetics*, Humanities*, Chem. w/ Lab*, OChem. w/ Lab*, Physics w/ Lab*, Psych.*, Social Sciences*, Rhetoric, and Logic.	AP credits accepted as long as they are listed on undergraduate transcript.
MEHARRY MEDICAL COLLEGE SCHOOL OF MEDICINE	Bio. w/ Lab, Biochem., Engl.*, Chem. w/ Lab, OChem. w/ Lab, and Physics w/ Lab.	Calc. and Genetics.	AP credits accepted.
UNIVERSITY OF TENNESSEE HEALTH SCIENCE CENTER COLLEGE OF MEDICINE	Chem. w/ Lab, OChem. w/ Lab, Physics w/ Lab, Bio. w/ Lab, and Engl.	Psych., Sociology, Biochem., Cell Bio., Comparative Anatomy, Embryology, Genetics, Histology, Immunology, Mammalian Physio., Microbio., Higher Mathematics, Comp. Science, For. Lang., Lit., Philosophy, History, Etymology, Political Sciences, Econ., and Stats.	AP credits accepted. Students are required to take upper level coursework if AP credit satisfied any science requirements. Students are encouraged, but not required, to take upper level coursework if AP credit satisfied the English requirement.
VANDERBILT UNIVERSITY SCHOOL OF MEDICINE	N/A	Biochem.*, Bio. w/ Lab*, Engl.*, Chem. w/ Lab*, OChem. w/ Lab*, Physics w/ Lab*, and Social Sciences*.	AP credits accepted. Students are strongly encouraged to take upper level coursework in the area that AP credit satisfied prerequisites.

For the number of hours required for prerequisite courses, and for the most up-to-date information, please refer to the individual school websites.

*A.P. credit satisfies the requirement.

** When A.P. credit is awarded, upper-level coursework in the same subject area is required.

*** A.P. credit may satisfy the requirement on a case by case basis.

TEXAS

School	Required	Recommended	Notes
BAYLOR COLLEGE OF MEDICINE	College Math (Biostats. rec.), Expository Writing, Humanities/Social Sciences, OChem., Biochem., and Advanced Bio.	Highly recommended: Genetics and Cell/Molecular Bio. Other recommendations: Spanish.	AP credits not accepted for required prerequisites. However, AP credits are accepted for other coursework as long as they appear on the undergraduate transcript. Additional upper-level coursework recommended in areas that AP credit was given.
MCGOVERN MEDICAL SCHOOL AT THE UNIVERSITY OF TEXAS HEALTH SCIENCE CENTER AT HOUSTON	Bio. w/ Lab*, Engl.*, Chem. w/ Lab*, OChem. w/ Lab***, and Physics w/ Lab*.	Biochem., Stats., Psych., and Sociology.	AP credits accepted as long as they are listed on undergraduate transcript.
PAUL L. FOSTER SCHOOL OF MEDICINE TEXAS TECH UNIVERSITY HEALTH SCIENCES CENTER	Biochem., Bio. w/ Lab*, Calc./Stats*, Engl.*, Chem. w/ Lab*, OChem. w/ Lab*, and Physics w/ Lab*.	Behav. Sciences, Cellular/Molecular Bio., Genetics, Humanities, and Social Sciences.	AP credits accepted.
TCU AND UNTHSC SCHOOL OF MEDICINE	Biochem.***, Engl.***, Genetics***, Humanities***, Physio.***, Social/Behav. Sciences***, and Stats./Biostats.***.	N/A	AP credits accepted on a case-by-case basis.

For the number of hours required for prerequisite courses, and for the most up-to-date information, please refer to the individual school websites.

*A.P. credit satisfies the requirement.

** When A.P. credit is awarded, upper-level coursework in the same subject area is required.

*** A.P. credit may satisfy the requirement on a case by case basis.

TEXAS A&M UNIVERSITY HEALTH SCIENCE CENTER COLLEGE OF MEDICINE	Advanced Bio. Sciences, Biochem., Bio. w/ Lab*, Engl.*, Chem. w/ Lab*, Math-based Stats.***, OChem. w/ Lab*, and Physics w/ Lab*.	N/A	AP credits accepted, although prerequisites taken at a four-year institution are preferred.
TEXAS TECH UNIVERSITY HEALTH SCIENCES CENTER SCHOOL OF MEDICINE	Biochem.***, Bio. w/ Lab, Engl.*, Chem. w/ Lab, OChem. w/ Lab, Physics w/ Lab, and Stats.*.	Genetics, Psych.*, and Social Sciences*.	AP credits accepted as long as they are listed on undergraduate transcript.
THE UNIVERSITY OF TEXAS AT AUSTIN DELL MEDICAL SCHOOL	Biochem.*, Bio. w/ Lab*, Engl.*, College Math*, Chem. w/ Lab*, OChem. w/ Lab*, and Physics w/ Lab*.	Genetics.	AP credits accepted as long as they are listed on undergraduate transcript.
THE UNIVERSITY OF TEXAS HEALTH SCIENCE CENTER AT SAN ANTONIO JOE R. AND TERESA LOZANO LONG SCHOOL OF MEDICINE	Biochem.*, Bio. w/ Lab*, Engl.*, Chem. w/ Lab*, OChem. w/ Lab*, Physics w/ Lab*, and Stats.*.	N/A	AP credits accepted as long as they are listed on undergraduate transcript.
THE UNIVERSITY OF TEXAS MEDICAL BRANCH AT GALVESTON SCHOOL OF MEDICINE	Bio. w/ Lab*, Engl.*, Chem. w/ Lab*, OChem. w/ Lab*, and Physics w/ Lab*.	Biochem.* and Genetics*.	AP credits accepted.
THE UNIVERSITY OF TEXAS RIO GRANDE VALLEY SCHOOL OF MEDICINE	Engl., Bio. w/ Lab, Biochem., Chem. w/ Lab, OChem. w/ Lab, Physics w/ Lab, and Stats.	Behav. Sciences, Comp. Science, Genetics, Psych., and Social Sciences.	AP credits accepted as long as they are listed on undergraduate transcript.
THE UNIVERSITY OF TEXAS SOUTHWESTERN MEDICAL SCHOOL	Bio. w/ Lab, Biochem., Chem. w/ Lab, OChem. w/ Lab, Engl., Math, and Physics w/ Lab.	N/A	AP credits accepted as long as they are listed on undergraduate transcript.

For the number of hours required for prerequisite courses, and for the most up-to-date information, please refer to the individual school websites.

*A.P. credit satisfies the requirement.

** When A.P. credit is awarded, upper-level coursework in the same subject area is required.

*** A.P. credit may satisfy the requirement on a case by case basis.

School	Required	Recommended	Notes
UNIVERSITY OF HOUSTON COLLEGE OF MEDICINE	Bio. w/ Lab, Advanced Bio., Chem. w/ Lab, OChem. w/ Lab, Biochem., Physics w/ Lab, Stats., and Engl. Comp.	For. Lang. and other biology courses: Molecular, Genetics, Human Physio., and Immunology	AP credits accepted as long as they are listed on undergraduate transcript.

UTAH

School	Required	Recommended	Notes
UNIVERSITY OF UTAH SCHOOL OF MEDICINE	Chem. w/ Lab*, OChem. w/ Lab, Phsyics w/ Lab, Writing/Speech, Bio. (1 course must be in Cell. Bio. or Biochem.), Social Science, and Humanities.	Anatomy, Behav. Sciences, College Math, Genetics, Human Behavior, Psych., Research Methods, and Stats.	AP credits (score 4+) only accepted for one semester of General Chemistry.

VERMONT

School	Required	Recommended	Notes
THE ROBERT LARNER, M.D. COLLEGE OF MEDICINE AT THE UNIVERSITY OF VERMONT	Bio. w/ Lab*, Chem. w/ Lab*, OChem. w/ Lab*, and Physics w/ Lab*.	Biochem., Molecular Genetics, Behav. Sciences, Engl., College Math, Humanities, Social Sciences, and Stats.*.	AP credits accepted as long as they are listed on undergraduate transcript.

VIRGINIA

School	Required	Recommended	Notes
EASTERN VIRGINIA MEDICAL SCHOOL	Bio. w/ Lab*, Chem. w/ Lab*, OChem. w/ Lab*, and Physics w/ Lab*.	Biochem. is strongly recommended.	AP credits accepted.

For the number of hours required for prerequisite courses, and for the most up-to-date information, please refer to the individual school websites.
*A.P. credit satisfies the requirement.
** When A.P. credit is awarded, upper-level coursework in the same subject area is required.
*** A.P. credit may satisfy the requirement on a case by case basis.

UNIVERSITY OF VIRGINIA SCHOOL OF MEDICINE	N/A	Cell Bio., Biochem., Human Behav., and Stats.	AP credits accepted as long as they are listed on undergraduate transcript.
VIRGINIA COMMONWEALTH UNIVERSITY SCHOOL OF MEDICINE	Bio. w/ Lab*, Engl.*, College Math*, Chem. w/ Lab*, OChem. w/ Lab*, and Physics w/ Lab*.	Biochem., Cell Bio., Anatomy, Embryology, Genetics, Microbio., Molecular Bio., Immunology, Neuroscience, Psych., and Sociology.	AP credits accepted as long as they are listed on undergraduate transcript.
VIRGINIA TECH CARILION SCHOOL OF MEDICINE	N/A	Biochem., Cell Bio., Comparative Anatomy, Genetics, Microbio., Physio., Psych., and Sociology.	AP credits accepted as long as they are listed on undergraduate transcript.

WASHINGTON

School	Required	Recommended	Notes
UNIVERSITY OF WASHINGTON SCHOOL OF MEDICINE	Bio.*, Chem., Calc.*, Humanities*, Physics*, and Social Sciences*.	Biochem., OChem.*, Genetics, Psych.*, Ethics, Anatomy/ Comparative Anatomy, Human or Mammalian Physio., and Embryology.	AP credits accepted as long as they are listed on undergraduate transcript.

For the number of hours required for prerequisite courses, and for the most up-to-date information, please refer to the individual school websites.

*A.P. credit satisfies the requirement.

** When A.P. credit is awarded, upper-level coursework in the same subject area is required.

*** A.P. credit may satisfy the requirement on a case by case basis.

| WASHINGTON STATE UNIVERSITY ELSON S. FLOYD COLLEGE OF MEDICINE | Bio. w/ Lab* (Genetics and Molecular Bio. pref.), OChem. w/ Lab*, Physics w/ Lab*. | Humanities*, Engl.*, College Math*, Sociology*, Human Development/ Embryology, Ethics, Genetics*, Anatomy or Comparative Anatomy, Stats., For. Language (Spanish pref.), Research coursework or Data Management, Psych.*, and Human or Mammalian Physio. | AP credits accepted as long as they are listed on undergraduate transcript. |

WEST VIRGINIA

School	Required	Recommended	Notes
MARSHALL UNIVERSITY JOAN C. EDWARDS SCHOOL OF MEDICINE	Behav. Sciences*, Biochem., Bio. w/ Lab*, Engl.*, Chem. w/ Lab*, OChem. w/ Lab, Physics w/ Lab*, and Social Sciences*.	Stats/Biostats, Epidemilogy, and Cellular and Molecular Bio.	AP credits accepted as long as they are listed on undergraduate transcript and upon successful completion of an advanced course in that field.
WEST VIRGINIA UNIVERSITY SCHOOL OF MEDICINE	N/A	Advanced Cell. & Molecular Bio.*, Behav./ Social Sciences*, Biochem.*, Bio.*, Engl.*, Chem.*, OChem.*, Physics*, Social Sciences*, and Laboratory Experience.	AP credits accepted.

For the number of hours required for prerequisite courses, and for the most up-to-date information, please refer to the individual school websites.

*A.P. credit satisfies the requirement.

** When A.P. credit is awarded, upper-level coursework in the same subject area is required.

*** A.P. credit may satisfy the requirement on a case by case basis.

WISCONSIN

School	Required	Recommended	Notes
MEDICAL COLLEGE OF WISCONSIN	Advanced Bio., Biochem., Bio., College Engl.*, College Math*, Chem.*, OChem.*, Physics*, and Social Sciences*.	Behav. Sciences*, Bio./Zoology*, Calc.*, Genetics, Humanities, Oral Communication*, and Psych.*.	AP credits accepted.
UNIVERSITY OF WISCONSIN SCHOOL OF MEDICINE AND PUBLIC HEALTH	Biochem., Bio./ Zoology w/ Lab*, Chem. w/ Lab*, Intensive Writing Course (that requires a research paper)***, OChem., Physics w/ Lab*, and Stats.*	Behav. Sciences, College Engl.*, Humanities*, Psych., and Social Sciences.	AP credits accepted as long as they are listed on undergraduate transcript.

For the number of hours required for prerequisite courses, and for the most up-to-date information, please refer to the individual school websites.

*A.P. credit satisfies the requirement.

** When A.P. credit is awarded, upper-level coursework in the same subject area is required.

*** A.P. credit may satisfy the requirement on a case by case basis.

CHAPTER 9

TOP 20 MEDICAL SCHOOLS

Rank	School	Website
#1	Harvard Medical School	https://hms.harvard.edu/
#2	New York University Grossman School of Medicine	https://med.nyu.edu/our-community/about-us
#3	Duke University School of Medicine	https://medschool.duke.edu/
#4	University of Missouri-Columbia School of Medicine	https://medicine.missouri.edu/
#5	Stanford University School of Medicine	http://med.stanford.edu/
#6	University of California, San Francisco School of Medicine	https://medschool.ucsf.edu/
#7	Johns Hopkins University School of Medicine	https://www.hopkinsmedicine.org/som/
#8	University of Washington School of Medicine	https://www.uwmedicine.org/school-of-medicine
#9	The Raymond and Ruth Perelman School of Medicine at the University of Pennsylvania	https://www.med.upenn.edu/
#10	Yale School of Medicine	https://medicine.yale.edu/
#11	Mayo Clinic Alix School of Medicine	https://college.mayo.edu/academics/school-of-medicine/
#12	Washington University in St. Louis School of Medicine	https://medicine.wustl.edu/
#13	University of Pittsburgh School of Medicine	https://www.medschool.pitt.edu/
#14	Vanderbilt University School of Medicine	https://medschool.vanderbilt.edu/
#15	Northwestern University Feinberg School of Medicine	https://www.feinberg.northwestern.edu/
#16	University of Michigan Medical School	https://medicine.umich.edu/medschool/home
#17	Icahn School of Medicine at Mount Sinai	https://icahn.mssm.edu/
#18	University of Chicago Division of the Biological Sciences, The Pritzker School of Medicine	https://pritzker.uchicago.edu/
#19	Weill Cornell Medicine	https://weill.cornell.edu/
#20	University of California, San Diego School of Medicine	https://medschool.ucsd.edu/Pages/default.aspx

Source: https://www.usnews.com/best-graduate-schools/top-medical-schools/research-rankings

CHAPTER 10

MEDICAL SCHOOLS BY AVERAGE MCAT SCORE

MD Schools	MCAT
San Juan Bautista School of Medicine	498
Ponce Health Sciences University School of Medicine	499
Universidad Central del Caribe School of Medicine	499
Marshall University Joan C. Edwards School of Medicine	502
Meharry Medical College School of Medicine	503
Mercer University School of Medicine	504
Morehouse School of Medicine	504
Howard University College of Medicine	505
University of Houston College of Medicine	505
University of Mississippi School of Medicine	505
University of New Mexico School of Medicine	505
University of Puerto Rico School of Medicine	505
Southern Illinois University School of Medicine	506
Louisiana State University School of Medicine in Shreveport	506
Northeast Ohio Medical University College of Medicine	507
University of North Dakota School of Medicine and Health Sciences	507
Boonshoft School of Medicine Wright State University	508
Central Michigan University College of Medicine	508
University of South Dakota Sanford School of Medicine	508
East Tennessee State University James H. Quillen College of Medicine	508
The Florida State University College of Medicine	508
University of Kentucky College of Medicine	508
University of South Carolina School of Medicine, Columbia	508
University of California, Riverside School of Medicine	508
University of Arkansas for Medical Sciences College of Medicine	508
Michigan State University College of Human Medicine	509
University of Missouri-Columbia School of Medicine	509
University of Missouri-Kansas City School of Medicine	509
LSU Health Sciences Center School of Medicine in New Orleans	509
The Brody School of Medicine at East Carolina University	509
University of Louisville School of Medicine	509
University of South Carolina School of Medicine, Greenville	509
West Virginia University School of Medicine	509
University of Nevada, Reno School of Medicine	509

MD Schools	MCAT
Oakland University William Beaumont School of Medicine	510
The University of Toledo College of Medicine and Life Sciences	510
Medical University of South Carolina College of Medicine	510
TCU and UNTHSC School of Medicine	510
Texas Tech University Health Sciences Center School of Medicine	510
The University of Texas Rio Grande Valley School of Medicine	510
Uniformed Services University of the Health Sciences, F. Edward Hébert School of Medicine	510
University of Alabama School of Medicine	510
Loma Linda University School of Medicine	510
The University of Arizona College of Medicine – Tucson	510
Washington State University Elson S. Floyd College of Medicine	510
Albany Medical College	511
Medical College of Wisconsin	511
Rush Medical College of Rush University Medical Center	511
Florida International University Herbert Wertheim College of Medicine	511
The University of Texas Medical Branch at Galveston School of Medicine	511
Tulane University School of Medicine	511
University of Oklahoma College of Medicine	511
University of South Alabama College of Medicine	511
Cooper Medical School of Rowan University	512
Drexel University College of Medicine	512
Geisinger Commonwealth School of Medicine	512
Jacobs School of Medicine and Biomedical Sciences at the University at Buffalo	512
Penn State College of Medicine	512
The Robert Larner, M.D. College of Medicine at the University of Vermont	512
Indiana University School of Medicine	512
Loyola University Chicago Stritch School of Medicine	512
University of Kansas School of Medicine	512
Nova Southeastern University Dr. Kiran C. Patel College of Allopathic Medicine	512
Paul L. Foster School of Medicine Texas Tech University Health Sciences Center	512
Virginia Tech Carilion School of Medicine	512

MD Schools	MCAT
California University of Science and Medicine – School of Medicine	512
Oregon Health & Science University School of Medicine	512
University of California, Davis School of Medicine	512
University of Nevada, Las Vegas School of Medicine	512
University of Washington School of Medicine	512
Hackensack-Meridian School of Medicine at Seton Hall University	513
Lewis Katz School of Medicine at Temple University	513
New York Medical College	513
State University of New York Upstate Medical University College of Medicine	513
University of Connecticut School of Medicine	513
Carle Illinois College of Medicine	513
Chicago Medical School at Rosalind Franklin University of Medicine and Science	513
Creighton University School of Medicine	513
University of Illinois College of Medicine	513
University of Minnesota Medical School	513
University of Nebraska College of Medicine	513
University of Wisconsin School of Medicine and Public Health	513
Wayne State University School of Medicine	513
Charles E. Schmidt College of Medicine at Florida Atlantic University	513
Eastern Virginia Medical School	513
Georgetown University School of Medicine	513
McGovern Medical School at The University of Texas Health Science Center at Houston	513
Medical College of Georgia at Augusta University	513
Texas A&M University Health Science Center College of Medicine	513
The George Washington University School of Medicine and Health Sciences	513
University of Tennessee Health Science Center College of Medicine	513
Virginia Commonwealth University School of Medicine	513
Wake Forest School of Medicine	513
California Northstate University College of Medicine	513
John A. Burns School of Medicine University of Hawaii at Manoa	513
University of Utah School of Medicine	513
Frank H. Netter MD School of Medicine at Quinnipiac University	514
Rutgers, Robert Wood Johnson Medical School	514

MD Schools	MCAT
Sidney Kimmel Medical College at Thomas Jefferson University	514
State University of New York Downstate Medical Center College of Medicine	514
Saint Louis University School of Medicine	514
University of Central Florida College of Medicine	514
University of Maryland School of Medicine	514
University of Miami Leonard M. Miller School of Medicine	514
University of Colorado School of Medicine	514
Albert Einstein College of Medicine	515
New York University Long Island School of Medicine	515
Rutgers New Jersey Medical School	515
Tufts University School of Medicine	515
University of Iowa Roy J. and Lucille A. Carver College of Medicine	515
The University of Texas at Austin Dell Medical School	515
University of Florida College of Medicine	515
University of North Carolina School of Medicine	515
The University of Arizona College of Medicine – Phoenix	515
Geisel School of Medicine at Dartmouth	516
Renaissance School of Medicine at Stony Brook University	516
University of Massachusetts Medical School	516
Western Michigan University Homer Stryker M.D. School of Medicine	516
David Geffen School of Medicine at UCLA	516
Kaiser Permanente School of Medicine	516
University of California, Irvine School of Medicine	516
The Warren Alpert Medical School of Brown University	517
The Ohio State University College of Medicine	517
University of Cincinnati College of Medicine	517
Emory University School of Medicine	517
The University of Texas Health Science Center at San Antonio Joe R. and Teresa Lozano Long School of Medicine	517
USF Health Morsani College of Medicine	517
Keck School of Medicine of the University of Southern California	517
University of California, San Diego School of Medicine	517
Boston University School of Medicine	518
Donald and Barbara Zucker School of Medicine at Hofstra/Northwell	518

MD Schools	MCAT
University of Pittsburgh School of Medicine	518
University of Rochester School of Medicine and Dentistry	518
University of Michigan Medical School	518
Baylor College of Medicine	518
The University of Texas Southwestern Medical School	518
University of California, San Francisco School of Medicine	518
Icahn School of Medicine at Mount Sinai	519
Weill Cornell Medicine	519
Case Western Reserve University School of Medicine	519
Duke University School of Medicine	519
Stanford University School of Medicine	519
Harvard Medical School	520
Mayo Clinic Alix School of Medicine	520
Northwestern University Feinberg School of Medicine	520
University of Virginia School of Medicine	520
Yale School of Medicine	521
University of Chicago Division of the Biological Sciences, The Pritzker School of Medicine	521
Washington University in St. Louis School of Medicine	521
Johns Hopkins University School of Medicine	521
Vanderbilt University School of Medicine	521
Columbia University Vagelos College of Physicians and Surgeons	522
New York University Grossman School of Medicine	522
The Raymond and Ruth Perelman School of Medicine at the University of Pennsylvania	522
CUNY School of Medicine	N/A

CHAPTER 11

MEDICAL SCHOOLS BY COST OF ATTENDANCE

MD Schools	Tuition (In-State)	Tuition (Out-of-State)	COA (Out-of-State)
Uniformed Services University of the Health Sciences, F. Edward Hébert School of Medicine	$0.00	$0.00	$0.00
New York University Grossman School of Medicine	$0.00	$0.00	$30,110.00
New York University Long Island School of Medicine	$0.00	$0.00	$33,924.00
Kaiser Permanente School of Medicine	$0.00	$0.00	$34,600.00
University of Puerto Rico School of Medicine	$16,000.00	$16,000.00	$44,631.00
The Brody School of Medicine at East Carolina University	$23,134.00	$23,134.00	$49,256.00
Texas Tech University Health Sciences Center School of Medicine	$17,411.00	$17,411.00	$51,203.00
Southern Illinois University School of Medicine	$33,474.00	$33,474.00	$55,761.00
McGovern Medical School at The University of Texas Health Science Center at Houston	$18,604.00	$26,125.00	$58,268.00
West Virginia University School of Medicine	$20,124.00	$40,824.00	$58,311.00
University of Mississippi School of Medicine	$31,197.00	$31,197.00	$60,190.00
University of Minnesota Medical School	$26,794.00	$38,452.00	$60,250.00
University of Houston College of Medicine	$24,264.00	$37,362.00	$60,960.00
The University of Texas Rio Grande Valley School of Medicine	$19,639.00	$32,739.00	$61,056.00
Washington State University Elson S. Floyd College of Medicine	$40,380.00	$40,380.00	$61,880.00
Paul L. Foster School of Medicine Texas Tech University Health Sciences Center	$18,378.00	$31,478.00	$63,690.00
Baylor College of Medicine	$19,425.00	$32,525.00	$64,735.75
The University of Texas Health Science Center at San Antonio Joe R. and Teresa Lozano Long School of Medicine	$16,921.00	$33,587.00	$64,841.00

MD Schools	Tuition (In-State)	Tuition (Out-of-State)	COA (Out-of-State)
The University of Texas Southwestern Medical School	$22,651.00	$35,751.00	$65,775.00
Texas A&M University Health Science Center College of Medicine	$21,760.00	$34,860.00	$66,016.00
The University of Texas at Austin Dell Medical School	$21,086.00	$35,406.00	$66,726.00
The Florida State University College of Medicine	$19,696.00	$45,733.00	$66,797.00
Mercer University School of Medicine	$42,586.00	$42,586.00	$66,910.00
East Tennessee State University James H. Quillen College of Medicine	$32,834.00	$42,684.00	$69,206.00
The University of Texas Medical Branch at Galveston School of Medicine	$20,271.00	$34,981.36	$69,290.76
University of Florida College of Medicine	$37,130.00	$49,390.00	$69,970.00
University of Cincinnati College of Medicine	$32,980.00	$51,244.00	$74,781.00
Central Michigan University College of Medicine	$43,952.00	$64,062.00	$74,991.00
San Juan Bautista School of Medicine	$35,280.00	$45,280.00	$75,378.00
Penn State College of Medicine	$50,960.00	$50,960.00	$75,772.00
Marshall University Joan C. Edwards School of Medicine	$23,094.00	$54,772.00	$76,267.00
Medical College of Wisconsin	$53,080.00	$56,780.00	$77,265.00
Albany Medical College	$57,598.00	$57,723.00	$78,376.00
Howard University College of Medicine	$46,610.00	$46,610.00	$78,778.00
University of California, Irvine School of Medicine	$35,220.00	$47,465.00	$78,862.00
University of New Mexico School of Medicine	$15,946.00	$44,023.76	$79,379.76
USF Health Morsani College of Medicine	$33,726.00	$54,916.00	$79,424.00
The Ohio State University College of Medicine	$30,636.00	$55,556.00	$81,044.00

MD Schools	Tuition (In-State)	Tuition (Out-of-State)	COA (Out-of-State)
University of Miami Leonard M. Miller School of Medicine	$48,663.00	$48,663.00	$81,133.00
University of Iowa Roy J. and Lucille A. Carver College of Medicine	$37,768.50	$58,543.50	$81,438.50
University of California, Davis School of Medicine	$41,927.00	$54,172.00	$81,471.00
Boonshoft School of Medicine Wright State University	$35,464.00	$54,342.00	$81,628.95
Michigan State University College of Human Medicine	$32,252.00	$59,808.00	$82,076.00
Ponce Health Sciences University School of Medicine	$39,218.00	$62,400.00	$82,262.00
Virginia Tech Carilion School of Medicine	$54,653.00	$54,653.00	$82,328.00
University of Central Florida College of Medicine	$29,680.00	$56,554.00	$82,375.00
Rush Medical College of Rush University Medical Center	$47,166.00	$47,166.00	$82,455.00
Medical University of South Carolina College of Medicine	$31,001.00	$53,001.00	$82,663.00
Lewis Katz School of Medicine at Temple University	$53,406.00	$56,628.00	$82,720.00
The University of Arizona College of Medicine – Tucson	$34,914.00	$55,514.00	$82,914.00
Morehouse School of Medicine	$45,208.00	$45,208.00	$83,044.00
Drexel University College of Medicine	$58,978.00	$58,978.00	$83,273.00
University of Virginia School of Medicine	$50,004.00	$61,114.00	$83,364.00
University of Wisconsin School of Medicine and Public Health	$39,636.00	$55,812.00	$83,492.00
Loma Linda University School of Medicine	$59,452.00	$59,452.00	$83,667.00
New York Medical College	$55,670.00	$55,670.00	$83,689.00
University of Rochester School of Medicine and Dentistry	$61,500.00	$61,500.00	$83,798.00
California University of Science and Medicine – School of Medicine	$60,000.00	$60,000.00	$83,991.00
Saint Louis University School of Medicine	$60,360.00	$60,360.00	$84,358.00

MD Schools	Tuition (In-State)	Tuition (Out-of-State)	COA (Out-of-State)
Eastern Virginia Medical School	$33,105.00	$56,382.00	$84,759.00
University of Missouri-Kansas City School of Medicine	$34,583.00	$67,037.00	$84,765.00
University of California, San Diego School of Medicine	$38,753.00	$50,998.00	$85,190.00
University of Pittsburgh School of Medicine	$57,684.00	$59,930.00	$85,509.00
Icahn School of Medicine at Mount Sinai	$60,405.00	$60,405.00	$85,920.00
University of California, San Francisco School of Medicine	$35,214.00	$47,459.00	$85,931.00
Chicago Medical School at Rosalind Franklin University of Medicine and Science	$63,223.00	$63,223.00	$86,026.00
University of North Dakota School of Medicine and Health Sciences	$34,762.00	$61,630.00	$86,033.00
University of Nebraska College of Medicine	$35,360.00	$57,290.00	$86,265.00
University of Tennessee Health Science Center College of Medicine	$34,566.00	$60,489.00	$86,465.00
Creighton University School of Medicine	$61,696.00	$61,696.00	$86,696.00
Sidney Kimmel Medical College at Thomas Jefferson University	$60,314.00	$60,314.00	$86,875.00
Loyola University Chicago Stritch School of Medicine	$61,000.00	$61,000.00	$87,105.00
The University of Toledo College of Medicine and Life Sciences	$32,924.64	$64,771.20	$87,471.62
The George Washington University School of Medicine and Health Sciences	$63,920.00	$63,920.00	$87,859.00
Frank H. Netter MD School of Medicine at Quinnipiac University	$61,040.00	$61,040.00	$87,878.00
Albert Einstein College of Medicine	$55,052.00	$55,052.00	$87,924.00
Western Michigan University Homer Stryker M.D. School of Medicine	$63,500.00	$63,500.00	$87,928.00
Donald and Barbara Zucker School of Medicine at Hofstra/Northwell	$54,525.00	$54,525.00	$87,967.00
Louisiana State University School of Medicine in Shreveport	$29,343.25	$61,165.25	$87,995.25

MD Schools	Tuition (In-State)	Tuition (Out-of-State)	COA (Out-of-State)
University of Chicago Division of the Biological Sciences, The Pritzker School of Medicine	$57,681.00	$57,681.00	$88,165.00
Oakland University William Beaumont School of Medicine	$58,218.00	$58,218.00	$88,296.00
State University of New York Upstate Medical University College of Medicine	$43,020.00	$65,160.00	$88,411.00
University of California, Riverside School of Medicine	$42,537.00	$53,652.00	$88,558.00
Medical College of Georgia at Augusta University	$28,926.00	$57,850.00	$88,695.00
The University of Arizona College of Medicine – Phoenix	$34,380.00	$54,980.00	$88,820.00
University of Michigan Medical School	$42,282.00	$61,680.00	$88,930.00
University of South Alabama College of Medicine	$31,860.00	$62,864.00	$88,980.00
Johns Hopkins University School of Medicine	$58,000.00	$58,000.00	$89,126.00
Weill Cornell Medicine	$61,110.00	$61,110.00	$89,130.00
Wake Forest School of Medicine	$61,200.00	$61,200.00	$89,292.00
Cooper Medical School of Rowan University	$40,479.00	$64,240.00	$89,581.00
University of Louisville School of Medicine	$41,778.00	$63,530.00	$89,646.00
The Robert Larner, M.D. College of Medicine at the University of Vermont	$37,070.00	$64,170.00	$89,676.00
Wayne State University School of Medicine	$39,280.00	$67,479.00	$89,850.00
Indiana University School of Medicine	$35,000.00	$60,000.00	$89,851.00
TCU and UNTHSC School of Medicine	$60,318.00	$60,318.00	$89,896.00
Washington University in St. Louis School of Medicine	$65,001.00	$65,001.00	$90,030.00
David Geffen School of Medicine at UCLA	$43,726.00	$55,971.00	$90,291.00
Meharry Medical College School of Medicine	$52,617.00	$52,617.00	$90,420.00

MD Schools	Tuition (In-State)	Tuition (Out-of-State)	COA (Out-of-State)
Emory University School of Medicine	$52,000.00	$52,000.00	$90,590.00
Geisel School of Medicine at Dartmouth	$67,532.00	$67,532.00	$90,743.00
University of Nevada, Reno School of Medicine	$30,210.00	$57,704.00	$91,236.00
Carle Illinois College of Medicine	$46,608.00	$61,342.00	$91,845.00
LSU Health Sciences Center School of Medicine in New Orleans	$32,936.95	$61,114.29	$91,866.22
Boston University School of Medicine	$66,702.00	$66,702.00	$91,870.00
Case Western Reserve University School of Medicine	$67,440.00	$67,440.00	$92,937.00
University of Missouri-Columbia School of Medicine	$36,688.00	$70,977.00	$93,090.00
University of Kansas School of Medicine	$37,891.00	$67,086.00	$93,130.00
University of Washington School of Medicine	$39,012.00	$69,444.00	$93,140.00
University of Oklahoma College of Medicine	$31,082.00	$65,410.00	$93,357.00
Jacobs School of Medicine and Biomedical Sciences at the University at Buffalo	$43,670.00	$65,160.00	$94,357.00
Northwestern University Feinberg School of Medicine	$64,262.00	$64,262.00	$94,378.00
Duke University School of Medicine	$63,310.00	$63,310.00	$94,478.00
Virginia Commonwealth University School of Medicine	$33,751.00	$56,577.00	$94,709.00
The Raymond and Ruth Perelman School of Medicine at the University of Pennsylvania	$61,586.00	$61,586.00	$94,927.00
University of Alabama School of Medicine	$33,067.00	$66,079.00	$95,047.00
Geisinger Commonwealth School of Medicine	$56,800.00	$63,100.00	$95,083.00
Mayo Clinic Alix School of Medicine	$58,900.00	$58,900.00	$95,196.00
Tufts University School of Medicine	$66,354.00	$66,354.00	$95,537.00
University of Arkansas for Medical Sciences College of Medicine	$33,010.00	$65,180.00	$96,091.00

MD Schools	Tuition (In-State)	Tuition (Out-of-State)	COA (Out-of-State)
The Warren Alpert Medical School of Brown University	$66,110.00	$66,110.00	$96,140.00
University of Massachusetts Medical School	$36,570.00	$62,899.00	$96,365.00
Renaissance School of Medicine at Stony Brook University	$43,670.00	$66,160.00	$96,860.00
Charles E. Schmidt College of Medicine at Florida Atlantic University	$28,111.00	$62,532.00	$97,094.00
Georgetown University School of Medicine	$56,586.00	$56,586.00	$97,135.00
Yale School of Medicine	$66,160.00	$66,160.00	$97,349.00
University of Nevada, Las Vegas School of Medicine	$27,000.00	$56,000.00	$97,746.00
Keck School of Medicine of the University of Southern California	$66,150.00	$66,150.00	$98,156.00
University of Kentucky College of Medicine	$38,920.00	$71,400.00	$98,241.00
University of North Carolina School of Medicine	$34,932.00	$62,325.00	$98,293.00
Tulane University School of Medicine	$69,308.00	$69,308.00	$98,952.00
University of Utah School of Medicine	$41,784.00	$77,991.00	$99,177.00
Harvard Medical School	$66,284.00	$66,284.00	$99,416.00
State University of New York Downstate Medical Center College of Medicine	$43,670.00	$65,160.00	$99,457.00
Vanderbilt University School of Medicine	$63,610.00	$63,610.00	$99,938.00
Columbia University Vagelos College of Physicians and Surgeons	$66,814.00	$66,814.00	$100,060.00
Hackensack-Meridian School of Medicine at Seton Hall University	$65,404.00	$65,404.00	$100,539.00
Rutgers New Jersey Medical School	$43,345.00	$66,882.00	$100,820.00
Oregon Health & Science University School of Medicine	$46,752.00	$70,580.00	$101,270.00
California Northstate University College of Medicine	$62,648.00	$62,648.00	$101,630.00

MD Schools	Tuition (In-State)	Tuition (Out-of-State)	COA (Out-of-State)
Rutgers, Robert Wood Johnson Medical School	$43,345.00	$66,882.00	$101,760.00
University of South Dakota Sanford School of Medicine	$31,787.00	$76,173.00	$102,734.00
John A. Burns School of Medicine University of Hawaii at Manoa	$36,672.00	$71,328.00	$105,132.00
Florida International University Herbert Wertheim College of Medicine	$32,739.00	$62,739.00	$105,626.00
University of Connecticut School of Medicine	$40,287.00	$74,367.00	$106,761.00
University of Colorado School of Medicine	$41,520.00	$77,474.00	$107,066.00
University of Maryland School of Medicine	$37,810.00	$66,905.00	$107,442.00
Nova Southeastern University Dr. Kiran C. Patel College of Allopathic Medicine	$55,671.00	$62,390.00	$110,120.00
University of Illinois College of Medicine	$45,360.00	$78,537.00	$111,226.00
University of South Carolina School of Medicine, Greenville	$44,612.00	$88,874.00	$111,497.00
University of South Carolina School of Medicine, Columbia	$42,888.00	$87,150.00	$113,145.00
Northeast Ohio Medical University College of Medicine	$44,204.00	$83,674.00	$115,042.00
Stanford University School of Medicine	$82,924.00	$82,924.00	$131,860.00
CUNY School of Medicine	$41,600.00	N/A	N/A
Universidad Central del Caribe School of Medicine	N/A	N/A	N/A

CHAPTER 12

MEDICAL SCHOOLS BY NUMBER OF INCOMING STUDENTS

Medical School	# enrolled in 2020
New York University Long Island School of Medicine	24
University of Houston College of Medicine	30
Carle Illinois College of Medicine	47
Virginia Tech Carilion School of Medicine	48
Nova Southeastern University Dr. Kiran C. Patel College of Allopathic Medicine	50
The University of Texas at Austin Dell Medical School	50
Kaiser Permanente School of Medicine	50
The University of Texas Rio Grande Valley School of Medicine	55
TCU and UNTHSC School of Medicine	60
University of Nevada, Las Vegas School of Medicine	60
San Juan Bautista School of Medicine	63
Charles E. Schmidt College of Medicine at Florida Atlantic University	65
University of North Dakota School of Medicine and Health Sciences	67
University of South Dakota Sanford School of Medicine	69
University of Nevada, Reno School of Medicine	70
East Tennessee State University James H. Quillen College of Medicine	72
University of South Alabama College of Medicine	74
Universidad Central del Caribe School of Medicine	75
CUNY School of Medicine	76
John A. Burns School of Medicine University of Hawaii at Manoa	77
University of California, Riverside School of Medicine	78
Southern Illinois University School of Medicine	80
Marshall University Joan C. Edwards School of Medicine	80
Washington State University Elson S. Floyd College of Medicine	80
Western Michigan University Homer Stryker M.D. School of Medicine	84
The Brody School of Medicine at East Carolina University	86
University of Chicago Division of the Biological Sciences, The Pritzker School of Medicine	90
Stanford University School of Medicine	90
Geisel School of Medicine at Dartmouth	92
Frank H. Netter MD School of Medicine at Quinnipiac University	94
Vanderbilt University School of Medicine	94
University of New Mexico School of Medicine	97
Donald and Barbara Zucker School of Medicine at Hofstra/Northwell	99
University of South Carolina School of Medicine, Columbia	99

Medical School	# enrolled in 2020
Yale School of Medicine	100
The University of Arizona College of Medicine – Phoenix	100
California Northstate University College of Medicine	101
New York University Grossman School of Medicine	102
University of Rochester School of Medicine and Dentistry	102
Central Michigan University College of Medicine	103
Washington University in St. Louis School of Medicine	104
University of California, Irvine School of Medicine	104
Mayo Clinic Alix School of Medicine	105
Morehouse School of Medicine	105
Weill Cornell Medicine	106
University of South Carolina School of Medicine, Greenville	108
University of Connecticut School of Medicine	110
Paul L. Foster School of Medicine Texas Tech University Health Sciences Center	110
University of Puerto Rico School of Medicine	110
Cooper Medical School of Rowan University	111
West Virginia University School of Medicine	112
Geisinger Commonwealth School of Medicine	115
Meharry Medical College School of Medicine	115
The University of Arizona College of Medicine – Tucson	117
Boonshoft School of Medicine Wright State University	118
Howard University College of Medicine	118
Florida International University Herbert Wertheim College of Medicine	120
The Florida State University College of Medicine	120
University of Central Florida College of Medicine	120
Duke University School of Medicine	121
Johns Hopkins University School of Medicine	121
Hackensack-Meridian School of Medicine at Seton Hall University	122
The Robert Larner, M.D. College of Medicine at the University of Vermont	124
University of Missouri-Kansas City School of Medicine	124
Oakland University William Beaumont School of Medicine	125
Mercer University School of Medicine	125
University of Utah School of Medicine	125
University of California, Davis School of Medicine	127

Medical School	# enrolled in 2020
University of Missouri-Columbia School of Medicine	128
California University of Science and Medicine – School of Medicine	130
University of Nebraska College of Medicine	131
University of California, San Diego School of Medicine	133
University of Florida College of Medicine	135
Renaissance School of Medicine at Stony Brook University	136
Emory University School of Medicine	136
Columbia University Vagelos College of Physicians and Surgeons	138
Icahn School of Medicine at Mount Sinai	140
Albany Medical College	143
The Warren Alpert Medical School of Brown University	144
Wake Forest School of Medicine	145
Louisiana State University School of Medicine in Shreveport	148
University of Pittsburgh School of Medicine	149
Oregon Health & Science University School of Medicine	150
Ponce Health Sciences University School of Medicine	150
Northeast Ohio Medical University College of Medicine	151
Eastern Virginia Medical School	151
Boston University School of Medicine	152
Penn State College of Medicine	152
University of Iowa Roy J. and Lucille A. Carver College of Medicine	152
University of Maryland School of Medicine	152
The Raymond and Ruth Perelman School of Medicine at the University of Pennsylvania	155
Rush Medical College of Rush University Medical Center	155
University of Virginia School of Medicine	155
University of Colorado School of Medicine	155
University of Louisville School of Medicine	159
State University of New York Upstate Medical University College of Medicine	160
Northwestern University Feinberg School of Medicine	160
University of Massachusetts Medical School	162
University of Oklahoma College of Medicine	164
University of Mississippi School of Medicine	165
Creighton University School of Medicine	167
Harvard Medical School	168

Medical School	# enrolled in 2020
University of Michigan Medical School	168
Loma Linda University School of Medicine	168
Uniformed Services University of the Health Sciences, F. Edward Hébert School of Medicine	169
Loyola University Chicago Stritch School of Medicine	170
University of Tennessee Health Science Center College of Medicine	170
University of Wisconsin School of Medicine and Public Health	171
Medical University of South Carolina College of Medicine	173
University of Arkansas for Medical Sciences College of Medicine	173
Rutgers, Robert Wood Johnson Medical School	174
Texas A&M University Health Science Center College of Medicine	175
David Geffen School of Medicine at UCLA	175
The University of Toledo College of Medicine and Life Sciences	176
Rutgers New Jersey Medical School	178
The George Washington University School of Medicine and Health Sciences	178
University of California, San Francisco School of Medicine	178
Texas Tech University Health Sciences Center School of Medicine	180
Jacobs School of Medicine and Biomedical Sciences at the University at Buffalo	182
University of Cincinnati College of Medicine	182
Albert Einstein College of Medicine	183
Saint Louis University School of Medicine	183
Baylor College of Medicine	186
University of Alabama School of Medicine	186
Virginia Commonwealth University School of Medicine	186
Keck School of Medicine of the University of Southern California	186
Michigan State University College of Human Medicine	188
Chicago Medical School at Rosalind Franklin University of Medicine and Science	189
USF Health Morsani College of Medicine	189
Tulane University School of Medicine	190
University of North Carolina School of Medicine	193
LSU Health Sciences Center School of Medicine in New Orleans	196
Tufts University School of Medicine	200
Georgetown University School of Medicine	203
University of Miami Leonard M. Miller School of Medicine	204

Medical School	# enrolled in 2020
The Ohio State University College of Medicine	205
University of Kentucky College of Medicine	205
State University of New York Downstate Medical Center College of Medicine	207
University of Kansas School of Medicine	211
New York Medical College	212
The University of Texas Health Science Center at San Antonio Joe R. and Teresa Lozano Long School of Medicine	212
Case Western Reserve University School of Medicine	214
Lewis Katz School of Medicine at Temple University	218
The University of Texas Southwestern Medical School	228
The University of Texas Medical Branch at Galveston School of Medicine	230
McGovern Medical School at The University of Texas Health Science Center at Houston	240
Medical College of Georgia at Augusta University	240
University of Minnesota Medical School	241
Medical College of Wisconsin	266
Drexel University College of Medicine	267
Sidney Kimmel Medical College at Thomas Jefferson University	270
University of Washington School of Medicine	270
Wayne State University School of Medicine	291
University of Illinois College of Medicine	299
Indiana University School of Medicine	365

CHAPTER 13

OSTEOPATHIC MEDICAL SCHOOLS BY CITY/STATE

DO Schools	City	State	Website
Edward Via College of Osteopathic Medicine (VCOM - Auburn Campus)	Auburn	AL	https://www.vcom.edu/
Alabama College of Osteopathic Medicine (ACOM)	Dothan	AL	https://www.acom.edu/
Arkansas College of Osteopathic Medicine (ARCOM)	Fort Smith	AR	https://acheedu.org/arcom/
New York Institute of Technology College of Osteopathic Medicine at Arkansas State (NYITCOM)	Jonesboro	AR	https://www.nyit.edu/arkansas
Midwestern University Arizona College of Osteopathic Medicine (MWU/AZCOM)	Glendale	AZ	https://www.midwestern.edu/academics/our-colleges/arizona-college-of-osteopathic-medicine.xml
A.T. Still University, School of Osteopathic Medicine in Arizona (ATSU-SOMA)	Mesa	AZ	https://www.atsu.edu/school-of-osteopathic-medicine-arizona
California Health Sciences University College of Osteopathic Medicine (CHSU-COM)	Clovis	CA	https://osteopathic.chsu.edu/
Western University of Health Sciences College of Osteopathic Medicine of the Pacific (WesternU/COMP)	Pomona	CA	https://www.westernu.edu/osteopathic/
Touro University College of Osteopathic Medicine-California (TUCOM)	Vallejo	CA	http://com.tu.edu/
Rocky Vista University College of Osteopathic Medicine (RVUCOM)	Parker	CO	http://www.rvu.edu/rvu-su/college-of-osteopathic-medicine/
Lake Erie College of Osteopathic Medicine-Bradenton (LECOM-Bradenton)	Bradenton	FL	https://lecom.edu/
Nova Southeastern University Dr. Kiran C. Patel College of Osteopathic Medicine (NSU-KPCOM-Clearwater)	Clearwater	FL	https://osteopathic.nova.edu/index.html
Nova Southeastern University Dr. Kiran C. Patel College of Osteopathic Medicine (NSU-KPCOM)	Fort Lauderdale	FL	https://osteopathic.nova.edu/index.html
Philadelphia College of Osteopathic Medicine South Georgia (PCOM South Georgia)	Moultrie	GA	https://www.pcom.edu/south-georgia/

DO Schools	City	State	Website
Philadelphia College of Osteopathic Medicine Georgia (PCOM Georgia)	Suwanee	GA	https://www.pcom.edu/campuses/georgia-campus/
Des Moines University College of Osteopathic Medicine (DMU-COM)	Des Moines	IA	https://www.dmu.edu/do/
Idaho College of Osteopathic Medicine (ICOM)	Meridian	ID	https://www.idahocom.org/
Midwestern University Chicago College of Osteopathic Medicine (MWU/CCOM)	Downers Grove	IL	https://www.midwestern.edu/academics/degrees-and-programs/doctor-of-osteopathic-medicine-il.xml
Marian University College of Osteopathic Medicine (MU-COM)	Indianapolis	IN	https://www.marian.edu/osteopathic-medical-school
University of Pikeville Kentucky College of Osteopathic Medicine (UP-KYCOM)	Pikeville	KY	https://www.upike.edu/osteopathic-medicine/
Edward Via College of Osteopathic Medicine-Monroe Campus (VCOM - Monroe Campus)	Monroe	LA	https://www.vcom.edu/louisiana
University of New England College of Osteopathic Medicine (UNECOM)	Biddeford	ME	https://www.une.edu/com
Michigan State University College of Osteopathic Medicine (MSUCOM-MUC)	Clinton Twp	MI	https://com.msu.edu/
Michigan State University College of Osteopathic Medicine (MSUCOM-DMC)	Detroit	MI	https://com.msu.edu/
Michigan State University College of Osteopathic Medicine (MSUCOM)	East Lansing	MI	https://com.msu.edu/
Kansas City University of Medicine and Biosciences College of Osteopathic Medicine (KCU-COM)	Kansas City	MO	http://www.kcumb.edu/programs/college-of-osteopathic-medicine
A. T. Still University Kirksville College of Osteopathic Medicine (ATSU-KCOM)	Kirksville	MO	https://www.atsu.edu/kirksville-college-of-osteopathic-medicine

DO Schools	City	State	Website
William Carey University College of Osteopathic Medicine (WCUCOM)	Hattiesburg	MS	https://www.wmcarey.edu/College/Osteopathic-Medicine
Campbell University Jerry M. Wallace School of Osteopathic Medicine (CUSOM)	Lillington	NC	https://medicine.campbell.edu/
Rowan University School of Osteopathic Medicine (RowanSOM)	Stratford	NJ	https://som.rowan.edu/
Burrell College of Osteopathic Medicine (BCOM)	Las Cruces	NM	https://bcomnm.org/
Kansas City University of Medicine and Biosciences College of Osteopathic Medicine (KCU-COM-Joplin)	Joplin	NO	http://www.kcumb.edu/programs/college-of-osteopathic-medicine
Touro University Nevada College of Osteopathic Medicine (TUNCOM)	Henderson	NV	https://tun.touro.edu/programs/osteopathic-medicine/
Lake Erie College of Osteopathic Medicine - Elmira (LECOM-Elmira)	Elmira	NY	https://lecom.edu/
Touro College of Osteopathic Medicine (TouroCOM-Middletown)	Middletown	NY	https://tourocom.touro.edu/
Touro College of Osteopathic Medicine (TouroCOM-Harlem)	New York	NY	https://tourocom.touro.edu/
New York Institute of Technology College of Osteopathic Medicine (NYITCOM)	Old Westbury	NY	https://www.nyit.edu/medicine
Ohio University Heritage College of Osteopathic Medicine (OU-HCOM)	Athens	OH	https://www.ohio.edu/medicine/
Ohio University Heritage College of Osteopathic Medicine in Dublin (OU-HCOM-Dublin)	Dublin	OH	https://www.ohio.edu/medicine/
Ohio University Heritage College of Osteopathic Medicine in Cleveland (OU-HCOM-Cleveland)	Warrensville Heights	OH	https://www.ohio.edu/medicine/
Oklahoma State University Center for Health Sciences College of Osteopathic Medicine - Tahlequah (OSU-COM Tahlequah)	Tahlequah	OK	https://health.okstate.edu/com/index.html

DO Schools	City	State	Website
Oklahoma State University Center for Health Sciences College of Osteopathic Medicine (OSU-COM)	Tulsa	OK	https://health.okstate.edu/com/index.html
Western University of Health Sciences College of Osteopathic Medicine of the Pacific-Northwest (WesternU/COMP-Northwest)	Lebanon	OR	https://www.westernu.edu/northwest/
Lake Erie College of Osteopathic Medicine-Erie (LECOM)	Erie	PA	https://lecom.edu/
Lake Erie College of Osteopathic Medicine - Seton Hill (LECOM-Seton Hill)	Greensburg	PA	https://lecom.edu/
Philadelphia College of Osteopathic Medicine (PCOM)	Philadelphia	PA	https://www.pcom.edu/
Edward Via College of Osteopathic Medicine-Carolinas Campus (VCOM - Carolinas Campus)	Spartanburg	SC	https://www.vcom.edu/carolinas
Lincoln Memorial University DeBusk College of Osteopathic Medicine (LMU-DCOM)	Harrogate	TN	https://www.lmunet.edu/debusk-college-of-osteopathic-medicine/index.php
Lincoln Memorial University DeBusk College of Osteopathic Medicine - Knoxville (LMU-DCOM Knoxville)	Knoxville	TN	https://www.lmunet.edu/debusk-college-of-osteopathic-medicine/index.php
University of North Texas Health Science Center Texas College of Osteopathic Medicine (UNTHSC/TCOM)	Fort Worth	TX	https://www.unthsc.edu/texas-college-of-osteopathic-medicine/
Sam Houston State University College of Osteopathic Medicine	Huntsville	TX	https://www.shsu.edu/academics/osteopathic-medicine/
University of the Incarnate Word School of Osteopathic Medicine (UIWSOM)	San Antonio	TX	https://osteopathic-medicine.uiw.edu/
Rocky Vista University College of Osteopathic Medicine (RVUCOM-SU Campus)	Ivins	UT	http://www.rvu.edu/rvu-su/college-of-osteopathic-medicine/
Noorda College of Osteopathic Medicine	Provo	UT	https://noordacom.org/

DO Schools	City	State	Website
Edward Via College of Osteopathic Medicine (VCOM-Virginia Campus)	Blacksburg	VA	https://www.vcom.edu/virginia
Liberty University College of Osteopathic Medicine (LUCOM)	Lynchburg	VA	https://www.liberty.edu/lucom/
Pacific Northwest University of Health Sciences College of Osteopathic Medicine (PNWU-COM)	Yakima	WA	https://www.pnwu.edu/
West Virginia School of Osteopathic Medicine (WVSOM)	Lewisburg	WV	https://www.wvsom.edu/

CHAPTER 14

DENTAL SCHOOLS BY CITY/STATE

Dental Schools	City	State	Website
University of Alabama at Birmingham School of Dentistry	Birmingham	AL	https://www.uab.edu/dentistry/home/
Midwestern University College of Dental Medicine-Arizona	Glendale	AZ	https://www.midwestern.edu/academics/our-colleges/college-of-dental-medi-cine%E2%80%93arizona.xml
Arizona School of Dentistry & Oral Health	Mesa	AZ	https://www.atsu.edu/arizona-school-of-dentistry-and-oral-health
California North State College of Dental Medicine	Elk Grove	CA	http://dentalmedicine.cnsu.edu/
Loma Linda University School of Dentistry	Loma Linda	CA	https://dentistry.llu.edu/
Herman Ostrow School of Dentistry of USC	Los Angeles	CA	https://dentistry.usc.edu/
University of California, Los Angeles, School of Dentistry	Los Angeles	CA	https://www.dentistry.ucla.edu/
Western University of Health Sciences College of Dental Medicine	Pomona	CA	https://www.westernu.edu/dentistry/
University of California, San Francisco, School of Dentistry	San Francisco	CA	https://dentistry.ucsf.edu/
University of the Pacific Arthur A. Dugoni School of Dentistry	San Francisco	CA	https://www.dental.pacific.edu/
University of Colorado School of Dental Medicine	Aurora	CO	http://www.ucdenver.edu/academics/colleges/dentalmedicine/Pages/DentalMedicine.aspx
University of Connecticut School of Dental Medicine	Farmington	CT	https://dentalmedicine.uconn.edu/
Howard University College of Dentistry	Washington	DC	http://healthsciences.howard.edu/education/colleges/dentistry
Lake Erie College of Osteopathic Medicine School of Dental Medicine	Bradenton	FL	https://lecom.edu/academics/school-of-dental-medicine/
Nova Southeastern University College of Dental Medicine	Davie	FL	https://dental.nova.edu/index.html

Dental Schools	City	State	Website
University of Florida College of Dentistry	Gainesville	FL	https://dental.ufl.edu/
Dental College of Georgia at Augusta University	Augusta	GA	https://www.augusta.edu/dentalmedicine/
The University of Iowa College of Dentistry & Dental Clinics	Iowa City	IA	https://www.dentistry.uiowa.edu/
Southern Illinois University School of Dental Medicine	Alton	IL	http://www.siue.edu/dental/
University of Illinois at Chicago College of Dentistry	Chicago	IL	https://dentistry.uic.edu/
Midwestern University College of Dental Medicine-Illinois	Downers Grove	IL	https://www.midwestern.edu/academics/our-colleges/college-of-dental-medicine%E2%80%93illinois.xml
Indiana University School of Dentistry	Indianapolis	IN	https://dentistry.iu.edu/
University of Kentucky College of Dentistry	Lexington	KY	https://dentistry.uky.edu/
University of Louisville School of Dentistry	Louisville	KY	https://louisville.edu/dentistry
Louisiana State University Health New Orleans School of Dentistry	New Orleans	LA	https://www.lsusd.lsuhsc.edu/
Boston University Henry M. Goldman School of Dental Medicine	Boston	MA	http://www.bu.edu/dental/
Harvard School of Dental Medicine	Boston	MA	https://hsdm.harvard.edu/
Tufts University School of Dental Medicine	Boston	MA	https://dental.tufts.edu/
University of Maryland School of Dentistry	Baltimore	MD	https://www.dental.umaryland.edu/
University of New England College of Dental Medicine	Portland	ME	https://www.une.edu/dentalmedicine
University of Michigan School of Dentistry	Ann Arbor	MI	https://www.dent.umich.edu/
University of Detroit Mercy School of Dentistry	Detroit	MI	https://dental.udmercy.edu/
University of Minnesota School of Dentistry	Minneapolis	MN	https://www.dentistry.umn.edu/

Dental Schools	City	State	Website
University of Missouri-Kansas City School of Dentistry	Kansas City	MO	https://dentistry.umkc.edu/
Missouri School of Dentistry & Oral Health	Kirksville	MO	https://www.atsu.edu/missouri-school-of-dentistry-and-oral-health
University of Mississippi Medical Center School of Dentistry	Jackson	MS	https://www.umc.edu/sod/SOD_Home.html
University of North Carolina at Chapel Hill Adams School of Dentistry	Chapel Hill	NC	https://www.dentistry.unc.edu/
East Carolina University School of Dental Medicine	Greenville	NC	https://www.ecu.edu/cs-dhs/dental/
University of Nebraska Medical Center College of Dentistry	Lincoln	NE	https://www.unmc.edu/dentistry/
Creighton University School of Dentistry	Omaha	NE	https://dentistry.creighton.edu/
Rutgers, The State University of New Jersey, School of Dental Medicine	Newark	NJ	http://sdm.rutgers.edu/
University of Nevada, Las Vegas, School of Dental Medicine	Las Vegas	NV	https://www.unlv.edu/dental
University at Buffalo School of Dental Medicine	Buffalo	NY	http://dental.buffalo.edu/
Touro College of Dental Medicine at New York Medical College	Hawthorne	NY	https://dental.touro.edu/
Columbia University College of Dental Medicine	New York	NY	https://www.dental.columbia.edu/
NYU College of Dentistry	New York	NY	https://dental.nyu.edu/
Stony Brook University School of Dental Medicine	Stony Brook	NY	https://dentistry.stonybrookmedicine.edu/
Case Western Reserve University School of Dental Medicine	Cleveland	OH	https://case.edu/dental/
The Ohio State University College of Dentistry	Columbus	OH	https://dentistry.osu.edu/
University of Oklahoma College of Dentistry	Oklahoma City	OK	https://dentistry.ouhsc.edu/

Dental Schools	City	State	Website
Oregon Health & Science University School of Dentistry	Portland	OR	https://www.ohsu.edu/school-of-dentistry
The Maurice H. Kornberg School of Dentistry, Temple University	Philadelphia	PA	https://dentistry.temple.edu/
University of Pennsylvania School of Dental Medicine	Philadelphia	PA	https://www.dental.upenn.edu/
University of Pittsburgh School of Dental Medicine	Pittsburgh	PA	https://www.dental.pitt.edu/
University of Puerto Rico School of Dental Medicine	San Juan	PR	https://dental.rcm.upr.edu/
Medical University of South Carolina James B. Edwards College of Dental Medicine	Charleston	SC	https://dentistry.musc.edu/
University of Tennessee Health Science Center College of Dentistry	Memphis	TN	https://www.uthsc.edu/dentistry/
Meharry Medical College School of Dentistry	Nashville	TN	https://home.mmc.edu/school-of-dentistry/
Texas A&M College of Dentistry	Dallas	TX	https://dentistry.tamu.edu/
Texas Tech University Health Sciences Center El Paso Woody L. Hunt School of Dental Medicine	El Paso	TX	https://elpaso.ttuhsc.edu/sdm/
The University of Texas School of Dentistry at Houston	Houston	TX	https://dentistry.uth.edu/
UT Health San Antonio School of Dentistry	San Antonio	TX	https://www.uthscsa.edu/academics/dental
University of Utah School of Dentistry	Salt Lake City	UT	https://dentistry.utah.edu/
Roseman University of Health Sciences College of Dental Medicine – South Jordan, Utah	South Jordan	UT	https://dental.roseman.edu/
Virginia Commonwealth University School of Dentistry	Richmond	VA	https://dentistry.vcu.edu/
University of Washington School of Dentistry	Seattle	WA	https://dental.washington.edu/

Dental Schools	City	State	Website
Marquette University School of Dentistry	Milwaukee	WI	https://www.marquette.edu/dentistry/
West Virginia University School of Dentistry	Morgantown	WV	https://dentistry.wvu.edu/

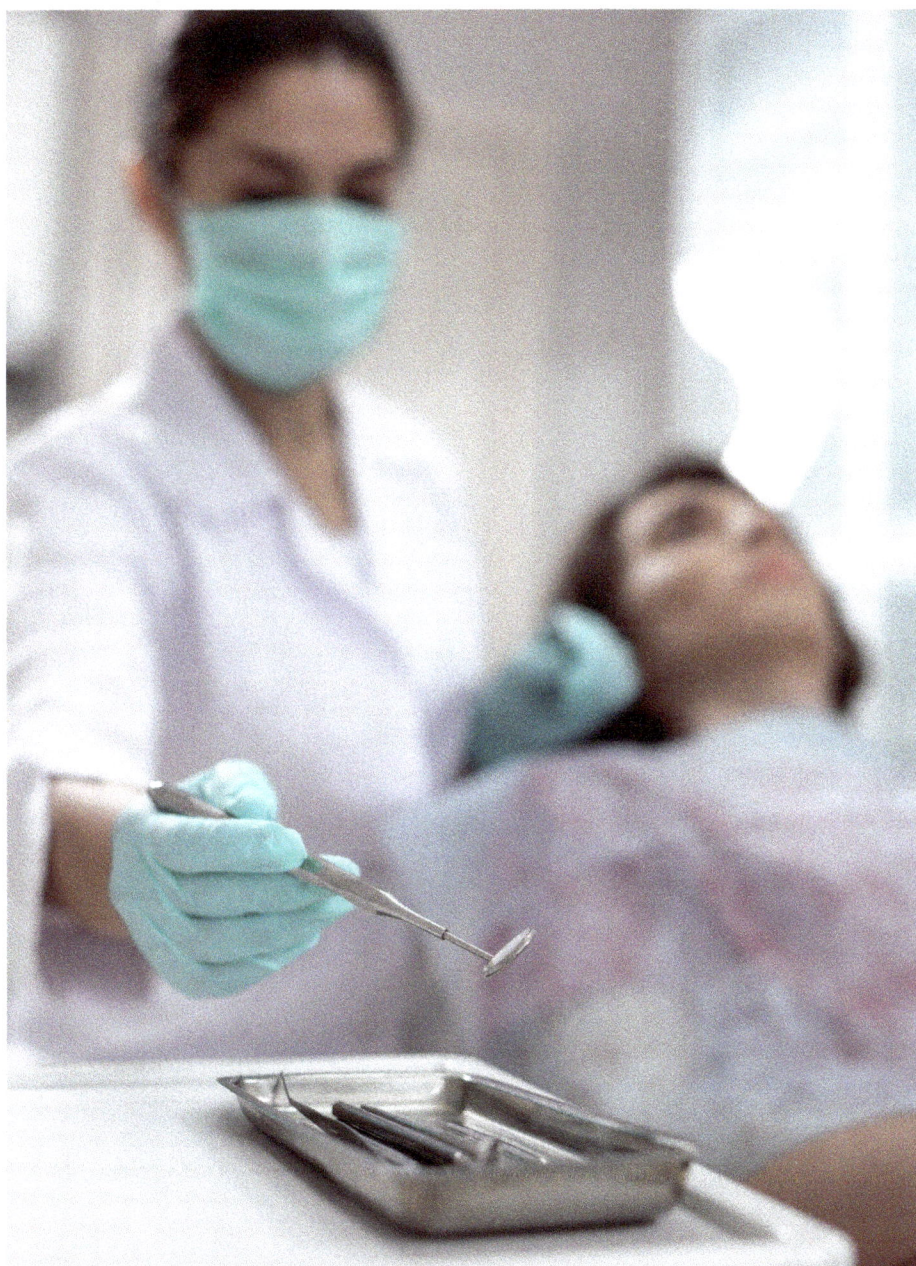

CHAPTER 15

PHYSICIAN ASSISTANT SCHOOLS BY CITY/STATE

PA School	City	State	Website
University of Washington - MEDEX Northwest, Anchorage	Anchorage	AK	https://depts.washington.edu/medex/pa-program/
University of Alabama at Birmingham	Birmingham	AL	http://www.uab.edu/shp/cds/physician-assistant
Samford University	Homewood	AL	https://www.samford.edu/healthprofessions/master-of-science-in-physician-assistant-studies
University of South Alabama	Mobile	AL	https://www.southalabama.edu/colleges/alliedhealth/pa/
Faulkner University	Montgomery	AL	https://www.faulkner.edu/graduate/graduate-degrees/physican-assistant-studies-ms-pas/
University of Arkansas	Little Rock	AR	http://healthprofessions.uams.edu/programs/physicianassistant/
Harding University	Searcy	AR	http://www.harding.edu/PAprogram/
Midwestern University - Glendale	Glendale	AZ	https://www.midwestern.edu/academics/degrees-and-programs/master-of-medical-sciences-in-physician-assistant-studies-az.xml
A.T. Still University - Arizona School of Health Sciences	Mesa	AZ	https://www.atsu.edu/physician-assistant-degree
Northern Arizona University	Phoenix	AZ	http://www.nau.edu/pa
University of Southern California	Alhambra	CA	https://keck.usc.edu/physician-assistant-program/
Marshall B. Ketchum University	Fullerton	CA	https://www.ketchum.edu/pa-studies
Chapman University	Irvine	CA	https://www.chapman.edu/crean/academic-programs/graduate-programs/physician-assistant/index.aspx
University of La Verne	La Verne	CA	https://artsci.laverne.edu/physician-assistant/

Physician Assistant	City	State	Website
Loma Linda University	Loma Linda	CA	http://www.llu.edu/allied-health/sahp/pa
Charles R. Drew University	Los Angeles	CA	https://www.cdrewu.edu/cosh/PA
Samuel Merritt University	Oakland	CA	http://www.samuelmerritt.edu/physician_assistant
Western University of Health Sciences	Pomona	CA	http://prospective.westernu.edu/physician-assistant/welcome-14/
California Baptist University	Riverside	CA	https://calbaptist.edu/programs/master-of-science-physician-assistant-studies/
University of California, Davis	Sacramento	CA	https://health.ucdavis.edu/nursing/admissions/programs/mhs-pa.html
University of the Pacific	Sacramento	CA	http://pacific.edu/PAprogram
California State University, Monterey Bay	Salinas	CA	http://csumb.edu/mspa
Point Loma Nazarene University	San Diego	CA	https://www.pointloma.edu/graduate-studies/programs/physician-assistant-ms-m#applicationinformation
Dominican University of California	San Rafael	CA	https://www.dominican.edu/directory/physician-assistant-studies
Stanford University	Stanford	CA	https://med.stanford.edu/pa
Touro University California	Vallejo	CA	http://cehs.tu.edu/paprogram/
Southern California University of Health Sciences	Whittier	CA	https://www.scuhs.edu/academics/csih/master-of-science-physician-assistant-program/
Red Rocks Community College	Arvada	CO	https://www.rrcc.edu/physician-assistant
University of Colorado	Aurora	CO	http://www.ucdenver.edu/academics/colleges/medicalschool/education/degree_programs/PAProgram/Pages/Home.aspx

Physician Assistant	City	State	Website
Colorado Mesa University	Grand Junction	CO	https://www.coloradomesa.edu/kinesiology/graduate/pa-program/index.html
Rocky Vista University	Parker	CO	https://www.rvu.edu/admissions/mpas/
Yale University	New Haven	CT	http://www.paprogram.yale.edu/
University of Bridgeport	Bridgeport	CT	http://www.bridgeport.edu/academics/schools-colleges/physician-assistant-institute/physician-assistant-ms
Sacred Heart University	Fairfield	CT	https://www.sacredheart.edu/majors--programs/physician-assistant-studies---mpas/
Quinnipiac University	Hamden	CT	http://www.quinnipiac.edu/gradphysicianasst
University of Saint Joseph	West Hartford	CT	https://www.usj.edu/academics/academic-schools/sppas/physician-assistant-studies/admissions/
George Washington University	Washington	DC	https://smhs.gwu.edu/physician-assistant/
Keiser University	Fort Lauderdale	FL	https://www.keiseruniversity.edu/master-of-science-in-physician-assistant/
Nova Southeastern University - Fort Lauderdale	Fort Lauderdale	FL	http://www.nova.edu/chcs/pa/fortlauderdale/index.html
Nova Southeastern University - Orlando	Fort Lauderdale	FL	https://healthsciences.nova.edu/pa/orlando/index.html
Florida Gulf Coast University	Fort Myers	FL	https://www2.fgcu.edu/mariebcollege/HS/MPAS/index.html
Nova Southeastern University - Fort Myers	Fort Myers	FL	https://healthsciences.nova.edu/pa/fort-myers/index.html
University of Florida	Gainesville	FL	https://pap.med.ufl.edu/
Nova Southeastern University - Jacksonville	Jacksonville	FL	https://healthsciences.nova.edu/pa/jacksonville/index.html

Physician Assistant	City	State	Website
Barry University - Miami	Miami	FL	http://www.barry.edu/physician-assistant/
Barry University - St. Petersburg	Miami	FL	http://www.barry.edu/physician-assistant/
Florida International University Herbert Wertheim College of Medicine	Miami	FL	https://medicine.fiu.edu/academics/degrees-and-programs/master-in-physician-studies/index.html
Miami Dade College	Miami	FL	http://www.mdc.edu/physicianassistantas/
AdventHealth University	Orlando	FL	https://www.ahu.edu/academics/ms-physician-assistant
South University, West Palm Beach	Royal Palm Beach	FL	https://www.southuniversity.edu/west-palm-beach/physician-assistant-ms
Gannon University - Ruskin	Ruskin	FL	https://www.gannon.edu/academic-offerings/health-professions-and-sciences/graduate/master-of-physician-assistant-science/admission-requirements/
Florida State University	Tallahassee	FL	https://med.fsu.edu/index.cfm?page=pa.home
South University, Tampa	Tampa	FL	http://www.southuniversity.edu/tampa/areas-of-study/physician-assistant/physician-assistant-master-of-science-ms
University of South Florida	Tampa	FL	https://health.usf.edu/medicine/pa/
University of Tampa	Tampa	FL	https://www.ut.edu/graduate-degrees/physician-assistant-medicine-program
Emory University	Atlanta	GA	http://med.emory.edu/pa/
Mercer University	Atlanta	GA	http://chp.mercer.edu/academics-departments/physician-assistant-studies/
Morehouse School of Medicine	Atlanta	GA	http://www.msm.edu//physicianassistantprogram/index.php

Physician Assistant	City	State	Website
South College - Atlanta	Atlanta	GA	https://www.south.edu/programs/master-health-science-physician-assistant-studies/atlanta/
Augusta University	Augusta	GA	https://www.augusta.edu/alliedhealth/pa/
Brenau University	Gainesville	GA	https://www.brenau.edu/healthsciences/physician-assistant-studies/
South University, Savannah	Savannah	GA	https://www.southuniversity.edu/savannah/areas-of-study/physician-assistant/physician-assistant-master-of-science-ms
PCOM - Georgia	Suwanee	GA	https://www.pcom.edu/academics/programs-and-degrees/physician-assistant-studies/georgia.html
University of Washington - MEDEX Northwest, Kona	Kealakekua	HI	https://depts.washington.edu/medex/pa-program/
St. Ambrose University	Davenport	IA	http://www.sau.edu/master-of-physician-assistant-studies
Des Moines University	Des Moines	IA	https://www.dmu.edu/pa/
University of Dubuque	Dubuque	IA	http://www.dbq.edu/Academics/OfficeofAcademicAffairs/GraduatePrograms/MasterofScienceinPhysician-AssistantStudies/
University of Iowa	Iowa City	IA	http://www.medicine.uiowa.edu/pa/
Northwestern College	Orange City	IA	https://www.nwciowa.edu/graduate/physician-assistant
Idaho State University - Caldwell	Caldwell	ID	https://www.isu.edu/pa/
Idaho State University - Meridian	Meridian	ID	https://www.isu.edu/pa/
Idaho State University - Pocatello	Meridian	ID	https://www.isu.edu/pa/
Southern Illinois University	Carbondale	IL	https://www.siumed.edu/paprogram

Physician Assistant	City	State	Website
Northwestern University	Chicago	IL	http://www.feinberg.northwestern.edu/sites/pa/
Rush University	Chicago	IL	http://www.rushu.rush.edu/pa-program
Midwestern University - Downers Grove	Downers Grove	IL	https://www.midwestern.edu/admissions/apply/master-of-medical-sciences-in-physician-assistant-studies-in-downers-grove.xml
Rosalind Franklin University of Medicine	North Chicago	IL	https://www.rosalindfranklin.edu/academics/college-of-health-professions/degree-programs/physician-assistant-practice-ms/
Dominican University of Illinois	River Forest	IL	https://www.dom.edu/admission/graduate/health-sciences-programs/mmspas
Trine University	Angola	IN	http://www.trine.edu/academics/majors-and-minors/graduate/master-physician-assistant-studies/index.aspx
University of Evansville	Evansville	IN	https://www.evansville.edu/majors/physicianassistant/
University of Saint Francis	Fort Wayne	IN	http://pa.sf.edu/
Franklin College	Franklin	IN	https://franklincollege.edu/academics/graduate-programs/master-science-physician-assistant/
Butler University	Indianapolis	IN	http://www.butler.edu/physician-assistant/
Indiana University School of Health and Human Sciences	Indianapolis	IN	https://shhs.iupui.edu/admissions/graduate-professional/master-physician-assistant-studies.html
Indiana State University	Terre Haute	IN	https://www.indstate.edu/health/program/pa
Valparaiso University	Valparaiso	IN	https://www.valpo.edu/physician-assistant-program/programs/admission/

Physician Assistant	City	State	Website
Wichita State University	Wichita	KS	http://www.wichita.edu/thisis/home/?u=pa
University of Kentucky - Lexington	Lexington	KY	http://www.uky.edu/chs/academic-programs/physician-assistant-studies
Sullivan University	Louisville	KY	https://www.sullivan.edu/programs/master-of-science-in-physician-assistant
University of Kentucky - Morehead	Morehead	KY	https://www.uky.edu/chs/academic-programs/physician-assistant-studies
University of the Cumberlands	Williamsburg	KY	http://gradweb.ucumberlands.edu/medicine/mpas/overview
University of the Cumberlands, Northern Kentucky Campus	Williamsburg	KY	https://www.ucumberlands.edu/academics/graduate/programs/master-science-physician-assistant-studies
Franciscan Missionaries of Our Lady University	Baton Rouge	LA	https://www.franu.edu/academics/academic-programs/physician-assistant-studies
Lousiana State University - New Orleans	New Orleans	LA	http://alliedhealth.lsuhsc.edu/pa/
Xavier University of Louisiana	New Orleans	LA	https://www.xula.edu/physician-assistant-program-about
Louisiana State University Health Sciences Center Shreveport	Shreveport	LA	https://lsuhscshreveportedu.finalsite.com/departments/allied-health-professions-departments/physician-assistant
Boston University School of Medicine	Boston	MA	http://bu.edu/paprogram
MCPHS - Boston	Boston	MA	https://www.mcphs.edu/academics/school-of-physician-assistant-studies/physician-assistant/physician-assistant-studies-mpas

Physician Assistant	City	State	Website
MGH Institute of Health Professions	Boston	MA	http://www.mghihp.edu/academics/school-of-health-and-rehabilitation-sciences/physician-assistant-studies/default.aspx
Northeastern University	Boston	MA	https://bouve.northeastern.edu/physician-assistant/ms/
Tufts University	Boston	MA	https://medicine.tufts.edu/education/physician-assistant
Bay Path University	East Longmeadow	MA	https://www.baypath.edu/academics/graduate-programs/physician-assistant-studies-ms/
Springfield College	Springfield	MA	https://springfield.edu/programs/physician-assistant-studies
Westfield State University	Westfield	MA	https://www.westfield.ma.edu/academics/master-of-science-in-physician-assistant-studies/
MCPHS - Worcester	Worcester	MA	https://www.mcphs.edu/academics/school-of-physician-assistant-studies/physician-assistant/physican-assistant-studies-mpas-accelerated
University of Maryland Baltimore/Ann Arundel Community College	Arnold	MD	https://graduate.umaryland.edu/mshs-pa-umb/
Towson University CCBC - Essex	Baltimore	MD	https://www.towson.edu/chp/departments/health-sciences/grad/physician-assistant/
Frostburg State University	Hagerstown	MD	https://www.frostburg.edu/academics/majorminors/graduate/ms-physician-assistant/index.php
University of Maryland Eastern Shore	Princess Anne	MD	http://www.umes.edu/pa
University of New England	Portland	ME	http://www.une.edu/wchp/pa

Physician Assistant	City	State	Website
Concordia University Ann Arbor	Ann Arbor	MI	https://www.cuaa.edu/academics/programs/physician-assistant-masters/index.html#overview
University of Detroit Mercy	Detroit	MI	http://healthprofessions.udmercy.edu/academics/pa/grad.php
Wayne State Unversity	Detroit	MI	http://www.pa.cphs.wayne.edu/
University of Michigan - Flint	Flint	MI	https://www.umflint.edu/physician-assistant-ms/
Grand Valley State University - Grand Rapids	Grand Rapids	MI	http://www.gvsu.edu/pas
Western Michigan University	Kalamazoo	MI	http://www.wmich.edu/pa
Central Michigan University	Mount Pleasant	MI	https://www.cmich.edu/colleges/CHP/hp_academics/srms/physician_assistant/Pages/PA-Program-at-CMU.aspx
Grand Valley State University - Traverse City	Traverse City	MI	https://www.gvsu.edu/pas/traverse-city-campus-89.htm
Eastern Michigan University	Ypsilanti	MI	http://www.emich.edu/pa
College of St. Scholastica	Duluth	MN	http://www.css.edu/graduate/masters-doctoral-and-professional-programs/areas-of-study/ms-physician-assistant.html
Augsburg University	Minneapolis	MN	http://www.augsburg.edu/pa/
Mayo Clinic School of Health Sciences	Rochester	MN	https://college.mayo.edu/academics/health-sciences-education/physician-assistant-program-minnesota/
Saint Catherine University	Saint Paul	MN	https://www.stkate.edu/academic-programs/gc/physician-assistant-studies-mpas

Physician Assistant	City	State	Website
Bethel University	St. Paul	MN	https://www.bethel.edu/graduate/academics/physician-assistant/
Stephens College	Columbia	MO	https://www.stephens.edu/academics/graduate-programs/master-in-physician-assistant-studies/
University of Missouri-Kansas City	Kansas City	MO	http://med.umkc.edu/pa/
Saint Louis University	Saint Louis	MO	https://www.slu.edu/doisy/degrees/graduate/physician-assistant-mms.php
Missouri State University	Springfield	MO	http://www.missouristate.edu/pas
Mississippi College	Clinton	MS	http://www.mc.edu/academics/departments/pa/
Mississippi State University - Meridian	Meridian	MS	https://www.meridian.msstate.edu/academics/physician-assistant/
Rocky Mountain College	Billings	MT	http://pa.rocky.edu/
Gardner-Webb University	Boiling Springs	NC	https://gardner-webb.edu/academic-programs-and-resources/colleges-and-schools/health-sciences/schools-and-departments/physician-assistant-studies/index
Wake Forest University - Boone	Boone	NC	http://www.wakehealth.edu/Physician-Assistant-Program/
Campbell University	Buies Creek	NC	https://cphs.campbell.edu/academic-programs/physician-assistant/master-physician-assistant-practice/
UNC-Chapel Hill	Chapel Hill	NC	http://www.med.unc.edu/ahs/unc-pa
Duke University	Durham	NC	http://pa.duke.edu/
Elon University	Elon	NC	https://www.elon.edu/u/academics/health-sciences/physician-assistant/
Methodist University	Fayetteville	NC	http://www.methodist.edu/paprogram
East Carolina University	Greenville	NC	http://www.ecu.edu/pa

Physician Assistant	City	State	Website
Wingate University - Hendersonville	Hendersonville	NC	https://www.wingate.edu/academics/hendersonville/physician-assistant
High Point University	High Point	NC	http://www.highpoint.edu/physicianassistant/
Pfeiffer University	Misenheimer	NC	https://www.pfeiffer.edu/mspas
Wingate University	Wingate	NC	http://pa.wingate.edu/
Wake Forest University - Winston Salem	Winston-Salem	NC	http://www.wakehealth.edu/Physician-Assistant-Program/
University of North Dakota	Grand Forks	ND	http://med.und.edu/physician-assistant/index.cfm
University of Nebraska Medical Center - Kearney	Kearney	NE	https://www.unmc.edu/alliedhealth/education/pa/
Union College	Lincoln	NE	http://www.ucollege.edu/pa
College of Saint Mary	Omaha	NE	http://www.csm.edu/academics/health-human-services/master-science-degree-physician-assistant-studies
Creighton University	Omaha	NE	https://medschool.creighton.edu/program/physician-assistant-mpas
University of Nebraska Medical Center - Omaha	Omaha	NE	https://www.unmc.edu/alliedhealth/education/pa/
MCPHS - Manchester	Manchester	NH	https://www.mcphs.edu/academics/school-of-physician-assistant-studies/physician-assistant/physican-assistant-studies-mpas-accelerated
Franklin Pierce University	West Lebanon	NH	http://www.franklinpierce.edu/academics/gradstudies/programs_of_study/mpas/index.htm
Saint Elizabeth University	Morristown	NJ	https://cse.smartcatalogiq.com/en/2019-2020/academic-catalog/academic-programs/physician-assistant/ms-in-physician-assistant

Physician Assistant	City	State	Website
Seton Hall University	Nutley	NJ	https://www.shu.edu/academics/ms-physician-assistant.cfm
Kean University	Union	NJ	https://www.kean.edu/academics/programs/physician-assistant-studies-ms
Thomas Jefferson University - New Jersey	Voorhees	NJ	https://www.jefferson.edu/university/health-professions/departments/physician-assistant-studies/degrees-programs/graduate/ms-new-jersery.html
Monmouth University	West Long Branch	NJ	https://www.monmouth.edu/graduate/ms-physician-assistant/
Rutgers University	West Piscataway	NJ	https://shp.rutgers.edu/physician-assistant/master-of-science-physician-assistant-program/
University of New Mexico	Albuquerque	NM	http://goto.unm.edu/pa
University of St. Francis	Albuquerque	NM	http://www.stfrancis.edu/academics/physician-assistant-studies
Touro University Nevada	Henderson	NV	https://tun.touro.edu/programs/physician-assistant-studies/
University of Nevada, Reno	Reno	NV	https://med.unr.edu/physician-assistant
Albany Medical College	Albany	NY	https://www.amc.edu/academic/PhysicianAssistant/index.cfm
Daemen College	Amherst	NY	https://www.daemen.edu/academics/areas-study/physician-assistant/physician-assistant-studies-ms
Mercy College	Bronx	NY	https://www.mercy.edu/degrees-programs/ms-physician-assistant

Physician Assistant	City	State	Website
Long Island University	Brooklyn	NY	https://www.liu.edu/Brooklyn/Academics/Schools/School-of-Health-Professions/Dept/Physician-Assistant/MS-PAS
SUNY Downstate Medical Center	Brooklyn	NY	https://sls.downstate.edu/admissions/chrp/pa/index.html
Canisius College	Buffalo	NY	https://www.canisius.edu/academics/programs/physician-assistant
D'Youville College	Buffalo	NY	http://www.dyc.edu/academics/pa/
Touro College - Long Island	Central Islip	NY	https://shs.touro.edu/programs/physician-assistant/physician-assistant-long-island/
Touro College - NUMC	East Meadow	NY	https://shs.touro.edu/programs/physician-assistant/physician-assistant-long-island/
Hofstra University	Hempstead	NY	https://www.hofstra.edu/academics/colleges/nursing-physician-assistant/physician-assistant/
Ithaca College	Ithaca	NY	https://www.ithaca.edu/academics/school-health-sciences-and-human-performance/graduate-programs/physician-assistant-studies
CUNY York College	Jamaica	NY	http://www.york.cuny.edu/academics/departments/health-professions/physician-assistant
Pace University - Lenox Hill Hospital, NYC	New York	NY	http://www.pace.edu/college-health-professions/explore-programs/physician-assistant-program
The CUNY School of Medicine	New York	NY	https://www.ccny.cuny.edu/csom/
Touro College Manhattan	New York	NY	https://shs.touro.edu/programs/physician-assistant/physician-assistant-manhattan/

Physician Assistant	City	State	Website
Weil Cornell Graduate School of Medical Sciences	New York	NY	https://gradschool.weill.cornell.edu/programs/health-sciences-physician-assistants
Yeshiva University, Katz School of Science and Health	New York	NY	https://www.yu.edu/katz/programs/graduate/physician-assistant
New York Institute of Technology	Old Westbury	NY	http://www.nyit.edu/pa
Pace University - Pleasantville	Pleasantville	NY	https://www.pace.edu/college-health-professions/graduate-degree-programs/physician-assistant-program-pleasantville
Clarkson University	Potsdam	NY	http://www.clarkson.edu/pa
Marist College	Poughkeepsie	NY	http://www.marist.edu/science/physassist/
St. John's University	Queens	NY	https://www.stjohns.edu/academics/programs/physician-assistant-master-science
Rochester Institute of Technology	Rochester	NY	http://www.rit.edu/healthsciences/graduate-programs/physician-assistant
Stony Brook University Southhampton	Southampton	NY	https://healthtechnology.stonybrookmedicine.edu/programs/pa/elpa
St. Bonaventure University	St. Bonaventure	NY	https://www.sbu.edu/academics/physician-assistant-studies
Wagner College	Staten Island	NY	http://wagner.edu/physician-assistant/
Stony Brook University Health Science Center	Stony Brook	NY	https://healthtechnology.stonybrookmedicine.edu/programs/pa/elpa
Le Moyne College	Syracuse	NY	https://www.lemoyne.edu/pa
SUNY Upstate Medical Center	Syracuse	NY	http://www.upstate.edu/chp/programs/pa/index.php
University of Mount Union	Alliance	OH	https://www.mountunion.edu/physician-assistant-studies

Physician Assistant	City	State	Website
Ashland University	Ashland	OH	https://www.ashland.edu/conhs/majors/master-science-physician-assistant-studies
Baldwin Wallace University	Berea	OH	https://www.bw.edu/graduate/physician-assistant/
Mount St. Joseph University	Cincinnati	OH	http://www.msj.edu/PA
Case Western Reserve University	Cleveland	OH	http://case.edu/medicine/physician-assistant/
Ohio Dominican University	Columbus	OH	http://www.ohiodominican.edu/academics/graduate/physician-assistant-program
University of Dayton	Dayton	OH	https://udayton.edu/education/departments_and_programs/pa/index.php
Ohio University	Dublin	OH	https://www.ohio.edu/chsp/rcs/pa/
University of Findlay	Findlay	OH	https://www.findlay.edu/healthprofessions/physicianassistant-ma/
Kettering College	Kettering	OH	http://kc.edu/academics/physician-assistant/
Marietta College	Marietta	OH	https://www.marietta.edu/pa-program
Lake Erie College	Painesville	OH	http://www.lec.edu/pa
Mercy College of Ohio	Toledo	OH	https://mercycollege.edu/academics/programs/graduate/physician-assistant-studies
University of Toledo	Toledo	OH	http://www.utoledo.edu/med/grad/pa/
Northeastern State University	Muskogee	OK	https://academics.nsuok.edu/healthprofessions/Degree-Programs/Graduate/Physician-Assistant-Studie
Oklahoma City University	Oklahoma City	OK	https://www.okcu.edu/physician-assistant/home
University of Oklahoma - Oklahoma City	Oklahoma City	OK	https://medicine.ouhsc.edu/Prospective-Students/Degree-Programs/Physician-Associate-Program

Physician Assistant	City	State	Website
Oklahoma State University Center for Health Sciences	Tulsa	OK	https://medicine.okstate.edu/pa/index.html
University of Oklahoma - Tulsa	Tulsa	OK	http://www.ou.edu/tulsa/community_medicine/scm-pa-program
Pacific University	Hillsboro	OR	http://www.pacificu.edu/pa
George Fox University	Newberg	OR	https://www.georgefox.edu/pa/index.html
Oregon Health & Science University	Portland	OR	https://www.ohsu.edu/school-of-medicine/physician-assistant
DeSales University	Center Valley	PA	https://www.desales.edu/academics/graduate-studies/master-of-science-in-physician-assistant-studies-(mspas)
Misericordia University	Dallas	PA	https://www.misericordia.edu/page.cfm?p=655
Salus University	Elkins Park	PA	http://www.salus.edu/Colleges/Health-Sciences/Physician-Assistant.aspx
Gannon University - Erie, PA	Erie	PA	http://www.gannon.edu/academic-departments/physician-assistant-department/
Mercyhurst University	Erie	PA	https://www.mercyhurst.edu/academics/physician-assistant-studies-program
Arcadia University	Glenside	PA	https://www.arcadia.edu/academics/programs/physician-assistant
Seton Hill University	Greensburg	PA	https://www.setonhill.edu/academics/graduate-programs/physician-assistant-ms/
Thiel College	Greenville	PA	https://www.thiel.edu/graduate-degrees/physician-assistant
Penn State University	Hershey	PA	https://med.psu.edu/physician-assistant
Lock Haven University	Lock Haven	PA	https://paportal.lhup.edu/PA/

Physician Assistant	City	State	Website
Saint Francis University	Loretto	PA	https://www.francis.edu/Physician-Assistant-Science/
Drexel University	Philadelphia	PA	http://drexel.edu/cnhp/academics/departments/Physician-Assistant/
Philadelphia College of Osteopathic Medicine (PCOM)	Philadelphia	PA	https://www.pcom.edu/academics/programs-and-degrees/physician-assistant-studies/
Temple University Lewis Katz School of Medicine	Philadelphia	PA	https://medicine.temple.edu/education/physician-assistant-program
Thomas Jefferson University - City Center	Philadelphia	PA	https://www.jefferson.edu/university/health-professions/departments/physician-assistant-studies/degrees-programs/graduate/ms-center-city.html
Thomas Jefferson University - East Falls	Philadelphia	PA	https://www.jefferson.edu/university/health-professions/departments/physician-assistant-studies/degrees-programs/graduate/ms-east-falls/applying.html
University of the Sciences	Philadelphia	PA	https://www.usciences.edu/samson-college-of-health-sciences/physician-assistant-studies/index.html
Chatham University	Pittsburgh	PA	http://www.chatham.edu/mpas/
Duquesne University	Pittsburgh	PA	http://www.duq.edu/academics/schools/health-sciences/academic-programs/physician-assistant
University of Pittsburgh	Pittsburgh	PA	https://www.shrs.pitt.edu/PAProgram
Marywood University	Scranton	PA	http://www.marywood.edu/pa-program
Slippery Rock University	Slippery Rock	PA	http://www.sru.edu/academics/graduate-programs/physician-assistant-studies-master-of-science

Physician Assistant	City	State	Website
West Chester University	West Chester	PA	https://www.wcupa.edu/healthSciences/physicianAssistant/default.aspx?gclid=EAIaIQobCh-MInYy7kYO36wIVAeWzCh-2qzAkbEAAYASAAEgItF-vD_BwE
King's College	Wilkes-Barre	PA	https://www.kings.edu/academics/undergraduate_majors/physicianassistant
Pennsylvania College of Technology	Williamsport	PA	https://www.pct.edu/academics/nhs/physician-assistant/physician-assistant-studies
San Juan Bautista School of Medicine	Caguas	PR	https://www.sanjuanbautista.edu/education/programs/pa-program.html
Johnson & Wales University	Providence	RI	http://www.jwu.edu/PA
Bryant University	Smithfield	RI	http://gradschool.bryant.edu/health-sciences.htm
Charleston Southern University	Charleston	SC	http://www.csuniv.edu/pa
Medical University of South Carolina	Charleston	SC	https://education.musc.edu/students/enrollment/bulletin/colleges-and-degrees/health-professions/ms-in-physician-assistant
Presbyterian College	Clinton	SC	https://www.presby.edu/academics/graduate-professional/physician-assistant-program/
University of South Carolina SOM	Columbia	SC	http://www.southalabama.edu/alliedhealth/pa
North Greenville University	Greer	SC	http://www.ngu.edu/pa-medicine.php
University of South Dakota	Vemillion	SD	http://www.usd.edu/pa
Lincoln Memorial University	Harrogate	TN	https://www.lmunet.edu/school-of-medical-sciences/pa-harrogate/index.php

Physician Assistant	City	State	Website
Lincoln Memorial University - Knoxville	Knoxville	TN	https://www.lmunet.edu/school-of-medical-sciences/pa-knoxville/index.php
South College - Knoxville	Knoxville	TN	https://www.south.edu/programs/master-health-science-physician-assistant-studies/knoxville/
Christian Brothers University	Memphis	TN	https://www.cbu.edu/pa
University of Tennessee Health Science Center	Memphis	TN	http://www.uthsc.edu/allied/pa
Milligan University	Milligan	TN	http://www.milligan.edu/pa
Lipscomb University	Nashville	TN	https://www.lipscomb.edu
South College - Nashville	Nashville	TN	https://www.south.edu/programs/master-health-science-physician-assistant-studies/nashville/
Trevecca Nazarene University	Nashville	TN	https://www.trevecca.edu/programs/physician-assistant
Bethel University (TN)	Paris	TN	https://www.bethelu.edu/academics/degrees-and-programs/physician-assistant-studies
Hardin-Simmons University	Abilene	TX	https://www.hsutx.edu/pa
University of Mary Hardin-Baylor	Belton	TX	https://go.umhb.edu/graduate/physician-assistant/home
University of Texas Southwestern Medical Center	Dallas	TX	http://www.utsouthwestern.edu/pa
University of Texas Rio Grande Valley	Edinburgh	TX	https://www.utrgv.edu/pa/
U.S. Army Medical Center of Excellence IPAP	Fort Sam Houston	TX	https://medcoe.army.mil/ipap
University of North Texas HS Center Fort Worth	Fort Worth	TX	https://www.unthsc.edu/school-of-health-professions/physician-assistant-studies/

Physician Assistant	City	State	Website
University of Texas Medical Branch at Galveston	Galveston	TX	http://shp.utmb.edu/PhysicianAssistantStudies/
Baylor College of Medicine	Houston	TX	https://www.bcm.edu/education/school-of-health-professions/physician-assistant-program
University of Texas Health Science Center - Laredo	Laredo	TX	https://www.uthscsa.edu/academics/health-professions/programs/physician-assistant-studies-ms/laredo-pa-extension-program
Texas Tech University Health Sciences Center	Midland	TX	https://www.ttuhsc.edu/health-professions/master-physician-assistant-studies/
University of Texas Health Science Center - San Antonio	San Antonio	TX	http://www.uthscsa.edu/shp/pa/
University of Utah	Salt Lake City	UT	https://medicine.utah.edu/dfpm/physician-assistant-studies/program/
Rocky Mountain University of Health Professions	South Provo	UT	https://rm.edu/academics/master-of-physician-assistant-studies/
South University, Richmond	Glen Allen	VA	https://www.southuniversity.edu/richmond/physician-assistant-ms
James Madison University	Harrisonburg	VA	http://www.healthsci.jmu.edu/PA/
Shenandoah University - Loudoun	Leesburg	VA	https://www.su.edu/physician-assistant/masters-of-science-in-physician-assistant-studies/
University of Lynchburg	Lynchburg	VA	http://www.lynchburg.edu/graduate/physician-assistant-medicine/
Emory & Henry College	Marion	VA	http://www.ehc.edu/academics/programs/school-health-sciences/shs-programs/school-health-sciences-graduate-programs/physician-assistant-pa/

Physician Assistant	City	State	Website
Eastern Virginia Medical School (early assurance, too)	Norfolk	VA	http://www.evms.edu/education/masters_programs/physician_assistant_program/
Mary Baldwin University	Roanoke	VA	https://go.marybaldwin.edu/health_sciences/pas/
Radford University Carilion	Roanoke	VA	https://www.radford.edu/content/grad/home/academics/graduate-programs/pa.html
Shenandoah Universityn - Winchester	Winchester	VA	https://www.su.edu/physician-assistant/masters-of-science-in-physician-assistant-studies/
University of Washington - MEDEX Northwest, Seattle	Seattle	WA	https://depts.washington.edu/medex/pa-program/
University of Washington - MEDEX Northwest, Spokane	Spokane	WA	https://depts.washington.edu/medex/pa-program/
University of Washington - MEDEX Northwest, Tacoma	Tacoma	WA	https://depts.washington.edu/medex/pa-program/
University of Wisconsin - La Crosse	La Crosse	WI	https://www.uwlax.edu/grad/physician-assistant-studies/
University of Wisconsin-Madison	Madison	WI	https://www.med.wisc.edu/education/physician-assistant-pa-program/
Concordia University - Wisconsin	Mequon	WI	https://www.cuw.edu/academics/programs/physician-assistant-masters/
Marquette University	Milwaukee	WI	http://www.marquette.edu/physician-assistant
Caroll University	Waukesha	WI	http://www.carrollu.edu/gradprograms/physasst/admission.asp
University of Charleston	Charleston	WV	http://www.ucwv.edu/pa/
Marshall University Joan C. Edwards School of Medicine	Huntington	WV	https://jcesom.marshall.edu/students/physician-assistant-program/
West Virginia University	Morgantown	WV	https://medicine.hsc.wvu.edu/physician-assistant-studies/

Physician Assistant	City	State	Website
Alderson-Broaddus University	Philippi	WV	http://ab.edu/academics/master-of-science-in-physician-assistant-studies/
West Liberty University	West Liberty	WV	http://www.westliberty.edu/physician-assistant/

CHAPTER 16

PHARMACY SCHOOLS BY CITY/STATE

Pharmacy Schools	City	State	Website
Auburn University Harrison School of Pharmacy	Auburn	AL	https://pharmacy.auburn.edu/
Samford University McWhorter School of Pharmacy	Birmingham	AL	https://www.samford.edu/pharmacy/
University of Arkansas for Medical Sciences College of Pharmacy	Little Rock	AR	https://pharmacy.uams.edu/
Harding University College of Pharmacy	Searcy	AR	https://www.harding.edu/academics/colleges-departments/pharmacy
Midwestern University College of Pharmacy-Glendale	Glendale	AZ	https://www.midwestern.edu/academics/our-colleges/college-of-pharmacy%E2%80%93glendale.xml
University of Arizona College of Pharmacy	Tucson	AZ	https://www.pharmacy.arizona.edu/
Keck Graduate Institute (KGI) School of Pharmacy and Health Sciences	Claremont	CA	https://www.kgi.edu/academics/school-of-pharmacy-and-health-sciences/overview/
California Health Sciences University College of Pharmacy	Clovis	CA	https://pharmacy.chsu.edu/
California Northstate University College of Pharmacy	Elk Grove	CA	https://pharmacy.cnsu.edu/
Marshall B. Ketchum University College of Pharmacy	Fullerton	CA	https://www.ketchum.edu/pharmacy
Chapman University School of Pharmacy	Irvine	CA	https://www.chapman.edu/pharmacy/index.aspx
University of California, San Diego Skaggs School of Pharmacy & Pharmaceutical Sciences	La Jolla	CA	https://pharmacy.ucsd.edu/
Loma Linda University School of Pharmacy	Loma Linda	CA	https://pharmacy.llu.edu/
West Coast University School of Pharmacy	Los Angeles	CA	https://westcoastuniversity.edu/programs/doctor-pharmacy.html
University of Southern California School of Pharmacy	Los Angeles	CA	https://pharmacyschool.usc.edu/
Western University of Health Sciences College of Pharmacy	Pomona	CA	https://www.westernu.edu/pharmacy/
University of California, San Francisco School of Pharmacy	San Francisco	CA	https://pharmacy.ucsf.edu/

Pharmacy Schools	City	State	Website
American University of Health Sciences School of Pharmacy	Signal Hill	CA	https://www.auhs.edu/academics/pharmacy/
University of the Pacific Thomas J. Long School of Pharmacy	Stockton	CA	https://www.pacific.edu/academics/schools-and-colleges/thomas-j-long-school-of-pharmacy.html
Touro University - California College of Pharmacy	Vallejo	CA	http://cop.tu.edu/
University of California, Irvine*	Irvine	CA	https://pharmsci.uci.edu/pharm-d/
University of Colorado Anschutz Medical Campus Skaggs School of Pharmacy and Pharmaceutical Sciences	Aurora	CO	http://www.ucdenver.edu/academics/colleges/pharmacy/Pages/SchoolofPharmacy.aspx
Regis University Rueckert-Hartman College for Health Professions School of Pharmacy	Denver	CO	https://www.regis.edu/academics/colleges-and-schools/rueckert-hartman/pharmacy/index
University of Connecticut School of Pharmacy	Storrs	CT	https://pharmacy.uconn.edu/
University of Saint Joseph School of Pharmacy and Physician Assistant Studies	West Hartford	CT	https://www.usj.edu/academics/academic-schools/sppas/
Howard University College of Pharmacy	Washington	DC	http://pharmacy.howard.edu/
Nova Southeastern University College of Pharmacy	Fort Lauderdale	FL	https://pharmacy.nova.edu/index.html
University of Florida College of Pharmacy	Gainesville	FL	https://pharmacy.ufl.edu/
Larkin University College of Pharmacy	Miami	FL	https://ularkin.org/pharmacy/
Florida Agricultural & Mechanical University College of Pharmacy and Pharmaceutical Sciences	Tallahassee	FL	https://pharmacy.famu.edu/
University of South Florida Health Taneja College of Pharmacy	Tampa	FL	https://health.usf.edu/pharmacy
Palm Beach Atlantic University Lloyd L. Gregory School of Pharmacy	West Palm Beach	FL	https://www.pba.edu/academics/schools/gregory-pharmacy/index.html
University of Georgia College of Pharmacy	Athens	GA	https://rx.uga.edu/

Pharmacy Schools	City	State	Website
Mercer University College of Pharmacy	Atlanta	GA	https://pharmacy.mercer.edu/
South University School of Pharmacy	Savannah	GA	https://www.southuniversity.edu/degree-programs/pharmacy
Philadelphia College of Osteopathic Medicine - Georgia School of Pharmacy	Suwanee	GA	https://www.pcom.edu/academics/programs-and-degrees/doctor-of-pharmacy/
University of Hawaii at Hilo Daniel K. Inouye College of Pharmacy	Hilo	HI	https://pharmacy.uhh.hawaii.edu/
Drake University College of Pharmacy and Health Sciences	Des Moines	IA	https://www.drake.edu/cphs/
University of Iowa College of Pharmacy	Iowa City	IA	https://pharmacy.uiowa.edu/
Idaho State University College of Pharmacy	Pocatello	ID	https://www.isu.edu/pharmacy/
University of Illinois at Chicago College of Pharmacy	Chicago	IL	https://pharmacy.uic.edu/
Chicago State University College of Pharmacy	Chicago	IL	https://www.csu.edu/collegeofpharmacy/
Southern Illinois University Edwardsville School of Pharmacy	Edwardsville	IL	https://www.siue.edu/pharmacy/
Midwestern University Chicago College of Pharmacy	Downers Grove	IL	https://www.midwestern.edu/academics/degrees-and-programs/doctor-of-pharmacy-il.xml
Rosalind Franklin University of Medicine and Science College of Pharmacy	North Chicago	IL	https://www.rosalindfranklin.edu/academics/college-of-pharmacy/
Roosevelt University College of Pharmacy	Schaumburg	IL	https://www.roosevelt.edu/colleges/pharmacy
Butler University College of Pharmacy and Health Sciences	Indianapolis	IN	https://www.butler.edu/cophs
Manchester University College of Pharmacy, Natural and Health Sciences	North Manchester	IN	https://www.manchester.edu/academics/colleges/college-of-pharmacy-natural-health-sciences
Purdue University College of Pharmacy	West Lafayette	IN	https://www.pharmacy.purdue.edu/

Pharmacy Schools	City	State	Website
University of Kansas School of Pharmacy	Lawrence	KS	https://pharmacy.ku.edu/
University of Kentucky College of Pharmacy	Lexington	KY	https://pharmacy.uky.edu/
Sullivan University College of Pharmacy	Louisville	KY	https://www.sullivan.edu/colleges/college-of-pharmacy-and-health-sciences
University of Louisiana at Monroe College of Pharmacy	Monroe	LA	https://www.ulm.edu/pharmacy/
Xavier University of Louisiana College of Pharmacy	New Orleans	LA	https://www.xula.edu/collegeofpharmacy
MCPHS University School of Pharmacy - Boston	Boston	MA	https://www.mcphs.edu/
Northeastern University Bouvé College of Health Sciences School of Pharmacy	Boston	MA	https://bouve.northeastern.edu/pharmacy/
Western New England University College of Pharmacy	Springfield	MA	https://www1.wne.edu/pharmacy-and-health-sciences/
MCPHS University School of Pharmacy - Worcester	Worcester	MA	https://www.mcphs.edu/
University of Maryland School of Pharmacy	Baltimore	MD	https://www.pharmacy.umaryland.edu/
Notre Dame of Maryland University School of Pharmacy	Baltimore	MD	https://www.ndm.edu/colleges-schools/school-pharmacy
University of Maryland Eastern Shore School of Pharmacy and Health Professions	Princess Anne	MD	https://www.umes.edu/pharmacy/
Husson University School of Pharmacy	Bangor	ME	https://www.husson.edu/pharmacy/
University of New England College of Pharmacy	Portland	ME	https://www.une.edu/pharmacy
University of Michigan College of Pharmacy	Ann Arbor	MI	https://pharmacy.umich.edu/
Ferris State University College of Pharmacy	Big Rapids	MI	https://www.ferris.edu/pharmacy/
Wayne State University Eugene Applebaum College of Pharmacy and Health Sciences	Detroit	MI	https://cphs.wayne.edu/
University of Minnesota College of Pharmacy	Duluth	MN	https://www.pharmacy.umn.edu/

Pharmacy Schools	City	State	Website
University of Missouri-Kansas City School of Pharmacy	Kansas City	MO	https://pharmacy.umkc.edu/
St. Louis College of Pharmacy	St. Louis	MO	https://www.uhsp.edu/
William Carey University School of Pharmacy	Biloxi	MS	https://www.wmcarey.edu/School/Pharmacy
University of Mississippi School of Pharmacy	University	MS	https://pharmacy.olemiss.edu/
University of Montana College of Health Professions and Biomedical Sciences Skaggs School of Pharmacy	Missoula	MT	http://health.umt.edu/pharmacy/
Campbell University College of Pharmacy and Health Sciences	Buies Creek	NC	https://cphs.campbell.edu/
University of North Carolina Eshelman School of Pharmacy	Chapel Hill	NC	https://pharmacy.unc.edu/
High Point University Fred Wilson School of Pharmacy	High Point	NC	http://www.highpoint.edu/pharmacy/
Wingate University School of Pharmacy	Wingate	NC	https://www.wingate.edu/academics/graduate/pharmacy
North Dakota State University College of Health Professions School of Pharmacy	Fargo	ND	https://www.ndsu.edu/pharmacy/
University of Nebraska Medical Center College of Pharmacy	Omaha	NE	https://www.unmc.edu/pharmacy/
Creighton University School of Pharmacy and Health Professions	Omaha	NE	https://spahp.creighton.edu/
Fairleigh Dickinson University School of Pharmacy	Florham Park	NJ	https://view2.fdu.edu/academics/pharmacy/
Rutgers, the State University of New Jersey Ernest Mario School of Pharmacy	Piscataway	NJ	https://pharmacy.rutgers.edu/
University of New Mexico College of Pharmacy	Albuquerque	NM	https://hsc.unm.edu/college-of-pharmacy/
Roseman University of Health Sciences College of Pharmacy	Henderson	NV	https://pharmacy.roseman.edu/
Albany College of Pharmacy and Health Sciences School of Pharmacy and Pharmaceutical Sciences	Albany	NY	https://www.acphs.edu/

Pharmacy Schools	City	State	Website
Long Island University Arnold and Marie Schwartz College of Pharmacy and Health Sciences	Brooklyn	NY	https://liu.edu/Pharmacy
D'Youville College School of Pharmacy	Buffalo	NY	http://www.dyc.edu/academics/schools-and-departments/pharmacy/
University at Buffalo The State University of New York School of Pharmacy & Pharmaceutical Sciences	Buffalo	NY	http://pharmacy.buffalo.edu/
Binghamton University State University of New York School of Pharmacy and Pharmaceutical Sciences	Johnson City	NY	https://www.binghamton.edu/pharmacy-and-pharmaceutical-sciences/
Touro New York College of Pharmacy	New York	NY	https://tcop.touro.edu/
St. John's University College of Pharmacy and Health Sciences	Queens	NY	https://www.stjohns.edu/academics/programs/doctor-pharmacy
St. John Fisher College Wegmans School of Pharmacy	Rochester	NY	https://www.sjfc.edu/schools/school-of-pharmacy/
Ohio Northern University Raabe College of Pharmacy	Ada	OH	https://www.onu.edu/college-pharmacy
Cedarville University School of Pharmacy	Cedarville	OH	https://www.cedarville.edu/Academic-Schools-and-Departments/Pharmacy.aspx
University of Cincinnati James L. Winkle College of Pharmacy	Cincinnati	OH	https://pharmacy.uc.edu/
Ohio State University College of Pharmacy	Columbus	OH	https://pharmacy.osu.edu/
University of Findlay College of Pharmacy	Findlay	OH	https://www.findlay.edu/pharmacy/
Northeast Ohio Medical University College of Pharmacy	Rootstown	OH	https://www.neomed.edu/pharmacy/
University of Toledo College of Pharmacy and Pharmaceutical Sciences	Toledo	OH	https://www.utoledo.edu/pharmacy/
University of Oklahoma College of Pharmacy	Oklahoma City	OK	https://pharmacy.ouhsc.edu/

Pharmacy Schools	City	State	Website
Southwestern Oklahoma State University College of Pharmacy	Weatherford	OK	https://www.swosu.edu/academics/pharmacy/index.aspx
Oregon State University College of Pharmacy	Corvallis	OR	https://pharmacy.oregonstate.edu/
Pacific University School of Pharmacy	Hillsboro	OR	https://www.pacificu.edu/academics/colleges/college-health-professions/school-pharmacy
Lake Erie College of Osteopathic Medicine School of Pharmacy	Erie	PA	https://lecom.edu/academics/school-of-pharmacy/
Temple University School of Pharmacy	Philadelphia	PA	https://pharmacy.temple.edu/
Thomas Jefferson University Jefferson College of Pharmacy	Philadelphia	PA	https://www.jefferson.edu/university/pharmacy.html
University of the Sciences Philadelphia College of Pharmacy	Philadelphia	PA	https://www.usciences.edu/philadelphia-college-of-pharmacy/
Duquesne University School of Pharmacy	Pittsburgh	PA	https://www.duq.edu/academics/schools/pharmacy
University of Pittsburgh School of Pharmacy	Pittsburgh	PA	https://www.pharmacy.pitt.edu/
Wilkes University Nesbitt School of Pharmacy	Wilkes-Barre	PA	https://www.wilkes.edu/academics/colleges/nesbitt-school-of-pharmacy/index.aspx
University of Puerto Rico Medical Sciences Campus School of Pharmacy	San Juan	PR	https://farmacia.rcm.upr.edu/academic-programs/doctor-of-pharmacy-program/
University of Rhode Island College of Pharmacy	Kingston	RI	https://web.uri.edu/pharmacy/
Medical University of South Carolina College of Pharmacy	Charleston	SC	https://pharmacy.musc.edu/
Presbyterian College School of Pharmacy	Clinton	SC	https://pharmacy.presby.edu/
University of South Carolina College of Pharmacy	Columbia	SC	https://www.sc.edu/study/colleges_schools/pharmacy/index.php

Pharmacy Schools	City	State	Website
South Dakota State University College of Pharmacy and Allied Health Professions	Brookings	SD	https://www.sdstate.edu/pharmacy-allied-health-professions
Union University College of Pharmacy	Jackson	TN	https://www.uu.edu/programs/pharmacy/
East Tennessee State University Bill Gatton College of Pharmacy	Johnson City	TN	https://www.etsu.edu/pharmacy/
South College School of Pharmacy	Knoxville	TN	https://www.south.edu/programs/doctor-pharmacy/
University of Tennessee Health Science Center College of Pharmacy	Memphis	TN	https://www.uthsc.edu/pharmacy/
Lipscomb University College of Pharmacy and Health Sciences	Nashville	TN	https://www.lipscomb.edu/pharmacy
Belmont University College of Pharmacy	Nashville	TN	http://www.belmont.edu/pharmacy/index.html
University of Texas at Austin College of Pharmacy	Austin	TX	https://pharmacy.utexas.edu/
University of Texas at El Paso School of Pharmacy	El Paso	TX	https://www.utep.edu/pharmacy/
University of North Texas Health Science Center UNT System College of Pharmacy	Fort Worth	TX	https://www.unthsc.edu/college-of-pharmacy/
University of Houston College of Pharmacy	Houston	TX	https://www.uh.edu/pharmacy/
Texas Southern University College of Pharmacy and Health Sciences	Houston	TX	http://www.tsu.edu/academics/colleges-and-schools/college-of-pharmacy-and-health-sciences/
Texas A & M University Health Science Center Irma Lerma Rangel College of Pharmacy	Kingsville	TX	https://pharmacy.tamu.edu/
Texas Tech University Health Sciences Center Jerry H. Hodge School of Pharmacy	Lubbock	TX	https://www.ttuhsc.edu/pharmacy/default.aspx
University of the Incarnate Word Feik School of Pharmacy	San Antonio	TX	https://pharmacy.uiw.edu/
University of Texas at Tyler Ben and Maytee Fisch College of Pharmacy	Tyler	TX	https://www.uttyler.edu/pharmacy/
University of Utah College of Pharmacy	Salt Lake City	UT	https://pharmacy.utah.edu/

Pharmacy Schools	City	State	Website
Hampton University School of Pharmacy	Hampton	VA	http://wp.hamptonu.edu/pharmacy/
Appalachian College of Pharmacy	Oakwood	VA	https://www.acp.edu/
Virginia Commonwealth University at the Medical College of Virginia Campus School of Pharmacy	Richmond	VA	https://pharmacy.vcu.edu/
Shenandoah University Bernard J. Dunn School of Pharmacy	Winchester	VA	https://www.su.edu/pharmacy/
University of Washington School of Pharmacy	Seattle	WA	https://sop.washington.edu/
Washington State University College of Pharmacy and Pharmaceutical Sciences	Spokane	WA	https://pharmacy.wsu.edu/
University of Wisconsin-Madison School of Pharmacy	Madison	WI	https://pharmacy.wisc.edu/
Concordia University Wisconsin School of Pharmacy	Mequon	WI	https://www.cuw.edu/academics/schools/pharmacy/index.html
Medical College of Wisconsin School of Pharmacy	Milwaukee	WI	https://www.mcw.edu/education/pharmacy-school
University of Charleston School of Pharmacy	Charleston	WV	https://www.ucwv.edu/academics/schools/school-of-pharmacy/
Marshall University School of Pharmacy	Huntington	WV	https://www.marshall.edu/pharmacy/
West Virginia University School of Pharmacy	Morgantown	WV	https://pharmacy.wvu.edu/
University of Wyoming School of Pharmacy	Laramie	WY	http://www.uwyo.edu/pharmacy/

CHAPTER 17

VETERINARY SCHOOLS BY CITY/STATE

Vet Schools	City	State	Website
Auburn University College of Veterinary Medicine	Auburn	AL	https://www.vetmed.auburn.edu/
Tuskegee University School of Veterinary Medicine	Tuskegee	AL	https://www.tuskegee.edu/programs-courses/colleges-schools/cvm
Midwestern University College of Veterinary Medicine	Glendale	AZ	https://www.midwestern.edu/academics/our-colleges/college-of-veterinary-medicine.xml
University of Arizona College of Veterinary Medicine	Oro Valley	AZ	https://vetmed.arizona.edu/
University of California, Davis School of Veterinary Medicine	Davis	CA	https://www.vetmed.ucdavis.edu/
Western University of Health Sciences College of Veterinary Medicine	Pomona	CA	https://www.westernu.edu/veterinary/
Colorado State University College of Veterinary Medicine and Biomedical Sciences	Fort Collins	CO	https://vetmedbiosci.colostate.edu/dvm/
University of Florida College of Veterinary Medicine	Gainesville	FL	https://education.vetmed.ufl.edu/
University of Georgia College of Veterinary Medicine	Athens	GA	https://vet.uga.edu/
Iowa State University College of Veterinary Medicine	Ames	IA	https://vetmed.iastate.edu/
University of Illinois College of Veterinary Medicine	Urbana	IL	https://vetmed.illinois.edu/
Purdue University College of Veterinary Medicine	West Lafayette	IN	https://www.purdue.edu/vet/
Kansas State University College of Veterinary Medicine	Manhattan	KS	https://www.vet.k-state.edu/
Louisiana State University School of Veterinary Medicine	Baton Rouge	LA	https://www.lsu.edu/vetmed/
Tufts University School of Veterinary Medicine	North Grafton	MA	https://vet.tufts.edu/
Michigan State University College of Veterinary Medicine	East Lansing	MI	https://cvm.msu.edu/
University of Minnesota College of Veterinary Medicine	St. Paul	MN	https://vetmed.umn.edu/
University of Missouri - Columbia College of Veterinary Medicine	Columbia	MO	https://cvm.missouri.edu/

Vet Schools	City	State	Website
Mississippi State University College of Veterinary Medicine	Mississippi State	MS	https://www.vetmed.msstate.edu/
North Carolina State University College of Veterinary Medicine	Raleigh	NC	https://cvm.ncsu.edu/
Cornell University College of Veterinary Medicine	Ithica	NY	https://www.vet.cornell.edu/
Long Island University School of Veterinary Medicine	Brookville	NY	https://liu.edu/vetmed
Ohio State University College of Veterinary Medicine	Columbus	OH	https://vet.osu.edu/
Oklahoma State University College of Veterinary Medicine	Stillwater	OK	https://vetmed.okstate.edu/
Oregon State University College of Veterinary Medicine	Corvallis	OR	https://vetmed.oregonstate.edu/
University of Pennsylvania School of Veterinary Medicine	Philadelphia	PA	https://www.vet.upenn.edu/
Lincoln Memorial University College of Veterinary Medicine	Harrogate	TN	https://www.lmunet.edu/college-of-veterinary-medicine/index.php
University of Tennessee College of Veterinary Medicine	Knoxville	TN	https://vetmed.tennessee.edu/
Texas A&M University College of Veterinary Medicine & Biomedical Sciences	College Station	TX	https://vetmed.tamu.edu/
Texas Tech University School of Veterinary Medicine	Amarillo	TX	https://www.depts.ttu.edu/vetschool/
Virginia Tech Virginia-Maryland College of Veterinary Medicine	Blacksburg	VA	http://www.vetmed.vt.edu/
Washington State University College of Veterinary Medicine	Pullman	WA	https://www.vetmed.wsu.edu/
University of Wisconsin-Madison School of Veterinary Medicine	Madison	WI	https://www.vetmed.wisc.edu/

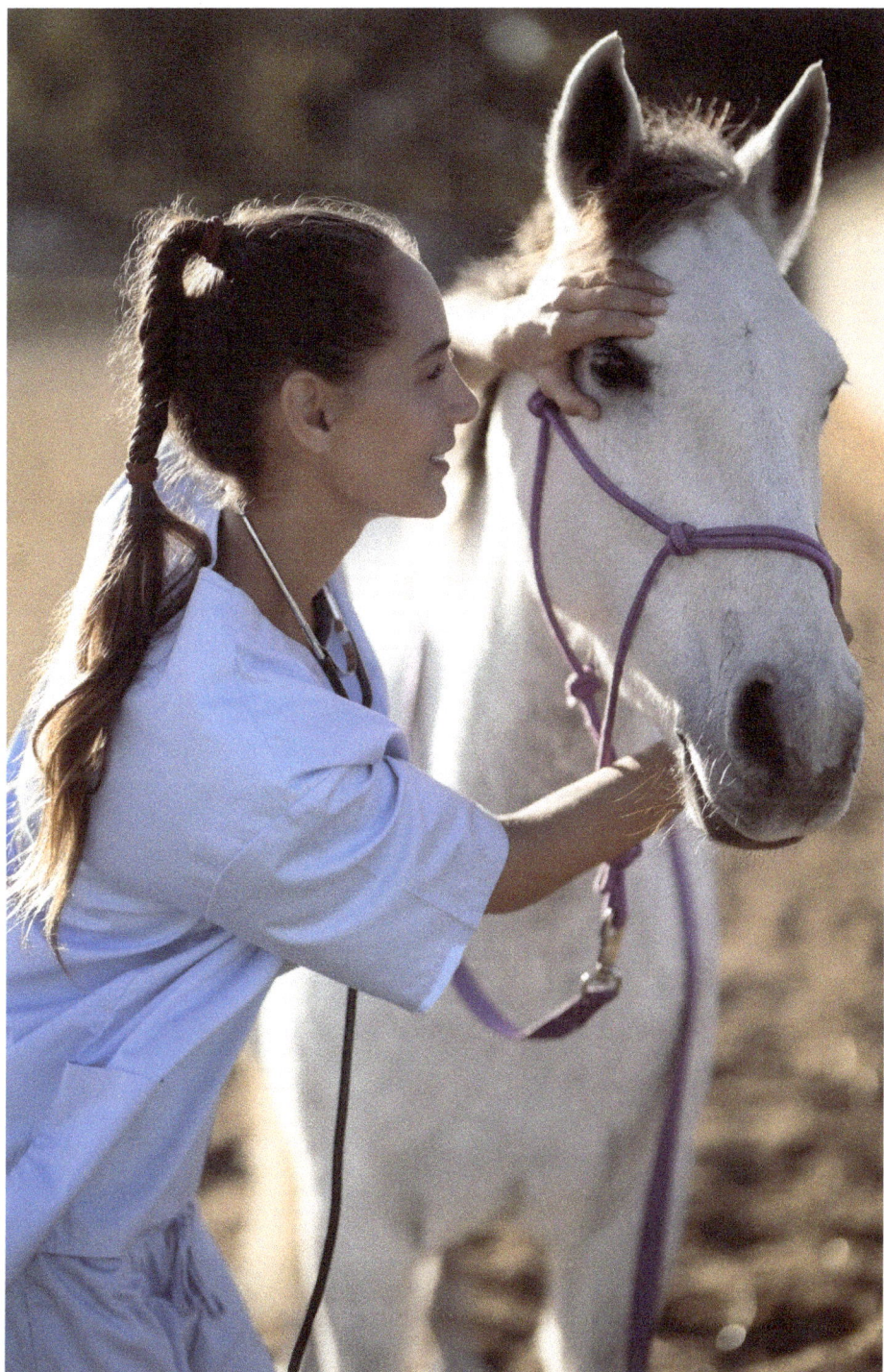

COMPREHENSIVE HEALTH CARE SERIES

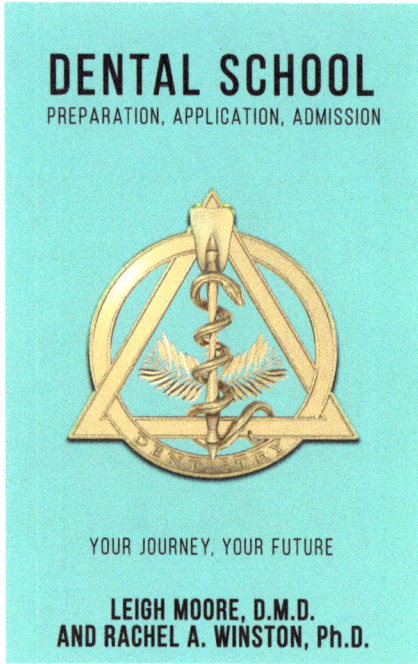

DENTAL SCHOOL
PREPARATION, APPLICATION, ADMISSION

YOUR JOURNEY, YOUR FUTURE

**LEIGH MOORE, D.M.D.
AND RACHEL A. WINSTON, Ph.D.**

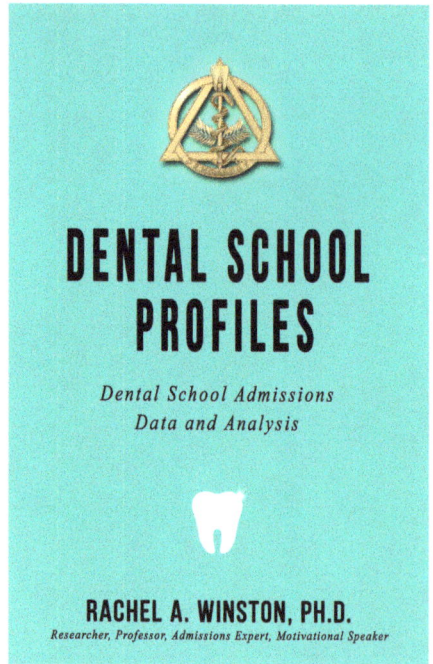

DENTAL SCHOOL PROFILES

*Dental School Admissions
Data and Analysis*

RACHEL A. WINSTON, PH.D.
Researcher, Professor, Admissions Expert, Motivational Speaker

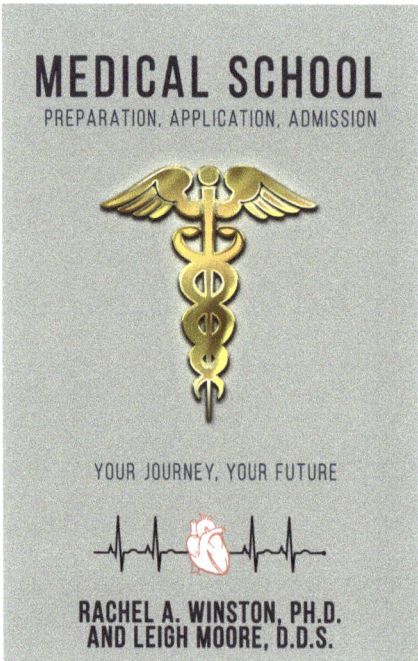

MEDICAL SCHOOL
PREPARATION, APPLICATION, ADMISSION

YOUR JOURNEY, YOUR FUTURE

**RACHEL A. WINSTON, PH.D.
AND LEIGH MOORE, D.D.S.**

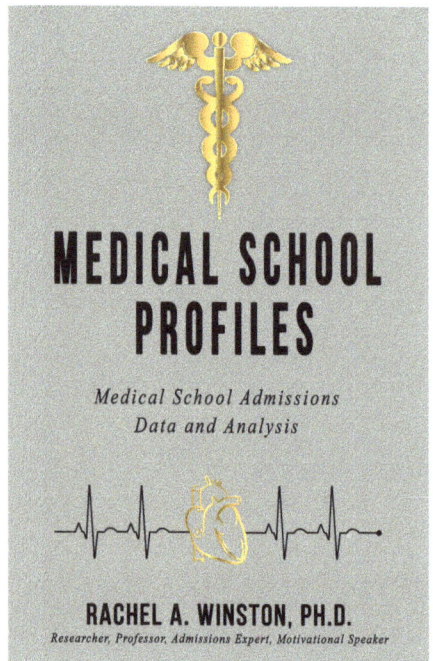

MEDICAL SCHOOL PROFILES

*Medical School Admissions
Data and Analysis*

RACHEL A. WINSTON, PH.D.
Researcher, Professor, Admissions Expert, Motivational Speaker

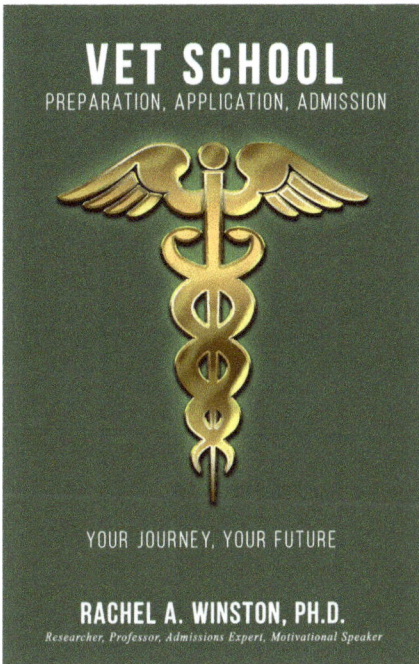

VET SCHOOL
PREPARATION, APPLICATION, ADMISSION

YOUR JOURNEY, YOUR FUTURE

RACHEL A. WINSTON, PH.D.
Researcher, Professor, Admissions Expert, Motivational Speaker

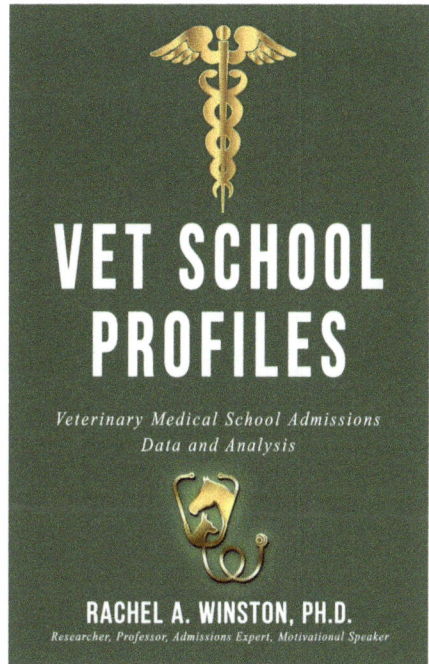

VET SCHOOL PROFILES

Veterinary Medical School Admissions Data and Analysis

RACHEL A. WINSTON, PH.D.
Researcher, Professor, Admissions Expert, Motivational Speaker

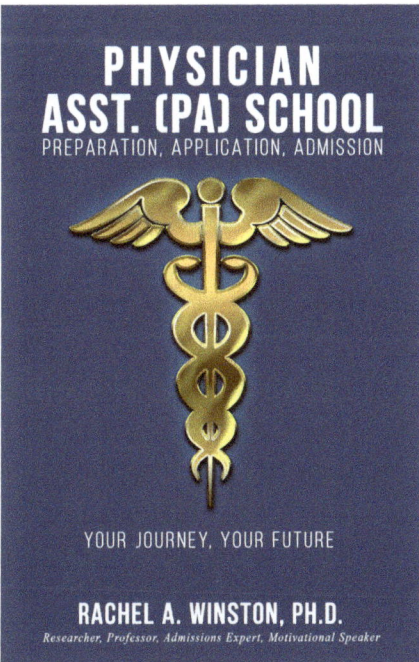

PHYSICIAN ASST. (PA) SCHOOL
PREPARATION, APPLICATION, ADMISSION

YOUR JOURNEY, YOUR FUTURE

RACHEL A. WINSTON, PH.D.
Researcher, Professor, Admissions Expert, Motivational Speaker

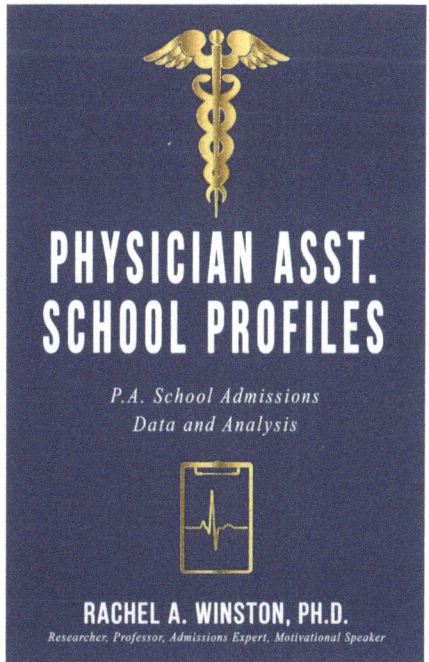

PHYSICIAN ASST. SCHOOL PROFILES

P.A. School Admissions Data and Analysis

RACHEL A. WINSTON, PH.D.
Researcher, Professor, Admissions Expert, Motivational Speaker

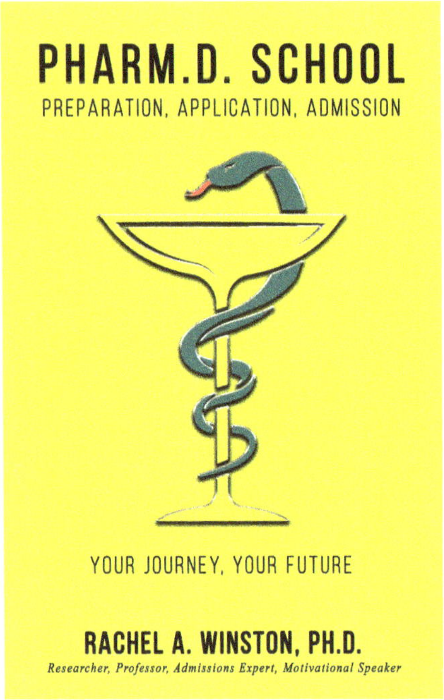

PHARM.D. SCHOOL
PREPARATION, APPLICATION, ADMISSION

YOUR JOURNEY, YOUR FUTURE

RACHEL A. WINSTON, PH.D.
Researcher, Professor, Admissions Expert, Motivational Speaker

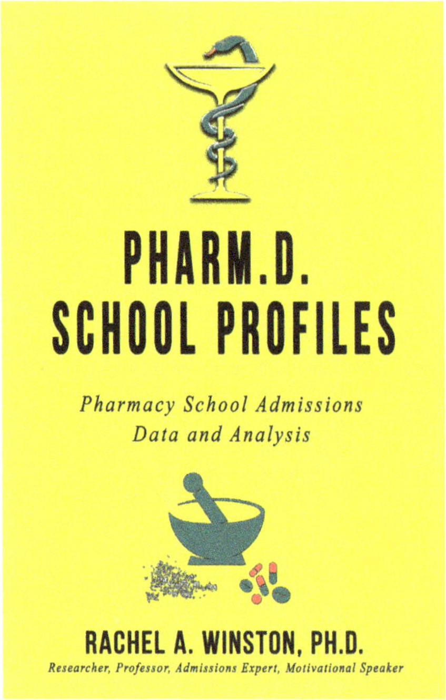

PHARM.D. SCHOOL PROFILES

Pharmacy School Admissions Data and Analysis

RACHEL A. WINSTON, PH.D.
Researcher, Professor, Admissions Expert, Motivational Speaker

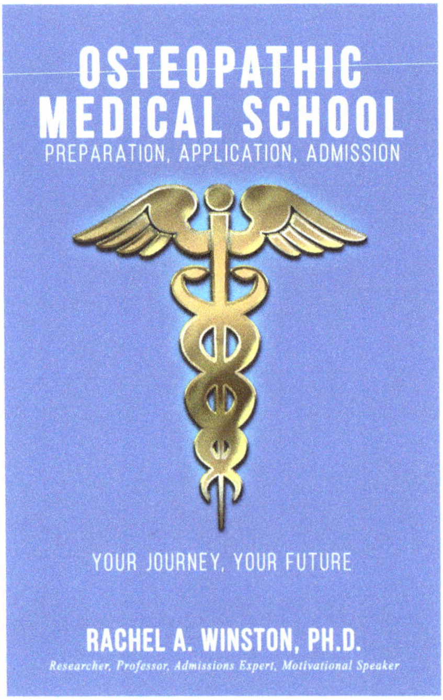

OSTEOPATHIC MEDICAL SCHOOL
PREPARATION, APPLICATION, ADMISSION

YOUR JOURNEY, YOUR FUTURE

RACHEL A. WINSTON, PH.D.
Researcher, Professor, Admissions Expert, Motivational Speaker

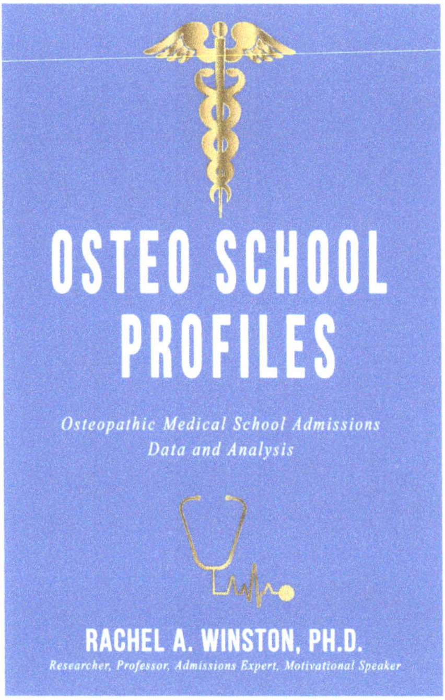

OSTEO SCHOOL PROFILES

Osteopathic Medical School Admissions Data and Analysis

RACHEL A. WINSTON, PH.D.
Researcher, Professor, Admissions Expert, Motivational Speaker

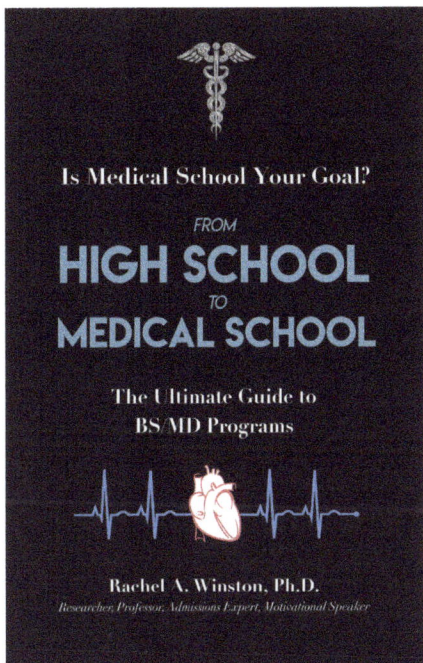

This comprehensive healthcare series is designed in full color to aid the growing number of applicants seeking clear, comprehensive materials. As a college admissions expert and former UCLA College Counseling Certificate Program faculty member, Dr. Winston is dedicated to helping students obtain the information they need.

FOR MORE INFORMATION

bsmdguide.com
medschoolexpert.com

Purchase books at Lizard-publishing.com

SERVICES OFFERED BY LIZARD EDUCATION:

- College Counseling
- Admissions News/Resources
- Essay Support and Editing
- Interview Preparation
- Road Trips to Visit Colleges
- Career Planning/Majors/Resumes
- BS/MD, BS/DO, BS/JD, BS/DDS
- Medical School
- Graduate School (Masters & Doctorate)
- Film Studio and Editing

- Portfolio Assistance/SlideRoom
- Athletics Recruiting/Highlight Films
- International Admissions/Visa/ TOEFL
- Financial Aid and Scholarships
- UCs, Ivy Leagues, and Colleges Nationwide
- Book Publishing
- Engineering, Robotics, STEM
- Art Portfolios

Email: collegeguide@yahoo.com
Website: collegelizard.com

LIZARD

INDEX

K

L

M

N

O

P

R

S

T

U